Wake Rites

The Florida James Joyce Series

UNIVERSITY PRESS OF FLORIDA

Florida A&M University, Tallahassee
Florida Atlantic University, Boca Raton
Florida Gulf Coast University, Ft. Myers
Florida International University, Miami
Florida State University, Tallahassee
New College of Florida, Sarasota
University of Central Florida, Orlando
University of Florida, Gainesville
University of North Florida, Jacksonville
University of South Florida, Tampa
University of West Florida, Pensacola

Wake Rites

The Ancient Irish Rituals of *Finnegans Wake*

George Cinclair Gibson

University Press of Florida
Gainesville/Tallahassee/Tampa/Boca Raton
Pensacola/Orlando/Miami/Jacksonville/Ft. Myers/Sarasota

First cloth printing, 2005
First paperback printing, 2026

31 30 29 28 27 26   6 5 4 3 2 1

Library of Congress Cataloging-in-Publication Data
Gibson, George Cinclair.
Wake rites : the ancient Irish rituals of Finnegans Wake /
George Cinclair Gibson.
p. cm. — (The Florida James Joyce series)
Includes bibliographical references and index.
ISBN 978-0-8130-2870-5 (cloth) | ISBN 978-0-8130-8183-0 (pbk.)
1. Joyce, James, 1882–1941. Finnegans wake. 2. Joyce, James, 1882–1941—Knowledge—Mythology.
3. Rites and ceremonies in literature. 4. Mythology, Celtic, in literature. 5. Ireland—in literature. 6. Brigit (Celtic deity).
7. Ritual in literature. 8. Saint Brigid's Day.
I. Title. II. Florida James Joyce series.
PR6019. O9F588 2005
823'.912—dc22   2005051925

The University Press of Florida is the scholarly publishing agency for the State University System of Florida, comprising Florida A&M University, Florida Atlantic University, Florida Gulf Coast University, Florida International University, Florida State University, New College of Florida, University of Central Florida, University of Florida, University of North Florida, University of South Florida, and University of West Florida.

University Press of Florida
PO Box 140239
Gainesville, FL 32614
floridapress.org

GPSR EU Authorized Representative: Mare Nostrum Group B.V, Doelen 72, 4831 GR Breda, The Netherlands, gpsr@mare-nostrum.co.uk

For The Shining Ones—
Past, Present, and Future

Contents

Figures

Tables

Foreword

The *Teamhur Feis*, for fifth-century Druidical Ireland, was a cross between Woodstock and a Republican National Convention, if such a thing can be imagined. A combination of celebration, ceremony, confrontation, and combat, the dark rites of the *Feis* reached a dramatic climax in A.D. 433, when St. Patrick usurped the ritual to light his Paschal fire. This event, held at Tara on Easter Sunday, has an extraordinary importance for *Finnegans Wake*: without a knowledge of these rites, it now appears, the *Wake* can simply not be understood.

George Cinclair Gibson examines the significance of this conclusion to the rituals of the *Teamhur Feis* on the setting, plot, character, language, and theme of *Finnegans Wake*, and the significance turns out to be enormous. With painstaking thoroughness, all previous work on the *Feis* rituals, from Latin manuscripts to discredited folklorists to contemporary Joycean critics, is brought to bear on the implications for the *Wake*. Similarly, when the argument reaches a celebrated crux in *Wake* studies (such as the identity of Magrath, or the charge against the Festy King), the major criticism on that crux is cited, sifted, and sorted, affording a rare clarity to the readings of problematic moments in the text. This is precisely the kind of book for which the Florida Joyce Series was invented: *Wake Rites* provides a crucial new way of reading the *Wake*, which may in turn open the way for the *Wake* to be more widely read and more generally understood.

What Gibson does is quite simply make sense of the *Wake*: if you were ever confused about Issy's doubling as the two Granias, the two Isoldes, the two Brigits, and the two Guineveres, this is the book that will sort you out. If you have ever wanted to know where the thunderwords came from, Gibson will introduce you to the Sacred Wheel, and even show you how to make one. Gibson makes absolutely clear that every ritualized action in the *Wake* has its roots in a single event: all roads in this narrative lead to Tara.

Some of the recoveries (the *Feis* included ritual combat between repeatedly transforming "Twins"; the high king of the *Feis* is called "ECH," who dies and is reborn in a fertility rite) seem almost too good to be true: either this is a revolutionary work, or, as Oliver Gogarty said about the *Wake* itself, it's the biggest hoax since *Ossian*. But of course it's all true, and all carefully attested: it's extraordinary how well *Wake Rites* works as a general guide to *Finnegans Wake*.

More than a book on *Wake* rites, then, this is a book on *Wake* character, *Wake* plot, *Wake* theme, and the *Wake* reader, spellbound before the tale of the *Teamhur Feis*. Throughout this extraordinarily dense material, the author is a very clear and compelling guide: it's as if Yeats's *Vision* had been written with a desire to be comprehended in mind. In George Cinclair Gibson, *Wake* criticism has a new bard, a *Fili* who with certain tone and real narrative skill gives us (finally!) the real story of the *Wake*.

Sebastian D. G. Knowles
Series Editor

Preface

This present work is the outcome of an event that occurred several years ago, while I was living in a cottage on the bank of a beautiful river bordering a wilderness preserve called The Joyce Sanctuary. For many weeks, I spent my waking hours immersed in *Finnegans Wake* to the exclusion of everything else; and one morning I realized I had reached the point of complete saturation. I closed the *Wake* and took the first book off the shelf—a text on ancient Celtic lore—and opened it at random to an arcane poem describing one of the great mythic events of Irish paganism. At that moment, I had a true Joycean epiphany: in a flash, I saw a deliberate connection between *Finnegans Wake* and this ancient Irish event—and I saw this connection as the elusive pattern that makes sense of the *Wakean* chaos. In Joycean terms, the soul of the *Wake*, the "whatness" that is its underlying pattern, leapt out to me from the vestment of its chaotic appearance. The connection I perceived between this arcane Irish event and Joyce's magnum opus formed the central thesis of my doctoral dissertation; and after much revision, and the addition of an introductory chapter, my dissertation developed into this present work.

Wake Rites focuses on the connections, the common structural patterns, and the striking parallels between *Finnegans Wake* and the arcane Irish event known as the *Teamhur Feis*, the "Rites of Tara." Obviously, for readers of *Wake Rites*, some knowledge of both *Wakean* and archaic Irish lore is necessary to follow the arguments made herein. To this end, I have revisited some of the earlier *Wakean* scholarship and have provided brief summaries of the *Wakean* episodes and characters discussed in this work. I have also included explanations and summaries of arcane Irish terms and concepts, mythological references, and ancient rituals presented throughout *Wake Rites*. The inclusion of this explanatory material will, I hope, serve to make *Wake Rites* accessible to any reader, regardless of the degree of familiarity with either *Finnegans Wake* or the Irish esoteric tradition.

Many people have been helpful to me in my project; but the composition of *Wake Rites* was greatly facilitated by seven in particular to whom I owe much gratitude: my parents, Blanche and George, who, through their considerable trust and largesse, supported me on many different levels; Dr. James Olney, who, at the inception of this project, defended it singlehandedly against its many detractors; Dr. John Gordon, who, throughout the course of this project, provided valuable guidance through his excellent and detailed critiques of my work; Ms. Patricia Walsh, who patiently acted as my foil by listening to, questioning, and evaluating each section of my work before it was written; Mr. Francis Broussard, who, acting through his insight and intuition, literally handed to me the rare and primary sources used in *Wake Rites*; and the late Mr. Jan "Duke" Kunst, who gave me sustenance and support more than he ever knew, and who, like the *Wake* itself, began and ended his own unique journey on the beautiful river he loved.

Abbreviations

FW Joyce, James. *Finnegans Wake*. New York: Penguin, 1967.

ICT Mercier, Vivian. *The Irish Comic Tradition*. Oxford: Clarendon Press, 1962.

IPC Macalister, R.A.S. *Ireland in Pre-Celtic Times*. New York: Benjamin Blom, 1921.

IU Tymoczko, Maria. *The Irish Ulysses*. Berkeley and Los Angeles: University of California Press, 1994.

JJII Ellmann, Richard. *James Joyce*. Rev. ed. New York: Oxford University Press, 1983.

Letters I, II, III Joyce, James. *The Letters of James Joyce*. 3 vols. Vol. 1, edited by Stuart Gilbert. Vols. 2 and 3, edited by Richard Ellmann. New York: Viking, 1966.

MC O'Curry, Eugene. *On the Manners and Customs of the Ancient Irish*. Vols. 1–3. Edited by W. K. Sullivan. New York: Scribner, Welford, and Company, 1873.

P Joyce, James. *A Portrait of the Artist as a Young Man*. New York: Penguin, 1985.

SH Joyce, P. W. *A Social History of Ancient Ireland*. Vols. 1 and 2. New York: Benjamin Blom, 1968.

SL Macalister, R.A.S. *The Secret Languages of Ireland*. Cambridge: Cambridge University Press, 1937.

T Macalister, R.A.S. *Tara: A Pagan Sanctuary of Ancient Ireland*. New York and London: Charles Scribner's Sons, 1931.

TB Macalister, R.A.S. "Temair Breg: A Study of the Remains and Traditions of Tara." In *Proceedings of the Royal Irish Academy* 34, sec. 100: 231–399. Dublin: Hodges, Figgs, and Company, 1919.

1

Introduction

Talismanic Darkness

For James Joyce, February 2 was, in Richard Ellmann's words, a "talismanic" day: a point on the great wheel of time where an event of the present could resonate in "sacred coincidence" with correlative events of an earlier cycle, thus imbuing the present with a potency that is at once symbolic, mythic, or even numinous.[1] On February 2, 1939, Joyce, with his family and friends, celebrated his own birth fifty-seven years earlier as well as the "birth" of his magnum opus—the arrival of the first printed copy of *Finnegans Wake*.

This "talismanic" day, February 2, also coincides with the ancient Irish feast of Imbolc, one of the four great holy days in the Celtic wheel of the year. (Imbolc's bowdlerized vestiges can still be found in both Candlemas and Groundhog Day.) Imbolc is sacred to the goddess Brigit, the one-eyed patroness of Ireland's visionary poets (the *Filidh*), her mythologists, and her storytellers. In pagan Ireland, Imbolc, birthday of the ancient goddess, observed the arrival of light after long darkness; Imbolc celebrated the birth of a new cycle of life and also honored the goddess whose gifts—poetic insight, mnemonic ability, linguistic skill, knowledge of the ancient lore, and "fire in the head"—allowed her votaries to preserve and continue the ancient Irish tradition. Thus, the feast day of this archaic Irish goddess of poets is also the birthday of the modern Irishman who, perhaps more than any of his contemporaries, embodies the very gifts she was understood to bestow. And the day in ancient Ireland that celebrates the birth of light in the realms of darkness and obscurity becomes the birthday of the *Wake*, the text known more for its apparent darkness and obscurity than perhaps any other book conceived in modern times.

Even before its birth on Imbolc, *Finnegans Wake* was denounced by Joyce's family and many of his friends for this overwhelming darkness and obscurity. Writing to his brother in 1924, Stanislaus Joyce, after reading one installment of the *Wake* in the *transatlantic review*, describes it as "driveling rigmarole" within a "nightmarish production" that is, at once, "nebulous," "chaotic," and "wearisome" in its "witless wandering"; Stanislaus then suggests to his brother that this writing is evidence perhaps of "the beginning of softening of the brain" (*JJII*, 577). In 1927, Nora, after reading a section of the *Wake*, asks her husband: "Why don't you write sensible books that people can understand?" (*JJII*, 590). Joyce's benefactor, Harriet Shaw Weaver, in a well-known passage, dismisses the *Wake* as a waste of Joyce's talent: "I do not care for the output from your Wholesale Safety Pun Factory nor for the darknesses and unintelligibilities of your deliberately entangled language system. It seems to me you are wasting your genius" (*JJII*, 590). Prior to this denouncement, Weaver had suggested to Joyce that he meliorate the obscurity of his new book by publishing, "along with an ordinary edition, also an annotated edition (at double or treble price, say?)" (*JJII*, 584).

And the early critics of the *Wake* were nearly unanimous in *their* indictment of its apparent meaninglessness and obscurity. Ezra Pound could hardly have been more scathing: "Nothing would be worth plowing through this, except the Divine Vision" (*JJII*, 585). Oliver St. John Gogarty cynically dismisses the *Wake* as "the most colossal leg-pull in literature since McPherson's *Ossian*" (*JJII*, 394). The mythologist Joseph Campbell, whose overall attitude toward the *Wake* is almost adulatory, nonetheless concludes that the *Wake* is a "gigantic wheeling rebus" whose message remains a "monstrous enigma" (*Skeleton Key*, 3). William York Tindall describes the *Wake* as "an arabesque—the elaborate decoration of something so simple that it evades us," and adds, "What the *Wake* is not is easier to determine than what it is" (13, 14). Adaline Glasheen is emphatic in her assessment: "*FW* is willfully obscure. It was conceived as obscurity, it was executed as obscurity, it is about obscurity" (*Second Census*, xvii).

More recent assessments tend to dismiss these earlier suggestions that the *Wake* is a product of mental decline, or a hoax, or a baffling exercise in obscurity, and offer more tempered theories—for example, that the *Wake* is fundamentally a metatext; or it is an exploration and enactment of the dream-state; or the *Wake* is both the type-site and paradigm of deconstructionist philosophy; or the *Wake* is an experiment in surrealism that, though brilliant in flashes, fails as a whole. Each of these theories certainly has its supportive argument; each is nonetheless a partial explanation at best: there is always more that is not explained than is.

It is a truism in *Wakean* studies that, for some unknown reason, Joyce created the *Wake* as a kind of microcosm, and, as a result, nearly everything in the world is in some way represented in the *Wake*. Consequently, almost *any* theory can be applied as an exercise in explication: a case can be made, an argument presented, that nearly any belief, theory, idea, or concept is part of the construct of *Finnegans Wake*. Always, however, more of the *Wake* is left outside of the argument than is contained within it. As Tindall observes: "There are nine-and-sixty ways of looking at the *Wake* and all of them are right, in part at least—wrong too, in part" (25).

Joyce himself only deepened the *Wakean* enigma. Unlike with *Ulysses*, for which he deliberately provided the interpretive keys and connections, Joyce remained secretive regarding the *Wake*—even refusing to divulge its title until absolutely necessary for publication purposes. When Joyce did remark on the *Wake*, his comments were almost tricksterlike in their brevity and their tendency to undermine his earlier statements—compounding the obscurity rather than providing any clarification. And Joyce's own attitude regarding the *Wake* and his role as its creator remains enigmatic. One of the few certain things known about the *Wake* is that Joyce sincerely believed and understood the *Wake* to be the sacred canon of a new religion for the West, and that he, through its creation, was cast in the role of an Irish prophet. Though exactly how or why the *Wake* is a sacred canon has never been explained, Joyce's own perception of the *Wake* hardly suggests a literary hoax, a surrealistic experiment, or the elaborate and imaginative presentation of a literary, psychological, or scientific theory. And unlike nearly every one of his critics, Joyce perceived *Finnegans Wake*, and not *Ulysses*, as his great work, his magnum opus.

The depth and degree of the *Wake*'s darkness is easily apprehended by anyone willing to read (if "read" is the operative word) any section or episode of the *Wake*. Each is fragmented, disjunctive, and a definite non sequitur relative to the episodes that precede and follow it. Each episode itself usually relates some activity, situation, or event that appears to be meaningless, surrealistic, absurd, bizarre, or ridiculous; and this activity typically bears little if any perceived relationship to any other episode in the book, nor does the part make sense to the book as a whole. Usually in the *Wake*, the activities of each episode are conducted (or performed) by a few members of the *Wakean* cast, the *Sigla Group*; the *Sigla Group*, like the episodes its members present, bears no correspondence to anything recognizable outside of *Finnegans Wake* itself. Quite often the actions and performances of an episode are played out within the backdrop of some event or occasion that has never been satisfactorily identified. In some episodes, this event appears to be a raucous Irish wake; in other places, the allusions indicate a marriage; but there is also much evidence cited by various *Wakeans* for Easter, or the vernal equinox, or the old Celtic May Day festival known as Beltane; or the event may be entirely in and of a dream. And every episode is told in a language that is perhaps the darkest aspect of the entire book itself: language nearly incomprehensible in its polyglot logorrhea; language sometimes blathering, at other times ranting, ribald, profound, or scatological, and everywhere laden with absurd catalogues of everything; language rife with riddles, and riddled with puns, neologisms, and a plethora of polysemes and portmanteaus; language literally loaded with thousands of words misspelled and malformed, bent, folded, twisted, mutilated or torn into pieces—all of this according to a bizarre set of "rules" that consistently apply throughout the *Wake*, rules for a dark tongue that Joyce seems to have invented specifically for conveying the *Wakean* episodes to his audience. This apparent chaos, along with its absolutely obfuscating language, prompted John Bishop to succinctly state what most readers of the *Wake* have already come to believe, that "nothing will make *Finnegans Wake* not obscure" (*Book of the Dark*, 3). Over six decades after its talismanic birth on Imbolc, the ancient Irish festival of light and elucidation, the *Wake* still remains concealed in its enigmatic darkness.

Even with this darkness, however, there are *Wakeans* who have consistently held to the belief—or, perhaps, the intuition—that there *is* something more than the apparent chaos, that there *is* a structure, albeit hidden, that may indeed illuminate the *Wakean* darkness. And further, if this talismanic key *is* found, it will be found deep within the center of ancient Irish myth.

That the *Wake* may have an ancient and mythic key is an idea that certainly resonates well with Joyce himself. In *Scribbledhobble* (the notebook for the *Wake*), he indicates to us how to read the dream of the *Wake*: "dream thoughts are wake thoughts of centuries ago: unconscious memory: great recurrence: race memory" (Connolly, 104). As early as his notebook entries for *A Portrait*, Joyce knew that his true purpose as an artist was in "remembering ancient days" (Scholes and Kain, 63). And in *A Portrait*, Joyce clearly designates the strong connection between Irish mythic tradition and his own goals as an artist. In *A Portrait*, Stephen

Dedalus makes the momentous decision to leave Ireland, and he states his ultimate reason for this decision simply and emphatically: "the shortest way to Tara was *via* Holyhead" (250). Stephen/Joyce leaves Ireland, not totally rejecting his native land but rather as a way to acquire perspective in order to reconnect with Ireland's mythic center: Tara (*Teamhur*), the ancient Irish omphalos, her cultural and spiritual nexus, the great *nemeton* of her pagan religion, the matrix of her lore and mythology. At the outset of his career, Joyce clearly envisions a future connection with Ireland's mythic past, her ancient center, and his own artistic and spiritual quest.

There are reasons to believe that, for Joyce, his "way to Tara" culminated as *Finnegans Wake*. For Joyce, the most crucial moment in *all* of Irish history and the climactic and talismanic point in his own magnum opus are one and the same: the momentous confrontation at Tara between Saint Patrick and the Archdruid of Ireland. In Irish myth and in *Finnegans Wake*, the confrontation at Tara occurs as the pivotal point of a great Irish event already under way. There is evidence that this event, held at ancient Tara and known as the *Teamhur Feis*, bears a very significant relationship to *Finnegans Wake*—not only to its climactic final chapter but also to the meaning and construct of *Finnegans Wake* as a whole. Further, there is evidence that this pivotal event at Tara may provide the hidden structure that clarifies much of the *Wakean* chaos and darkness. The single most recognized feature of *Finnegans Wake* is darkness. "Teamhur," in its most ancient and fundamental sense, literally *means* "darkness"—and this "darkness" may also hold the talismanic key to the *Wake*'s elucidation.[2] And given the relatively arcane nature of the *Teamhur Feis* and its importance in this present work, an overview of the *Teamhur Feis* is certainly warranted at this point.

"crazy elegies around Templetombmount" (192.34–35): A Mythic Overview of the *Teamhur Feis*

The *Teamhur Feis* (also known as *Feis Temro*, *Oenach* of Tara, and the Rites of Tara) was the most important religious, mythic, sociopolitical, historical (and pseudohistorical) event conducted in pre-Christian Ireland. The *Teamhur Feis* was, according to Joyce's sources, neither the primitive fertility rite nor the literary fiction suggested by most modern historians.[3] Rather, the *Teamhur Feis* was an extraordinary and complex array of rites, rituals, mythic and historical reenactments, sacred drama, conclaves, assemblies, funeral and inaugural ceremony clustered around several major themes that, in turn, defined the structure and nature of the *Teamhur Feis* itself.

Like *Finnegans Wake,* the *Teamhur Feis* had its origin in the funeral and wake rites conducted for a great but fallen leader. These rites (collectively called the *Nosad*) were performed—as they are in the *Wake*—during a truce period, thus allowing a national gathering of mourners, Fianna, Druids, legislators, and other attendants. The *Nosad* at Tara included an array of events: elegies around the temple (that was also tomb and mount), keening, songs related to the deceased, drinking and feasting, Druidic divinations, fertility rites, sacred dances and mimes, athletic contests, and ritual combats between two young males known as the Twins. The national gathering and the truce period of the *Nosad* made the *Teamhur Feis* an opportune occasion for various groups already gathered for the *Nosad* to convene separately for their own specific purposes. The *Nosad* was thus associated with the national gatherings of the Irish Druids and the Fianna, as well as musicians and artists, judicial and legislative assemblies, along with a motley multitude of Irish revelers and onlookers.

As considerable as the events of the *Nosad* were, the most important proceedings at the *Teamhur Feis* were those comprising the inaugural cycle and ritual investiture of the Irish high king. For the Irish assembled at the *Teamhur Feis,* their high king, *ard rí,* was nothing less than the human vessel for "ECH," the great solar god who resided in his human vehicle as long as it was deemed suitable. Age, illness, infamy, the violation of the magical proscriptions known as *geissi,* or failing potency, would render this vessel unfit, thus necessitating replacement of an aged ruler with a younger and more virile successor. The fate of many a failed king was regicide—usually at the hands of a certain Druid known as "Mog Ruith," specially designated for this grim task.

The *Teamhur Feis* was the occasion for this dramatic royal spectacle to unfold. Consequently, a complex sequence of choreographed events were conducted: portents to assess the king's future, a review of his adherence to the royal *geissi,* tests of virility (often followed by formal charges), rejection by the Sovereign queen, Druidic curses and scathing ranns, a public trial and execution. Then, a series of magical tests and rites (including an important séancelike inquest) were enacted to identify and verify the new king; these were followed by inaugural rites involving a sacred mantle, horses, ritual bathing in a consecrated cauldron, a fourteen-part labyrinthine procession, baptism, and the lighting of a hallowed bonfire. The inaugural cycle culminated in the marriage of the king and his consort, the

Sovereign goddess Ana, personification of the land. The ancient name for this royal marriage, *Banais Righe* (literally, "wedding feast of kingship"), is frequently used in the mythological tracts to describe the entire inaugural event.

The date of the *Teamhur Feis* was also recognized as the birthday of the "Spirit of Vegetation" and was deliberately calculated to coincide with the vernal equinox, the day of renewal of both the sun and the earth. This is a deliberate act of sympathetic magic meant to underscore a fundamental goal of the *Teamhur Feis*: sustenance and renewal not only for the king and the seasons, but sustenance and renewal for the land, the people, and the Irish nation as a whole. To this end, the *Teamhur Feis* was deliberately constructed as a microcosm of Ireland and Irish culture: all of the knowledge, science, lore, and great events—historical, pseudohistorical, mythical, and religious—that created and defined Ireland and its people were retold, reenacted, re-created on this birthday of king, sun, and land. Through the skill of their visionary poets, the sum of Ireland's knowledge, lore, and history was thus conjured into the present—relived, reexperienced in real time at the Rites of Tara. Through this deliberate rite of creation, the king, the assembled populace, and the nation as a whole could begin life anew. Collectively, these events of the *Teamhur Feis*—the *Nosad*, the cycle of *Banais Righe*, the rites of renewal—constitute the single most important religious festival conducted in pagan Ireland.

The choreographed presentation of this complex of religious, sociopolitical, and magical events required a truly elaborate array of performers: human representatives of pagan divinities, personifications of natural forces, magistrates, divine functionaries, Druids, priestesses of the goddess Brigit, reenactors of the mythic dead. Through their performances at the *Teamhur Feis*, mortals were connected with their divinities, and the realm of the Irish gods and goddesses was made manifest upon earth. The ultimate purpose behind the performances at the *Teamhur Feis* was to reunite the populace with their pantheon—religion (Latin, *re*, "again" + *ligare*, "connect") in its most fundamental manifestation. The climactic moment in these religious performances was the lighting of the *torc caille*, the sacred bonfire, symbolizing the new light of a new dispensation. At the culmination of the *Teamhur Feis* in A.D. 433, Saint Patrick dramatically usurped this pagan ritual when he lit his Paschal fire nearby on the Hill of Slane. This event—Patrick's confrontation and victory at Tara—which heralded the end of Irish paganism, is also the pivotal and climactic moment of *Finnegans Wake*.

The Central Thesis

The *Wake*'s climactic moment is unquestionably focused on the lighting of the bonfire at Tara; and this moment can also be identified as the climactic and concluding ritual of the *Teamhur Feis*. Furthermore, an examination of the other specific events, characters, and themes that constitute the *Teamhur Feis* indicates a remarkable correspondence, a "sacred coincidence," with the other events, characters, and themes that constitute *Finnegans Wake*. Every one of the events and rituals alluded to in the above summary (and described in detail in the mythological accounts of the *Teamhur Feis*), along with the pagan cast necessary to enact them, has its parallel in *Finnegans Wake*. Conversely, *all* of the episodes in *Finnegans Wake*, along with Joyce's entire *Sigla Group*, have their corresponding equivalents at the *Teamhur Feis*. Herein is the central thesis of this present work: the *Teamhur Feis* is the secret structure of *Finnegans Wake*, and *Finnegans Wake* is James Joyce's deliberate re-creation of the most important and sacred event of Irish paganism.

Organization of the Argument

In order to address this very broad thesis, more specific claims are argued in the following chapters:

• Chapter 2, "The Day of the *Wake*," addresses the controversy regarding the date, occasion, or event of *Finnegans Wake*. Three separate events have been suggested as the specific event that forms the backdrop to the *Wake*: Easter, the vernal equinox, and the Celtic May Day (Beltane). Though the date and occasion of the *Teamhur Feis* have never been considered as a solution to this controversy, this event both subsumes and reconciles the current conflicting theories.

• Chapter 3, "The *Sigla Group* at the *Teamhur Feis*," focuses on the parallels between the *Sigla Group* and the functionaries who performed the Rites of Tara. The *Wakean* dramatis personae bear a striking resemblance—in their names, numbers, and functions—to the cast at the *Teamhur Feis*. If the functionaries at Tara had specific names or titles, Joyce, with slight variation, uses these original names for his *Wakean* counterparts: ECH becomes, in the *Wake*, HCE; the mother goddess Ana becomes Anna; the twenty-eight virgin priestesses from the temple of the goddess Brigit become the Twenty-Eight Virgins from Saint Brigit's Finishing School; the Druidic slayer of ECH at Tara, Mog Ruith, becomes the sinister nemesis of HCE, Magrath; Saint Patrick remains Saint Patrick. The other members of the *Sigla Group* (for example, the Four Elders, the Twelve Magistrates, the Twins, and so on) have their counterparts at the *Teamhur Feis* as well. Table 3.1 outlines the *Sigla Group*, their correlates at Tara, and their similar roles in both.

• Chapter 4, "The Fall of the All-Father," explains the parallels between rites, rituals, portents, tests, and events of the *Teamhur Feis* that lead to the demise of the king at Tara and their analogues in *Finnegans Wake*. Table 4.1 outlines these events and their parallel episodes in the *Wake*.

• Chapter 5, "The Funeral Games at Valleytemple," reviews the wake rites and other funerary events conducted at Tara and their reenactments in the *Wake*.

• Chapter 6, "The Return of Solsking the First," discusses the colorful and bizarre array of rituals and tests used at the *Teamhur Feis* to determine and inaugurate the new king and their correlative episodes in the *Wake*. Table 6.1 outlines these rituals at Tara and their reenactments in *Finnegans Wake*.

• Chapter 7, "The Etiological Myths," argues that the etiological myths underpinning the *Teamhur Feis* have their parallels in the themes and construction of the *Wake*.

• Chapter 8, "The Recovery of the Dark Tongue," considers what is perhaps the single most obfuscating aspect of *Finnegans Wake*—its absolutely absurd, baffling, and dark language—and offers a new theory for its appearance in the *Wake*. At the *Teamhur Feis*, many of the rituals were conducted in a language specifically designed for use by the choreographers of the *Teamhur Feis*, the *Filidh*, Druids, and poets. Called *bélra na filed*, this language was nearly incomprehensible in its polyglot logorrhea; language sometimes blathering, at other times ranting, ribald, profound, or scatological, and everywhere laden with absurd catalogues of everything; language rife with riddles, and riddled with puns, neologisms, and a plethora of polysemes and portmanteaus; language literally loaded with thousands of words misspelled and malformed, bent, folded, twisted, mutilated or torn into pieces—all of this according to a bizarre set of "rules" that consistently apply, rules known to the Druids and *Filidh* themselves. This language was so obscure it was generally referred to as the "Dark Tongue." Saint Patrick, soon after his victory at the *Teamhur Feis*, deliberately made the Dark Tongue illegal. James Joyce, in *Finnegans Wake*, re-creates the illegal Dark Tongue for his reenactment of the *Teamhur Feis*.

Sources for the Irish Lore

The central thesis of *Wake Rites*, as well as the more specific claims addressed in the separate chapters, obviously presuppose that James Joyce possessed considerable in-depth knowledge of Irish myth and the arcane practices of the old Celtic religion; that Joyce had access to sources of this material in Ireland, Trieste, Zurich, and especially while living in Paris, where he resided during the research and composition of *Finnegans Wake*; and that there are specific sources that Joyce utilized for his re-creation of the Rites of Tara. From early comments made by Joyce's biographers, to more detailed observations made by various bibliographers, to Maria Tymoczko's systematic and comprehensive survey of Joyce's Irish sources, the critical assessments evaluating Joyce's knowledge of Irish mythology concur that his knowledge of the Irish material was both extensive and deep, that this knowledge is manifest throughout his oeuvre, and that in *Finnegans Wake* Joyce manifests a mastery of Irish mythic lore.[4]

Stanislaus Joyce writes that while his brother was pursuing Irish studies while living in Dublin, the latter's interests ranged from the formal to the folkloric, and "extended in Ireland from Mangan and Yeats to the unlettered poets of the rugged glens, where a few years later Synge was to stake out his claim."[5] F. L. Radford, in his study of the Celtic substructures in *A Portrait*, notes that Synge and Joyce met in Paris in 1903 for discussion regarding Irish and Celtic lore. In Paris, Synge had studied extensively under the Celticist Henri d'Arbois de Jubainville, even acting as his assistant for a time.[6] Cóilín Owens, in his study of the Irish and Celtic lore in "Clay," concludes that, "Joyce's knowledge of popular folk customs and their roots in archaic tradition are both detailed and accurate" (338). John Kelleher and Maria Tymoczko note that while in Trieste, Joyce drew upon his knowledge of Irish lore and myth in several significant ways: the Trieste Lectures and the architectonics of "The Dead" (*IU*, 316). John Kelleher and Stanley Sultan (in *Eliot, Joyce, and Company*) both conclude that Joyce read and studied translations of early Irish myth *in extenso*.[7] In her essay on Irish mythic structures in Joyce's work, Tymoczko argues that "Revisionist critical work on Joyce has made it increasingly clear that in *Portrait, Ulysses,* and *Finnegans Wake* Joyce utilized structural features, mythopoeic imagery, formal elements, and linguistic resources found in his Irish heritage" ("Broken Lights," 763). Summarizing Joyce's use of Irish lore in *Finnegans Wake,* Ellsworth and Ellmann state that, "When, in his own last book, he deigned at last to make use of the materials of Irish folklore, he showed himself to be as much in tune with them as either Lady Gregory or Yeats" (Joyce, *Critical Writings,* 102). Tymoczko, at the conclusion of her comprehensive survey of Joyce's Irish sources, argues that Joyce manifests a knowledge and application of Irish myth, "more extensive and more various than that of most of his contemporaries among the writers of the Anglo-Irish literary revival"; and compared to the majority of the writers in the Anglo-Irish literary revival, "Joyce is more able . . . to transpose and reanimate, among other things, the humor, the sexuality, the ironies, the genres, and the formal properties of early Irish literature" (*IU,* 326). And it is in *Finnegans Wake*—where, as Tymoczko notes, the Irish material manifests as a "logical extension of Joyce's earlier work"—that Joyce's appropriation of Irish mythology reaches its furthest development (*IU,* 326). Tymoczko concludes that, in the *Wake,* it "can hardly be doubted" that Joyce manifests an "ability to see Irish tradition whole, to use Irish myth in ways that are less tainted and parochial than are those of his nationalist Irish contemporaries (including W. B. Yeats)" (*IU,* 326). In *Finnegans Wake,* Joyce's knowledge and application of Irish myth reaches fruition and wholeness. As Tymoczko suggests, the *Wake* manifests a depth of Irish mythic lore only beginning to be recognized—and this depth and expression of Irish myth is the very goal voiced by Stephen Dedalus in *A Portrait* so many years before.

As a young writer coming into his craft during Ireland's nationalistic resurgence and Celtic Revival, Joyce naturally would have become acquainted with the Anglo-Irish literary refractions, scholarly publications, translations, summaries, retellings, and critical discussions of Irish myth and lore that, in this period, were cathected with what William Irwin Thompson calls "nationalist power."[8] Included in this genre—and easily accessible to Joyce in Dublin and at University College—are the works by William Butler Yeats, Lady Gregory, P. W. Joyce, Kuno Meyer, Whitley Stokes, Standish O'Grady, Eugene O'Curry, Æ, Henri d'Arbois de Jubainville, Richard Best, Eoin MacNeill, and periodicals such as *Revue Celtique, All Ireland Review, Dana, Zeitschrift für celtische Philologie,* and *United*

Irishman. (As reported by Stanislaus Joyce, James Joyce read *United Irishman* every week, had it sent to him on the Continent, and called it "the only paper in Dublin worth reading" [*My Brother's Keeper*, 173].) As a student in Dublin, Joyce was thoroughly familiar with the Irish material resultant from the Celtic Revival: "Joyce situated himself in the cultural spectrum in such a way that he was among the best informed of those who used popular vehicles to instruct themselves about Irish literary and historical traditions" (*IU*, 254).

After leaving Ireland, evidence indicates that Joyce continued to deepen his knowledge of early Irish myth and literature. In Trieste, even though Joyce had access to relatively few books on Irish lore, he wrote to his Aunt Josephine during this period requesting Irish material and also received his regular subscription copies of *United Irishman* (*IU*, 317).

In Zurich, however, Joyce had access to "extensive materials that make it unnecessary to suppose that Joyce was dependent on either his personal library or his memory of texts read long since for his use of Irish myth" (*IU*, 317). In Zurich, Joyce worked almost daily in the Zentralbibliothek. Here, he had access to comprehensive studies of Irish and Celtic material, including works by German philologists (such as Heinrich Zimmer) who were at the forefront of Celtic studies in the early decades of the twentieth century; journals such as the *Revue Celtique* and *Zeitschrift für celtische Philologie*; the complete Todd Lecture Series and the entire run of *Cours de literature celtique* by Jubainville; works by Stokes, Meyer, O'Curry, P. W. Joyce, plus "an extensive collection of monographs on early Irish language and literature" (*IU*, 318). As a result of her broad study of Irish material available to Joyce at the Zentralbibliothek, Tymoczko observes that the Zentralbibliothek's collection of Irish material was superbly organized and emphasized scholarly work rather than popular editions of Irish material. Because of the excellent composition of Celtic materials and its easy accessibility, she concludes that "few libraries in Europe and the British Isles would have been better than Zurich's Zentralbibliothek for Joyce to have pursued his interests in early Irish literature, history, and language" (*IU*, 323).

Joyce lived in Paris during the period when he focused on the research and composition of *Finnegans Wake*. Paris, even more than Zurich, provided Joyce access to Irish material—virtually any source material needed for information on Irish myth in general and Tara in particular: "It is clear that once located in Paris, a major center of Celtic studies where d'Arbois de Jubainville had been professor, Joyce would have had access to virtually

any text or critical book on early Irish literature that he cared to work with" (*IU*, 317).

Though there is the consensus that Joyce possessed an impressive knowledge of Irish myth, and his access to this material was considerable, identifying specific sources remains problematic for several reasons:

1. Joyce, for reasons known only to himself, deliberately concealed and obscured almost everything in the *Wake* and everything pertaining to it; this certainly holds true regarding his Irish sources.

2. During the composition of *Finnegans Wake*, Joyce's eyesight deteriorated, and he relied much on information conveyed through discussion and reports from others; most of this information is not documented.

3. Joyce, like an ancient Irish *Fili*, possessed extraordinary mnemonic abilities; much of the Irish material in *Finnegans Wake* may have been recalled from earlier and undocumented sources.

4. The Irish material regarding myth and mythic Tara is problematic in its own right. True to its Celtic nature, there is no single monolithic tale describing the Rites of Tara. Rather, the Rites are described through stories, reports, narratives, and rituals interlaced throughout the varied collections of Fenian and Red Branch tales, the Cycle of the Kings, the Christian Apocryphal writings, the annals, histories, and pseudohistories. Furthermore, prior to the period of the *Wake*'s composition, a copious amount of material was published and readily available regarding Tara and Irish myth. Much of this material overlaps: there are multiple translations and editions of the same material, along with numerous commentaries; there are redactions, refractions, bowdlerizations, and versions designed for both scholarly audiences and the popular press.[9]

As problematic as it is to identify specific Irish sources used in the *Wake*, there are methods that have been used by Joyce's bibliographers to identify particular Irish sources:

1. Books and journals on Irish lore have been identified in Joyce's own library (for example, *Zeitschrift für celtische Philologie, United Irishman*).

2. As Atherton and others have stated, Joyce sometimes identifies a source of material for the *Wake* by naming the source in the *Wake* itself.

3. A passage in the *Wake* is so specific in its wording and phrasing that it can only have come from one source, and that source has been conclusively identified.

4. In an extant notebook or letter, Joyce names a particular Irish source used in the *Wake*.

With these criteria, specific sources can be identified; these constitute major sources of information used in *Wake Rites*.

Major Sources

All major sources for Irish lore used in *Wake Rites* were published prior to the composition of *Finnegans Wake* and were available to James Joyce. These sources contain important primary material regarding Tara, the Rites of Tara, the arcane rituals of the *Feis*, mythopoeic imagery, mythic patterns, kingship rites, wake customs, Fianna lore, and issues and imagery associated with the Sovereign. In *Wake Rites*, major sources are the following:

- *The Annals of the Four Masters* (the 1848–51 O'Donovan edition). The ostensible authors of *The Annals* are cited by Joyce in the *Wake*; *The Annals* is one of the sources of information used in the *Wake* that is clearly identified by all of Joyce's bibliographers.

- Richard Best. Richard Best makes a guest appearance in *Ulysses*; important essays and translations of early Irish material by Best are included in *United Irishman*.

- Whitley Stokes. Stokes is honored in the *Wake* with the accolade "Stout Stokes" (619.32).

- Kuno Meyer. Meyer is identified by Tymoczko as one of the certain sources used in the *Wake*.

- Giraldus Cambrensis. Giraldus is named in the *Wake*.

- P. W. Joyce. P. W. Joyce, called by James Joyce "my namesake," was highly recommended by James Joyce, who owned some of the works of his "namesake."

• E. Gwynn. Tymoczko cites Gwynn's translation of the *Dindshenchas* (called in the *Wake* "Dunshanagan" [417.31]) as a certain source in the *Wake*. Gwynn also edited and translated important sections of *The Book of Armagh*.

• Eugene O'Curry is identified by Tymoczko.

• Standish O'Grady is identified by Tymoczko.

• W. B. Yeats and Lady Wilde are identified in the *Wake* and by the bibliographers as certain sources of material for Joyce.

• Eoin MacNeill. MacNeill taught at University College during Joyce's matriculation and is cited by Tymoczko as a certain source.

• Muirchú maccu Machthene. The Irish scribe Muirchú maccu Machthene, in *The Book of Armagh,* relates one of the earliest extant accounts of Patrick's confrontation at Tara; in turn, Muirchú's account provides the basis for much of the later Patrician lore and commentary. In Muirchú's account of the Tara confrontation, a unique and peculiar phrase—"Fiat, Fiat"—plays an important role in his story. This same phrase also appears numerous times throughout the *Wake*—strongly suggesting that Muirchú's account in *The Book of Armagh* (which was translated and edited by both Gwynn and Stokes) is one of Joyce's important sources for Patrician lore, especially the lore related to Patrick's confrontation at Tara.

• *The Yellow Book of Lecan.* A large section of *The Yellow Book of Lecan, Auraicept na n-Éces* (*The Scholar's Primer*) was translated by George Calder and published in 1916 in Edinburgh. Roland McHugh (in his *Annotations*) identifies the *Wake*'s "Orange Book" (374.31) as *The Yellow Book of Lecan*—thus acknowledging *Auraicept na n-Éces* as one of Joyce's sources for the *Wake.*

In addition to the major sources listed above and identified by the bibliographers, I have used several other sources; these include: W. G. Wood-Martin (1902); J. Bonwick (1894); A. Macbain (1917); J. MacCulloch (1918); R. Holinshed (1577). Though the bibliographers have not identified these five sources, all five were available to Joyce prior to the composition of *Finnegans Wake*. The material taken from these five sources is general in nature, and provides information on Irish lore that Joyce could have acquired from any number of available sources.

The Post-*Wakean* Commentaries

As a supplement to these major sources used in *Wake Rites,* I have included some commentary by a selection of Celtic scholars whose works were clearly completed and published *after* 1939, the year *Finnegans Wake* was published. Relative to the major sources listed above, the post-*Wakean* commentaries are used sparingly in *Wake Rites,* and in all cases used strictly in an ancillary role, that is, they offer commentary on earlier texts, imagery, rituals, and mythic imagery that were available and known to James Joyce. In the following chapters, these post-*Wakean* commentaries offer observations on earlier primary material and are not sources for primary material itself. The post-*Wakean* commentators used in *Wake Rites* include the following:

• Alwyn and Brinley Rees (on the *Dindshenchas* related to the Rites of Tara, the role of the Twelve Magistrates at the Rites of Tara, Irish Bardic lore, and mythic imagery associated with the Sovereign at Tara).

• Joseph Falaky Nagy (on early Fianna tales, Patrician lore, and the ancient Druidic concept of liminality).

• Walter and Mary Brenneman (on the Welling rites and its imagery and lore, as found throughout the Red Branch and Fenian Cycles).

• Joseph Campbell (on banshees and Celtic rites of divination found in the *Wake*).

• Mary Condren (on Brigit, her priestesses, and their rites).

• Miranda Green (on investiture rites of the Irish king and imagery associated with the Sovereign as found in early Irish literature).

• Robert Graves (on the *Wake*'s Anna and her similarity to the old Irish triple goddess, Ana).

• Patricia Lysaght (on the banshees in early Irish myth and ritual).

• Adam McLean (on the triplicity of the ancient Sovereign goddess).

• Vivian Mercier (on the old Druidic language known as the Dark Tongue).

• Dáithí Ó hÓgáin (on imagery and lore associated with Finn, and Druidic curses as found in early Irish literature).

• Thomas O'Rahilly (on the etymology of "Ana").

• Thomas Garbáty (on the Welling ritual of the Celts).

• Anne Ross (on imagery and lore associated with the Celtic Welling rites).

• Maria Tymoczko (on Joyce's use of imagery associated with the Otherworld and the Sovereign).

The Primary Source: R.A.S. Macalister

Though none of the *Wakean* bibliographers (for example, Atherton, Radford, Kelleher, Tymoczko) even mention his name, R.A.S. Macalister is very likely the most important source of information on Irish lore and the Rites of Tara used in *Finnegans Wake*. During the early years of his tenure at University College, Dublin (where he was Professor of Celtic Archaeology from 1909 to 1943), Macalister delivered a series of lectures on the history and lore of Tara, the Rites of Tara, and its associated events, rituals, performers, themes, and imagery. This series was later published in January 1919 in *Proceedings of the Royal Irish Academy* under the title "Temair Breg: A Study of the Remains and Traditions of Tara." In 1931, after some rewriting, editing, and compression, the lectures were republished as *Tara: A Pagan Sanctuary of Ancient Ireland*. In both "Temair Breg" and *Tara*, Macalister initially revisits the earlier and more conservative work of George Petrie, *On the History and Antiquities of Tara Hill* (1839), then applies his own theories regarding comparative mythology, anthropology, occultism, shamanism, arcane Irish lore, as well as his own interpretations and explications of early Irish texts related to the events at Tara. As a result, Macalister presents a version of the *Teamhur Feis* that differs greatly from that of his contemporaries, and a version certainly at variance with the consensus of most present-day academics as well.

Macalister argues that the *Teamhur Feis* was an actual historical event with nationwide attendance and participation—neither the localized and primitive fertility rite nor the literary fiction that constitute the present-day majority views regarding the *Teamhur Feis*. In Macalister's analysis, the *Feis* at Tara was a highly complex and colorful assemblage of performances, rites, and rituals based upon underlying occult and magical concepts recognizable through comparative mythology and shamanism. The rituals themselves, deeply imbued in archaic and esoteric tradition, frequently require an occult perspective for their interpretation—an approach that many of Macalister's colleagues considered irrelevant at best and many Irish Christian readers found somewhat irreverent. Some of Macalister's theories (for example, his acknowledgment of Irish ritual cannibalism along with a sympathetic defense of the practice based upon occult principles) suggest to many that he belongs to the marginal realm of Irish studies.

One of the consistent charges leveled against Macalister (and a charge that he himself acknowledges) is his tendency to draw correspondences between events at Tara and apparently unrelated events occurring elsewhere in time and space. One of the correspondences Macalister made (that was subsequently rejected by most of his contemporaries) was that the *Feis* at Tara was held on the vernal equinox and thus related to a wider pagan and pan-European celebration on this date. Some of his other controversial claims include: a connection between ritual dance performed by the king at Tara and Finn MacCool; a spiral labyrinthine petroglyph indicating the pattern of a ritual procession at Tara; the mysterious voice of the thunder god, heard during the Rites at Tara and its true origin in the device known as the "bull-roarer" (though there was never any archaeological evidence to substantiate such a claim); the important role of a Druid known as Mog Ruith, the slayer of ECH at the Rites of Tara; and the characters known as the Twins (the young male offspring of their father, ECH, and mother, Ana), who perform important ritualized combat at the *Teamhur Feis*.

The majority of the academic community has never accepted these and other claims made by Macalister; and his occult orientation and proclivity to make connections unfathomable to most of his colleagues have made him a favorite bête noire for many. Recently, Edel Bhreathnach, in *Tara: A Select Bibliography,* notes, in her understated manner, that Macalister's version of the *Teamhur Feis* is laden with "strange conclusions" (135); his book *Tara: A Pagan Sanctuary of Ancient Ireland* received so little favorable criticism after its initial publication that it has never been reprinted.

Consequently, Macalister's "strange conclusions" are found nowhere else in the genre of Irish lore—nowhere else except in *Finnegans Wake*.

As discussed in the following chapters, Macalister's highly unique conclusions all have their parallels in *Finnegans Wake*; this strongly suggests that Macalister's work is indeed an important source used by Joyce. And the work of Macalister *has* been identified in *Finnegans Wake* by the *Wake*'s demographer, Adaline Glasheen, by Vivian Mercier, and by Ian MacArthur. Glasheen cites material so peculiar, so specific, and so unique that it could only have come from Macalister's *Secret Languages*; and although *Secret Languages* was published in 1937, there is conclusive evidence that Joyce, even at this late date in the *Wake*'s gestation, read and incorporated parts of Macalister's work into his own. (And in a curious coincidence, *Finnegans Wake* is also a subject of discussion in *Secret Languages*. Macalister was shown a short section of the *Wake* in circulation before its publication; in a lengthy passage in *Secret Languages*, Macalister discusses the linguistic techniques Joyce uses to compose the *Wakean* language and their *exact* parallels in the composition of an ancient Irish Druidic tongue.) Obviously, Joyce and Macalister knew one another's work, and each incorporated the other's work into his own. Macalister's unique assertions regarding Tara are enacted throughout the *Wake*, and Macalister's later work has been documented in the *Wake*—both of these points indicate that Joyce was certainly familiar with Macalister's earlier works regarding Tara.

A further connection between R.A.S. Macalister and James Joyce may be found through a consideration of the charges leveled against Macalister by his colleagues: the occultism and the strange correspondences and claims he makes. These charges have made Macalister's work on Tara both marginal and obscure; these are, however, the very charges that have been leveled at Joyce himself. Frank Budgen notes, "it is sometimes forgotten that in his early years in Dublin Joyce lived among the believers and adepts in magic gathered around the poet Yeats."[10] Joyce possessed considerable knowledge of the Western occult traditions (such as Neoplatonism, Hermeticism, Cabalism, and Celtic paganism) that were promulgated by the Golden Dawn and Theosophical Society, both of which flourished in Dublin in Joyce's student days.[11] As he describes himself in *A Portrait*, "all the hierarchs of initiation cast their spells upon him."[12] Stuart Gilbert, a close friend of Joyce, observes that Joyce "seemed inclined to give some credence to the theory held by certain occultists that essentially thoughts, like matter, are indestructible and persist in some 'repository' out of space and out of time, yet accessible in certain privileged moments" (*Letters I*, 30). Frank Budgen notes that Joyce, like the practitioners of ritual in the Golden Dawn (most notably Yeats and Mathers), believed the "repository" of the *Anima Mundi* could be accessed if his talismans were evoked in the right set and setting: "Yeats held that the borders of our mind are always shifting and form part of the universal memory. This universal mind and memory could be evoked by symbols. When telling me this Joyce added that in his own work he never used the recognized symbols, preferring instead to use trivial and quadrivial words and local geographical allusions. The intention of magical evocation, however, remained the same" (325).

Atherton notes that this magical belief permeates *Finnegans Wake* and accounts for Joyce's religious dedication to his project. Joyce "saw himself as the *Vates*, the poet and prophet," and the *Wake* as "the sacred book of a new religion"; and this belief and its concomitant sense of dedication allowed Joyce to continue for the seventeen long years at his self-imposed task (14). Joyce felt that if the *Wake* could be presented and written down correctly, it would have a power of its own: "Joyce was not in his own opinion simply writing a book, he was also performing a work of magic" (15). Atherton concludes that Joyce's archaic and occult attitude regarding the *Wake* "bordered, perhaps, on madness" (14).

Like Macalister, the other symptom of Joyce's borderline "madness" was his amazing proclivity to make outlandish correspondences, connections, and associations between apparently unrelated things. The most obvious and overwhelming manifestation of this ability is the language of *Finnegans Wake*. The thousands of outlandish puns, polysemes, portmanteau words, multiple etymologies, and multilevel neologisms all share the same property of making correspondences and connections where none have been recognized before. Frank O'Connor, after studying *Finnegans Wake* and listening to Joyce discuss his book, observed as Joyce framed a picture of the city of Cork with a frame he carefully and deliberately made *of* cork. O'Connor concluded (as others have) that Joyce suffered from a pathological condition he describes as "associative mania."[13] Macalister's inclination toward occult and esoteric interpretations, as well as his own version of "associative mania," would hardly have deterred Joyce from using him as a source for *Finnegans Wake*. Rather, Joyce would have seen these characteristics not as liabilities but as assets, if not actual requirements. And the fact that Macalister's works were rejected by most academics would, if anything, have been sufficient reason for Joyce to seek out these works and hold them in high esteem.

Irish mythology itself is deeply imbued with esoteric and occult principles. The Celtic certainty of the Otherworld (a point commented upon by many classical writers), the archaic wake rites, the Otherworld journeys and initiations that comprise the *echtra* and *immrama* tales, Finn's reincarnation, the bizarre ritual conducted at Tara known as the *Tarbh Feis*, the magical proscriptions, the shape-shifting shamans—all of which are found in *Finnegans Wake*—indicate a worldview different from that of most contemporary readers and academics. Joyce's belief in, and use of, pre-Christian occultism in *Finnegans Wake*—described by Atherton as near-madness—may actually be an appropriate means to the *Wake*'s interpretation.

The "associative mania" that both Joyce and Macalister share is, in the archaic Irish tradition, a gift from the goddess Brigit and a highly respected ability of the *Filidh*. Far from pathological, the power to perceive hidden correspondences and sacred coincidence was concomitant with the ability to discern the talismanic potency of certain words, and the ability to articulate a deeper level of reality: "From a mythological standpoint, such correspondences are neither accidents nor inventions. They are discoveries, their validity grounded in the inexhaustible analogical riches of the universe. Their magic has delighted and sustained the spirit of man throughout the ages, for it has the power to breach the constraining boundaries of the finite so that the light of eternity may transubstantiate that which is commonplace and fill it with mystery" (Rees and Rees, 351).

Joyce and Macalister share one further characteristic that has a relevance to this present work. In their respective pursuits, both men found themselves in marginalized roles with many of their peers believing them slightly mad. This particular social identity—the outcast with visionary abilities—is one of the important roles in Irish mythic tradition. Macalister and Joyce, as well as Stephen Dedalus, Shem, and HCE, along with the visionary poets of Ireland, all share characteristics with this ancient paradigm whose archetypal manifestation is Finn, the ultimate and titular hero of *Finnegans Wake* itself.

Given the nature of the charges leveled against Macalister—occultism and his own version of "associative mania"—as well as the outlandish, colorful, bizarre, esoteric spectacle that Macalister presents as the *Teamhur Feis*, Macalister's rendition of the *Teamhur Feis* would, for James Joyce, make the perfect model to appropriate for *Finnegans Wake*; and it is this model of the *Teamhur Feis* that is used throughout the present work. In *Wake Rites*, I have referred to the work of Macalister more than any other single source of Irish mythic material, and I have extensively utilized four of his most significant works on Irish lore: "Temair Breg: A Study of the Remains and Traditions of Tara" (1919); *Ireland in Pre-Celtic Times* (1921); *Tara: A Pagan Sanctuary of Ancient Ireland* (1931); and *The Secret Languages of Ireland* (1937). Two of these works in particular are cited repeatedly in the following chapters: "Temair Breg" and *Tara*. In *Wake Rites,* I have frequently chosen to quote from the 1931 edition of *Tara* rather than the 1919 edition of "Temair Breg" (even though Joyce's research for the *Wake* began a decade before *Tara* was published). When I do so, it is with the understanding that Macalister's ideas and conclusions, as presented in *Wake Rites,* are found in *both* of Macalister's works on Tara, but the expression of these ideas is clearer and more succinct in the book version (*Tara*) than in the lecture series ("Temair Breg"). I have also used sections from *Secret Languages;* as stated earlier, *Secret Languages* has already been documented as a source used in *Finnegans Wake.*

Methodology

In the early years of the twentieth century, a new method for elucidating mythopoeic texts emerged as a result of prior research in the field of comparative mythology. In this new mythopoeic paradigm, the myth itself has been stripped to its quintessential frameworks, condensed to its most basic patterns, and comes to be perceived as the substructure lying beneath the surface narrative of a text that, in turn, frequently appears to be fragmentary, confused, and obscure. Identifying the mythic patterns used as substructures allows for clarification of the surface narrative; the myth becomes "the subtext and the means by which the surface tale signifies" (*IU,* 340). This methodology proved to be especially appropriate in Celtic studies, for frequently mythic substructures must be identified and used to explain Celtic texts that are fragmentary or obscured in their surface narratives. In studies of Irish mythopoeic literature in particular, this method proved most useful, "even perhaps essential in establishing patterns in a mythology that was in many ways opaque" (*IU,* 340).

This method of using mythic patterns as subtext and signifier for a fragmented and obscure surface narrative was appropriated for the creation of literature by several important writers in the early decades of the twentieth century, perhaps most conspicuously by T. S. Eliot in *The Waste Land.* However, as Maria Tymoczko notes, James Joyce is generally credited not only with first utilizing this paradigm for literary creation but also with modifying this method to suit his own literary and artistic purposes:

> The extension of the methods of comparative mythology and folklore to the creation of literary texts was pioneered by James Joyce though he was not the sole practitioner of these techniques. Eliot himself in *The Waste Land* depends on comparative mythology, using . . . the basic pattern behind the myth, rather than the surface . . . to achieve his ends; lest we miss his deep structures, Eliot provides footnotes to spell out the patterns we need in order to understand the meaning of his poem. Joyce has dispensed with footnotes. (*IU*, 341)

Even without providing the "footnotes" that Eliot includes for *The Waste Land*, Joyce's narrative method in *Finnegans Wake* bears a strong resemblance to Eliot's poem, as William York Tindall, among many others, has noted: "The *Wake* is put together like a long poem, 'The Waste Land' again, of parts placed side by side without transition, parts in a variety of rhythms, shapes, and tones. Like the whole of such a poem the parts and whole of the *Wake* evade immediate understanding" (17). And the resemblance between *The Waste Land* and *Finnegans Wake* may actually be much deeper than the surface similarities observed by Tindall and others: the chaotic and fragmented surface tale of *The Waste Land* is signified by a substructure from Celtic myth; and, as is argued in this present work, Celtic myth is the signifier of the chaotic and fragmented surface tale that is *Finnegans Wake*.

Wake Rites identifies and uses Celtic myth—specifically, the mythic patterns of the *Teamhur Feis*—as the signifying substructure for *Finnegans Wake*. Putting it another way: *Wake Rites* provides the "footnotes" that Joyce dispensed with when he wrote *Finnegans Wake*. Each of the bizarre, fragmented, obscure, and seemingly absurd episodes that collectively form the surface narrative of *Finnegans Wake* can be explained—signified—by correlating the appropriate mythic pattern from the *Teamhur Feis* with its parallel event in the surface story of the *Wake*.

In *Wake Rites*, each of the *Wakean* episodes is addressed using this method. Every episode in *Finnegans Wake* can be shown to have its correlative in the *Teamhur Feis*; and every ritual, rite, and event enacted at the *Teamhur Feis* has its parallel reenactment in the bizarre surface narrative of *Finnegans Wake*. In addition to examining all of the episodes of *Finnegans Wake*, I have also addressed the other aspects of the *Wake* that collectively make it the obscure narrative that it is; these include the enigmatic underlying event in the *Wake*—the mysterious holiday, holy day, festival—that has never been identified; the absurd cast, the *Sigla Group*; the dream of the *Wake*; its microcosmic quality; and the nearly impenetrable language of the *Wake*. For each of these, I use the same method used for analysis of the *Wakean* episodes—that is, correlating the surface story with its mythic substructure from the *Teamhur Feis*. As related above, this methodology is especially appropriate for Irish mythopoeic texts, texts such as *Finnegans Wake*; this approach is certainly relevant for addressing *Finnegans Wake*, as it is based on the mythopoeic methods pioneered by James Joyce himself. And, finally, my intention with the application of this methodology is to show that the entire *Wake* and the ancient *Teamhur Feis* resonate in a sacred coincidence—a sacred coincidence that imbues *Finnegans Wake* with a potency symbolic, mythic and numinous, that has never been truly recognized since the *Wake*'s talismanic birth on Imbolc so many years ago.

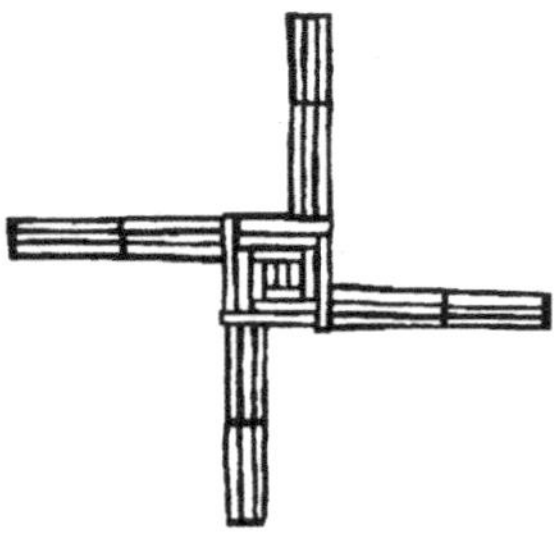

Figure 1. The Cross of Brigit, Patroness of the Irish *Filidh*. Graphic design by Mary Davis, Abita Springs, Louisiana.

2

The Day of the *Wake*

The Ricorso at Tara

Seventeen—the sacred number of regeneration for the pagan Irish—is also the number of renewal and resurrection in *Finnegans Wake*.[1] After sixteen chapters in the unconsciousness of sleep, night. and winter darkness, the seventeenth, the day of the *Wake*, begins with a rejoicing: "Sandhyas! Sandhyas! Sandhyas!" (593.1), a chant at once encompassing sanctity (Latin, *Sanctus*), peace (Sanskrit, *Samdhi*), and a new beginning (Sanskrit, *Sandhi*, "twilight of dawn"). The first ray of the sun, a shivering shaft of dawn light (597.24), suggests the inception of an ancient sunrise ritual as it illuminates primeval megaliths—this spearpoint of "dawnfire" (594.21) touches on the table stone at the center of a great circle of megaliths (594.21–22).

As this spearpoint of dawnfire waxes in strength, the cold and darkness of winter and night give way to the day of greening and spring: the "Dayagreening" (607.24 [Irish, *deo-greine*, "spark of the sun"; Swedish, *daggrynning*, "dawn"]) gains in "schlimninging" (607.24 [Swedish, *shymningen*, "dusk"]). The reign of darkness and snow slowly recedes (607.25). A mythic leader returns, renascent and newly incarnate, as foretold around the hearth sides (596.3–5). The primal sun king, "Solsking the Frist" (607.28), will soon arrive in great procession (607.28–29). And the sleeper, who has been having a sound night's sleep (597.2), and whose dreamthoughts are the obscure events of sixteen previous chapters, finally wakes in the seventeenth, when everything is about to "rolywholyover" (597.3).

One of the first acts of the awakened sleeper is lighting the domestic fire; and as the smoke rises, this fire is at once the fire lit by Saint Patrick centuries ago at pagan Tara. Commenting on the rising smoke they both see, Mutt and Jute reappear here at Tara (609.24), along with the crowd of thousands who wandered through the dreamed episodes of earlier chapters. The Twins note that this bonfire lit at Slane (609.34) has definitely angered the Archdruid (610.1–2). This modern yet ancient fire becomes the focus of confrontation between pagan Archdruid and Christian saint; and this singular event—the confrontation at Tara—is the transforming climax of the *Wake*: "Taawhaar?" (613.5) . . . "To trancefixureashone" (613.9). And though all who are present here were here before (613.13), the order is entirely "othered" (613.14), "Nought is nulled. *Fuitfiat*!" (613.14).

In the "Recorso" (usually spelled "Ricorso") section of *A Skeleton Key to "Finnegans Wake,"* Joseph Campbell and Henry Robinson identify this event as "the crucial moment of Book IV; the crucial moment indeed of history; the moment of the renovating impulse"; and it is at this crucial moment, more than anywhere else in the *Wake*, that "We behold . . . a curious convergence of many themes" (348). This curious convergence of themes in the Ricorso—the seasonal transformation, renewal and resurrection, the return of the "sun king," the relighting of a ritual bonfire, Patrick's Christian rituals, the pagan solar rites, the confrontation of antinomial forces, the festive crowd gathered at Tara prior to Patrick's arrival—has suggested to many *Wakean* scholars that underlying the Ricorso is some very significant date, holiday, holy day, seasonal festival, or pagan event. Joyce has used this method before, and with great effect (for example, in *Ulysses*, "Ivy Day," "The Dead," and "Clay"); and many *Wakeans* have felt that if the date or event of the Ricorso *could* be specifically identified, this identification could then be used to elucidate the obscure events in the *Wake* leading up to the Ricorso. Consequently, a host of *Wakean* scholars, past and present, have attempted to clarify the murky events preceding the Ricorso by first identifying the Ricorso occasion itself. The most comprehensive theories regarding the date of the Ricorso are independently presented by Clive Hart, Nathan Halper, John Gordon, and Michael Kaufmann. Their research presents three strong arguments for three completely different events: Easter, the vernal equinox, and the ancient pagan festival Beltane.

The Three Theories

1. The Easter Ricorso. Initially presented by Clive Hart, the most widely accepted theory is that the dream episodes and actions of *Finnegans Wake*

lead to the Ricorso of an Easter morning. Textual evidence in the *Wake* certainly supports this: for example, the crowd of Irish gathered for Hosty's ballad are pondering over the Roman Easter (43.10); HCE, frequently associated with Easter eggs (210.32, 220.21, 483.21), overhears an Easter greeting (376.36–377.1) the Saturday night before his own Easter reappearance (483.10); Paschal fires and candles (128.30, 213.18–19, 379.30, 397.26–27) illuminate the night in Ireland, the "two easter island" (188.10–11). And the major themes of Easter are totally in accord with certain episodes in the *Wake*: the trial of a king, the fourteen questions representing the *Via Crucis*, the death and funeral of a great and divine leader, the mysterious journey through the underworld, the sunrise and springtime resurrection, and HCE's reappearance as the sun king, all strongly suggest the imagery of Easter.

In concurrence with Clive Hart, Roland McHugh emphasizes that the Ricorso itself obviously begins with Saint Patrick lighting the Paschal fire. McHugh notes that among Saint Patrick's major exploits was his defiance of royal authority in lighting a fire at Slane on Holy Saturday, which led to the "vital clash" between Christian and pagan that occurred on Easter Sunday at Tara. The clash takes the form of a contest associated with light and darkness—and this "particular miracle" is featured in the Ricorso of the *Wake*.[2]

McHugh's account of the Ricorso confrontation is ultimately derived from the Irish Christian scribe Muirchú maccu Machthene, whose Latin version of the event (one of the oldest extant accounts) alludes to an unidentified pagan feast concurrent with the first Irish Easter.

> Sequente uers die, hoc est in die pascae, recumbentibus regibus et principibus et magis apud Loiguire—festus enim dies maximus apud eos erat—manducantibus illis et bibentibus uinum in palatio Temoriae sermocintibusque aliis et aliis cogitantibus de his quae facta fuerant, sanctus Patricius quinque tantum uiris, ut contenderet et uerbum faceret de fide sancta in Temoria coram omnibus nationibus, hostiis claussis secundum id quod de Christo legitur uenit.
>
> [The next day, that is, Easter, when kings, princes, and druids were reclining at Loegaire's table—for this day was the most important feast day among them—when they were eating and drinking wine in the palace of Tara, with some discussing and others pondering the things that had been done, holy Patrick with only five men came inside despite the closed doors, just as it can be read about Christ, in

order to contend and to preach the holy faith in Tara before all the nations.][3]

The accounts of both McHugh and Muirchú (as well as the *Wake*) suggest an unnamed pagan feast already under way when Patrick came to Tara at Easter. Professor Bury, however, in his *Life of St. Patrick,* addresses this issue and dismisses the notion of a concurrent pagan feast as merely a literary device: an argument that definitely supports Clive Hart's theory. Bury sees the idea of the first Easter fire flashing defiance across the plain of Meath to the heathen powers of Tara as both "bold and brilliant"—a verbal picture worthy of the best of myth makers who, for their own purposes, "transfigure the facts of history" (106–7). Bury emphasizes the fact that the calendar is disregarded in the story of the confrontation at Tara: "The idea is that Easter is to replace Beltane, the Christian to overcome the heathen fire; and it is a matter of no import that the day of Beltane was the first day of summer which could never fall on Easter Eve" (106–7).

The strongest evidence for the Easter Ricorso, though, is from Joyce himself. In a letter to his son, Joyce describes Tara as "the Mecca and Jerusalem of the ancient Irish," the sacred locus where the high king was crowned. Joyce summarizes the pivotal event of the *Wakean* Ricorso: "St. Patrick went there [Tara] to confront the druid priests. . . . Every fire in Ireland was supposed to be extinguished except the royal fire at Slane . . . Patrick raised the Druid's ire by lighting the Paschal fire. It was Holy Saturday."[4] Given the evidence cited above, the majority of *Wakeans* believe that Easter Sunday is the day of the *Wake* and the key event of the Ricorso.

2. The Vernal Equinox Ricorso. Throughout the *Wake,* however, there is at least as much evidence for the vernal equinox date as there is for Easter. In "The Date of Earwicker's Dream," Nathan Halper cites textual evidence for the vernal equinox and argues that this is the *only* event that clearly expresses the theme of balanced opposites so fundamental to the *Wake* and the Ricorso. Halper emphasizes the evidence in the *Wake* that winter is at an end and the sun is about to move into the "equinoctial Ram." At the pivotal moment of the Ricorso, there is parity, perfect equipoise between winter and summer, between night and day. Halper argues that, in the *Wake,* the "book of antinomies," this parity of day and night is the *only* pair we can numerically measure. It therefore becomes a gauge by which to measure *all* of the other antinomials converging at the Ricorso: "The time when they are equal is the time when Shaun and Shem, young-old, right-left . . . all opposites are equal" (75). And this time can *only* be the

vernal equinox, the Day of the Ram, which, as Halper notes, was celebrated in antiquity on the twenty-fifth day of March (89).[5]

John Gordon expands on Halper's argument for the vernal equinox, citing more textual evidence, the necessity of balanced opposites, and the promise of spring and a new beginning that are the requisites for the Ricorso event. Gordon cites a key passage in the *Wake*, where Shem clearly states that the activities of the *Wake* all occur about the "first equinarx" (347.02) in the calendar (347.2–3). The vernal equinox has, at various times, also been associated with the date of another ancient festival prominent in the *Wake*, Sechselauten (whose bells are sounded at 213.18–19). The equinox is the time for the rising "germinal" (354.34–35), the rising seed as well as the beginning of *Germinal*, on the vernal equinox; it is also the occasion for early spring dabbling (342.25), for gusts of spring wind (321.31), and for people to discard their furs and don mackintoshes (346.1–2). The vernal equinox is the day when the sun leaves Pisces the fish and enters Ares the ram; and as Gordon points out, in book I, chapter 1, "The Four Watchers," immediately after telling Finnegan to lie down and "Finn no more" (28.34), add that there is already a "big rody ram" (28.36) on the premises (28.35–36). Trist*ram* supplanting Finn is also ram (Aries) supplanting finny fish (Pisces)—the vernal equinox is thus strongly indicated throughout the *Wake* itself (*Plot Summary*, 38–39).

3. The Beltane Ricorso. Sir James Frazer, in *The Golden Bough*, arrives at yet a third interpretation for the confrontation between Patrick and Archdruid at Tara: the historical event at the time of their colloquy was the pagan festival of May Day, Beltane. Frazer bases his theory on earlier accounts, specifically the account of Muirchú as evidence for his own theory:

> Contigit uero in illo anno ut aliam idolatriae sollempnitatem, quam gentiles incantationibus multis et magicis inuentionibus nonnullisque aliis idolitriae superstitionibus congregates etiam regibus, satrapis, ducibus, principibus et optimatibus populi, insuper et magis, incantatoribus, auruspicibus et omnis artiis omnisque doni inuentoribus doctoribusque vocatis ad Loigaireum uelut quondam ad Nabucodonossor regem in Temoria istorum Babylone exercere consuerant, eadem nocte qua sanctus Patricius pasca illi illam adorarent exercerentque festiuitatem gentilem.
>
> [It so happened in that year that a feast of pagan worship was being held, which the pagans used to celebrate with many incantations and

> magic rites and other superstitious acts of idolatry. There assembled the kings, satraps, leaders, princes, and the nobles of the people; furthermore, the druids, the haruspecs, and the inventors and teachers of every craft and every skill were also summoned to king Loigiure at Tara, their Babylon, as they had been summoned at one time to Nabuchodonosor, and they held and celebrated their pagan feast on the same night on which holy Patrick celebrated Easter.][6]

Frazer, along with the overwhelming majority of folklorists and Celtic scholars reviewing the early accounts by Muirchú and other Christian scribes, argues that the weight of evidence supports Beltane rather than Easter, and that Muirchú and the other Christian scribes conflated Beltane with Easter for their own propaganda purposes (714–16). Citing the work of Sir James Frazer and concurring with him, Michael Kaufmann, in "Seasonal Change and Transformation in the Prankquean's Tale," identifies the Ricorso event as Beltane. Kaufmann associates the Paschal bonfire of Patrick with the "need fire" thought to have been lit by the pagans at Beltane, an annual event in which all fires and hearths were extinguished and then rekindled from the "need fire." Kaufmann acknowledges that there *is* a problem with this theory: the "need fire" was, according to the early written accounts, believed to be relit on Beltane morning, which falls well after the latest possible date for Easter. Kaufmann, Frazer, and others surmise, therefore, that Saint Patrick actually arrived at Tara on Beltane (Kaufmann, 452).

Kaufmann cites further evidence from Celtic paganism that supports the Beltane theory. On each of the Prankquean's visits to the Jarl, hilltop bonfires are burning. These bonfires provide important clues about each date, because bonfires such as these played an important part in several major festivals of the old Celtic year, including Beltane (May Day), Lugnasad (Lammas), and Samhain (All Hallows Eve). "The Prankquean's Tale" is placed in the first chapter of the *Wake*, and it plays out through the cycle of important Celtic festivals—strongly suggesting that the Prankquean episode and the other *Wakean* events (including the Ricorso) occur at the renewal of this Celtic cycle, that is, Beltane. The truce held by Irish Celts at this period, and the ritualistic "marriage" of the Jarl and the Prankquean, also indicate "her first visit on May Day" (438–46).

Kaufmann also finds evidence for the Beltane Ricorso in the multitude of transformations under way at the end of the *Wake*: "summer is dawning" and will soon replace the long winter; the representatives of antinomial transformations throughout the *Wake*, the Twins, are themselves transforming much like the seasons they represent; and the disputation on optics, the "final exchange" between Archdruid and Saint concludes as the season shifts at Beltane: "The point of change comes when the Archdruid reverses his disputation on optics from one on all colors to one on a single color: green. The green of May has come" (445–46).

Problems with the Theories

A few basic calculations clearly show the inherent problems with the three theories. Easter and the vernal equinox can certainly coincide, though it is extremely rare (once or twice a millennium); and these events did not coincide at all in the seventeen years Joyce composed *Finnegans Wake*. Easter and Beltane *never* coincide; nor can Beltane and the vernal equinox. This conundrum is of course recognized by Kaufmann, Gordon, Halper, and others, and they all offer compromises to their original theories: that Joyce, like some of the earlier scribes, ignored any historical accuracy and conflated Christian, pagan, and seasonal events to suit his own literary purposes. The compromise solution is, however, problematic in its own right in that it runs completely counter to Joyce's deliberate precision in dating many of his other works. Joyce, too, exhibits a strong penchant for associating some of his works with "talismanic" dates; combining or conflating dates would, in a sense, diminish this talismanic potency. Furthermore, these three theories, whether applied individually or in some conflated manner, have not provided the interpretive key for the bizarre episodes of the *Wake* preceding the Ricorso—and the discovery of this key is the primary reason for identifying the Ricorso event itself.

The problem is further compounded by the fact that most of the *Wake* is a dream and, as such, is not subject to the evaluations and explanations of waking consciousness. As John Bishop succinctly expresses it: "the book represents nothing; or, to modulate the phrase one degree, much of it represents much the same kind of nothing that one will not remember not having experienced in sleep last night" (*Book of the Dark*, 43). Consequently, many *Wakean* scholars believe *Finnegans Wake* has no structure or intrinsic meaning, and this in itself makes any speculation on the Ricorso occasion peripheral at best.

In a strangely appropriate way, the Ricorso event at the *Wake* enacts this problematic state of criticism about it. The three main participants—Archdruid, Saint, and King—all gather at the Ricorso fire, the climactic focus of their confrontation. The Archdruid, basing his interpretation on ancient Celtic tradition, sees only a pagan meaning. The Christian Patrick totally ignores his Druidic predecessor and sees only Easter. King Leary is leery of both and hedges his bets, suggesting that he sees both interpretations as either totally subjective or fundamentally meaningless. Like the Ricorso moment itself, the convergence of these theories results in a highly charged moment of stalemate.

A Synthesis of the Theories

Of the entire group of Celtic scholars who have addressed the issue of the Tara confrontation, R.A.S. Macalister alone offers a completely different view of the events at Tara—an interpretation that has considerable bearing on the *Wake*'s Ricorso controversy. Macalister states that there is absolutely no evidence that the pagan feast of Beltane was *ever* celebrated at Tara; this mistake was originally made by Irish Christian scribes who were both ignorant of, and hostile to, their pagan precursors. Later scholars—Sir James Frazer, Professor Bury, and others—continued the error when they used these same Christian scribes as their own sources. According to Macalister, however, there was indeed an actual historical pagan rite under way at Tara when Patrick lit his Paschal fire. And in the kind of incredible synchronicity that James Joyce reveled in—and the only time that this has *ever* happened in the history of Ireland—this pagan rite at Tara, Patrick's first Easter celebration, and the vernal equinox, *all occurred on the same day*.

In Macalister's view, on the evening of March 25, A.D. 433, the king of Tara, his entourage, Druids, Fianna, and hordes of pagan Irish were gathered at Tara where the rites, rituals, and events of the *Teamhur Feis*—not Beltane—were already under way. As part of these rites, all fires were extinguished and were to be rekindled from the *torc caille*, the sacred flame kept at Tara. At this key moment in the Rites of Tara, a fire is seen lighting up the horizon: Patrick's Paschal bonfire on the Hill of Slane, the fire that becomes the focus of confrontation between Archdruid and Saint. The confrontation between Patrick and Archdruid occurs on the vernal equinox, which also happened to be the last day of the *Teamhur Feis* and the first Easter Sunday in Ireland, "a piece of extraordinarily good luck that Easter fell on that particular day in that particular year, to teach us that in Tara . . . the Vernal Equinox was a day of celebration" (*T*, 183–84).

The *Teamhur Feis*, by far the most important religious, political, and social event conducted in pre-Christian Ireland, on this one day alone, occurred in sacred coincidence with the first Easter celebrated in Ireland and with the vernal equinox. If Joyce is using the *Teamhur Feis* as the fundamental event in the climactic point of the *Wake*—as is suggested here—then he is *not* conflating, combining, or confusing events for the *Wakean* Ricorso. Rather, he shows that he is so precise in his designation for the day of the *Wake* that only one day in all of Irish history manifests the talismanic potency necessary for the themes and events of the *Wakean* Ricorso: the *Teamhur Feis* conducted on Easter Sunday, A.D. 433.

If the Ricorso event *is* the *Teamhur Feis*, this theory allows for a synthesis of the three conflicting theories already proposed for the *Wakean* Ricorso: *all* of the significant themes and events cited by *Wakean* scholars as evidence for Easter, the vernal equinox, and Beltane, respectively, are defining components of the *Teamhur Feis* itself. Patrick lights his Paschal fire precisely when the Druids gathered at the *Teamhur Feis* are expecting the relighting of their *torc caille* that proclaims ascendancy for the one who lights it, the newly designated representative of divinity. The pagans at the *Feis* have been conducting a wake and funeral rites for their sun king, who was executed, sent to the Otherworld, and is resurrected at dawn that Sunday morning of Easter: Solsking the First, returning on his equinoctial birthday. At the *Teamhur Feis*, the pagan king, like the Christian King, enacts a sacred procession of fourteen parts. During the *Feis*, a truce is in effect throughout the realm. A great feast attended by thousands celebrates the *Banais Righe*, the royal marriage, of the sun king and his queen.

At no other point in the history of Ireland do all the polarities that permeate the *Wake* manifest in more perfect equipoise than that climactic day of Easter, equinox, and *Teamhur Feis*: the Archdruid of Ireland confronts the Christian saint, Native versus Invader, Celto-Nordic Pagan meets Roman Judeo-Christian, the representative of the Triple Goddess faces the spokesman for the Patriarchal Trinity, the Old Dispensation meets the New, the oral and esoteric tradition confronts the literal and orthodox, night and day, winter and summer, death and life, are all, for one brief point in time, in perfect balance. The evidence presented by Clive Hart for an Easter Ricorso, by Nathan Halper and John Gordon for a vernal equinox date, and by Michael Kaufmann for Beltane, is all in perfect accord with the single date and singular events of the *Teamhur Feis*.

That the day of the *Wake* might be the recollection of this ancient event certainly reflects Joyce's deep interest in the talismanic potency of special days, and it also reinforces Joyce's indication that the dream thoughts of the *Wake* are also the wake thoughts of centuries ago. Though it has eluded identification, the day of the *Wake* may be found in the synchronicity of evidence and events of the *Teamhur Feis*. If so, the dream episodes of the *Wake*, and the improbable cast of characters who perform them, may be much more than nocturnal nothingness—they may be the memory of wake events of centuries ago, resurrected from darkness in the seventeenth chapter of the *Wake*, the great recurrence of the Ricorso.

3

The *Sigla Group* at the *Teamhur Feis*

Joyce's Sigla Group

One of the truly striking features of *Finnegans Wake* is the bewildering farrago of characters that gathers for the strange proceedings. Hundreds, thousands, of Irish assemble for the unfolding dramatic events, the mythic reenactments, and the bizarre episodes that constitute the *Wake*. For the most part, these *Wakean* characters are observers, and, usually after a brief moment of acknowledgment, they return to the shifting and somewhat amorphous crowd and are rarely singled out again. Among the thousands gathered for the *Wake*, however, is a recurring group that becomes more distinctive and identifiable as the episodes unfold—a relatively small and improbable cast of characters that performs *all* of the *Wakean* drama.

In her *Third Census*, Adaline Glasheen, the demographer of *Finnegans Wake*, identifies the Porter Family as the primary actors in the *Wakean* cast:

• HCE. The aging patriarch of the Porter clan, the antiheroic HCE runs the tavern where much of the drama unfolds. HCE is frequently portrayed as a once powerful, but now failing, Irish king. More often than not, his role is reduced to that of the fallen leader, or the hapless cuckold, in the various romantic triangles from Celtic mythology reenacted throughout the *Wake*.

• Anna. The wife of HCE, Anna is the archetypal mother and bestower of gifts upon her children, who are all the Irish people. Anna is strongly identified with water: she *is* the rivers, springs, and wells of Ireland. Her young daughter and her elderly housekeeper are frequently portrayed as Anna in her two other aspects, strongly suggesting that Anna and the other two women represent a feminine Trinity present at the *Wake*.

• The Twins. Shem and Shaun, the sons of HCE and Anna, usually appear together and typically take opposing sides on every issue. Their main preoccupation in the *Wake* is fighting each other through an array of forms that suggest characters from the realm of magical realism: they fight as humans, as historical figures, as animals, as the personifications of abstract concepts, and even as varieties of food products.

• Issy. The younger sister of the Twins, Issy is the Maiden/Temptress aspect of the *Wake*'s feminine Trinity. Issy usually appears in dyadic form: with her mirror image, as a split personality, or in the company of her darker "sister." Issy plays the archetypal Celtic princess in all the various romantic triangles reenacted in the *Wake*. In the role of "Brigit," Issy leads her Twenty-Eight Girls from Saint Brigit's School, acting as their mentor and prototype.

Also included in the *Wakean* cast are, as Adaline Glasheen calls them, the "characters of the second rank":[1]

• Kate. The elderly housekeeper at the tavern, Kate frequently represents Anna in her later years. Kate typically plays the roles of crone, witch, and soothsayer. In her two most important roles, Kate plays the guardian who opens and enters the great tumulus, and a banshee in "The Washers at the Ford" episode.

• Sackerson. The butler, janitor, and handyman, the generally taciturn Sackerson maintains the day-to-day operation of the tavern. Even though Sackerson is presented as janitor, his few roles in the *Wake* where he does actually speak suggest he wields some level of authority beyond his apparent station.

• The Twelve. The Twelve Men linger at the tavern, acting as witnesses to the events played out, as representatives of various divisions and factions of Ireland, and as a jury for the legal proceedings in the *Wake*. Their presence at the *Wake* is ubiquitous; they rarely speak, and for some reason seem almost a prerequisite for the proceedings.

• The Four Elders. The Four Elders always travel together, are identified with numerous quadratures (for example, the Four Masters, Four Evangelists, compass points, traditional provinces of Ireland), and on occasion are accompanied by a talking donkey or ass. The main performance of the Four Elders is in the *Wake*'s longest and possibly most surrealistic episode, "The Inquest of Shaun." In "The Inquest," the Four conduct a psychic investigation over the supine body of an entranced Shaun; interrogating the various "entities" speaking through the boy, the Four Elders are deliberate and rigorous in completing their strange and secret agenda.

• The Twenty-Eight Girls from Saint Brigit's School. The Twenty-Eight Irish maidens (whose school seems to be located in Kildare) are associated with the twenty-eight-day lunar cycle, the twenty-eight days of February, budding sexuality, and early springtime. Their main roles in the *Wake* are as the dancers around the "sun god" in the "Mime" episode and as the target audience for Shaun's moralistic rant on the perpetuation of their virginity.

• Master Magrath. Magrath is probably the most enigmatic character of the *Wakean* cast. Magrath is the archenemy, the ritual adversary of HCE, who (though it is never explained how or why) obviously knows Magrath and is terrified of him. Magrath appears early in the *Wake*, where he accosts HCE in "The Encounter in the Park." Magrath, in a rage, curses a terrified HCE in "The Banging at the Gate." Magrath, known as a "Serpent," is apparently the slayer of the kingly but failing HCE. The sinister and important role of Magrath in *Finnegans Wake*, coupled with the bizarre details about Magrath given in the *Wake*, have suggested to many *Wakean* scholars that Joyce had a specific person, historical or mythical, in mind when he created this character. The search for Master Magrath, "whose identity has gravely troubled *FW* explicators" (McHugh, *The Sigla of FW*, 127), however, has generated no real answer to either his role or identity, suggesting to many that Magrath—like the rest of the cast—has no real identity or basis apart from what is found in *Finnegans Wake* itself.

James Joyce, in the early stages of the *Wake*'s composition, identified and designated his improbable cast of primary and secondary characters by assigning each of his characters, and each of his character groups (such as "the Four," "the Twelve," or "the Twenty-Eight") a symbol, known as a *Siglum* (plural, *Sigla*). All of the characters described above are assigned *Sigla*.

In addition, Joyce assigned a specific *Siglum* for Saint Patrick. In this collection of highly imaginative characters, Saint Patrick adds another aspect to the *Sigla Group*'s overall implausibility. Unlike all of the other characters designated with *Sigla*, Patrick shows up only once at the *Wake* events—the confrontation at Tara—and plays only one role, where he essentially makes a guest appearance as himself. In the entire *Sigla Group*, Patrick is also the only identifiable historical character; unlike all the others, the *Wakean* Patrick is known to have existed outside of the *Wake* itself, making him something of the anomaly in this surrealistic group of characters.[2]

Joyce's *Sigla Group*—the twelve characters or groups listed above—represent the *Wake*'s dramatis personae in their entirety: they perform *all* of the various roles in *all* of the *Wakean* episodes. The *Sigla Group*—as surrealistic, antiheroic, and ridiculous as they are—is the improbable array both necessary and sufficient to conduct all the services at the *Wake*.

The *Sigla* themselves, much like the characters they represent, are a strange and improbable mix. Some *Sigla* are identical to letters in the classical Greek alphabet; some *Sigla* are identical to letters in the Roman; others are geometric shapes not found in either Greek or Roman alphabets. Curiously—perhaps significantly—nearly identical representations of all of Joyce's *Sigla* are found in one early Greek alphabet, the Formello-Cervetri, which was used in Ireland by Druids and Bards for divinatory purposes as well as communication in their secret language.[3]

Much like early forms of Celtic and Germanic divination with ogham and runic characters, the *Sigla* have a life of their own and can convey different meanings depending upon their position and placement vis-à-vis their viewer. In *The Sigla of Finnegans Wake*, Roland McHugh (citing John Garvin) presents an example of this ability in the *Siglum* representing ECH, "E" in Joyce's Manuscript I.6.1. The *Siglum* "m" in the Manuscript changes in meaning as it changes in position. Garvin cites the passage at 131.9–11, where HCE's tiara of "scones" (131.10) was held unfillable until one "Liam Fail" (131.10) felled him in "Westmunster" (131.10–11), and notes that this refers to the *Lia Fail*, the sacred stone on which Irish kings were crowned at Tara and which may have been incorporated into the Coronation Chair at Westminster. This phrase also suggests identification of the *Siglum* "m" with Parnell, the "uncrowned King of Ireland," whose followers failed him in Westminster. Another meaning, related to "Tara of the Kings," associates HCE with the High King of Ireland. A further meaning relates to HCE, who in I.2 meets King William (Irish, *Liam*). When "m" is reversed, "Ш" signifies the murdered king of

Tara, the sleeping HCE, and the fall of Finnegan (McHugh, *Sigla of Finnegans Wake*, 11). The *Siglum* itself thus associates HCE with the failure and fall of Irish leaders and the regicide at Tara—both central events of the *Teamhur Feis*.

The *Sigla Group*, as most readers of the *Wake* come to realize, manifests other unique properties as well. At almost any given place in *Finnegans Wake*, when a few *Sigla* characters gather, they can usually resemble something outside of *Finnegans Wake*. The connection may be approximate; the method of analogy is usually, out of necessity, procrustean; and the resemblance is always fleeting, but it can be discerned nonetheless. At no point in *Finnegans Wake*, however, does the *Sigla Group* in its entirety resemble anything *but* itself, that is, the overall pattern of the *Group* is found nowhere but in *Finnegans Wake*. Joyce is deliberate in assigning his *Sigla* to specific characters, and the pattern the *Group* creates is apparently unique to *Finnegans Wake*.

These basic observations regarding the *Sigla Group*—the antiheroic qualities of some characters, the elements of surrealism and magical realism inherent in many, the overall nonpattern of the group, its self-referential identity—collectively present a strong core of evidence for the current assessments of the *Wake*, for example, the confusion of a dream, the type-site for postmodernism, a prototype of literary deconstruction, a major work of metafiction. The striking improbability of the *Sigla Group*, its nonpattern and inherent surrealism, is, in sum, a microcosmic reflection of *Finnegans Wake* as a whole.

The *Sigla Group* as the Dramatis Personae of the *Teamhur Feis*

As improbable as the *Sigla Group* itself may be, it bears an extraordinary resemblance to the dramatis personae required for the religious rites at the *Teamhur Feis*. In order to conduct and perform the complex array of rites and rituals, sacred mime, and inaugural ceremonies that constitute the events of the *Feis* at Tara, the king, his consort, various members of their entourage, Druids, priestesses, religious functionaries, and reenactors of the mythic dead participated as the performers in the Rites. Some of these religious performers acted as the human vehicles of various of the Irish gods and goddesses believed to manifest during the Rites; others became the personifications of natural forces or the complementary representatives of opposing abstract principles; some functioned as members of the legislative assembly convening during the Rites; and various Druids and priestesses performed the complex array of magical rites and tests connected with the wake, the royal marriage and the renewal rites—all indispensable to successfully perform the events that collectively comprise the *Teamhur Feis*.

To this pagan cast performing at the *Feis*, the anomalous Saint Patrick must be added, since he is, de facto, one of the main religious performers at the Rites of Tara. And with this inclusion of Patrick, the *Wakean Sigla Group* finds its ancient counterpart in the cast of performers necessary to conduct the *Teamhur Feis*—their numbers and functions are identical; and when the performers at the *Feis* had names or titles, Joyce hardly changed these from their ancient correlates. Table 3.1 outlines these correspondences between the *Wake*'s entire *Sigla Group*, their counterparts at the *Teamhur Feis*, and their functions at the *Wake* and the *Feis*. Each of these correspondences is, in turn, discussed at length in the following sections of this chapter.

HCE: The Once and Future ECH

ECH: The God-King at the Teamhur Feis

In the complex series of events that comprise the Rites of Tara, the most important male protagonist is the *ard rí*, the high king: "the royal occupant of Tara was a god upon earth; he was the living incarnation of one of the deities" (*T*, 125). The high king, through the array of tests and inaugural rites of the *Feis*, has been elevated to godhead; a divinity has chosen to inhabit the physical vehicle of the *ard-rí*. In the person of the high king, this god will be present with his people; and as long as this divinity remains with the king, the harvest will be plentiful; storms, famines and epidemics will be averted; peace and plenty will be assured for the Irish populace (*T*, 126).

The roles of this god-king were many. The *ard-rí* was the leader of the Irish; he was the representative of the sun god; he was the Spirit of Vegetation whose forces waxed and waned in the seasonal cycle; he was the royal consort of the Sovereign queen, a deity in her own right; he was the father of all the Irish; he was mystically identified with fox and horse. And the long history of these god-kings at Tara, as recorded in the famous *Annals of the Four Masters*, indicates that the same few names—all cognates—repeat throughout the entire regnal line: Eochu, Eocha, Eocho, Eochaid.

The *Wake's* ultimate source of "history," *The Annals of the Four Mas-*

Table 3.1. Comparison of the *Sigla Group* with the dramatis personae of the *Teamhur Feis*

The *Wake*	*Sigla*	The *Feis*	The Description
HCE	E	ECH	Father god of the Irish; Consort of Ana; God king at Tara; Elder Male in the Triangle at the Feis
Anna	△	Ana	Mother Goddess of Eire; Creator of rivers and springs; Triple Goddess; Consort of ECH; Sovereign of Eire
Issy	⊥	Ess, Brigit, Dyadic goddess	Maiden/Temptress Aspect of the Triple Goddess
Kate	K	Cailleach, the Crone	Crone Aspect of the Triple Goddess
The Twins	┘ ⊏	The Twins	Minor male deities; Offspring of ECH and Ana; Personifications of antinomial opposites; Brothers; Opponents in the Ritual Transformation Combats
The Twelve Morphios	O	The Twelve Magistrates	Royal Representatives to Rites and Assembly
The Four Elders	X	The Four Watchers	Four Elder Druids who perform the Shamanistic Inquest
The Twenty-Eight Girls from Saint Brigit's School	⬭	The Twenty-Eight Priestesses from the Sanctuary of the Goddess Brigit	Vestal Virgins of Tara; Entourage of Brigit; Participants in Fertility Rites and Rites of Lustration at *Feis*
Sackerson the Butler at the Mullingar Inn	S	Steward of the *Tech Midchuarta*	Steward and Seneschal during the *Feis* Events conducted in the House of the Circulation of Mead
St. Patrick	P	St. Patrick	Christian Colonizer; Ultimate Invader; Usurper of Pagan Rites
Magrath	F	Mog Ruith	Ritual Adversary of ECH; Powerful Druid and Slayer of the aging ECH at Tara; Possessor of a mysterious wooden device, the Roth Romach; Votary of goddess Ana

ters, ostensibly authored by Farfassa O'Mulconry, Peregrine O'Clery, Peregrine O'Duignan, and Michael O'Clery, emerges early in chapter 1 where Joyce praises both *The Annals* and its authors: after all that is "farfatch'd" (14.28), "peragrine" (14.28), "dingnant" (14.28) or "clere" (14.28) we lift our ears, our eyes in the darkness, from their tome (14.28–29). And as noted in the *Wake*, *The Annals* presents an important theme regarding the successive waves of invaders and colonizers: ever since the bouts between "Hebear" (14.35) and "Hairyman" (14.35–36 [Heber and Heremon, the first Irish Celts]), the "Formoreans" (15.5 [Fomorians, pre-Celtic invaders]) have battled the "tooath" (15.5–6) of the "Danes" (15.6 [Tuatha De Danaan]), and the "Oxman" (15.6 [Viking]) has been pestered by the "Firebugs" (15.6–7 [Fir Bolg, early colonizers of Ireland]); and these have "quadrilled" (15.9–10) across the span of centuries (15.10).

The events Joyce alludes to in the above passage, if investigated in the original *Annals*, manifest an important pattern regarding kingship at Tara. *The Annals of the Four Masters* states that the Fir Bolg, the "Firebugs," one of the earliest and most powerful groups of invaders and colonizers of Ireland, gained hegemony over the natives (the Cruithne) and established a Fir Bolg dynasty at Tara between 3267 and 3303 *anno mundi*. Their most prominent king is Eochu; his reign is described by the Masters as "the most golden of ages" that Ireland has ever seen. The Four Masters note that in Eochu's reign "there was no year without harvest, falsehood was banished from Ireland during his lifetime, and he it was who first established the rule of justice there."[4] The "Firebug" Eochu is the first great builder of Tara, a great patriarch and lawgiver.

The Annals then describes a later race of invaders and colonizers, the Tuatha De Danaan, who overthrow the Fir Bolg and establish their own dynasty at Tara. The kings of the Tuatha De Danaan reign between 3304 and 3500 *anno mundi*. The first king of the Tuatha De Danaan is Eochu, who is also given the accolades "Bres mac Elada" ("Son of Science," "Learned Man of Ireland"), "Eochu Oll-athair" ("Eochu the Great Father"), and Dagda ("The Good God"). Eochu of the Tuatha De Danaan is, like his Fir Bolg counterpart, the great patriarch, bringer of learning, and builder of Tara. As the Dagda, he brings a great cauldron to Tara that later figures prominently in the rituals of the *Feis*.

The next great wave of invaders and colonizers discussed in *The Annals* are the Celts, who are led to Ireland by "Hebear" and "Hairyman." The Celtic monarchy reigns at Tara from 3883 to 4019 *anno mundi*. The first Celtic king at Tara is again named Eochu, surnamed "Ollam Fodhla" ("The

Learned Man of Ireland"). The Celtic Eochu initiates another great building program at Tara. As Ollam Fodhla, he establishes the great Druidic College at Tara and the first of the *Teamhur Feis*. Eochu is given the agnomen "Gede of the Great Voice"—a reference to the thunder traditionally associated with both Eochu and the Rites established by him. And even before the great invasions, the aboriginal Cruithne named their first and best patriarch Eochu, surnamed Gede Olgudach and Ollamh, both surnames again associated with thunder and learning (*T*, 106). In *The Annals* (as well as in many other early Irish manuscripts), bearers of the name *Eochu* in its various spellings (and with numerous surnames and agnomens) include famous colonizers, kings, saints, bards, villains, patriarchs, and conquerors on horseback (MacKillop, *Dictionary*, 162). Indeed, the name *Eochu* is the ultimate name for *all* Irish patriarchs: "it is not for nothing that so many kings of Temair, in the official history, bore the name *Eochu. . . . Eochu Oll-athair* and *Eochu Oll-Flaith* . . . avatars . . . of the monarchy bore the name" (*TB*, 331). R.A.S. Macalister therefore surmises, "all the kings, as a matter of course, originally were called *Eochu*" (*TB*, 331).

Eoin MacNeill, writing in 1921, explores the name further and asserts a point that others have also suspected: all the Eochus, Eochaids, Eochas, and so on, in all the myths and legends, despite their different agnomens, are emanations of one primordial entity (MacKillop, *Dictionary*, 162). Even though he appears to be "more mob than man" (261.21–22), the actual identity of this singular being who manifests as All-Father, ultimate Irish Patriarch, Master Builder, Thunderer, Husband of Ana, Father of the Twins, and founder of the *Teamhur Feis* is the god whose original name is the ancient Celtic "ECH" (*TB*, 331).

The "cluekey": HCE as ECH

"ECH" is, of course, the reversal of "HCE," Joyce's name for the *Wake*'s ultimate male hero. And as William York Tindall and many other scholars recognize, the reversal of this name is a very important theme in the *Wake*: "Renewal [is] signalized in the *Wake* by reversal. . . . Such 'backwords' include initials: H.C.E., reversed becomes E.C.H. These 'tristurned initials' are the 'cluekey to a worldroom beyond the roomwhorld' (100.28–29)" (84). By applying Joyce's "cluekey," some important parallels emerge between ECH of the *Teamhur Feis* and HCE of the *Wake*.

ECH, as the "Good God" Dagda, hardly seems a powerful or attractive divinity. His youth has passed; he is heading into later middle age. A bit overweight, he drinks too much, and because of this, he is sometimes called "Dagda Deirgdeic" ("Dagda Red-Eyed"). At gatherings with friends and family, his eructation and flatulence are an embarrassing joke. His clothes are ill-fitting and he usually and inappropriately carries around a stick, club, or shillelagh.

The Dagda is certainly one of the most ancient and most powerful of the Irish Celtic gods and is, in the Irish pantheon, the primary male actor. But as portrayed in Irish mythology, the Dagda is remarkably different from most of the preconceived images regarding pagan deities—perhaps because these ideas are derived primarily from the mythic pictures of the Greek gods renowned for youth, grace, and beauty. The Dagda hardly presents a fine figure of refinement and slim muscularity but rather is overweight, aged, somewhat grotesque, and even slightly deformed. This untoward description of the Dagda is, of course, a perfect description for HCE.

Throughout *Finnegans Wake,* HCE is *always* dressed in his ubiquitous seven articles of differently colored clothing (for example, 22.34, 30.23–24, 35.8–10). HCE seems to be making a point (more than just a fashion statement) with this deliberately septenary outfit—though what his point exactly is has never been determined. But HCE's elusive message may be related to a sartorial trend initiated by his prototype, as recorded in *The Annals of the Four Masters, anno mundi* 3664:

> This was the first year of Eochaidh Eadghadhach, as king over Ireland. He was called Eochaidh Eadghadhach because it was by him the variety of colour was first put on clothes in Ireland, to distinguish the honour of each by his raiment, from the lowest to the highest. This was the distinction made between them: one colour in the clothes of slaves; two in the clothes of soldiers; three in the clothes of goodly heroes, or young lords of territories, six in the clothes of ollaves; seven in the clothes of kings and queens.

ECH's colorful septenary outfit is a perfect fit for HCE.

Like ECH Dagda, HCE has his problem with flatulence: "our cubehouse" (5.14 ["cubehouse" refers to the Ka'aba, the center of Islam; "our" Irish "cubehouse" was at Tara]) still rocks as "earwitness" (5.14) to the "thunder" (5.15) of his "arafatas" (5.14–15 [farts, Our Fathers, Arafata hill near Mecca, thunder of Mount Ararat]). Throughout the *Wake,* this minor rumbling may even be confused or conflated with thunder, as Joyce indicates with his pun on "arafatas." HCE, then, is certainly associated with some version of "thundering" that does relate to ECH as "Thunderer." It may be amusing to note here that in ancient Ireland the *Filidh*, like Joyce, also concocted a ridiculous pun to highlight the noisy parallel between flatulence and thunder. In *Cormac's Glossary* (edited by Whitley Stokes, "Stout Stokes" [619.32]), a compendium of ninth-century Irish pagan lore, one of the stranger entries is the pun that is the word "TON": "TON: ('anus') *a tonitro .i. on torainn bis inti* ('from the thunder that is in it') *vel a tono fograigim* ('I make a noise')" (162). Joyce evidently continues in the tradition of his pagan predecessors.

The word *ECH* itself means "horse," and is meant to convey the appellation of "Horseman of the Heavens," the great and powerful Irish sun god who traverses the heavens and provides light and warmth and seasonal fertility for all his Irish children (O'Rahilly, 202). ECH is a great equestrian and mounted warrior. In the Otherworld, he possesses a terrible weapon, a spear that harnesses the power of the sun, the *gae bulga*, a Celtic lightning rod that at once conveys the phallic potency synonymous with the Great Horseman as well as the power of the heavens in both its creative and destructive aspects. At the *Teamhur Feis*, the representative of ECH, the *ard rí*, carries a mundane facsimile of the *gae bulga* of ECH—a straight white rod—as the royal wand of office (*SH*, 1:46). In his recent incarnation in the *Wake*, HCE, the "mannork" (378.6) of all Ireland who heard his name in the thunder (378.7), is hardly ever without his ridiculous and ubiquitous stick: a pot on a pole (31.2–3), a staff (35.7), a "chopstick" (36.16), "ruling rod" (553.1), a "supershillelagh" (25.15), a "swaystick" (569.19) held aloft, a "Tullagrove pole" (284.4), and a plethora of limbs, branches, canes, and staffs.

In his essay on HCE and his sticks, Marion W. Cumpiano notes the obvious "royal," divine, and phallic themes conveyed when HCE carries his sticks of office. These sticks, "symbols of royal authority glorified in HCE's fantasies of power matching a king's," identify HCE with the chief "polemarch" (380.12), the unhappy last king of Ireland (20). Cumpiano notes that HCE's "pot on a pole" is linked to a voice from afar (3.9), suggesting that the staff is connected with the heavens and that there is divine power imbuing the staff itself: an aroused and aspiring HCE thought to touch "himmels" (191.35–36 [German, *Himmel*, "heaven"]) with the point of his risen "stiffstaff" (191.35–36) ("Flowerpot," 62–63). Like his ancient counterpart, ECH, HCE carries his own version of the *gae bulga*.

In addition to the *gae bulga*, horses themselves are strongly associated with the god and his representative at the *Feis*. The name *ECH* identifies the horse as a totem animal of the god, and several important rituals conducted during the *Teamhur Feis* focus on the relation between the king and his totem animal. In the *Wake,* HCE has his own curious connections with horses; these *Wakean* horses appear in several important episodes that directly parallel the ancient rituals.[5]

In addition to the equine theme connected with ECH and HCE, both share a curious association with foxes. The classical writers Athenaeus and Posidonius both relate that throughout the Celtic realm, kings were typically associated with the fox. Many a Celtic king fostered this vulpine totemism—especially between the second century B.C. and the fifth century A.D.—because it "implied that his initiation rites were connected with foxes; that it was an ancestral name . . . [and] implied intelligence."[6] Throughout the Celtic realm, vulpine names were taken by, or associated with, royalty: for example, *Lovern* (Briton), *Lovernios* (Gaulish), *Louarn* (Armorican), and, in Ireland, *Loarn* and *Crimthann.* (The father of High King Leary, for example, was named "Crimthann.") A fallen king, or king rejected by society, was known in Ireland as a "wild fox" (Nagy, *Angels,* 106). In *Finnegans Wake,* HCE's initial encounter with royalty involves a fox hunt (96.26–97.27): the king pauses from the fox hunt to give HCE a special epithet; this is when HCE begins carrying his royal sticks. Later, as the "wild fox" Festy King (now called "Reynard" [97.28], the famous fox of medieval fable), he is the fox hunted by an irate citizenry described as a pack of excited hounds. HCE uses some vulpine strategies to outmaneuver the hunters, but he is eventually caught. The "wild fox" is forced into a dark watery grave somewhere in the vicinity of Dublin as a ritual sacrifice intended to foster the wheat crop (76.35) and ginger up the tourism trade (76.35). The entire ritual is performed under the auspices of "Sowan" and "Belting" (77.4–5). ("Sowan and Belting" are Samhain and Beltane, Halloween and May Day, two of the important ritual days of the pagan Irish. Connected with Imbolc and Lugnasad, these four seasonal festivals form the cyclical calendar of the Celts.) HCE, the "wild fox," is ritualistically murdered and placed in a dark pool on a pagan holy day.

A curious parallel to the *Wake*'s vulpine murder emerged on Lugnasad (the Celtic feast intended to foster wheat crops) in 1984, when evidence of just such a ritual homicide as described by Joyce was discovered in a pool of black water at Lindow. The body of a Celtic male, preserved in peat for almost two thousand years, was uncovered. The evidence indicates that he was certainly of the nobility and quite possibly of royalty, and that he was ritually murdered. He was definitely vulpine: his skull still held a thick shock of red hair; his peat-stained corpse still wrapped in fox furs; the top of his head covered by a fox headdress, with the fox head in front so as to rest on his own forehead. The archaeologists named him "Lindow Man" after the dark bog where the corpse was discovered. "Lindow" in the old Celtic means "black pool," which is also the original meaning of "Dublin."[7] The vulpine allusions ascribed to HCE, fanciful as they are, resonate well with Irish mythic tradition and ancient Celtic ritual.

ECH travels through the seasons, waxing and waning with the seasonal, solar, and human cycles. Vegetation, the sun, and ECH are all reborn at the *Teamhur Feis* on the vernal equinox. The *Teamhur Feis* "need not have been the birthday of the man Loeguire mac Neill; but it was the natal day of the spirit of vegetation, of which Loeguire was incarnation and representative" (*TB*, 369–70). And the *Wakean* presentation of Loeguire mac Neill on this same day certainly indicates the "spirit of vegetation" manifest through him: High King Leary's "grassbelonghead"(611.33–34) shows all the color of "sorrelwood herbgreen" (611.34); the high king's costume appears as boiled spinach (611.36); his two golden torcs look like curling cabbages (612.2); his "verdant readyrainroof" appears as a bunch of laurel leaves (612.5); the eyes of the king look like thyme chopped on parsley (612.7); and the gem on his finger looks like "olive lentil" (612.2–10). The "spirit of vegetation" manifesting at the *Teamhur Feis* through the high king Leary finds its parodic reenactment through vegetable-laden High King Leary (611.33) at the *Wake*.

At the *Teamhur Feis*, the cyclical god ECH returns once more. Once again, he will become the virile consort of the Sovereign goddess Ana. He will be the father of the Twins, and the great builder, Thunderer, and Patriarch of all the Irish. ECH will remain as long as his mortal vessel is capable. Even for the gods, however, the "Ineluctable modality of the visible" (*Ulysses* 30.1) cannot be denied: "no amount of care and precaution can annul the laws of nature. . . . the insidious advance of old age cannot be averted. The god upon earth will inevitably come to a time of declining mental and bodily vigour" (*T*, 127). And when the aging ECH becomes unfit, he will be killed and replaced by a member of the *derbhfind*, a group comprised of the younger male members of the same royal family. ECH is thus superannuated by a younger version of himself. In *Finnegans Wake*, the gnawing fear in the heart of the aging HCE is his realization of inevitable downfall and replacement by his own sons.

When the new ECH resurrects during the *Teamhur Feis*, the ancient cycle continues: "The new king, no longer a man but a god, is to enjoy his office till a day shall come when a stronger than he shall arrive, to wrest from him the divine spark and to reign in his stead" (*T*, 149–50). ECH, the once and future king, dies at the *Teamhur Feis* to be born once more in *Finnegans Wake*—his "tristurned initials" thus indicating his cyclical return that is at the heart of the *Teamhur Feis* and of *Finnegans Wake* itself.

Anna: The Primordial Goddess

In the Name of Ana

In the *Filidh* tradition of ancient Ireland, the name of a powerful and important being is deliberately complex: a single name can carry many meanings, and many names are given to a single person. Quite possibly, the philological uncertainty that haunts the interpretation of many significant names in archaic Irish tradition is due in large part to their being puns and polysemes, "the clues to which have long been forgotten" (Rees and Rees, 348). The *Dindshenchas,* for example, frequently presents several alternative explanations and etymologies for the name of an important person or deity; but unlike the modern etymologist, the Irish *Filidh* did not single out one explanation as the true one. Rather, it was considered proper and respectful that the meaning of a significant name should be multifaceted, multifarious, and inscrutable. In archaic Irish tradition, many meanings can thus meet in a single name, and many names meet in a single person (Rees and Rees, 348).

In pagan Ireland, there was hardly a more significant name than that of the primeval goddess "Ana." The archetypal nature of Ana, her manifestation as a female trinity, her role as the fecund and nurturing creator of lands and rivers, her identity as the primeval queen and consort of the god ECH, and her important functions at the Rites of Tara meant that this goddess possessed a diverse host of emanations, epithets, etymologies, and characteristics. In *Finnegans Wake,* this ancient and multifaceted goddess manifests once again; and like her ancient namesake, many roles and many meanings meet once again "In the name of Annah" (104.1).

Archetype of the Feminine

In *The Archaeology of Ireland,* R.A.S. Macalister identifies the first known goddess of Ireland: "in the thin disguise of the *Mor-rigu,* 'the great queen,' otherwise suggestively named *Ana* . . . entered Ireland in the train of the Beaker people" (358–59). From the earliest migration of the Beaker People, to the time of the Fir Bolg, the Tuatha De Danaan, as well as the later Milesian Celts, *the* goddess of Ireland is Ana. Ana is the original Sovereign, the most ancient personification of the land itself. She is *Mor-Rigu*, "The Great Queen," who rules the land with her royal consort, ECH, and whose marriage rites are celebrated at the *Teamhur Feis*. She is *Danu*, "The Flowing One," the creator of rivers and springs (Ó hÓgáin, *Sacred Isle*, 65). She is the great Triple Goddess of the Celts, the divinity manifest as Maiden, Mother, and Crone. Ana is the *Dea Nutrix*, the matrix of feminine energy, nurture, and sustenance in Irish paganism. In *Cormac's Glossary*, Ana is called *Mater Deorum Hibernensium*, "mother of the gods of Ireland" (4). Ana, in the *interpretatio romana*, is known as *Magna Mater*, the "Great Mother." Ana is the mother of all the Irish as well as the mother of the Twins—the quarrelsome minor male deities who personify antinomial opposites. So primal is the maternal Ana that all of her various titles of "mother goddess" were converted into personages, Bo-ann, Brighid, Sion-ann, and so on, in the lore of early Ireland. In archaic Irish tradition, Ana is the archetype for every woman, for every goddess, and for the rivers and the land itself.

In *Finnegans Wake, the* paragon of women is Anna. Anna is the primeval personification of the land of Ireland and its rivers and waters. In one of her important *Wakean* emanations, Anna is the great and powerful Prankquean, who rules the land with her consort, HCE. Anna is "The Flowing One," the creator of all rivers and springs. Anna is a triple goddess, who manifests as Maiden (Isabel), Mother (Anna), and Crone (Kate). She is the matrix of feminine energy, nurture, and sustenance for all her Irish children. Anna is the Great Mother: one of our "original payrents" (576.27), the mother of us all, as well as the mother of the problematic Twins, the quarrelsome boys who personify antinomial opposites. The *Wakean* Anna is, like the ancient goddess, the archetype of the feminine; as Adaline Glasheen describes her, Anna is "Everywoman, Everygoddess, Everyriver" (*Third Census*, 10).

The Triple Goddess

Ana, the primordial *Mor-Rigu* and Sovereign, is, in one of her fundamental emanations, the ancient Triple Goddess of the pagan Irish: "the Irish goddess of sovereignty is frequently presented as a triad" (Green, *Celtic Goddesses*, 71). In the *Wake*, this triune manifestation is also one of Anna's strong characteristics; many readers of the *Wake* have sensed that the three main female protagonists—Isabel, Anna, and Kate—are all aspects of one individual. And Anna's triune manifestation bears a remarkable resemblance to that of the pagan Triple Goddess of Ireland.

In *The Triple Goddess,* Adam McLean notes that triplicity is one of the defining traits of the Sovereign Goddess's identity, and he further emphasizes that her triplicity is "not merely a multiplying by three, but rather a threefold manifestation; the Goddess reveals herself on three levels, in the three realms of the world, and of humankind" (14–15). For example, the macrocosm is a threefold manifestation: the heavens, the surface of the earth, and the chthonic world; and the Triple Goddess frequently possesses facets that link her to these three realms. The dimension of time is also triune—past, present, future—and here too, the goddess Ana frequently corresponds in a threefold manner as well. The most important of the triune aspects of the Triple Goddess is, however, her manifestation as Maiden/Mother/Crone. This is perhaps the easiest and most familiar representation of the Goddess, as her triplicity corresponds to the three phases of a woman's life. Yet another way of perceiving the Triple Goddess is by seeing her in various possible relationships with the masculine. The Goddess Ana can be seen as the Virgin or Temptress; Magna Mater or polyandrous Queen; and Wise Widow or bansheelike Crone (McLean, 14–15).

McLean's observation that the triplicity of the Goddess manifests through spatial relationships (high, middle, lower); through chronological relationships (past, present, future); and through relationship with the masculine (Maiden/Mother/Crone) fits well with her presentation in the *Wake.* The "three realms of the world" in which the goddess manifests are represented in the Mullingar house itself. The house is a three-story structure, with Issy living nearest the sky, Anna on the middle floor, and Kate on the lowest. As John Gordon notes, Issy is the "sky-goddess" and her room descriptive of the heavens (*Plot Summary,* 10–11). Her room has sky-blue wallpaper (396.11–12), with white stars decorating the ceiling (Issy recalls the "twinkly way" over her bed at 148.13–14). Issy is connected with stars (at 8.32 she is an astrologer, and at 340.30 she is remembered raising her legs to the constellations); and Issy is the damsel looking down over the "bannistars" (157.9) (*Plot Summary,* 10–11). Anna the mother occupies the middle realm, the middle floor of the Mullingar house; and like the activities of *middengeard,* middle earth, her concerns here are of the hearth and home. Kate is of *chthonos,* the goddess manifest in the lower realms. Kate lives on the lowest floor of the Mullingar house and spends much of her time in its basement. Her initial presentation in the *Wake* is in just such an "underworld" role, as the guide into an ancient Irish tumulus.

In her relationships to the masculine characters in the *Wake,* the Triple

Goddess also works well through the *Wakean* women. The Maiden/Temptress role is played to perfection by Issy. Young, pretty, and flirtatious, she is the object of desire in many of her various roles in the *Wake*. She is the goddess Julia Bride, the "prize" in the riddling contest "Find Me Colours." In her favorite role, Issy plays the part of Princess Grania of Tara in the three-cornered plot so central to the *Wake*. ALP is the archetypal Mother/Wife. Kate is the widow and perfect representation of the Crone. In her farewell soliloquy, ALP describes herself in all three aspects of the Triple Goddess as she flows out to sea. As she explains, through the three dimensions of time, she was Maiden, Mother, and Crone: "Three times in all . . . the pet of everyone" (626.26) as a "princeable girl" (626.27), then "married tell delth to uspart" (626.31), and now "it's me [the aged Anna] who's got to give" (626.32).

For nearly four decades, *Wakean* scholars have recognized the Triple Goddess in Isabel/Anna/Kate; one of the earliest observations is by William York Tindall: "ALP is a triple goddess, young, old, and middling at once. Isabel and Kate are two of her aspects. . . . A pity that Robert Graves, celebrating his three-cornered White Goddess, did not know of A.L.P., who . . . would have suited his taste entirely" (99). Actually, Robert Graves *did* know; and in *The White Goddess* he identifies the *Wakean* Anna as the ancient Irish deity decades before Tindall's commentary: "James Joyce playfully celebrates Anna's universality in his Anna Livia Plurabelle. And indeed if one needs a single, simple, inclusive name for the Great Goddess, Anna is the best choice" (372).

Personification of the Land and Rivers

Robert Graves refers to the goddess by yet another of her epithets, *Anna Perenna*, "The Perennial Ana," whose cyclical nature is at the core of her identity. In the *Wake*, Anna's cyclical aspect is perhaps most apparent in her identity with the rivers of Ireland. As the Maiden, Anna is a trickling rivulet emerging from a sacred spring in a *leitir*, a watery hill. As the Mother, she is a fecund river system, the mature and revered *Dea Nutrix*; and her fertile alluvial gifts and her water are the sustenance and lifeblood of the people. As the Old One, the exhausted and spent river, she flows to her death in the depths of the sea, and the cycle, as indicated by the last sentence and first word in the *Wake*, begins anew. As the *Wake* itself indicates: "Anna was at the beginning lives yet and will return" (277.12–13).

As the Sovereign, Ana personifies the land and the rivers, and on her depend the fortunes and wealth of her children and the creative power of the land itself (Green, *Celtic Goddesses,* 70). Ana's identification with the land is reflected in one of the oldest names of Ireland, *iath nAnann,* "the land of Ana" (Ó hÓgáin, *Sacred Isle,* 66). The mountains are her breasts (for example, *Da Chech nAnann,* "The Paps of Ana," southeast of Killarney); she *is* the rivers Bo-ann (Boyne) and Sion-ann (Shannon) that bear her name; and the sacred springs and wells that give life are her womb that provides the liquids of life itself.

The very name *Anna* conveys these characteristics of the ancient Irish Sovereign. Brendan O'Hehir, in *A Gaelic Lexicon for Finnegans Wake,* believes that the primary meaning of "Anna" derives from the Irish *eanach* (its genitive singular, *eanaigh,* and the nominative plural, *eanaighe,* are both pronounced "ani") that comes from the root *ean* [an] meaning "water" (355). An *eanach* is a watery place, generally a marsh, swamp, or fen; the terminal "-anny" meaning "of a fen." O'Hehir argues that Joyce's acceptance of *eanach* as the etymological basis of "Anna" is readily shown by recalling that "Fennyana" (55.5), a "fenemine" (93.14) person, is a "Fenny poor hex" (208.31) who is just as "fenny" (242.29) as he is "fulgar" (242.29). The association of "Anna" with water also produces "Fenegans Wick" (358.23) and "fenland" (589.22) (355). Offering a completely different etymology, Daíthí Ó hÓgáin cites the Old Irish *anae,* meaning "wealth" or "riches," as the origin of "Ana"; and much like an Irish *Fili,* Ó hÓgáin also suggests a second meaning, the variant *danu,* "the flowing one" as the etymological basis for "Ana" (*Sacred Isle,* 65–66). Bishop Cormac, in addition to describing "Ana" as the mother goddess, also gives a second meaning of "Ana" in a different entry in his *Glossary*: an "Ana" is a very valuable vessel kept at a well or spring and used to contain and convey water (7).

As the source of water, Ana is certainly *anae,* the wealth of a community: water for humans, animals, and crops; and alluvial deposits that provide fecund soil. In traditional Irish society where wealth was in large part defined by cattle and crop harvest, water was indeed the source of wealth and riches, and Ana the chief benefactor. In her emanation as Sion-ann, Ana travels to the Well of Conla and releases its waters for the benefit of Ireland; the river she creates from the release of waters is named after her, Shannon. In her emanation as Bo-ann, she travels to a secret and holy place, the well of Nechtan, the source of all knowledge. Bo-ann performs a ritual at the forbidden well, and her act—the "Welling" of Ana—releases the fertile waters of imagination and knowledge. The water she releases carries her name, the River Boyne. In *Finnegans Wake* (105.24–25), Anna thus proclaims: "*I have not Stopped Water Where It Should Flow.*" In the

Wake, the river goddess Anna gives her riches to all the Irish children: a Christmas package for each and every one of her children, the birthday gifts they dreamed about, the spoil she fleetly placed at their doors (209.27–29). The catalogue of gifts continues for several pages: gifts of food, candies, fertility, toys, animals, cradles, meat, virility, health, clothing, tools, masks, eggs, bread, rabbits and karma, all are the gifts from the *Dea Nutrix,* Anna.

Anna is the *ana,* the valuable vessel of life-bearing liquids; she is the personification of the watery place; she is Danu, "the flowing one." Moreover, for the Irish pagans, the flowing of this watery goddess—sometimes as her menstruation but more typically as her act of micturition—*is* the act of creation. Maria Tymoczko, in *The Irish Ulysses,* notes that Irish myth provides many such examples of urination and menstruation, symbols that are central to the linked destructive and procreative powers of Celtic mother goddesses (111). Charles Bowen, in his essay "Great-Bladdered Medb," notes that menstruation and micturition in early Irish literature are both centrally connected with the powers of the Celtic mother goddesses; the micturition of the mother goddess in Irish myth is strongly connected with the life-bringing powers and creative fertilization of water—rain, rivers, and amniotic fluid. Both Tymoczko and Bowen see this water symbolism as a link in identity of the Sovereign goddess with the Celtic river goddess—both aspects of the primal goddess Ana.[8]

In *Finnegans Wake,* this mythic pattern—micturition as creation—is reenacted on a *leitir* by Anna, our "wee wee mother" (598.34), when she creates the Liffey (and thereby gives life to Dublin) through her micturition, pouring her "pee, pure and simple" (204.12–13) on the spur of a hill (204.13). As the young river created through her micturition, Anna, the wiggling "livvly" (204.14 [lively, lovely, Liffey]) slips through a gap in the glen while Sally [willow trees on the banks] her nurse is sound asleep (204.15–16); Anna falls over a spillway before she finds her stride (204.16–17), then lies and wriggles in the stagnant black pool (204.17–18 [Dublin means "black pool"]). Like her ancient counterpart, Anna is the land, the rivers, their fecundity and wealth, the vessel of life liquids, and through her creative act associated with her micturition, she is the matrix of civilization.

Ana's Great Circle and Triangle

In his study of the goddess Ana, Thomas O'Rahilly finds the etymological origins of "Ana" in the Old Irish *an,* a polyseme that means "bright" or "fiery," with a second meaning as "traveler," and in the Old Irish *ainne,* meaning "ring," "circle," and "circuit." Collectively, these diverse etymologies associate Ana with the fiery sun in its cyclical travels through the heavens and through the wheel of the year (286–303). And as O'Rahilly indicates, these etymologies, in turn, also suggest two of Ana's central roles in the Irish pantheon: as queen and consort of the fiery sun king, and as a key participant in the great cyclical journey of the god-king himself.

The *ainne*, the great circle indicated in the name of "Ana," had its most important ritual dramatizations at Tara during the *Teamhur Feis*. The great circle begins at Tara on the vernal equinox birthday of Ana's consort. Later in the course of this cycle, the inevitable day arrives when, as a failing god-king, ECH can no longer fulfill his obligations to Ana; and when this occurs, Ana casts off the aging and failed king in a rite at the *Teamhur Feis* called the *Lommrad*. The goddess then seeks a new consort, one who through his youth, virility, adherence to her proscriptions (the *geissi*), and his righteousness, will foster the vitality of the land and its people. At the *Teamhur Feis*, the Queen thus engages herself in a great ritualistic triangle: she seeks out and selects a new consort, called the *tanaiste*, a younger and more virile male to replace the aging and failing ECH; but the one Ana selects is *always* mystically identified as ECH himself. (The *tanaiste* is sometimes referred to as the son of the aging king; this does not mean, as the Freudians would have it, that the *tanaiste* marries his mother. Rather, the wife of the *tanaiste* became the new vessel of the goddess Ana; if the *tanaiste* were single, he was required to marry before his inauguration.)

Ana's triangle leads to one of the fundamental events of the *Teamhur Feis*: the royal marriage of the goddess and the younger male who is at once the mystically renewed ECH. Ana thus practices a form of ritualized and cyclical polyandry as a central event of the Rites of Tara. The marriage rites of Ana and ECH, as performed at Tara (and called *Banais Righe*), also constitute the inaugural rites of the new king. And with the *Banais Righe*, celebrated on the vernal equinox birthday of ECH, the *ainne*, Ana's great circle, completes itself and begins once again. In the *Wake*, Anna, like her ancient prototype, is again cast in the role of queen and consort. As the Prankquean, Anna reviews and then rejects her royal consort in "The Prankquean's Tale"—much like the *Lommrad*, when the Queen casts off her failing and aged consort at the *Teamhur Feis*. And like the pagan goddess, Anna also practices her version of ritual polyandry.

In the *Wake*, Anna's polyandry is presented in a most appropriate setting. Chapter 8, "The Washers at the Ford," finds the three *Wakean* women at a river, Maiden on one bank, Crone on the other, Mother Anna the river flowing between them—the Triple Goddess reflecting on her own life. The women discuss Anna's philandering past: more than most, she must have been a gadabout in her day (202.4–5); Anna had quite a few men of her own (202.5–6), "Casting her perils before our swains" (202.8–9), linking with one while "knocking" (202.10) the next (202.10). As the river flows, the catalogue of Ana's serial consorts continues in the *Wake* for several pages. Like the goddess at the *Teamhur Feis*, the *Wakean* Anna is also presented as a Triple Goddess, identified with rivers, and polyandrous in nature.

Anna's polyandrous encounters and her cyclical marriages indicate one of the central themes of *Finnegans Wake*: the triangle that plays out in numerous variations throughout the *Wake*. William York Tindall explains this fundamental *Wakean* pattern: "The theme of this encounter is not only the young man challenging and replacing the old man but the son challenging and replacing the father and marrying the mother."[9] James Joyce declares that this encounter is the "basis" of *Finnegans Wake* itself (*Letters I*, 396). Anna's triangle, its cyclical and recurring nature, its replacement of the older male with the younger, its two males presented in the roles of "father" and "son," its culmination in a "marriage" that indicates the inception of a new cycle, shares the same defining characteristics as the triangles of the goddess Ana at Tara. These ritualistic triangles—the "basis" of the *Wake* and the central rite of the *Teamhur Feis*—are one and the same.

"Tea" and the Tea Party

One of Ana's epithets in particular, her primary appellation, has a special relevance for *Finnegans Wake*: "Houseanna! Tea is the Highest!" (406.25). At Tara, Ana was known simply as *Tea*, meaning both "The Goddess" (cf. *Dea, Thea*) and "The Dark One" (Old Irish, *Temel*, "Darkness"). At Tara, Tea is again consort of ECH. Tea is the founder of *Teamhur* (Tara), and the royal center is named after her: *Tea-mur*, "The wall [city] of Tea" and *Temro*, "The Dark Mound." Tea and Big-Voice originate the celebration and rituals of the *Teamhur Feis*: the vernal equinox election of a king, a wake, a wedding, a three-cornered plot, the antics of the minor male deities known as "the Twins," the activities of the Four Watchers, and Druidic divinations. Tea's celebration is conducted in the geodetically aligned Royal Hall or near the Dark Mound, which is a *leitir*, a tumulus with a flowing well. The *Teamhur Feis* is in honor of Tea; and in this sense, the *Feis* is the ultimate and original "Tea Party."

According to the "professor" in *Finnegans Wake*, the *Wake* itself is the recovery of a mysterious letter ("litter") by a hen (the totem animal of the *Mor-Rigu*) at a wet tumulus (110.22). This metatextual artifact, called by the professor the "Mamafesta" (104.4 [Manifesto, Mama Fest]), the "darkumound" (386.20–21 [document, dark mound]), and the Tea-stained Letter (or *leitir*), finally appears at 111.10–20. As the professor notes (at 117.27–28), both the *Wake* and the "Mamafesta" are an old world epistle of the ancient weatherings, marrying, burying and natural selections that have tumbled down to us fresh, like an old cup of "tay" (117.29–30). The letter itself describes a tea party held in Ireland in warm weather, a seasonal beginning, a wedding, a funeral, royal elections, the Twins, the Four, and is "signed" by "Tea" (as is the *Wake*). In his further commentary on the Mamafesta, the professor notes that the plot is an old familiar story (113.18), the three-cornered plot, the ancient triangle of Ana/Anna. He observes that the layout of the darkumound shows "ruled barriers" (114.7) aligned along "cardinal points" (114.7), suggesting pagan geodetic alignments: such crossing is "antechristian" (114.11), and it is seriously believed that the intention of this crossing may have been "geodetic" (114.15). The professor then refers to two ancient forms of divination that he finds in the darkumound and believes are clues to its interpretation: "kapnimancy" and "infusionism" may both fit as right as two trivets (117.33–34). "Infusionism" is divination by tea (or Tea), a succinct way of expressing the ancient Irish rites of sovereignty. "Kapnimancy" is divination by smoke; the ritual of kapnimancy was about to be performed by the Druids at Tara but was usurped by Patrick when *he* lit the Paschal fire. The Manuscript then refers to the "Serpents" banished from the scripture (that is, Tara Druids [known as "Serpents"] who were defeated by Patrick [121.14–15]), causing the story to take an utterly unexpected "sinistrogyric return" (120.27) to one particular "sore point" (120.28) in the past (120.28). This "sore point" in the past that is at the core of *Finnegans Wake* is the antechristian Tea Party, the Mama Fest of pre-Christian Ireland, celebrating a seasonal beginning, a wedding, a funeral, royal elections, and held at the geodetically aligned Dark Mound on that vernal equinox so long ago.

Issy: The Sovereign as Maiden

Adaline Glasheen summarizes the character of Issy (a.k.a. "Iss" and "Isabel") as "inconsequent, affected, blithe and treacherous—Gertie Macdowell playing at being an Irish princess" (*Third Census*, 137). In her main roles in *Finnegans Wake*, Issy does indeed play an array of Maiden princesses from Celtic mythology. In the elaborate "Mime," Issy assumes the role of the young goddess Bride ("Brigit") who will marry the sun god. She is Guinevere and Isolde, the objects of desire for aging kings and their young nephews. In her most significant role, Issy plays princess Grania, where, in the *Filidh* tradition, she is presented through acknowledgment of her entire royal lineage: "Ineen MacCormick MacCoort MacConn O'Puckins MacKundred" (376.1–2).

Grania MacCormick, her Brythonic Celtic counterparts Guinevere and Isolde, and Brigit, all share characteristics identical to the Sovereign of Ireland, the Triple Goddess, in her Maiden aspect: her manifestation in numerous dyadic forms, her association with vision and light, her intrinsic connection with wells and springs, and her important role as Temptress in the variations of the romantic triangle that appear throughout Celtic mythology.[10] And Issy, through her main roles in *Finnegans Wake*, manifests all of the characteristics of the Sovereign goddess in her Maiden aspect.

The Dyadic Goddess

One of the defining characteristics of the Sovereign Maiden is her tendency to manifest as a doublet. In Irish mythology, this dyadic propensity appears in several variant forms: as princess sisters; Mother and Daughter; *puella/senilis*; twin solar goddesses; mirror images; as the split personality of one woman; and as a woman and her shadowy female companion, a Gaelic version of the *doppelganger* called *comimeadh*, "the Co-Walker," (literally, "the one who accompanies"). Issy, who states that she is more divine when she is doubled (527.18–19), appears in all of these traditional dyadic forms. In her "perfect apposition" (527.12), she is always "two goddesses" (508.31), who is matched in beauty only by her grateful "sister reflection" in a mirror (220.9). Issy and her double are the two "jinnies" (9.28 [*jinn*, "deity"]) at the *fionn uisce* well who make the blessed "Tarra's widdars" (Tara's waters, Tara's widows [9.21]) in "The Phoenix Park Incident." They are the king's "inseparable sisters" (322.7), two pretty peaches (57.5), Snowwhite and Rosered (64.27), and "Nuvoletta" and "Nuvoluccia" (157.24).

Brigit, daughter of ECH/Dagda, and one of Issy's important roles in the *Wake*, is one emanation of the Sovereign. Brigit is identified with vision, light, and fire, especially the "fire in the head" whose dual nature can manifest as either inspiration or madness. Brigit always presents herself as a duality. In her pagan rendition, one side of her body is portrayed as old and withered, her face ugly and eyeless; the other side of the goddess is young, beautiful, and with clear vision. Sometimes Brigit appears with her *comimeadh*, Darlughdacha ("Daughter of the sun god Lugh"). For both Brigit and Issy, issues related to vision, potential schizophrenia, and madness are themes strongly associated with their split psyches.

Issy also doubles as the two Guineveres, the pair of "quinnyfears" (389.23). In some early versions of the Arthurian myth, Arthur, before he is king, fathers a child by a Guinevere he does not marry; and then as king, marries a Guinevere who then remains childless. These two women are known as the "false Guinevere" and the "true Guinevere." As in the *Wake*, the illusive nature of this dyad suggests themes related to perception, appearance, and the chimerical nature of her identity.

"Issy" is an abbreviated version of "Isolde," who, like Guinevere, is a doublet: Isolde of Ireland ("The Fair") and Isolde of Brittany ("The White Hands"), or in other versions Esylt Fynwen ("White Neck") and Esylt Fyngue ("Slender Neck") (Ellis, *Celtic Women*, 64). Like Arthur and his two Guineveres, Tristan is involved with both halves of the Isolde dyad: he marries one Isolde but remains in love with the other.

Grania, as well, is essentially dyadic in her nature. She and her sister, Ailbe, are a complementary pair of princesses nearly equal in age. At different times, both women are married to Finn MacCool. Grania exhibits a split personality, suggested in the Fenian lore through wordplay on her name: *Grain* means "beautiful"; *Grainne* means "hideous." At various times in the Fenian stories, she is either Grain or Grainne.

In her dyadic manifestations in the *Wake*—as Brigit, Guinevere, Isolde, Grania—Issy enacts the important dyadic characteristics of the Sovereign Maiden. The dual nature of the Sovereign Maiden indicates her fundamentally illusory nature, her chimerical ability to simultaneously appear as young and old, gorgeous and hideous, enlightened and insane, false and true, dark and fair, blonde and brunette. Her ability to cast such a powerful glamour reflects her essentially inscrutable nature—an inscrutability that in turn makes her bewitchingly attractive to most males. The dyadic nature of the Sovereign Maiden also indicates other aspects of her character: she possesses power that is potentially both creative and destructive, along with a mercurial temperament that can be both blithe and treacherous. Issy as the dyadic Irish princess exhibits all of these characteristics in common with the Sovereign Maiden.

Goddess of Vision and Light

One of Issy's favorite preoccupations is the gazing that she finds so very pleasing (527.8). As the Maiden Temptress, she is certainly the object of much male gazing; but she performs her own gazing as well. More often, Issy gazes at her own double with her ubiquitous mirror, her "alluring glass" (528.17–18), where she sees herself as more divine because she has two of everything (527.18–19). And she commands: "Mirror do justice" to "meemly us two, meme idol" (527.22–24). During "The Quiz Show" (page 126), Question 10 is directed to her; her response is delivered as she gazes into her mirror. In her amorous letter (457.25–461.32), she responds with her looking-glass girl, "Sosy" (459.4), calling her "Sosy" ["double"] because she is "sosiety" for Issy (459.10).

"Issy" is, throughout the *Wake*, Joyce's pun on "I see" (Glasheen, *Third Census*, 137); and the Maiden princesses Issy portrays—Isolde, Guinevere, Brigit, Grania—are also strongly identified with vision and its concomitant imagery: sunlight, firelight, perception, gazing, and eyesight. Isolde, after drinking the magic potion, is destined to fall in love with the first man upon whom she gazes. Called "eyesoult" (222.27) and "Sol di" (280.23) in the *Wake*, the name *Isolde* is itself derived from the Brythonic Celtic *Adsiltia*, and literally means "she who must be gazed upon," alluding to both her physical beauty as well as her divine power associated with vision (Ellis, *Celtic Women*, 64). Guinevere, too, is characterized by light and visual imagery. The name *Guinevere* is derived from the Welsh *gwyn* ("shining," "bright") and *hwyvar* ("phantom"), conveying at once the beauty and power of the goddess along with her illusory and deceptive nature. Brigit is *the* patron goddess of vision, both physical sight and poetic vision. And like her Nordic counterpart, Wotan, she is one-eyed—her physical vision traded for poetic insight. Brigit's wells are always associated with the acquisition and repair of sight. Cormac believes her name derives from *breo-aigit*, "a fiery arrow," suggesting both acuity and brilliance in her visionary abilities (*Cormac's Glossary*, 23).

Issy's most important role in the *Wake*, Grania, also has strong associations with light and vision. The chaos and tragedy resulting from the Finn/Grania/Diarmaid triangle begins with Grania's fatal gaze at the mysterious and compelling *ball seirce* "love spot" on Diarmaid's face. Closely related to Grania is "Grian," the ancient name of the Irish sun maiden (*grian*, "sun"). In Irish paganism, the Maiden "Grian" is, like the other dyadic princesses, paired so often that her dual nature is represented in a variety of relationships. Grian is frequently paired with her double, Aine (Ana). Grian and Aine are also described as twin sisters, or as "a mother-daughter dyad" (McGrath, 63–68). Sometimes Aine and Grian are portrayed as rivals for the affection of Finn MacCool, much like the relationship of Anna, Issy, and HCE. As with the other Maidens, Grian's appearance shifts—from beautiful to ugly—through the different seasons of the year (McGrath, 63–68).

Like her sisters from Celtic mythology, Issy too is identified with sunlight. Issy is "Iris," the Rainbow Princess (285.27), (354.25), (528.23), (612.20), personification of the seven prismatic colors. Issy is "Princess Sunbeam," whose white light reflects Seven Rainbow Girls (Glasheen, *Third Census*, 137). And at ancient Tara, "Princess Sunbeam" of the *Wake* has an especially close counterpart.

Closely related to the name of Grania is *grianan*, which means "abode of the sun" (Glasheen, *Third Census*, 137). In Irish mythology, a *grianan* was a place apart, a sanctuary for women, a location specifically selected to maximize the ingress of sunlight, sometimes located on top of a house or special building of "crystal," which was also the home of a fey Irish beauty. At Tara, there was a *grianan* at the top of the high king's dwelling; and herein lived "Princess Sunbeam." The mythic "Princess Sunbeam" of Tara is, like Issy and her counterparts, a dyadic Sovereign, and known as Ess and Mess.[11] Princess Sunbeam becomes quite beautiful at puberty. Her father, the aging king Eochaid, places the Maiden in a confined tower, the upper room of a castle. The young beauty is watched over by two brothers. Ess and Mess are princesses at Tara, but there is a dark side to their position at court—the implication of incest between father and daughter. Accordingly, the Maiden is described as "the sister of her mother" (Rees and Rees, 220–21). In the tower of Princess Sunbeam there are no windows, only a single shaft open to the sky. Threatened by her incestuous father, who lives in the castle below, she remains alone in her room. The Maiden, though, is able to entice birds—her sole companions—down the open flue in her room for company.

In his description of Issy alone in her room at the Mullingar, John Gordon describes a very close *Wakean* counterpart to Princess Sunbeam in her *grianan* at Tara. Issy's room at the top floor of the Mullingar contains a fireplace through which the young princess attempts to call birds, trying to decoy more "nesters" to come down the flue (28.09). Gordon notes that a "nester" is also a "Nestor," that is, HCE in his old-man incarnation, "who calls for Issy every time" (*Plot Summary*, 12).

Many of the images associated with Issy languishing in her upper-floor room of the Mullingar clearly reflect the themes of the earlier myth of Princess Sunbeam at Tara: the dyadic Maiden associated with sunlight who manifests as mother/daughter or as two sisters, her "confinement" in an upper-story room, the two brothers who (at times) act as her guardians, her totemic connection with birds, the incestuous father. Princess Sunbeam of the *Wake* thus bears an especially close resemblance to the Sovereign Maiden of Tara.

Goddess of Wells and Springs

Issy and the Sovereign Maidens of Irish paganism share yet another important common trait: their affiliation with wells and springs. The Insular Celts believed that wells and springs had an inherent connection with the dyadic Maiden, her association with vision and glamour, her sovereignty, and her creative powers (McGrath, 57). Celtic goddesses of water typically manifest as a pair of beautiful maidens, usually making their appearance at or near a sacred well or spring; their appearance is typically "glamorous" in the sense of visually engaging and illusory, and their appearance is related to their sovereign powers and their creative force (McGrath, 55). In the *Wake*, these dyadic maidens, the "jinnies" (*jinn*, "deity"), appear at the spring in Phoenix Park, the *fionn uisce* ("bright water"), their activities and the gazing that ensues constitute the important *Wakean* episode known as "The Phoenix Park Incident."

The Temptress in the Triangle

Issy's most important roles at the *Wake* are in the various triangles reenacted from Celtic myth, all of which follow the same mythic pattern: the young beautiful princess or queen (Guinevere, Isolde, Grania) is betrothed to the aging ruler (Arthur, Mark, Finn); she generates strife and chaos through her selection of the younger male (Lancelot, Tristran, Diarmaid) as her mate. In the *Wakean* reenactments of these Celtic Triangles, Issy is perfect in her role of Maiden Temptress; HCE is always the aging ruler; and one of the Twins plays the role of the young *tanaiste*.

The main reenactment of this triangle at the *Wake* is the Tara version: Grania MacCormac, the princess of Tara, though betrothed to Finn MacCool, the aging leader of the Fianna, generates much chaos and strife when she chooses Finn's young nephew Diarmaid O'Duibhne, rather than the aging leader, as her lover and mate. Though presenting herself as the passive onlooker, Grania is the one with real power: she is the one who chooses her mate; she is the one able to control and select the men (Green, *Celtic Goddesses*, 117, 135). (It may be worth noting here that in early Irish society, the relation of uncle and nephew was frequently a bond more akin to father and son, thus exacerbating the tensions already inherent in the triangle.) In Irish mythology, the most complete version of the Finn/Grania/Diarmaid triangle is related in "The Pursuit of Diarmaid and Grania." In the *Wake*, there are more allusions, references, and reenactments from the Tara version of the triangle (as found in "The Pursuit of Diarmaid and Grania") than from any of the other variant accounts found in Celtic myth.

Alwyn and Brinley Rees and Miranda Green (among others) have noted that the Tara version of the triangle (as well as the similar stories involving Grania's counterparts, Isolde and Guinevere) all contain a very deliberate allegory of seasonality, the death of the old year and the beginning of the new, as reflected in the ascendancy of youth over age.[12] As an allegory of the changing seasonal cycle, the aged leader obviously represents the old solar cycle; the young *tanaiste* personifies the new solar cycle; and the Maiden's selection occurs at Tara on the seasonal transition of the vernal equinox.

There is also a strong connection between the Tara Triangle and the rites of sacral kingship that played out at Tara as part of the *Teamhur Feis*. In the Tara Triangle, the great conflict between the young man and the established and older ruler "comes sharply into focus as a challenge for the kingship" (Green, *Celtic Goddesses*, 135). In this interpretation of the Tara Triangle, the aging Finn plays the role of the waning god-king, ECH; Diarmaid becomes the young *tanaiste*, mystically related to the aging ruler, and successor to his throne; Grania, Princess of Tara, is the Sovereign in her Maiden aspect. At Tara, at the transition of the seasons, and through the Rites of Tara, the Sovereign goddess of Ireland rejects the aged and failing ECH and unites with his younger and more potent successor. "The Pursuit of Diarmaid and Grania," alluded to and reenacted throughout the *Wake*, is in its origin an important mythical account of inaugural rites conducted at Tara during the seasonal transition of the vernal equinox. The triangle alluded to throughout the *Wake* is in its origin directly connected to the role of the Sovereign in Irish myth and to the kingship rites at the *Teamhur Feis*. Issy's main role in *Finnegans Wake*—Temptress in the

Celtic Triangle—directly connects her with the ancient pattern of the Sovereign. The triangles she enacts in the *Wake* originate in the rites of sacral kingship conducted at the seasonal transition. Issy's other important performances in the *Wake*—as the dyadic goddess in "The Phoenix Park Incident," and as Bride in "The Mime"—like the ancient triangle, have their correlates in the ancient Rites of Tara as well. (These are discussed at length in the upcoming chapters).

Kate: The Sovereign as Crone

The Wake*'s Chthonic Termagant*

Kate, the third constituent of the *Wakean* Triple Goddess, is the old and witchlike housekeeper at the Mullingar Inn. Many of Kate's activities at the *Wake* are of a dark and arcane nature, and she has a strong connection with the telluric and chthonic realms. Like the mythological Crones, Morrigan and Cerridwen, Kate exhibits many of the traits and talents of an old Wiccan priestess. Kate has her own cauldron (142.5); she tells fortunes (221.12); she has "The Two Sights," which allow her to see ghosts (556.31–557.12). She secretly teaches Issy the ways of the old religion. She is a witch on the heath (468.35); and, as John Gordon observes, she practices rites of divination (221.12) usually ascribed to the ancient Celts. Gordon notes that Kate's necromantic practices are "very much of the druidical past, whether remembered censoriously (520.13–14) or nostalgically (79.14–26)" (*Plot Summary*, 70). Kate is associated with banshees, with nature religions, and with magic. As the old nurse, she has taught Issy all of her runes, to the point that Issy is prepared to take her place as a pagan priestess at their "Drewitt's altar" (279.20–27). With Kate as her Druidic teacher, young Issy becomes a "sourceress" singing a "song of a witch" (251.11–12), and a "Holy moon priestess" (360.25) (Gordon, *Plot Summary*, 70).

In her introduction at the *Wake*, the old Hag appears, appropriately enough, darkly veiled, an apron for her "mask" (11.33–34). Kate wanders alone through Ireland, collecting the *disjecta membra* of history in her "nabsack" (11.18): cartridges and buttons, stockings, flags (and flasks) from many nations, clavicles and scapulas, cloth, maps, keys, pennies, ills, ells, and bells, among other things (11.19–21), bringing the varied relics back to her dark tumulus. During the truce (11.15), held "toomourn" (11.14 [to mourn; tomorrow; Temora, a.k.a. Tara]), Kate is praised for this activity, her strange habit of preserving the forgotten detritus from which history is constructed: how beautiful of her, even when it was strongly forbidden, to steal our historical presents from the "past postprophetica1s" (11.30–31), in order to make us all lordly heirs of a very nice "kettle of fruit" (11.32).

Like the witch Cerridwen, Kate has the power to shape-shift into her totem animal, the hen, a "peacefugle" (11.9), a "parody's bird" (11.9), who picks here and pecks there (11.8–12). In her totem form, Biddy the Hen, Kate haunts the sacred tumulus at Tara, the site where the Irish race began (80.16), where the "Allhighest" (80.20) Patrick spoke of Christianity for the propagation of the faith (80.19–20), and where this "timberman torchpriest" (80.26–27) lit the sacred fire in the woods (80.26–28). Picking through the scattered and buried debris of the sacred darkumound of Tara, she recovers the mysterious Litter/Letter—the ancient and fragmented source of *Finnegans Wake.*

Kate's first major performance at the *Wake* is in the role of "janitrix" (8.8) of the "museyroom" (8.9), the hollow chamber beneath a massive mound (8.1), capped by a megalith (8.1). Kate is the guide as well as guardian and interpreter of the relics contained within the tumulus, the "Tip" (8.9). The "Tip" that Kate refers to is, as Adaline Glasheen suggests, "tipping rubbish into a dump or rubbish tip," as well as the "dump," that is, the tumulus itself (*Third Census,* 153). In her other major performance at the *Wake,* Kate plays a banshee figure in "The Washers at the Ford" episode, gazing into the stream, rinsing the clothing of one soon to die.

In her *Third Census,* Adaline Glasheen argues that much of Kate's identity originates with the dyadic Cathleen ni Houlihan, Æ's rendition of the Sovereign, who, after many bitter centuries of repressed isolation, finally emerged in her Crone aspect: "Æ wrote after the 'troubles' . . . the generations for 700 years fought for the liberation of beautiful Cathleen ni Houlihan, and when they set her free she walked out a fierce vituperative old hag" (153). In all of her dark and chthonic roles at the *Wake,* Kate presents a striking resemblance to the traditional representations of the Sovereign in her Crone aspect, the *Cailleach.*

Kate as the Cailleach

In the Insular Celtic tradition, the Sovereign as Crone is known by an array of descriptive appellations that collectively describe many of the attributes of Kate: she is *Caillagh ny Groamagh* (Manx, "Old Woman of Gloominess," "Sullen Witch"), and *Caillagh ny Gueshag* ("Old Woman of the Spells"). In Ireland, she is known as *Cailleach* ("The Veiled One," "The Old Woman") and *Caile* ("The One Who Keeps"). Bishop Cormac calls her *Caile*, which he defines as "an old woman who keeps a house" (*Cormac's Glossary*, 70). The *Cailleach*, like Kate, is typically portrayed with a dark veil masking her face and a long apron that doubles as a collecting sack. The *Cailleach* secretly wanders Ireland, collecting in her "nabsack" the shards, the accrual, and the historical detritus of the land and its people. She traditionally resides in the chamber deep within a hollow tumulus, especially a tumulus topped with a megalith. The *Cailleach*, "The One Who Keeps," preserves the relics of history in her "Tip." The Sovereign as Crone is also the mythological origin of the banshee, the hag usually portrayed at rivers washing the cerements of a dying king—in archaic Irish lore, "The Washer at the Ford."[13]

These two patterns traditionally identified with the Crone, that is, the *Cailleach*, and "The Washer at the Ford," provide the mythic paradigms for two important rites conducted in ancient Ireland at the *Teamhur Feis*—the first, a divinatory rite held within the hollow of a tumulus, the second, a scrying ritual performed by two Druidesses on the banks of a stream. Both of these rites are performed once again by Kate in the course of the *Wake*.

Twin Troubles at the *Wake* and the *Feis*

The Twins at the Wake

HCE and Anna have two sons—the Twins—Shem and Shaun, who appear throughout the *Wake* under dozens of jingling or alliterative pseudonyms: Mick and Nick, Brutus and Cassius, Burrus and Caseous, Root and Rock, Butt and Taff, Mutt and Jute, Mookse and Gripes, Glugg and Chuff, Penman and Postman, Piggott and Parnell, Swift and Sterne, Camal and Gamal (guardians at Tara), James and John. Shem is favored by the mother and Shaun by the father. The Twins have developed talents in different but complementary directions. Shem is penman, artist, outlaw, alchemist, forger, shaman, introvert, Fianna, and esoteric. Shaun is the postman, practical, orthodox, policeman, rational, linear, extrovert, popular, Tuatha, and exoteric. The Twins share a mutual hostility for each other; they are rivals, enemies, personifications of opposing forces, and representations of complementary laws and principles. Adaline Glasheen notes that, as a general consensus in *Wakean* criticism, "the twins illustrate the theory of the identity of opposites. . . . They represent men at war with one another and man at war with himself. The war is the same whether fought with fists or philosophical principles" (*Third Census*, 119). In the *Wake*, their hostility manifests through numerous duels, fights, and arguments that play out through a myriad of bizarre permutations. And in all of their various battles, the Twins both personify and parody the antinomials they represent.

The Twins of Tara

Like their parents, the Twins have their close counterparts in the religion of pagan Ireland. In addition to the cults of ECH and Ana, another and almost equally ancient sect developed in Ireland and had its center at Tara: the Cult of the Twins. And as early as the fourth century B.C., classical writers recognized the importance of the Cult of The Twins in Ireland. The Greek writer Timaeus (writing in the fourth century B.C.) is later quoted by Diodorus Siculus: "The Celts that live on the shore of the ocean [that is, the Irish] chiefly honor the Dioscuri."[14] Archaeological evidence at Tara supports this classical reference and indicates that Tara was in all probability the center of the Twin Cult in Ireland. Two stones on the western side of the ancient site at Tara (known as the "Monument of Cú and Cethen") mark the graves of Cú and Cethen, workers in the Mead Hall who managed to kill each other in their feuding (*T*, 43). Nearby are the stones of Blocc and Bluicne, equally powerful but rival Druids. To the east, the mounds of the Twins Dall and Dorcha ("Blind" and "Dark") recall these famous opponents who murdered each other while fighting over gifts they received (*T*, 56–58). R.A.S. Macalister argues that this extant evidence indicates a cult of "Dioscuric couplets" at Tara, and that Tara was, from its outset, one of the great "Twin-towns" of antiquity, "connected with the twin-cult" from the beginning of its existence (*T*, 112–13).

Two indigenous chronicles, *The Pictish Chronicle* and *The Annals of the Four Masters*, corroborate the classical and archaeological evidence for the Twin Cult at Tara. The regnal lists from these sources cite numerous versions of the Twins at Tara, from the earliest Cruithne kings, to the Fir Bolg royalty, to the later dynasties of the Milesian Celts. As with most of Joyce's Twins, the Tara Twins all have distinctive alliterative names. Among the Cruithne Twins are the Dioscural kings Brude Pant and Brude Urpant, Brude Gant and Brude Urgant, Brude Gnith and Brude Urgnith. *The Annals* notes that the Fir Bolg kings at Tara include the Twins Genn and Genann. The Milesian Celts had Twins at Tara from the outset of their control: Eber and Eremon, Cú and Cethen, Blocc and Bluicne, Dall and Dorcha, Iuchar and Iucharba, Brian and Cian.

Like Shem and Shaun, the Tara Twins functioned as complementary pairs: "There is usually a dominant and recessive member. The recessive one may be associated with plebian activities in contrast to his more aristocratic brother" (*T*, 112). Each of the young men—the Tara Twins are always young males—is favored by one or the other of their divine parents, ECH and Ana. They have complementary personalities: one is always bright and extroverted, the other always darkly introspective. Each develops abilities appositional to his brother. They become minor deities, culture heroes, and creators in various arts. The Twins were thus identified "with a whole range of other polarities" (Rees and Rees, 291).

Like their *Wakean* counterparts, the pagan Twins are antagonistic rivals. As *The Annals of the Four Masters* relates, Eremon and Eber, the first Celtic colonizers of Ireland and prototypical Celtic Twins, exhibit mutual hostility from their first days in Ireland. After gaining possession of Tara, the brothers quarrel over the kingship, and an agreement is made to split Ireland: Eremon takes the North, Eber, the South; Eremon takes an odd number of chieftains with him; Eber takes an even number. Eremon takes the first Celtic poet in Ireland to the North; Eber, with the first Celtic harper, heads to the South. The personal attributes of Eremon become the typical characteristics of the northern Irish, those of Eber, the southern people. The complementary division only exacerbates their innate hostility, and the fighting between the Twins continues.

In their final fight, Eremon kills Eber. But the brother-battle continues between the descendants of the Twins, so that throughout the period of Irish independence, dynastic succession at Celtic Tara typically took the form of alternation between two feuding factions who both traced their lineage back to the original Celtic Duo. As with the Shem and Shaun fights, the Eber and Eremon quarrel, even at its very inception, carried implications beyond fraternal rivalry. The Twin battle was also one of conceptual, abstract, and political polarities: North opposing South, intellect against emotion, the poet as opposed to the harper, science versus art, even numbers against the odds. The personal, political, and philosophical antinomials of Shem and Shaun and the ancient polarities of the Tara Twins are essentially identical.

The other great sociopolitical division of pagan Ireland, Fianna and Tuatha, much like the rift in the Celtic royal line, has *its* origin in another set of Tara Twins, the brothers Fiacha (the Shem type) and Tuathal (the Shaun type). In *The Colloquy of the Ancients*, Cailte mac Ronan, the Fianna poet and friend of Finn MacCool, explains how Ireland was split into two complementary realms, each identified with one of the Twins.

> [Cailte:] "There was a king of Ireland named Feradach the Prosperous, and he had two sons, Tuathal and Fiacha. When Feradach died, his two sons made a division of Ireland between them: to the one went the country's treasures, valuables, goods, herds, cattle-drivings, rings, ornaments, forts, strongholds, and towns; to the other went Ireland's cliffs, river mouths, nuts, fruits, beautiful speckled salmon, and game. . . ."
>
> "That was not a fair division," said the nobles of Ireland.
>
> "Which portion would you have preferred?" asked Ossian.
>
> [The nobles responded:] "The portion that includes the feasts, houses, and the benefits that come with them as opposed to the portion of woods, wilderness, and game."
>
> "The portion which they think is inferior seems to us [the Fianna] the better one," said Cailte.[15]

The differences between Fiacha and Tuathal quickly expand into a rivalry between the social organizations they represent: Fianna, and its associations with nature, freedom, risk, shamanism, poetry, intuition, and fluid identities; and Tuatha, and its qualities of urbanity, society, status, security, material wealth, rationality, practicality, and fixed social roles. Like the Twins, the brothers Fiacha and Tuathal and their organizations come to represent the range of polarities in which Irish Celtic culture functioned, a polarization that reached its climax with Finn MacCool, the seventeenth, the greatest, and the last leader of the Tara Fianna.

Other Irish narratives relate versions of the Twin quarrels and frequently give the Twins extraordinary powers of shape-shifting. Because the Twin feud in pagan tradition always has ramifications in many dimensions, the Twins acquire the shamanistic ability to take any shape and perpetuate their battle of antinomials throughout any dimensions of time and space—a Twin tradition that J. A. MacCulloch and others refer to as the "Transformation Combat" (MacCulloch, 353). The story "Cophur in da' muccida," "The Two Swine-Herds"—the introductory tale in the *Táin*—relates the Transformation Combat of two antinomial rivals, Rucht and Friuch. When their quarrel breaks out, they argue as swineherds from rival provinces; then they fight as equally matched ravens, then in human form again, then as water beasts, human warriors, hideous demons, stags, dragons, and finally as two contesting worms in a well in Connaught. Laramiere, in his collection of West Irish tales, records a folktale analogue of the Transformation Combat. Two Irish boys quarrel until they are old men, then continue as puppies, old dogs, young bulls, stallions, and finally as fighting birds; one bird is mortally wounded, and his falling body kills his own slayer.[16]

A consideration of some of the bizarre manifestations of the Shem and Shaun quarrel shows just how close Joyce's presentation of the Transformation Combat is to the ancient tradition. Shem and Shaun fight as boys; they confront each other as Native (Mutt) and Invader (Jute), Confederate and Federal warriors, as insects, as ancient Roman rivals, as time and space, Archdruid and Saint, writer and postman, even butter and cheese. The *Wake*'s fantastic shape-shifting combats, usually explained as the phantasmagoria of dream, are in perfect concurrence with the Twin traditions of Tara and Irish myth.

Periodically throughout the *Wake*, the Twins shift the focus of their hostility from each other to the Old Man, as pranksters, usurpers, or successors, generating at least some of the anxiety gnawing away at the psyche of HCE. As Brutus (Shaun) and Cassius (Shem), they plot against Caesar (HCE). As soldiers in the Napoleonic wars, they shoot Wellington off his horse. Shem as Buckley shoots HCE in his role as the Russian General. As the Porter Twins, Shem and Shaun are constantly scheming to put one over on the Old Man. And on more than one occasion, the dark musings of HCE regarding his problematic Twins are exacerbated by the moaning sound of the mysterious "thunder" that presents itself almost as a death knell throughout the *Wake*.

Rendell Harris believes this dire combination—Twin boys and thunder—is a potent factor in the origin of the old Celtic religion. Harris argues that in the earlier religion, "these two fears are closely involved in one another," and that "much of religious practice and belief is traceable to one or other of these."[17] And at both the *Wake* and the Rites of Tara, terrible Twins and ominous thunderings become dire components in their dark proceedings.

The Twins at the Teamhur Feis

The Twins (or the two young males personifying these minor deities) certainly play a key role in the religious rites of the *Teamhur Feis*. At Tara, the Twins represented the great polarities of nature as well as the antinomial forces within an individual or society. Through ritualized combats, battles of wit, and mock conflicts representing opposing forces and their inevitable transformations, the Twins dramatized the workings of the gods; the fights of the Tara Twins can also be perceived as "rationalized versions—parodies, rather—of a theomachia, a contest between the gods of summer and winter, day and night, light and darkness, good and ill" (*T*, 116). Joyce's presentation of the Twins in their stylized fights, debates, and contests throughout the *Wake* provides an accurate correlate to this ancient rite, the theomachia of the Twins, as performed during the *Teamhur Feis*.

One further aspect of the Tara Twin Cult has a certain relevance to the adventures of the Twins in *Finnegans Wake*. The battles originally enacted as ritual theomachia at Tara have survived in Irish folklore in a much-denigrated form: as the ribald misadventures of a nasty pair of Irish Tricksters. One commentator notes that typically, "these narratives are very disagreeable . . . often repulsively blasphemous, and the reader has to force himself to bear in mind that what he is perusing is merely a pagan legend of the Dioscuri" (*T*, 118–19). One of the standard scenarios for these deteriorated Twins places the two malicious brethren at an inn. The plot turns on the schemes the boys concoct to outwit and humiliate the cheating innkeeper: a perfect description of Shem and Shaun, those "rather unpleasant young men" (Glasheen, *Third Census*, 119), at the Mullingar Inn.

The Twelve Magistrates at the *Wake* and the *Feis*

The Twelve at the Wake

Initially presented in the *Wake* as the twelve regular patrons at the Mullingar Inn, this "mysterious and recurring group" always appears as a set, but in a variety of different roles (Glasheen, *First Census*, 135). The Twelve are associated with Irish government, as suggested by Joyce's wordplay on Dáil: the Twelve are the choir of the "O'Daley O'Doyles doublesixing" (48.13). The "twolve" (76.2) witness the burial rites of HCE and are the Twelve Mourners at the *Wake*. During "The Quiz Program," in Question 7 (142.8–29), the "professor" correlates the Twelve with component parts of Irish society (148.8), and with the zodiac (148.17), and then identifies them as magistrates, the keepers of the laws (148.24), and as the Twelve Apostles (148.27–28). The Twelve are associated with the divisions of Ireland and are referred to as the "twelve territorials" (147.5).

During the debate between Mercius and Justius, Cathmon and Carbery

(194.2 [brothers in Macpherson's *Temora*]) describe the Twelve as the "retainers" (194.8) to the "royal one" (194.6). The Twelve are witnesses to inaugural rites (194.8–30) leading to a royal "consummation" (194.6–7). The Twelve hear the "tremours of Thundery" (194.14), the mysterious thunder that was part of the rites at Temora. The Twelve participate in the "tipsy wake" (194.29) held for the "royal one."

At the wake celebration in the tavern (chapter 11), the Twelve are again described as the witnesses to royal rites (375.2). They observe a high king coming to an inn and court (369.18). As the "twelfth correctional" (375.11), the Twelve act as jurors (375.2). The Twelve present the case against HCE and inform him of its inevitable outcome: in the tradition of the Matter of Britain, the old king will be replaced by a younger successor. The Twelve Magistrates thus announce to HCE to wait until they [the Twelve] send him to sleep [or death] by "jurors' cruces" (374.5 [jurisprident]); then the old HCE will be "blasted" (375.6 [murdered, replaced]) by the "youthful herald" (375.6) who once he was, and the new one will be the chosen one in the "matter of Brittas" (375.4–8).

During "The Inquest," the Twelve are discussed by a mysterious entity calling himself "Jaun." Jaun surfaces during the strange interview conducted by the Four and berates his rival Shem. Jaun threatens to bring "proceedings" (443.11) against the "joyboy" (443.11) and cites the Twelve as the group of "magistrates" (443.12) and the jury of twelve good men (443.12). At dawn on the Easter equinox, the Twelve are again presented as a jury: at each "juridicial" (557.13) session at night, these good men twelve and true tried old HCE in their role as "juremembers" (557.15); and by a "reverendum" (557.16) they found him guilty (557.13–16).

In the court case of "Honuphrius" (572.21), another version of HCE, the Twelve act as judges, twelve upright "judaces" (575.35–37). And when HCE and Anna are in their sleeping chambers (566.7), they are described as a royal couple with the Twelve present, this time in the role of twelve representatives of the realm: the Twelve are Ireland's "chief barons" (566.12) standing by to put down all excursions and false alarms, and afterward to return to their forums and the compilation of their charters (566.12–15).

The Twelve Magistrates at the Rites of Tara

This "mysterious and recurring group"—whose members are at once legislators, magistrates, symbols of the land and the seasonal cycle, royal representatives, witnesses to kingship rites, and apostles—is analogous to the group of twelve royal representatives who symbolized Ireland and served the *ard rí* at Tara. Ancient Ireland consisted of four quarters, and every quarter was further divided into three sections, making twelve divisions in all. These twelve sections sent men to the annual meeting at Tara and to the Rites of Tara who are referred to as the "Twelve Magistrates" (Rees and Rees, 151).

Examples and analogues of the Twelve Magistrates are found throughout Irish tradition. Conchobar mac Nessa and his twelve heroes are a Red Branch equivalent to the Tara tradition of high king at the center of twelve men. According to *Críth Gablach,* twelve was the company of a king of a *tuath,* and there were twelve couches in a royal house. In "The Wooing of Emer," the king of Munster has his entourage of twelve under-kings. When Conaire proceeded to the *Tarbh Feis* (an important Druidic ritual performed during the Rites of Tara), through which he was chosen king, three minor kings were waiting for him on each of the four roads to Tara. And before Conaire's death at Da Derga's Hostel, the Twelve, like the zodiac surrounding the sun, were positioned in a circle around the king's room.[18] During the *Teamhur Feis,* the Twelve were participants in the legislative Assembly held on this occasion. The Twelve were magistrates, royal representatives, and the official witnesses to inaugural and funeral rites of the king. The Twelve were symbols of the divisions of both the land and the heavens. In the sense that they were subordinates to the god-king of Tara, they were twelve apostles. Sitting in the Mullingar Inn—the *Wakean* rendition of the *Tech Midchuarta* (the Mead Hall of Tara)—the Twelve, now in their role as patrons of HCE, reenact every one of the diverse roles once ascribed to their pagan predecessors.

The Four Elders

The Wakean *Quaternity*

Early in the *Wake,* Joyce introduces the Four Elders: "fore old porecourts" (5.36), "Four things" (13.20), four fathers (57.4), the "four of them" (57.8). Shadowy and fleeting characters at first, the Four acquire substance and individual identities and become the dominant characters in one of the most bizarre episodes of *Finnegans Wake,* "The Inquest" (chapter 15). In this extensive section (the longest chapter in the *Wake*), the strange performance of the Four is described by Adaline Glasheen as "half-inquest, half-séance" (*First Census,* 42).

In a letter to Harriet Shaw Weaver (December 10, 1923), Joyce outlines the basic patterns that the Four acquire in the *Wake*. The Four correspond to the Four Evangelists, Matthew (Matt Gregory), Mark (Marcus Lyons), Luke (Luke Tarpey), and John (Johnny MacDougall). They also correspond to the Four Masters, the compilers of *The Annals of the Four Masters*: Peregrine O'Clery, Michael O'Clery, Farfassa O'Mulconry, Peregrine O'Duignan. They represent the Four Provinces, Ulster, Munster, Leinster, Connacht; four metals, gold, silver, steel and iron; the four cardinal points, and the four winds.[19] Each of the Four is tightly bound to his numerical position in the quaternity, and each has a distinctive dialect and speech pattern that allows him to be identified as an individual. In addition to the religious, historical, geomantic, seasonal, and metallurgical correspondences, the Four Elders are associated with the Four Hallows of the Celts located at Tara (219.9–13), where they are presented as the "four coroners" (219. 10) of the high king (219.13). The Four Elders are so resonant with other quaternities that Adaline Glasheen remarks, "Joyce worked out his Four with such finicky care, that it is a wonder he had time to do anything else with *FW*" (*First Census*, 42).

The Four Elders of the Teamhur Feis

Joyce notes that the Four Elders at the *Wake* are also the "four coroners" to the high king; and indeed, there were Four Elders connected with the high king at Tara. Four senior Druids, known as the "Four Elders" or the "Four Watchers," performed one of the most important rites required for the selection of a new king, the *Tarbh Feis*, a shamanistic investigation that quite accurately could be described as "half-inquest, half-séance." The Four Elders of Tara are indeed "coroners" in the sense that during the *Tarbh Feis* they lean over an unconscious body while conducting a psychic investigation. They are the pagan evangelists: they deliver the word on the resurrected god-king. They are associated with the geomantic and territorial correspondences inherent in the design of Tara. The performance of the *Tarbh Feis* itself—the main function of the Four Elders at the *Teamhur Feis*—is reenacted in great detail as "The Inquest" section of the *Wake*.

The Twenty-Eight Girls from Saint Bride's School

The Twenty-Eight Girls at the Wake

The Twenty-Eight Girls from Saint Bride's School, though their appearances are few, play several important roles at the *Wake*. Most notably, the

Girls act as the entourage of their leader (played by Issy) in the "Find Me Colours" riddling game (chapter 9). The *Wake* describes the "Girl Scouts from St. Bride's Finishing Establishment" (220.3–4) as a "month's bunch" of attractive maidens who form the "guard" for Issy (220.3–6).

In this episode, the Girls select a suitable male to play the role of sun god and "husband" for their leader named "Bride" and then perform a circular dance around the chosen male. The Girls also figure prominently as "Jaun's" audience for his "Sermon" (432.4–455.29), his ranting exhortation on the virtues of sexual abstinence. The Girls from Saint Bride's are identified with early spring; they are the twenty-nine sweet reasons why "blossomtime's the best" (64.5–36). They are associated with marriage and bells; and when their "bride" was married, all the "belles" began to ring—"A ring a ring a rosaring!" (147.18–19). They carry evergreens, holly and mistletoe (147.10), and cakes (147.24). They are symbolic of the twenty-eight days of February, the "phalanx" (470.4) of the daughters of February (470.4). They are associated with candles and light (10.25). The Girls may reside in Kildare: they are driving home to Kildare (436.30–32); and Saint Biddy and the Kildare oaks, and Kildare's Brigits are mentioned at 210.25–29.

The Pagan Brigit

Saint Bride of Kildare, also known as Saint Brigit, is the Christianized version of the goddess Brigit, acknowledged by Bishop Cormac in his *Glossary* as "daughter of the Dagda," "the female sage," "the woman of wisdom," and "the goddess whom poets adored, because very great and very famous was her protecting care" (23). The goddess Brigit, like Issy and her entourage, is associated with early spring, light, candles, evergreens, bells, special cakes, and the month of February. Brigit's most prominent sanctuaries in pagan Ireland were located at Kildare, and later at Tara, where she was the patroness of a college of priestesses.

At these citadels, the goddess transformed herself into a Christian saint. R.A.S. Macalister argues that, with "scarcely any doubt," there was at Kildare, "from prehistoric times, a sanctuary of a fire-goddess Brigindo, Brigit, whose cult is found over the whole Celtic area" (*T*, 197). This sanctuary was tended by a college of virgin priestesses, whose leader was regarded as an incarnation of the goddess Brigit, and who officially bore her name. The last leader of this pagan lineage accepted the teachings of Christianity. In her new enthusiasm—or perhaps through her deliberate attempt at syncretism—she accomplished the tremendous feat of transforming the pagan sanctuary into a Christian shrine, "a feat for which she will be held in everlasting honour, and one incomparably more marvelous than the pointless juggleries with which her mediaeval panegyrists insult her memory and our intelligence" (*T*, 197). Saint Brigit thus has her origins in the pagan Irish goddess, whose name, in turn, was assumed by her human representatives, at both Kildare and at Tara.

The Twenty-Eight Virgins of the Goddess Brigit

Tara, like Kildare, had a college dedicated to the worship of Brigit, which was comprised of a group of Irish virgin priestesses equivalent to that of the Vestal Virgins of Rome. The Tara priestesses were known as the "royal daughters" dedicated to the service of the high king. At Tara, the priestesses fulfilled functions similar to those of the Vestal Virgins of Rome—performing rites intended to uphold the reign of the high king and maintain the peace, welfare, and stability of Tara, which was the quintessence of ancient Ireland (Condren, 70). The virginity of these Irish priestesses was, somewhat paradoxically, perceived as a source of the fruitfulness of the king, the Sovereign, and the state itself. The importance of virginity among the Irish priestesses may have arisen from the perception that sexual purity was desirable when in contact with the divine world, but also perhaps, because virgins were regarded as especially potent symbols of fertility and regeneration: their sexual energy had not been squandered on mortals but rather was intact, preserved for the gods themselves. Through their virginity, the Irish priestesses of Brigit acquired magical energy and a powerful collective aura that reflected on the leaders of Ireland, providing them with the magical and symbolic authority to rule.[20]

The virgin priestesses at Kildare and Tara functioned as a two-tiered hierarchy. Nineteen priestesses were selected to maintain a perpetual fire, the number representing the nineteen-year cycle of the Celtic "Great Year." (The Great Year, the coincidence of the Celtic solar calendar and lunar Metonic cycle, was approximated by the ancient Celts; the actual period of coincidence is 18.61 years in the Gregorian reckoning, or almost 19 years exactly in Julian reckoning [Walker, 117]). A curious corroboration of the tradition of nineteen priestesses at Brigit's college is found in the *Chronicle* of the twelfth-century writer Giraldus Cambrensis, who is identified in the *Wake* at 151.31–32. Reporting on his tour of Ireland, Giraldus composed a short essay entitled "How the Fire Is Kept Alive by Saint Brigit on Her Night." Giraldus reports that in the time of Saint Brigit, twenty nuns were engaged at Kildare "in the Lord's welfare"—

Brigit herself being the twentieth. After her death, "nineteen have always formed the society, the number having never been increased." Each of these nineteen nuns tends the sacred fire for a single night in turn; and on the evening before the twentieth night, the last nun, after building up the fire, says: "Brigit, take charge of your own fire; for this night belongs to you." The nineteenth nun then leaves the fire, and in the morning it is found that the fire has not gone out, and that the usual quantity of fuel has been used (*Chronicle*, 97). In addition to these nineteen priestesses, the college of Brigit also included a special group of nine women, called the "Nine Barrigenae" by the classical writer Pomponius Mela (iii.c.vi), the "Nine Brig" in the ancient Irish law tracts, but more commonly referred to as the "Nine Women of Judgments."[21] The Nine were also virgins and powerful Druidesses; they were legal advocates for Irish women and advisors to the Queen of Tara (Condren, 72). Both groups of virgin priestesses were led by a single Druidess who assumed the name of the goddess herself: the Twenty-Eight Virgins from Saint Bride's Finishing School, located in Kildare, and led by a dyadic woman named "Bride."

The priestesses performed several important rituals during the *Teamhur Feis*. One, a fertility rite, involves their selection of a male candidate to represent the sun god and their performance of the *deosil*, the circle dance representing the solar cycle. A second rite, known in the *interpretatio romana* as the *Februa*, is a ritual lustration. In *Finnegans Wake*, these rituals are reenacted as the "Find Me Colours" mating game, and as "Jaun's Sermon to the Twenty-Eight."

Sackerson the Steward

The Dual Roles of "S"

Of the entire *Sigla Group*, Sackerson is the character mentioned the least and with the fewest and shortest appearances. This minor status, however, is offset by the two seemingly incompatible roles he plays throughout the *Wake*. Sackerson is the janitor, handyman, and butler at the Mullingar Inn, and he performs a host of menial tasks, including serving up flasks, scaring off jack and jills from time to time, emptying wastebaskets, polishing bottles, covering all fires during the night, watching for burglars, sharpening knives, and serving drinks (141.8–15). At the Inn, "S" is responsible for maintenance of the establishment, for the logistics of supplying food and drink to the patrons, for the security of the premises, for policing the kitchen, and for seeing to the arrangements and comfort of the guests.

Sackerson, however, is also an official spokesman of relatively high status and is recognized as such by both patrons and residents of the Mullingar. Somewhat incongruously, the butler is referred to as "constable Sistersen" (186.19), "boufeither Soakersoon" (566.10), "patrolman Seekersenn" (586.28), and "exsearfaceman" (429.20 ["ex-serviceman"]). In perhaps his most significant performance at the *Wake*, Sackerson stands before an angry mob intent on doing harm (186.19). Through his presence, and with very few words, the steward silences the rabble and gains control of a dangerous situation: the crowd apparently recognizes the steward in his official capacity and responds accordingly.

This curious and dual role—menial steward and official spokesman—assigned to the *Wake*'s janitor is recognized by Grace Fredkin in her essay on Sackerson, "'S' in *Finnegans Wake*." Fredkin notes that while the problematic Sackerson has been placed in the HCE/Anna household apparently as a mere handyman and servant, "closer scrutiny" of Sackerson's divergent roles "poses some difficulty to such rapid role assignment" (190). Sackerson's incongruous roles at the *Wake* have remained problematic.

"S" as Steward at Tara

As with the other members of the *Sigla Group*, Sackerson has his counterpart in the ancient events conducted at Tara. During the *Teamhur Feis*, many of its most important events—such as "Drinking the Feast of Tara," the placement of guests according to their rank and function, and the apportioning of the feast itself—occurred within the Mead Hall, the *Tech Midchuarta*. The Steward of the *Tech Midchuarta*, the *Rechtaire*, was responsible for the practical and logistical aspects of the *Feis* conducted within the Hall. The *Rechtaire*, or house-steward, who was also called *Taísech-teglaig*, "chief of the house" or *Fer-thaigis*, "man of the household," held an office considered by the Irish Celts to be one of great dignity and honor. The *Rechtaire* at Tara arranged the guests in their proper places at table (a potentially dangerous assignment since the seating arrangements themselves were indicative of each participant's rank, social status, and honor); the *Rechtaire* also assigned sleeping quarters (which could also become problematic), and each morning determined the supplies of food needed for the day. If a dispute arose on any matter connected with the arrangements for receiving, placing, or entertaining the guests, he decided it; and his decision was final. When the *Rechtaire* stood up to speak, "all were silent, so that a needle might be heard if it dropped on the floor" (*SH*, 1:64).

Though a minor figure in the overall events of the *Teamhur Feis*, the *Rechtaire*, much like Sackerson, was given a certain official recognition and status well beyond that of butler or domestic. The *Rechtaire*'s roles as both steward and official speaker strongly suggest the dual roles assigned to Sackerson at the *Wake*. The correlation of Sackerson with the ancient Steward at Tara may thus explain the incongruous roles of the *Wakean* "S," who is at once both a handyman and an honored state official.

Saint Patrick at the *Teamhur Feis*

The Wakean *Hostility toward Ireland's Patron Saint*

In the *Wakean* version of Irish history, the victory of Saint Patrick at the *Teamhur Feis* is hardly a cause for Irish celebration. At Tara, Patrick and his modus operandi suggest more the machinations of a manipulator and usurper than they do the work of a spiritual missionary for the dissemination of an enlightened religion. The *Wake*'s utterly unflattering assessment of Ireland's patron saint has certainly been recognized by *Wakean* scholars, many of whom have summarized the character of Patrick and his questionable tactics:

- Campbell and Robinson: "Practical, hard-headed Saint Patrick . . . though unable quite to follow the trend of the druid's transcendentalist argument, knows well enough how to give a popular reply" (*Skeleton Key*, 347).

- O'Sullivan: "Patrick will use any tactic to sway the crowd; he represents a Christianity of the marketplace that recognizes political realities and manipulates the ignorance of the populace" (74). "Patrick represents Christ and Caesar most happily hand in glove" (75).

- Kopper: Patrick's victory at Tara is the victory of "forms over spontaneity" (89). Patrick is a "black magician, ironically, coming to convert the bedimmed Druids" (89).

- Gordon: Patrick's victory at Tara is the "*Wakean* Armageddon" (*Plot Summary*, 269).

An examination of several of the rituals used by Patrick at the *Teamhur Feis*—and at the *Wake*—may help to explain the *Wakean* hostility toward Ireland's patron saint.

"Fiat, Fiat" at the Feis

A fitting leitmotif for the *Wake*'s hostile attitude toward Saint Patrick is found in the strange chant "Fiat, Fiat"—"that deliberately occulted phrase," as John Bishop calls it (*Book of the Dark*, 55)—that recurs throughout *Finnegans Wake*. The chant appears at least a dozen times in the *Wake* (in several variant forms), has never really been explained, and in its final occurrence is sung by the multitudes at Tara shortly after Patrick's victory. The origin and significance of the incantation are found in an ancient Patrician legend.

Long before Patrick arrives at Tara and lights the Ricorso bonfire, dire portents herald his arrival. One of these is a strange chant, "Fiat, Fiat." The chant itself is derived from a Druidic ritual; and the origin of the chant is explained by Muirchú maccu Machthene in *The Book of Armagh*:

> In illis autem diebus quibus haec gesta sunt in praedictis regionibus fuit rex quidam magnus ferox gentilisque, imperator barbarorum regnans in Temoria, quae [tunc] erat caput [regni] Scotorum, Loiguire nominee filius Neill, origo stirpis regiae huius pene insolae. Hic autem scious et magos et aurispices et incantatores et omnis malae artis inuentores habuerat, qui poterant omnia scire et prouidere ex more gentilitatis et idolitriae antequam essent, e quibus duo prae caeteris praeferebantur, quorum nomina haec sunt: Lothroch qui est Lochru, et Lucetmael qui et Ronal, et hii duo ex sua arte magica crebrius profetabant morem quondam exterum futurum in modium regni cum ignota quadam doctrina molesta longinquo trans maria aduectum, a paucis dictatum, a multis susceptum, ab omnibus honorandum, regna subuersurum, resistentes reges occissurum, turbas seducturum, omnes corum deos distructurum, et iectis omnibus illorum artis operibus in saccula regnaturum. Portantem quoque suadentemque hunc morem signauerunt et profetauerunt hiis uerbis quasi in modem uericuli crebro ab hiisdem dictis, maxime in antecedentibus aduentum Patricii duobus aut tribus annis. Haec autem sunt uersiculi uerba, propter linguae idioma non tam manifesta: "Aduenit ascicaput cum suo lingo curuicapite, / ex sua domu capite perforata incantabit nefas / a sua mensa ex anteriore parte domus suae, / respondebit ei sua familia tota 'fiat, fiat.'" Quod nostris uerbis potest manifestius expraemi. "Quando ergo haec omnia fiant, regnum nostrum, quod est gentile, non stabit."

> [In those days, when these events took place in the aforesaid region [Ireland], there was a certain great king, ferociously pagan, an emperor of barbarians reigning in Tara, which was then the capital of the kingdom of the Irish, by the name of Loegaire, son of Niall, the founder of the royal dynasty [that reigned over] almost [all of] this island. This Loegaire, moreover, had [in his court] seers and druids, fortune tellers and magicians, and devisers of all manner of wicked art, who were able to know and foresee everything before it happened, by means of the technique[s] of paganism and idolatry. Two of these were preferred over the others, and their names were Lothroch, or Lochru, and Lucet Mael, or Ronal. Utilizing their magic art, these two would frequently prophesy on a certain alien practice in the future, like a kingdom with an unfamiliar, troublesome doctrine that would be brought over the seas from far away, dictated by the few but accepted by the many, to be honored by all, that would subvert kingdoms, kill resistant kings, seduce the masses, destroy all their gods, and with all the accomplishments of their art rejected, would reign forever. They also foretold of the one who would bring and urge this practice and prophesied in words like a little poem, often spoken by them, primarily in the two or three years preceding the arrival of Patrick. These are the words of the little poem, not very clear on account of the idiom of the language: "Adze-head will come, the end of his staff bent, / From his house, with a perforated head, he will chant abomination, / From his table, in the front of his house, / All of his household will respond to him, 'fiat, fiat' ('so be it, so be it')." Which can be expressed more clearly in our words: "When all these things will come to pass, our kingdom, which is pagan, will not survive."][22]

As foretold in the prophetic vision of the Tara Druids, Adze-head (a sarcastic allusion to Patrick's tonsure) did come from across the sea, wearing a cloak with a hole in its head (his hooded robe) and carrying a stick bent in the head (his crozier). (Both "hole in the head" and "bent in the head," of course, suggest mental aberration.) And the people of Ireland did chant the abomination, the foreign phrase, as a sign of their conversion: at the climax of the Ricorso, the Irish loudly sing "*Fuitfiat!*" (613.14). As portrayed in the *Wake*, the troublesome doctrine from overseas, dictated by the few, does indeed seduce the masses, destroy their mythology, and cause them to reject and ultimately forget the accomplishments of their ancient traditions. The Patrician leitmotif, *Fiat Fiat,* thus gives voice to the same theme in the *Wake* as it did centuries ago at Tara: the spiritual coup d'etat of Ireland by the manipulative and aberrant Christian Invader.

Patrick's Usurpation of Druidic Ritual

Another Druidic ritual, used at Tara, present in the *Wake,* and appropriated by the Invader, is the *Feth-fiadha* (or *Fe-fiada*), an incantation used by Irish Druids to cast a glamour that allows, for example, Druidic magicians to appear not as humans, but as deer. P. W. Joyce notes that the *Feth-fiadha,* while undoubtedly Druidic in origin, reappears as a Christian hymn used by Patrick against the Druids themselves: "Saint Patrick's well-known hymn [the *Lorica*] was a *Fe-fiada,* and it is openly called so in old authorities: for it made Patrick and his company, as they went towards Tara, appear as a herd of deer to those who lay in wait to slay them" (*SH* 1:246–47).

The *Lorica* of Saint Patrick appears in the *Wake* during "The Inquest," when a mysterious entity speaking through the body of "Yaun" foretells of the arrival of the Saint at Tara. To the surprise of the Four Elders, the entity claims to hear the cries of the deer being hunted (500.11–12); then, this entity begins chanting a parodic version of the Patrician *Lorica*: "Christ in our irish times! Christ on the airs independence! Christ hold the freedman's chareman! Christ light the dully expressed!" (500.14–16).

Through his use of the *Lorica,* Patrick achieves a profound victory over his Druidic enemies. Patrick learns the pagan incantation, alters its wording, and changes the name of the ritual from its native Gaelic *Feth-fiadha* to the Roman *Lorica* ("Shield"). Chanting the appropriated ritual, Patrick and his entourage escape the ambush on the road to Tara by using the native weapon against the natives themselves.

Patrick's success with the *Lorica,* however, is a victory for him on another level as well: in his appropriation of the *Feth-fiadha,* Patrick also subsumes important components related to its underlying mythology. The *Feth-fiadha,* along with its concomitant glamour, "has an especially pointed ideological dimension" in relation to the Irish rites of kingship (Nagy, *Angels,* 88). In these rites, the hero sometimes wins kingship through success in a ritualized deer hunt; the prey is typically a supernatural being using the *Feth-fiadha* to appear in disguise. Success in the ritual hunt is usually contingent upon the hero piercing the illusion, dispelling the glamour. Patrick's escape by using the *Feth-fiadha* thus makes use of this mythic motif especially relevant to the Druidic rites of kingship then under way at Tara—the important Druidic motif completely unperceived by the Tara Druids themselves.

Patrick uses this same technique—appropriation of pagan ritual—at the Rites of Tara as he does through chanting the *Lorica* on his way to Tara. Dáithí Ó hÓgáin notes that Patrick, by using "the rites and tabus of Tara as his theme," and by appropriating imagery "borrowed from the pre-Christian culture," becomes the triumphant one in the context of the indigenous tradition (*Sacred Isle,* 201). In the *Wake,* when Patrick lights the bonfire at Slane, he usurps the pagan tradition, becoming "the new champion, the new Lugh or Conaire or Cormac" (*Sacred Isle,* 201).

Whether working the *Lorica* on his way to Tara or lighting the fire at the *Feis,* Patrick's methods are the same. Patrick steals the magic, ritual, and mythology of his enemies and claims this powerful force as his own. Then the saint uses this same power for his own purposes: suppressing the indigenous traditions and replacing them with a much narrower and orthodox regime. The fact that Patrick is celebrated for this takeover prompted J. Colm O'Sullivan to describe Patrick's mission as "the most successful invasion of Ireland ever completed" (75).

Wakean history recognizes Patrick's victory at the *Teamhur Feis* as more loss than gain. The shamrock, Patrick's famous emblem of the new religion, is, through the *Wakean* lens, perceived as an illusory scam, the "Shamwork" (613.10). "Slypatrick" (51.8) himself is likened to a con artist working the old shell game: he is the pea trick (361.3–4). In *Wakean* terms, Patrick's victory at Tara meant the defeat, suppression, and forgotten memory of the other and earlier tradition. This loss results in collective amnesia—which then spawns its own array of problems. James Joyce sought to remedy this amnesia and endeavored to redress the loss wrought by Patrick at Tara through the seventeen-year labor of *Finnegans Wake.*

Magrath: Servant of the Sacred Wheel

Magrath at the Wake

In Joyce's *Sigla Group,* or indeed in the entire course of the *Wake,* there is no more well-defined, sinister, and enigmatic character than Master Magrath. Magrath is, for some undisclosed reason, the mortal enemy of HCE; and HCE, who seems fully aware of the evil intent of his adversary, is terrified of him. Magrath is the "Cad in the Park" who accosts HCE and warns him of his impending doom. Magrath is in all probability the mysterious character known as the "Banger at the Gate," who late at night stands at the threshold of the Mullingar and hurls violent execrations at a horrified HCE cowering inside the Inn. Magrath is frequently referred to as a "Serpent." He is probably a murderer. He has been punished by God. He is the closest character in the *Wake* to the "Adversary." Magrath is partially blind and has a young male associate who assists him in his mysterious agenda. He has traveled in Asia Minor. He is married to a beautiful woman named "Kinsella." He possesses a mysterious wooden device that holds strange powers. And Magrath has a curious and secret relationship with HCE's consort, Anna.

The first allusion to this mysterious character in the *Wake* is in the "Overture" of chapter 1, where Joyce introduces most of the major themes. Paragraph 4 announces the matter of conflict, the clash of wills (4.1), and Magrath, a.k.a. "Malachus Micranes" (4.4), is presented as the adversary of the "Verdons" (4.4), a name associated with Irish kingship (the Verdons are the possessors of Brian Boru's sword) as well as the bloody Battle of Verdun (McHugh, *Annotations*, 4). At the very outset of the *Wake*, Magrath is presented as the willful and murderous antagonist to Irish royalty.

In "The Encounter with the Cad" (34.30–36.34), HCE, alone in the park, is accosted by a mysterious man speaking Gaelic in a very sinister tone (35.15). The man asks HCE if he knows what time it is; at this moment, a clock, a deep thunderous "toller" (35.31–32) striking twelve, gives an ominous answer. William York Tindall notes that the nature of Magrath's question "implies that the old man is through—especially when the time is twelve, the end of one temporal cycle and the beginning of another" (59). There is the suggestion here of death for HCE at the end of a cycle and at the hands of the Cad, Magrath.

Magrath's next encounter with HCE is more vicious and directly threatening. Calling himself a "process server" (63.32), Magrath places himself at the threshold of HCE's residence (69.15) and screams out threats and abuses (70.12) in an unidentifiable archaic tongue (70.4). Ranting at a frantic and wicked rate (70.32), Magrath curses HCE (73.7) and threatens to kill him.

Shortly after "The Banging at the Gate," HCE as Festy King is arrested by the Assembly (97.28), tried, and found wanting. Festy King escapes (97.29–98.4) but soon meets his adversary once again. Immediately before this fateful encounter, Festy hears a strange roaring sound that drives him "blem [mad], blem, stun blem" with fear (98.3–4). The Adversary then reappears, now occupying the physical body of Cornelius Magrath (98.7–9).

At this point in the *Wake* (98.8–35), Joyce provides most of his strange details about Magrath. Magrath has traveled to Asia Minor, where, in the company of royalty, he enjoys watching a certain belly dancer perform in opulent settings: as a "Turk of the theater" (98.10–11) and guest of the king (98.9–10), Magrath had "bepiastered" (98.12 [that is, thrown piastres, Turkish coins]) to the "buikdanseuses" (98.12 [belly dancer]) from his royal "omnibox" (98.12–13). For some undisclosed crime, Magrath is then judged by God—recalled and scrap-heaped by the "Maker" (98.17). Magrath is punished through a mysterious disease that possibly leaves him partially blind, an infamous and private ailment that closed his "vicious circle" (98.18–19). Then, partially blind, Magrath walks to a stagnant lily pond, considers it, but does not drink its "demifrish" water (98.20–24). Instead, he provides water for everyone from another source, when he "did drinks from a pumps" (98.25). A mysterious workman presents Magrath with a strange wooden instrument imbued with magical potency: "Mr. Whitlock" (98.25) gives him a piece of wood, with "words of power" (98.26) made fast between them—"*acnomina*" (98.27 [surnames]) "*ecnumina*" (98.27 [outside the power of the gods]). Much speculation then arose regarding Magrath's wooden device. Some noted that it resembled a stick, a "baton" (98.29); some observed that it made a strange whirring sound like a "punsil shapner" (98.30 [a pencil sharpener]); some said that Magrath's wooden device reminded them of a cup-and-ball toy (98.31). And Magrath's wooden instrument has a powerful symbolic meaning: this wood is, in some way, representative of "the world" (98.35).

During "The Inquest," Yawn tells the Four that Magrath was involved in a fight at a wedding ceremony—Magrath was the "wedding beastman" (511.2). Yawn notes that the irreverent Mister Magrath was in search of the stammering cuckold (HCE), intent on kicking the bedding out of the "old sexton" (511.7–8). HCE, alone in the pub, wake games in the background, thinks about "Mawgraw" (377.4) and wonders about the fight—whether he will use guns (377.6) or a hangman's noose (377.8). The rumors of HCE's impending death at the hands of Magrath suggest both regicide and ritual—a real murder, of the royal and Rosicrucian variety (99.26–28).

Throughout the *Wake*, Magrath is called "Serpent" and is given various serpentine appellations, such as "MacCrawls" (618.1) and "Mr. Sneakers" (618.5). And Anna, who exhibits a strange ambivalence toward Magrath, calls him "Hwemwednoget" (243.3 [Danish, *hvem ved noget*, "who knows something"]) and refers to Magrath as her solicitor. And in Anna's final letter, she relates that Magrath is married to a woman named "Kinsella" (618.4), and that Magrath is indeed the mysterious adversary and mortal enemy of HCE known as the Cad (618.3).

Theories Regarding Magrath

Given the weird details about Magrath, coupled with his important thematic role in the *Wake*, many *Wakean* scholars believe that this character may be a major key to the *Wakean* enigma. Roland McHugh, in "The Magrath Mystery," sees the association of Magrath and Serpent as especially important, and points to a similar role between Magrath and HCE, and the Norse Loki who kills the sun god Balder (*Sigla*, 126–32). John Gordon, in "McGrath," connects the biblical Serpent Adversary with the thematic role of McGrath but also suggests, "McGrath does not exist apart from the dreamer's imagination" (*Plot Summary*, 58). McGrath, then, is the dreamer's fear projected as a Shadow figure. Brendan O Hehir, in "Magrath," reviews the biographies of several persons named "Magrath" in Irish history who may have contributed to the *Wakean* character, but he concedes that he "can do little to elucidate the elusive personality of Magrath in *Finnegans Wake*" (423). Adaline Glasheen's assessment of Magrath in *The First Census* underscores the importance and the enigma of this character in the overall plan of the *Wake*:

> Magrath—to me, [is] one of the major mysteries of *FW*. I believe that if he were completely identified and his place in the scheme of *FW* understood, much of the obscurity of *FW* would disappear. A few things are certain. Magrath is the Cad with a Pipe, he is the Snake, he is the Devil, he is HCE's enemy. . . . He is married to Lily Kinsella. His servant is Sully the Thug. Magrath is perhaps to be identified with the Druid Mog Ruith who made a great wheel that ran around the sky. (81–82)[23]

Adaline Glasheen's theory—that Magrath and the Druid Mog Ruith may be identical—bears some interesting results when investigated through the two arcane and opposing traditions that relate the story of Mog Ruith: the Irish Christian Apocryphal tradition and the Irish Druidic tradition.

Mog Ruith in Irish Christian and Irish Druidic Lore

In the Irish Christian Apocryphal tradition, an attempt was made by medieval scribes to incorporate the great Druid Mog Ruith (also spelled "Mogh Ruith," "Mug Ruith," and "Mog Roth") into their own Christian lore. *The Book of Ui Maine*, one of the arcane Christian sources relating the lore of Mog Ruith, states that the Druid left Ireland to study in Asia Minor under the infamous biblical magician Simon Magus (Simon Magus appears in Acts 8:8–25). In Asia Minor, Mog Ruith is befriended by the evil King Herod and is entertained in the opulent settings of the royal palace. As he does in the *Wake*, Mog Ruith especially enjoys the seductive belly dance of Salomé. After her voluptuous performance, she demands the death of John the Baptist. No one dares to execute the divine prophet until Mog Ruith is approached. Mog Ruith agrees to murder John the Baptist, and for his diabolical deed Mog Ruith is punished by God, partially blinded and stricken with a strange disease. Mog Ruith returns to Ireland and continues his life as a nefarious magician; but because of his blindness he relies heavily on his servant and pupil Ceanm to help carry out his Druidic rituals and functions.[24]

Back in Ireland, Mog Ruith's story continues in "The Siege of Druim Damhgaire." In "The Siege," the High King of Tara, Cormac mac Art, orders his Druids to dry all the wells and ponds in Munster as a punishment for the insubordination of the provincial king, Fiacha. King Fiacha then hires Mog Ruith to counter this Druidic drought. Mog Ruith succeeds; he indeed "did drinks from a pumps," as the *Wake* relates, for the people of Munster. For his success, King Fiacha rewards Mog Ruith by permitting him to marry the most beautiful woman in Munster, from the Kinsale area in Corchaille, that is, the *Wake*'s Lily Kinsella.

While the Christian accounts of Mog Ruith can explain some of the curious allusions to the *Wakean* Magrath, his real significance surfaces from an examination of the role of Mog Ruith in Irish paganism. The name *Mog Ruith*, in Druidic tradition, is not a name at all but rather a title. The prefix "Mog" or "Mug" imparts a theophorous sense to a name and also indicates that the second element of the name in which it occurs is something divine, if not actually a divinity. "Ruith" or "Roth" means "wheel," therefore, a divine or sacred wheel. "Mog Ruith," then, is a title, meaning "Servant of the Sacred Wheel" (*TB*, 346).

R.A.S. Macalister argues that evidence indicating "Mog Ruith" is a title and *not* a name can be found in Keating's *History* (I.T.S. edition, II, 320). In

Keating's work, Mug Ruith is described as a "water-finder," who lived through the reigns of nineteen kings: "a passage most easily explained by supposing that the functionary called 'Mug Ruith' was referred to in various records relating to these reigns, and that the 'official historians' mistook it for a personal name" (*TB*, 356). "Mog Ruith," then, is a title, indicating a Druid in a ritualistic association with a "Sacred Wheel."

One meaning of this Sacred Wheel is identical to the Sacred Wheel that is the theme of *Finnegans Wake*: the great wheel of birth, life, death, and rebirth—the Celtic wheel of the soul and the seasons. At the ritual celebration of this Sacred Wheel in pagan Ireland, the *Teamhur Feis*, Mog Ruith was one of the most important participants: Mog Ruith was the Ritual Adversary of the sun god, ECH. If the king failed the ritual tests, if he were no longer a suitable vehicle for ECH, he was formally confronted and accused by Mog Ruith (enacted in the *Wake* as "The Encounter in the Park"). Mog Ruith would perform a powerful Druidic curse and direct this deathly execration at the failed king (in the *Wake*, the episode known as "The Banging at the Gate"). Mog Ruith was the Ritual Slayer of the god-king, truly the Cad, the personification of terror and death for an aging ruler. Mog Ruith *was* a Serpent, an ancient appellation for a Druid. He was a murderer and he was the Adversary. He was a "beastman" as described in the *Wake*: unlike other Druids, Mog Ruith wore the skins of animals rather than traditional Druidic robes.[25] And like his *Wakean* counterpart, Mog Ruith had a secret and ambivalent relationship with Ana: the Goddess Ana was Mog Ruith's patron deity; he was her particular solicitor and problem.

As evidence of Mog Ruith's role as Ritual Slayer and Adversary, R.A.S. Macalister refers back to the Christian overlay, the "delirious nonsense" written by Christian scribes about Mog Ruith murdering John the Baptist. John the Baptist's Day—the calendar day of his "murder"—is the summer solstice, the very day the sun god ECH enters his "dying" phase. The Christian eschatologists "drew on the resources of ancient pagan tradition," and reworked the dying god of Irish paganism into the Christian saint, and the Druid Mog Ruith into his Adversary (*TB*, 352). The *Wakean* details regarding Magrath agree completely with this early lore regarding Mog Ruith.

There is, however, a second meaning to the Sacred Wheel of Mog Ruith that has a special relevance to both the *Teamhur Feis* and the *Wake*: Mog Ruith and his connection with a mysterious sound called the "Voice of Fal." Many of the early Irish texts containing accounts of the inaugural rites at Tara—*Dindshenchas Erenn, Sil Chonaire Mor, Baile an Scail, Lebor Gabála Érenn, The Book of Ballymote, The Book of Lecan*—refer to an enigmatic cry heard near the *Lia Fail* (Stone of Fal), the phallic monolith at Tara known also as the "Stone of Destiny." Described as a peal of thunder, a rumbling, a screaming, or a low moaning, the strange sound was given the name the "Voice of Fal." During the *Teamhur Feis*, the *Lia Fail* and the enigmatic Voice of Fal comprised an important test for kingship: the Voice of Fal, if heard during the inaugural rites, confirmed the legitimacy of the new king.

According to the *Lebor Gabála Érenn*, the *Lia Fail* was brought to Tara by the Tuatha De Danaan after their victories over the indigenous inhabitants of Ireland: "It is the Tuatha De Danaan who brought with them the great Fal, that is, the Stone of Knowledge, which was in Temair, whence Ireland bears the name of 'The Plain of Fal.' He under whom it should utter a cry was King of Ireland."[26]

Throughout the cycle of *Wake* rites are numerous allusions to the Stone of Destiny. The *Wake* describes the "stone of destiny" (40.19–20) as colder than a man's knee or a woman's breast (40.18–20); HCE reigns until one "Liam Fail" felled him (131.9–10). The Voice of Fal, the "cry of Stena" (608.16), comes from the "stone that moans when stricken" (94.5), also called the "liamstone" (331.4), and the "Linfian Fall" (600.13).

HCE himself actually hears the cry of the Stone of Destiny. In the old pagan ceremony, many of the inaugural rites were conducted in or near the royal hall at Tara, and consequently the Voice of Fal was traditionally heard by the king in proximity to the hall, the *Tech Midchuarta*, "House of the Circulation of Mead." HCE, in bed with his consort, hears a mysterious "cry" (558.32) off in the distance (as the rightful king should), and to his amazement and confusion thinks he is now in the ancient Mead Hall of Tara, the "House of the cedarbalm of mead" (558.35).

The mysterious cry of "the stone that moans" was heard, not just at the inaugural and wedding events of the Irish king but also during the wake rites conducted at Tara. The sound was, for the Irish pagans, the aural credential of a divine authority: the Voice of Fal was both the death knell for a failed king and the unearthly voice of approval for his legitimate successor. The sound itself, claimed by the organizers of the wake to be of divine origin, was of course created by the choreographers themselves: "That it was some trick on the part of the druids . . . may be taken for granted" (*TB*, 344). The "trick" originates with a shamanistic instrument used by certain Irish Druids, known in Old Irish as the *Roth Romach*, referred to by Bishop Cormac as *Foi*, described by classical writers as the "sacred thunder maker" (*rhombus*), and commonly known to anthropologists as the *bull-roarer*. The Voice of Fal was created by the whirring moan of the *Roth Romach*, secretly wielded by designated Druids to dramatically punctuate key moments in the wake and marriage rites of the *Teamhur Feis*.[27]

The earliest accounts of the *Teamhur Feis* describe this mysterious sound, a "remarkable accompaniment" that was, at times, a low moaning; at other moments, a shrieking or a thundering roar intended to strike fear in those who heard it (*IPC*, 299). The sound "penetrated the hearts of the people, so that men lost their colour and their strength, women the children in their wombs, boys and girls their reason"; the *Roth Romach* created "a mysterious noise that brought destruction to unauthorized persons that came within its influence" (*TB*, 351). The origin of this mysterious sound was never disclosed to the participants at the wake; the Druids told them that this sound was the voice of the thunder god (*TB*, 351).

The *Roth Romach* is a deceptively simple device to construct. From hardwood (traditionally, an oak hit by lightning) or a piece of flat bone, a small paddlelike lath—usually four-sided and inscribed with Ogham characters or sacred designs—is whittled; and as Macalister notes, it is delivered with "some mysterious and outlandish 'word of power'" (*TB*, 347). In one end of the lath, a perforation is made through which a length of cord is fastened; traditionally, this length is the exact distance from the center of the heart to the furthest extension of the right arm. To operate the *Roth Romach*, the Druid or shaman holds the cord by its free end and then whirls the lath in a deosil circle overhead—the "Wheel in the Sky" that Adaline Glasheen mentions. The lath then strikes the air rapidly and obliquely and begins to rotate axially at the end of the cord, "like a screw propeller at the end of its shaft," as Andrew Lang describes it; and this axial vibration produces, in Lang's words, "a most horrible and unexampled din," a roaring "hideous and unearthly" (137–38). As the thunder wheel continues to whirl, the cord becomes more and more tightly coiled, until it cannot tighten any further. The axial rotation of the *Roth Romach*, like a "perne in a gyre," then actually reverses direction in midair flight and continues in this manner until it reverses again. The strange sound of the *Roth Romach* is therefore not continuous although the deosil rotation is uniform. The sound rises and falls; and in the hands of a skillful performer, the *Roth Romach* can even produce a sharp crack like an imitative thunderclap (Lang, 137).

In *The Books at the Wake*, James Atherton observes that James Joyce is obviously familiar with the *Roth Romach*. Atherton cites a particular occurrence in the episode known as "The Inquest" (464.18–19), where

"Dave" recalls the killing of a king and the strange noise that accompanies this event: "Joyce is referring to the 'Bull-roarer' . . . that made a roaring noise when it was swung round on the end of a string. It . . . is believed to have been used by the Druids to produce the effect of a singing stone when a king stood on a sacred stone such as the famous Lia Fail" (228).

The wielding of the *Roth Romach* at the *Teamhur Feis* "centers in the personality of a certain magician known as Mug Ruith" (*T*, 139). On pages 98 and 99 of the *Wake*, Joyce describes the strange wooden device possessed by Magrath, a description that certainly reinforces Atherton's statement that Joyce uses the *Roth Romach* in the *Wake*. Joyce states that a certain "Mr. Whitlock" (98.25) gave Magrath a piece of wood (98.26). "Whitlock" is a portmanteau word: "Whit" plus "lock" implies knowledge concealed; "Whitl" plus "ock" suggests whittled oak. That this wooden device is, as Macalister states, delivered with a "word of power" is indicated through the "words of power" (98.26) that were made fast between Whitlock and Magrath: "*acnomina ecnumina*" (98.26–27). Then Joyce notes that some believe Magrath's device to be a stick, a "baton" (98.30); held laterally, viewed sideways, a *Roth Romach* does look like a stick. Some guessed the device was a "cup and ball" (98.31); a *Roth Romach* fastened to the hand by its string does indeed suggest this child's toy. Magrath's wooden device is whirled and makes a strange sound, reminding one person of the whirring of a pencil sharpener (98.30). Joyce provides an extremely accurate description of both Mog Ruith and his strange shamanistic device.

Throughout the *Wake*, punctuating the funeral and marriage rites at dramatic intervals, are the sounds of thunder—in the form of the famous hundred-letter "thunderwords" (for example, 3.15–17, 23.5–7, 44.20–21, 90.31–33, 113.9–11, 257.27–28, 314.8–9, 332.5–7, 414.19–20). And Joyce (through reference to Vico) tells his readers—the audience and participants at the *Wake*—that these thunder sounds are the voice of the thunder god. The mysterious thunderwords that punctuate the *Wake* rites are nothing less than Joyce's rendition of the ancient Voice of Fal, thundering his sanction through the Servant of the Sacred Wheel. Not only does Joyce precisely describe Mog Ruith and his wooden instrument, he, like the Druids at the Rites of Tara, explains the mysterious rumblings as the voice of the thunder god. Joyce thus uses the same cover story that was used by the choreographers of the Rites of Tara to explain the Voice of Fal nearly sixteen hundred years ago, when it provided a thundering backdrop for both the rise and fall of the All-Father.

4

The Fall of the All-Father

The Descending Arc of the Great Wheel

For the pagan Irish, the *Feis* at Tara was a talismanic point on the great wheel of birth, life, death, and rebirth—the great wheel enacted by ECH, implied in the name of "Ana," and served by the Druid Mog Ruith. The *Teamhur Feis* presented, through its rituals, its rites, and its choreographed spectacle, the downward arc of this great wheel: the turn of events involving the fall, divestiture, and death of an Irish god-king. And as with the god-king at Tara, as with Ana, and as with Mog Ruith, the events at the *Feis* leading to the king's demise are themselves imbued with concepts unique to archaic Irish paganism; the two most important of these are *Fir Flathemhan* and the *geis*.

Fir Flathemhan: *The Truth of a Ruler*

One of the fundamental concepts underlying the divestiture rites of the *Teamhur Feis* is the archaic principle referred to in the mythological texts as *Fir Flathemhan* ("truth of a ruler," "justice of a leader"). *Fir Flathemhan* encompasses an array of qualities—physical, moral, and magical—requisite for Irish kingship: youthfulness, virility, generosity, fecundity of the land and people, as well as the absence of certain negative traits, especially immorality, unseemliness, weakness, and niggardliness. The reign of an Irish king was deemed legitimate as long as the defining traits of *Fir Flathemhan* were acknowledged by his subjects and recognized in his reign; when, at the *Feis*, a king's manifestation of *Fir Flathemhan* was measured, weighed, and found wanting, his fate was sealed.

The Geissi: *The Proscriptions of Ana*

Closely related to *Fir Flathemhan* and sacral kingship is the distinctively Irish concept of the *geis* (plural, *geissi*) a magical proscription or idiosyncratic taboo. The imposition of a *geis* upon a famous leader is a frequent element in Irish Celtic myth and the later romances. The *geis*, however, has its source in the rituals of sacral kingship as practiced at Tara. As a sacred being whose function it was to maintain the weal and stability of the land and its people, the life of the god-king was circumscribed by magical principles, and he therefore had to consistently make the correct decisions relative to his divine and magical functions. The imposition of the *geis* specified what his approach should be. Significantly, the early mythological literature "focuses in particular on the varieties of *geis* associated with kings of the great cultic centre, Tara" (Ó hÓgáin, *Encyclopedia*, 237). The implication is that the *geissi*, in their earliest form, were integral aspects of the kingship rites conducted at the *Teamhur Feis*.

The concept of the royal *geis* originates in the belief that the Sovereign goddess Ana imposed certain conditions upon her royal consort; and the *geissi* placed upon a high king by the Sovereign were frequently very specific and applicable to this person alone. A few *geissi* in Irish mythology, however, are repeatedly imposed on numerous high kings and seem to be applicable to all. These include prohibitions on activities involving sacred springs, sacred sod, and sacred fire—all three of these realms are under the dominion of the Sovereign Ana and are therefore subject to her control, especially through the imposition of *geissi*.

The Rites of Divestiture

Accordingly, the rites conducted at the *Feis* that were used to determine the success (or failure) of the *ard rí* were essentially assessments of the king's *Fir Flathemhan* and his adherence to the royal *geissi*. One of these rites was divinatory in nature and conducted within a burial tumulus, the *Forradh*, and meant to augur the future of the reigning monarch. Others were public tests of the king's strength and virility, and reviews of his adherence to the various *geissi*. Failing these reviews, a king was subject to the rite of the *Lommrad* (literally, "the shearing away"), where the Sovereign, now manifest in her negative aspect, takes back her gifts of fertility, power, and children from her failing consort. Another key event, the *briamon is meth righe*, a *rann* (a traditional verse form, usually a four-line stanza and frequently satirical in nature) against the king, was publicly performed by Bards and designed to incite public opinion against the king by focusing on his failures regarding *Fir Flathemhan*. At some point in these proceedings, Mog Ruith would deliver the dreaded *glam dichenn*, the most powerful of all Druidic execrations, against the hapless king. The king, now divested of all power and privilege, is then murdered by the Servant of the Sacred Wheel. And in the religion of the pagan Celts, the god ECH, who had taken up temporary abode in the person of the king, now enters *Tir na Nog*, Land of the Ever-Young. In *Tir na Nog*, ECH reunites with the Sovereign in her most beautiful and youthful aspect. And in *Tir na Nog*, the god-king EÇH is mystically regenerated and renewed prior to his return to the earth plane.

Each of the events described above is an integral component in the descending arc of an Irish god-king as it was enacted at the *Teamhur Feis*; and each event described above is reenacted in *Finnegans Wake*. Table 4.1 outlines these events at the *Teamhur Feis* and their correlate episodes in the *Wake*. Each is then discussed at length in this chapter.

Portents in the Museomound

The Sidh *in the Wake*

The great tumulus, described as the "museomound" (8.5) and the "Shee" (9.7), the pronunciation of the Old Irish *sidh*, is arguably the most fecund locus of drama and history in the entirety of the *Wake*. The *sidh* in the *Wake*, like many passage-graves in Ireland, is a hollow hill (7.33–34), with a womblike chamber in its center, reminiscent of the womb-tomb at "tarabom" (7.34). The *bruthain*, the chamber within the center of the mound, the "museyroom" (8.9), is a reliquary containing artifacts belonging to the great leader, the Great Horseman: weapons, banners, regalia, even the celestial and totemic white horse ("Hopeinhaven") that belonged to the leader himself. The museyroom chamber has two portals that are usually closed and guarded by Kate (8.8), the crone of the barrow, the "janitrix" (8.8) with her "passkey" (8.8); she is a *Bean-tighe* ("Fairy Housekeeper"), a "fairy ann" (9.14). On top of the "Shee," as William York Tindall notes, is a single large erect stone where "Willingdone" gets the "band up" (*bander*, French slang for getting an erection) with his "Sexcaliber hrosspower" (8.35–36)—suggesting strong phallic and sexual associations with the monolith (37). The tumulus is the site of the great leader's fall and the place of his interment: his feet of clay, now swaddled in verdant grass, stick up starkly where he last fell, by the "mund" (7.29–31). The "Shee" is the location for much of the wake that follows the death of

Table 4.1. The events leading to the divestiture and demise of the king at the *Teamhur Feis* and the corresponding events in *Finnegans Wake*

The event at the *Feis*	Description of Event	Correspondence in *Finnegans Wake*
Opening the *Forradh* of a dead king	An Elder Seer opens the passage grave, enters, and utters mantic prophecy.	Kate enters "Museyroom," the chambered tumulus, and utters dire predictions regarding HCE.
The King's Ritual Dance	As a test of his virility and competency, the King must shoulder a sack of earth and perform a ritual dance; if he falls, he fails as King.	The Great Fall of HCE, told as the Fall of the hod-carrier Finnegan who fails to shoulder the load he is required to carry.
Royal *Geis* on Wells and Welling Ritual	The King is forbidden to intrude upon the Welling Rituals of the goddess Ana.	HCE's crime of voyeurism in "The Phoenix Park Incident."
Royal *Geis* on the Sacred Sod	The King is forbidden to use "Sacred Sod" for personal hygienic purposes.	In "Buckley and the Russian General," the leader is killed for using sacred sod.
Geis on *Torc Caille*	The King must not misappropriate the *torc caille*, the "pig of the fire," from which the seasonal bonfires are relit.	In "The Trial of Festy King," misappropriation of a "pig" is the main charge against the King.
The Rite of *Lommrad*, "The Shearing Away"	The Queen manifests in her negative aspect, takes back from a failing King her gifts of power and fertility.	The "Prankquean" takes back her gifts from the failed Jarl.
Performance of *Bria-mon is meth righe*	Bards perform a satirical Rann against the King in an attempt to incite opinion against him.	"Hosty" the Bard composes and performs his vicious "Rann" against the failed HCE.
The Encounters with Mog Ruith	Mog Ruith formally charges the King; performs the ritual execration, the *glam diccen*; slays King.	Magrath vs. HCE in: "The Encounter in the Park"; "The Banger at the Gate"; "The Murder of HCE."
The King Returns to *Tir na Nog*	A magical ship conveys the King to "Land of Youth" where he returns to youthful state with a beautiful goddess.	HCE recovers youth, and sails on honeymoon voyage with "Isolde."

the great one; the mound is part of the complex of tree, stone, well, and tavern where the wake ceremonies are conducted. The mound is the site of the Assembly, where the huge crowd gathers for the *Wake* and later listens to Patrick in his confrontation with the Archdruid. The mound is the *leitir* (hill) of *Tea*, where all the ceremonies of her "*Tea* party" take place. And as John Bishop notes, the Dark Mound is also the locus for Otherworldy activities: "Dead to the world" as HCE may be, "he continues highlyfictional, tumulous under his chthonic exterior" [hce] (261.17–18). In the Dark Mound, the signs of tumultuous and chthonic activity in the tumulus (or tomb) suggest that Otherworldly spirits haunt our "mounding's mass" (479.23–24). Hollow yet all-hallowed, the "darkumound" (386.20–21) of which the *Wake*, as literary "document," is a "present(i)ment," now is presented as the "ollollowed ill" (hill) and the locus of spirits (7.33–34): "Spooksbury" (442.7), "Soulsbury" (511.29), "Haunted Hillborough" (340.34), or "Finsbury" (374.28) (Bishop, *Book of the Dark*, 80).

The hallowed tumulus, the "darkumound," is also the site where the *Wake* itself was buried. Long ago in a different age, the *Wake* existed (or was conducted) at this mound. This ancient *Wake* ended and was long forgotten—buried and scattered throughout the mound. Fragments were found here; then Joyce began the task of piecing the *Wake* back together—recovered at the very site of its earlier demise.

On this special occasion—the initial episode of the *Wake*—both portals of the museyroom are opened, much like the older pagan custom of opening the *bruthain* (chamber) of a royal tumulus on designated ritual days. Under the guidance of Kate, certain guests are allowed into the museyroom. Within the chamber, Kate, rapidly speaking in a mantic staccato, directs attention to the various relics of significance and then offers her interpretation of their importance. Kate's story of the great leader interred therein is told primarily through allusions to "Willingdone" (8.16); Wellington, in her interpretation, is the great fallen leader who undergoes his demise, his Waterloo, when knocked off his celestial white horse onto his "big wide harse" (8.21). Kate's tale of the great Irish war chief and horseman unhorsed and defeated is a portent of events that soon follow, a prefiguring of the fall, defeat, and death of HCE. When her rant is over, Kate ushers all out of the chamber (10.22–23).

Curiously, Kate's prophecy of doom for the great leader is framed in language suggesting a symbolic birth. William York Tindall observes that the phrases, "Mind your hats goan in" (8.9), the advice to "Penetrators" at the beginning of the episode, and "Mind your boots goan out" (10.22) at the end strongly suggest the begetting and birth of a child, and the nine "tips" the nine months of gestation (36). This prenatal and natal symbolism noted by Tindall is also strongly associated with many Irish passage-graves. Dáithí Ó hÓgáin observes that in Irish pagan tradition, caves, tumuli, and openings in the earth are ancient symbols of the womb and of maternity—the construction and the figuration of many Irish court-cairns and passage-graves are deliberately suggestive of the female reproductive organs. This calculated symbolism indicates that "regeneration was one of the principal functions of these structures," and that allusions to death and birth were certainly employed in the rituals conducted within (*Sacred Isle,* 15).

The Museomound at the Teamhur Feis

The museomound and its connection with spirits and portents, its association with both birth and death, strongly suggest a *Wakean* version of an ancient Irish ritual mound; the museomound's connection with both Irish assemblies and Irish chieftains, living and dead, strongly suggests an ancient Irish inaugural site. In ancient Ireland, the primary inaugural site was, of course, Tara. Many of the inaugural rites conducted at Tara were focused on a place, usually thought of as the cultural omphalos, the center of the *tuath,* which was "the place both of creation and of death, in that the chief was inaugurated there and buried there" (Brenneman and Brenneman, 24). The physical form of this center was that of a mound. The shape and location of an inaugural mound provided its power; the magical and spiritual power of the mound "lay within it, that is, in its interior rather than on top of it. Nearby was located, as part of the center complex, a sacred tree, or *bile,* a sacred stone, and a holy well" (Brenneman and Brenneman, 24).

> Behold the *Sidh* before your eyes,
> It is manifest to you that it is a king's mansion,
> Which was built by the firm Daghda;
> It was a wonder, a court, an admirable hill.[1]

In the rites associated with inauguration, some of the most arcane ceremonials "took place within the tombs. This would be the area where the official seers—perhaps in dissociated states of consciousness—would communicate with the forces which they felt were at work in the mystery of existence" (Ó hÓgáin, *Sacred Isle,* 14). In one important ritual conducted within the *sidh,* the passage-grave of a great king is opened on the occasion of the *Feis* by one of the elder seers. A select group of the assembly is invited into the inner chamber, both the reliquary of the dead king and the portal to the Otherworld. (So strong was this association between the *sidh* and Irish kingship that the word itself, *sidh*, was a deliberate pun in pagan Ireland meant to emphasize this connection. *Sidh* in Old Irish means both "Otherworld mound" and "peace": legitimate kingship always has its true source in the Otherworld, and peace and plenty always mark the reign of a righteous ruler.) This hallowed chamber, the *bruthain*, is thus the matrix for rites and prophecies concerning future kings, especially at the beginning of a *Feis* when the old king may soon die and a new one may be selected. One of the elder Druids skilled in seership enters the chamber, and in an entranced state utters a mantic prophecy concerning the king in question. If the prophecy is dire—as it is in the *Wake*—this ritual event is the beginning of the end for an Irish king. In "The Expulsion of the Dessi," just such a ritual is performed as part of the inaugural rites at the *Feis* of Tara. An elder seer, Dil, on the morning of the *Feis* opens the *sidh*, enters the hollow reliquary in its center, and utters a dire prophecy regarding the present king.

When Kate goes into the museomound chamber and utters her ranting sequence of battles and defeats, of a king unhorsed and deposed in humiliation, the prophecy is indeed dire. And as at the *Teamhur Feis*, succeeding tests and events in the *Wake* prove the accuracy of her grim prediction.

The Ominous Fall

The Fall of HCE at the Wake

Of all the shortcomings, failures, crimes, and blunders that HCE commits (or is accused of committing) in Book I of the *Wake*, "the fall" is his most important and symbolic. The mysterious fall is his original sin, and it seems to initiate the entire cycle of *Wakean* events that follow: "The fall" (3.15) of "oldparr" (3.17) is retold through all of Christian minstrelsy, and the great fall of HCE/Finnegan promptly sends an enquiring one well to the "west in quest" (3.15–21). The primordial fall of HCE is enacted by Tim Finnegan in the ballad "Finnegan's Wake":

> Tim Finnegan lived in Walker Street
> An Irish gentleman, mighty odd,
> He'd a bit of a brogue, so neat and sweet
> And to rise in the world, Tim carried a hod.

But Tim had a sort of tippling way:
With a love of liquor Tim was born,
And to help him through his work each day,
Took a drop of the creature every morn.

Chorus:
Whack! Hurroo! Now dance to your partner!
Welt the flure, your trotters shake;
Isn't it the truth I've told ye,
Lots of fun at Finnegans Wake?

One morning Tim was rather full,
His head felt heavy and it made him shake;
He fell from the ladder and broke his skull,
So they carried him home, his corpse to wake.

Finnegan is identified with Finn MacCool; and William York Tindall argues that the hod-carrying Finnegan and the tottering, sack-bearing HCE are also identical in this episode—proven by HCE's initials embedded in proletarian "*h*od, *c*ement and *e*difices" and in Imperial "*H*aroun Childeric *E*ggeberth" (33). And throughout chapter 1 of the *Wake*, HCE, like Finnegan/Finn, also shoulders his own sack of earth, variously described as his "whole bag" (26.10), his "kis" (26.03 [Irish *cis*, "basket"]), a "suspicious parcel" (62.28–29), and the "sack" (61.12) that helped him (61.12). Joyce describes Finnegan's movement up and down the ladder (4.18–5.4) as a kind of ritual dance performed by the Finn/HCE avatar: the strength, virility and agility of Finnegan allow him not only to carry bricks up a ladder but also to convey earth to heaven. His dance unites matter with spirit, the above with the below, male and female, yin and yang. The ritual dance of Finnegan creates culture and creates children: "Take up your partner" means dancing, but "tuck up your part inher," the dance of life (Tindall, 33). The dance highlights Finnegan's potency both sexually and as the creative father of civilization. The fact that Finnegan/HCE *can* shoulder his sack of earth with its symbolic weight and then perform his ritual dance is proof indeed of his virility and his vitality.

Immediately following the description of Finnegan's ritual dance, the narrator relates that the dancer himself is of the most ancient royalty: he was of the first to bear arms and a name (5.5). This primeval king has a crest of heraldry (5.6) containing antlers and horns, an ancient oak on green, suggesting a primordial cuckold, or even the original Celtic cuckold, Cernunnos, "The Horned One."

On that tragic thunder-day, "tragoaday thundersday" (5.13), the ritual dance of this ancient royal one ends with his fall: his head felt heavy (6.8), his "hod" did shake (6.8–9); he staggered from the "latter" (6.10), and "Damb! He was dud" (6.10). Reasons for the fall are suggested: it may have been a misfired brick (5.26), or it might be due to a collapse of his "back promises" (5.27–28). The physical fall of Finn/HCE, especially his failure to shoulder his "suspicious parcel" in the symbolic dance, results in his overall downfall and death. The relatives of HCE, the Irish populace, the Druids, and Fianna assemble for the funeral. Their activities and events constitute the subsequent episodes of the *Wake*.

The Fall of ECH at the Feis

In his reconstruction of the various rituals performed during the Rites of Tara, R.A.S. Macalister describes an event that bears a striking resemblance to the ritual dance of the sack-bearing HCE. At the beginning of the *Feis*, the high king, median between heaven and earth, builder of Tara, ultimate vessel of Irish virility, and physical vehicle of ECH, was required to perform a symbolic dance as a test of his fitness for royal office. The king had to shoulder a sack of earth and perform publicly; he had to shoulder the load and dance the dance of fitness and virility. He could keep the kingship, "so long as he can perform the feat of dancing publicly with a sack of earth on his back" (*T*, 129). The dance of the king was certainly a test of physical endurance and virility, which in turn would indicate his prowess in other performance arenas. The dance too was rich with symbolic meaning related to the Sovereign (the earth itself was identified with the goddess), and related to the play of opposites so integral to Irish ritual. As in the *Wake*, the successful dance of an Irish king at the Rites of Tara united heaven and earth, male and female, spirit and matter—all requisite for civilization to continue and flourish.

At some point in the reign of a high king, however, the task of the dance will prove beyond his physical ability; when he falls, the ramifications are numerous and serious. A fallen king is no longer a worthy vehicle for divinity. When he drops "the sack that helped him," that "suspicious parcel," he is obviously not virile enough to remain consort of the earth goddess: both literally and symbolically, he has proven to be incapable of handling and supporting her. Macalister cites a parallel in a story of Finn: "We may also recall how the fairy maiden Donait consented to retain Finn as her husband for so long as he could leap once a year over a certain deep chasm. When he failed to do so he would be superannuated" (*T*, 128). At the *Feis* of Tara, the fall of the king initiates the great cycle of death and renewal that is symbolically enacted through the ritual episodes that follow in his wake.

The Phoenix Park Incident and the Welling Rite of Ana

The Phoenix Park Incident: A Summary

Late in the evening, HCE as "Porter," walking alone in a wooded and apparently deserted section of Phoenix Park, spies two young women in a secluded glen at *fionn uisce* (bright water), the spring in the park from which the name *Phoenix* is derived.[2] The girls may be exposing themselves, may be urinating, and may or may not be aware of Porter, who is at once sexually aroused, fearful, and guilt-ridden by his voyeuristic activity. A short distance away, three males witness the entire scene. The three males might be soldiers: all three wear some kind of uniform and headgear and are apparently armed. The soldier in the center appears larger and older than the other two. The Incident occurs in a "freakfog" (48.2), and only garbled accounts of it survive. These reports of Porter's transgression at *fionn uisce* circulate throughout all Ireland and throughout the entire course of the *Wake*. Kate alludes to the Incident in her museyroom prophecies as the "jinnies" (8.31) making their "war" (8.32) on "Willingdone" (8.31–33 [Wellington Monument in Phoenix Park, Well and Stone, welling done]). The "narrator" of the *Wake*, mustering his considerable circumlocutional abilities and circumventing the facts in an attempt to meliorate the "crime," admits to having behaved with ungentlemanly immodesty while opposite a pair of dainty maidservants in the concealment of a rush-cloaked hollow, where mother nature in all innocence had spontaneously sent them both (34.12–22). More allusions to the Incident appear throughout the *Wake*, and the scene, refreshed and reviewed, was never to be forgotten (55.10–11). The dyadic maidens are "two goddesses" who are "liable to sue" HCE for his transgression (508.31). The girls at the well are the Peequeens, the "prettiest pickles of unmentionable mute antes" HCE ever peeped at (508.26–28); they are a pair of sloppy sluts, quite plainly showing all of their "Unmentionability" (107.6–7), two quite white village girls who show themselves while giggling amongst the foliage (8.3–4). They are two early "*spring dabbles*," showing HCE a clean pair of hides (342.23–26). The two maidens are "evesdripping" (89.1), making waters "most improper" (96.14) in their "possing of the showers" (51.2); at their "wetting" (314.33), they made "whole waters" (312.14).

The Incident of that "fatal wellesday" (58.29) acquires mythic and religious dimensions: "Unquestionably his [Porter's] predicament is of the nature of Original Sin: he shares the shadowy guilt that Adam experienced after eating the apple" (Campbell and Robinson, *Skeleton Key*, 7). Porter's indiscretion haunts him throughout the *Wake*; never really convicted of the crime and never exonerated, the Incident stigmatizes Porter and singles him out and is one of the main reasons he remains the outsider. Much like the Fall of Adam, the Incident is a genesis, the "crime" itself necessitating the cycle of rebirth and renewal so intrinsic to the *Wake*. The strange episode of micturition and voyeurism at *fionn uisce* becomes, in some fundamental sense, a creation rite. The English mistranslation of the Gaelic name for the spring, *Fionnusige*, as "Phoenix," certainly plays into this theme very well. The *Fionnusige* Incident becomes, like the phoenix, both symbol and means for creation and renewal: "O foenix culprit [and *felix culpa*]! Ex nickylow malo comes mickelmassed bonum" (23.16–17).

The defining characteristics of the Phoenix Park Incident are in themselves a curious farrago: dyadic maidens almost twinlike in appearance; a secluded locale, the site of an ancient spring sacred to the early Celts; the primary act of micturition and/or exposing themselves; the secretive and almost ritualistic nature of the activity; the inherent sexuality of the place and the event; the crime of voyeurism that assumes a religious dimension; three uniformed, armed, and silent watchers; and, perhaps most important, the entire event representing a creation rite.

The Phoenix Park Incident as a Welling Rite

The defining characteristics of the Phoenix Park Incident are nearly identical to an ancient Irish ritual conducted at wells and springs during the seasonal festivals. Known as the "Welling" of Ana, this ancient Irish ceremony of sympathetic magic is based upon the beliefs and paradigms of the old religion. For the pagan Irish, the great natural cycle of water they experienced was such a profound metaphor it seemed synonymous with creation and the cycle of life itself. A striking example of this belief is found in the *Lebor Gabála Érenn*, where the Celtic invasion of Ireland is described. The Milesian Celts have not yet landed in Ireland. Off the coast of the land destined to become their new home, the Celts deliberately wait for the most auspicious time for their landing. Their plan is to colonize the seventeen plains of Ireland and then take control of the *tuatha* that comprise Meath and make Tara—the seventeenth *tuatha* of Meath—their capital. Offshore of Ireland, on the day of invasion—the seventeenth day after the full moon—Amairgen White-Knee, the first Celtic Druid in Ireland, composes the first Celtic poem of Ireland. Amairgen's verse is an incantation, a creation rite, designed to establish Celtic control over the new land. The chant is cyclical and prophetic: it moves from its periphery (their present location on the sea) to the center of Ireland in the future (their Welling ritual at the *Teamhur Feis*) and then back to the present and the sea offshore. In Amairgen's poem, the creation of Celtic Ireland is synonymous with the cycle of water itself.

I seek the land of Ireland,
Coursed be the fruitful sea,
Fruitful the ranked highland,
Ranked the showery wood,
Showery the river of cataracts,
Of cataracts the lake of pools,
Of pools the hill of a well,
Of a well of a people of assemblies,
Of assemblies of the king of Temair;
Temair, hill of peoples,
Peoples of the Sons of Mil,
Of Mil of ships, of barks;
The high ship Eriu,
Eriu, lofty, very green,
An incantation very cunning.[3]

Amairgen's incantation exemplifies what J. A. MacCulloch calls the Celt's "peculiar aptitude" for "water worship" (181). The cycle of water, synonymous with the cycle of life, was, for Amairgen White-Knee and other Celtic *Filidh*, an essentially feminine power identified with the goddess Ana, the mother of waters, in her many emanations: "Wherever springs emerge, Anu [*sic*], the great mother of gods, is venerated under a variety of titles" (Matthews and Matthews, *Encyclopedia*, 291). (James Joyce himself certainly possesses Amairgen's "peculiar aptitude." The first and last words of his own seventeen-part creation rite pay homage to the goddess and the power she personifies.)

Wells and springs are the sources of life, the matrices of fertility and creative energy. They are the loci of power for the goddess, a power called the *Toradh* ("fruitfulness," "fecundity") of Ana, whether she manifests as a single entity (such as Medb in the *Táin*) or in her dyadic form (as she appears to Niall of the Nine Hostages). The wells, consequently, are the site of the ritual called the "Welling," where the flowing waters—waters flowing from the womb of the goddess—are used as the medium for rites of *Toradh*: creation and fertility. During the points in the year when fertility was of paramount concern (such as the vernal equinox), the Welling rites were especially important: "As sources of fertility they had a place in the ritual of the great festivals" (MacCulloch, 184).

The mythic paradigm for the Welling ritual is found in the lore of the sovereign of Tara, Medb. Hugh Kenner, Marian Robinson, Maria Tymoczko, and others have demonstrated Joyce's incorporation of this goddess in the *Wake*: "Medb in her multiple matings, in her use of her daughter as surrogate and pawn, and in her identification with water and rivers is clearly a prototype for ALP" (Robinson, "Women Will Water," 19). In the *Táin*, the goddess Medb, representative of numerous sovereign goddesses, creates the great rivers of Ireland through her micturition, symbolizing "the life-bringing powers and creative fertilization of water—rain, rivers, and amniotic fluid . . . linking the territorial or sovereignty goddesses with the Celtic river goddesses" (*IU*, 111). For the Celts, every spring, well, or river was "haunted by divine beings, mainly thought of as beautiful females" (MacCulloch, 184). These numerous emanations of Ana/Medb have created many of the wells, springs, and rivers of Ireland in the manner of their prototype, thus enacting a fundamental theme in Irish ritual: "associations of the goddesses' urine with fertility" (*IU*, 112).

The various mythic themes associated with water and creation were ritually enacted at the wells: the flowing waters, the presence of "goddesses," gestures and acts to increase sexuality, fertility, and creation. The rituals were performed and attended only by the women of the *tuatha*; a *geis* was placed on all men, banning them from the Welling. Breaking such a *geis* was a serious offence, one that would invite severe, even fatal, retribution. MacCulloch suggests that many of the "old tabus concerning wells" that have survived in Irish folklore are the vestiges of these ancient proscriptions (191).

Given the overall circumstances under which the Welling rite was performed (that is, the seclusion and secrecy, the obvious sexual nature of the rite, the *geis*, the oral tradition of the pagans), written accounts of the Welling are rare but do exist. Thomas J. Garbáty, referring to the medieval lyric "Maiden in the Mor Lay," observes that this song—"about a girl who lay . . . by a well in order to conceive"—contains remnants of a very old and forgotten "fertility ritual," passed down through generations by word of mouth (31). The song plays on the dual meaning of the word *well*—"the pun on the word . . . referring to the rite of 'welling'" (657).

Maiden in the mor lay,
In the mor lay—
Seuenyst [seven nights] fulle, seuenist fulle.
Maiden in the mor lay,
In the mor lay—
Seuenistes fulle ant a day.

Welle was hire mete [food, sustenance].
Wat was hire mete?
The primerole ant the—
The primerole ant the—
Welle was hire mete.
Wat was hire mete?
The primerole ant the violet.

Welle was hire dryng [drink].
Wat was hire dryng?
The chelde water of the—
The chelde water of the—
Welle was hire dryng.
Wat was hire dryng?
The chelde water of the welle-spring.

Welle was hire bour [chamber].
Wat was hire bour?
The rede rose an te—
The rede rose an te—
Welle was hire bour.
Wat was hire bour?
The rede rose an te lilie flour. (Garbáty, 657–58)

A more detailed account of an actual Welling ritual—an eyewitness account from over a century ago—still conveys many of the pagan aspects of the old ritual: a secret creation rite at a secluded well; young women exposing themselves; definite acts of sympathetic magic connecting the well water and the women; the equating of liquids and fertility; the connection with the sun, suggesting a seasonal fertility rite; the ninefold pattern inherent in the *Toradh* of Ana; and the innate sexuality of the entire ritual.

This detailed account of the secret ritual was coaxed out of an eyewitness, who, like his voyeuristic counterpart in the *Wake*, hid in the bushes by a sacred well where he watched the clandestine proceedings.

> They took off their boots, their hose, and syne they rolled up their skirts and petticoats till their wames [wombs] were bare. The auld wife gave them the sign to step round her and one after the other, wi' the sun, round the spring, each one holding up her coats like she was holding herself to the sun. As each one came anent her. the auld wife took up the water in her hands and threw it on their wames. . . . Three times round they went. . . . Then they dropped their coats to the feet again, syne they opened their dress frae the neck and slipped it off their shoulders so that their paps sprang out. The auld wife gave them another sign. They doun on their knees afore her, across the spring; and she took up the water in her hands again, skirpit [sprinkled] on their paps, three times the three.[4]

Although the Welling rite is forbidden to males, archaeological evidence uncovered at many Insular pagan wells and springs indicates that a group of three males—whether they are human or Otherworldy is undetermined—played a role in the ritual. These three are always portrayed wearing identical outfits and headgear and are usually armed, suggesting uniforms or the battle-dress of Celtic warriors. They are "clearly themselves connected with fertility and with the cult of healing waters," and their portrayals are always found in close proximity to the wells (Ross, *Pagan Celtic Britain*, 241, 294). Sometimes they appear with the goddess (or dyadic goddesses), suggesting the goddess, her lover and two brothers (a frequent theme in Celtic tales). As portrayed on votive slabs and by statuary found at wells, the central of the three soldiers is typically presented as slightly taller than his brethren and with features reflecting more age than his counterparts, indicating "an older deity flanked by two youths" (Green, *Dictionary*, 104). Though they are frequently present at the sacred wells, the three males remain enigmatic. The exact role they play in the rituals has not been determined, and their indigenous names remain unknown. The Romans referred to them as *Genii Cucullati*, "The Hooded Ones"; Anne Ross believes the mysterious triad makes an appearance in the *Táin*, where the three soldiers are known as the "Three Watchful Ones" (*Pagan Celtic Britain*, 242).

As one of the primary seasonal rites of the old Irish religion, the Welling of Ana would have been an important vernal equinox ceremony at the

Rites of Tara; and the *Wakean* rendition of this ancient rite contains all the elements of the pagan original: the secluded sacred well, the dyadic maidens, micturition as the medium of fertility, the creation rite, the Three Watchful Ones, and the *geis* placed on the rite itself—making HCE's voyeurism the ritualistic crime that it is in the *Wake*.

The "Buckley" Episode and the *Geis* on the Sacred Sod

Salient Features of the "Buckley" Episode

The *Wakean* episode known as "Buckley and the Russian General" (337.22–354.36) is presented as a dialogue, a television skit, between two vaudevillian characters, "Butt" and "Taff," with Butt in the role of Buckley. The story, based upon a tale that Joyce's father used to tell, takes place during the Crimean War. Buckley, a young Irish soldier, finds himself in close proximity to the leader of the enemy, the "Russian General," who, unaware of Buckley's presence, has sought some privacy in order to relieve himself. Buckley, seeing his opportunity, takes aim at the General but is so impressed by the General's regal stature, uniform, and medals he cannot fire. Buckley quickly recovers and is about to shoot his royal enemy when the General drops his pants to defecate, exposing his old tailbottom by "manurevring" (344.17) in "open ordure" (344.16–17). Observing the General at this "cultic twalette" (344.12 [Celtic twilight, cultic toilet]), this all-too-human circumstance, Buckley again shows hesitancy (350.12) in killing his enemy, he "adn't the arts to" (345.2–3). Then the General grabs a piece of turf in order to wipe himself; Buckley sees this, refers cryptically to the "sourd" (353.14 [sod, sword] of "foemoe [former] times" (353.14–15) and immediately kills the squatting General for this insult to the sacred sod of Ireland (353.14–21).

The "sod of former times" used in the tale is not the only connection to ancient Ireland in this story. The General, the HCE/king figure, is identified with ancient high kings of Ireland, Nuad (344.36) and Conor (348.19). Butt's obscure rambling is replete with allusions, quotes, and passages from the various Fianna Tales contained in *The Youthful Exploits of Finn* and other collections of Fenian lore. (In the "Buckley" episode, the Fenian allusions considerably outnumber the allusions to the Crimean War itself.)[5] At the conclusion of his blathering narrative, when Butt finally beached the "bark" of his tale (358.17), he and Taff merge and become Finn MacCool (354.5–6). Butt and Taff, now one and the same person, fight to uphold the right, and are *"umbraged"* (354.9 [overshadowed]) by ancient Eire's magical and mythical *"mulattomilitiaman"* (354.10) who falls by Goll's gillie (354.7–13). (Finn MacCool is, as Joyce implies, "mulatto." Finn's father, Cumal, was of the indigenous Fir Bolg, traditionally portrayed as possessing much darker complexion and features than the ruling Milesian Celts, typically described as blond and fair. Finn's mother, Muirne, was of the Milesian aristocracy.) Butt/Taff/Buckley then states that he, without falter, has taken the pledge and the vow of the Fianna (354.18–20). (In ancient Ireland, the "pledge of fiannaship" [354.19] was publicly delivered during the *Teamhur Feis*, when each new member of the Fianna formally and legally dissolved any ties with relatives in the *tuatha*.)

Richard Ellmann relates that Joyce, during composition of the *Wake*, kept telling the Buckley story to his friends, "convinced that it was in some way archetypal."[6] Nathan Halper, in his analysis of the "Buckley" episode, addresses the connection between the clump of turf and Ireland and offers an explanation for the significance of the turf: "What is there about a clump of turf that makes it an insult to Ireland? . . . The answer to this question is found in the *Wake* itself. Joyce did not call it a 'piece': he called it a 'sob of turf'—that is, a sod of turf. . . . *Old Sod* is a phrase for Ireland" ("Another Anecdote," 90).

Nathan Halper argues that the underlying theme in this tale is the fight of the low-status Irish soldier to overthrow imperial authority: "I take it to mean that the lads, the Sons, are going to kill the Father. . . . Joyce saw Buckley in his own role of the ordinary Irishman in combat with imperial authority" ("Another Anecdote," 91). Joyce, in a letter to Stanislaus (August 29, 1920), alludes to several of the "Buckley" themes in reference to the arrival in Ireland of Sir Horace Rumbold, the "first Emperor of Ireland": "Please hang the Union Jack out of the scullery window at the exact instant when he ascends his ancestral throne of alabaster [that is, his toilet]. If a man named Buckley calls, asking to see His Majesty, he is on no account to be admitted" (*Letters III*, 13). Halper then suggests the allusion to Buckley is Joyce's way of expressing his unforgiving ill-will to Rumbold, wishing that when Rumbold acts like the General, some young Irishman will act like Buckley ("Another Anecdote," 92–93).

The interpretive commentary by Ellmann, Halper, and Joyce himself emphasizes certain defining characteristics of the Buckley tale: a young Irish soldier identified with Finn and the Fianna; a battle to overthrow (or unseat) the imperial authority; the person of imperial authority appearing at his most vulnerable, that is, at a toilet or latrine; the embarrassing defecation scene of the authority figure; the empathy of the young Irish soldier; the sod imbued with mythic and symbolic power, and identified with Ireland; the appropriation of the sod as tantamount to a death sentence; and the numerous Fenian allusions throughout the story.

The "Buckley" Episode at Tara

As Joyce suggests, the Buckley tale is indeed archetypal in the sense that it is a retelling of ancient myth with ritualistic origins. In the Fianna Tales (in the very collections alluded to throughout the Buckley yarn) are two analogues to the *Wakean* story that may explain some of its colorful images, especially Joyce's patriotic and sacred clump of toilet turf. As their main plot device, both of these mythic tales refer to what has to be the most bizarre of all the magical proscriptions placed upon the kings of Tara: the *geis* forbidding them to use the sacred sod for latrine duty.

In the first Fianna story, the role of Buckley is played by Caoilte mac Ronan, who, like Buckley, is a "buckley" (Irish, *bhuachailin*, "young man"); and like his *Wakean* counterpart, Caoilte is the narrator of his story, an actor in his story, a pledged Fianna, and an emanation of Finn MacCool himself. In Caoilte's tale, he, Finn, and other Fianna are at war with the imperial authority in the person of the high king Cormac mac Art. Caoilte's and Finn's goal is to unseat Cormac and make Finn king of Tara. In the course of their warring, Caoilte manages to infiltrate the royal hall at Tara, residence of the high king. One evening, "when the drinking was finished," Caoilte surreptitiously observes the king leaving for the latrine and he stealthily follows. Caoilte relates, "I sat on his right side, intent on doing him harm." The Fianna buckley observes the king squatting but then refrains from killing him in the act of defecation. Then the king moves to grab some turf to wipe himself. At this point, Caoilte decides he will "kill" the king in a ritualistic manner. Caoilte walks over to the squatting high king and hands him a piece of turf, actually the "sacred sod" from Sescann Uairbeoil, which he happened to have in his possession. Caoilte knows full well that the sacred sod of Sescann Uairbeoil has a royal *geis* upon it, and the *geis* is very specific: no high king must use the sacred sod to wipe himself; to do so will destroy his kingship. With this knowledge, Caoilte relates, "Nevertheless, I put a piece of it in his hand." When Cormac is handed the *geis*-imbued sod, he literally smells a trap, refusing to use the proffered turf, stating, "I am surprised by what you have given me . . . some moss from Sescann Uairbeoil with the smell of Caoilte's skin on it." The squatting king knows full well what the turf means if he uses it.[7]

Another Fianna tale, also taking place at Tara, repeats the same pattern. In this version, the buckley is played by one Maelodran; the General is Diarmaid, high king of Tara. Again, the Fianna and king are at war, and Maelodran furtively positions himself to do harm to the king. Maelodran follows the army to the edge of the island on Loch Gabur, where the king has gone for a feast.

Maelodran hides in a dwelling until nighttime and waits to row over. He steals a boat, rows to the island, and finds the revelers asleep. Maelodran stealthily waits near the door of the royal booth. Unbeknown to anyone, King Diarmaid walks outside to relieve himself. Once again, the high king, while squatting, finds himself without anything to use for wiping. Maelodran, armed with both a sword and a clump of sacred sod—the "sourd" of former times—enters the scene when the king is at his most human and most vulnerable.[8] As Joseph Falaky Nagy describes the scene: "The tricky enemy enters through the back door, both literally and metaphorically . . . during an act . . . that is symbolically a violation of bodily and social boundaries . . . when even a king is isolated and vulnerable" (*Wisdom*, 146).

All three of the Fianna boys—Buckley, Caoilte, and Maelodran—are young Irish soldiers of low social status. All three are enemies of the imperial monarch, and they seek to unseat him. They each gain control over the king/general while he is alone and vulnerable; all three Fianna boys literally and figuratively catch their royal enemy with his pants down. In all three, the ridiculous plot turns on the same strange device that gives each tale the outrageous blend of the scatological and the archetypal so loved by James Joyce: the *geis*-laden turf of Tara, a deadly device and a necessary commodity, and the magical emblem of Ireland herself. The *Wakean* king-figure, by appropriating the sacred sod, violates one of the strongest and oldest of the *geissi* placed on the kings of Tara—a violation that at the *Teamhur Feis* would have eventually led to the king's death—as it does in the *Wake*.

The *Geis* on the "Pig" and the Trial of Festy King

The Absurd Trial of Festy King

The narrative account of the Trial of Festy King (beginning at 85.20), his "crime conundrum" (85.22), is on its surface an event both bewildering and absurd. On or around the calends of March (85.27), Festy King (another emanation of HCE) is "haled up" (85.26) and indicted on two charges, each from an "equinoxious" point of view (85.28); "equinoxious" suggests the charges are both equally noxious and equinoctial, related to the vernal equinox in March. The initial charge leveled against Festy King is that he was "flying cushats" (85.29–30), a slang term for stealing coals (McHugh, *Annotations*, 85). The second charge: Festy was "making fesses immodst" (85.31 [immodest, amidst]) his forces on the field (85.31). "Fesses" is French for "buttocks" and suggestive of "feces," connecting Festy with the Russian General and his scatological demise. "Fesse" is also a term used in heraldry to describe a band on an escutcheon (McHugh, *Annotations*, 85). In addition, "Fesse" is close to the Gaelic *Feis*.

Festy King appears at the trial dressed in his ubiquitous seven articles of clothing, motley (85.33–35), identifying Festy with HCE and the motley-attired Feste in *Twelfth Night*. The ensuing deposition notes that Festy was arrested while trying to light a fire (85.36–86.5), probably a ritual bonfire since it was "wildfires night" on all the "bettygallaghers" (90.9–10 [hills]); Festy, too, refers to a god of the fires (91.29) during his self-defense.

More charges are brought against Festy. The king is accused of sneaking into a fair, a *feis*, or an agricultural festival (a gathering convened by the Irish Agricultural and Pre-pastoral Organization [86.20–21]) with a "pedigree pig" (86.14). As recounted in the deposition, the pedigree pig's activities are somehow central to Festy's "crime." The pig is placed in its own wooden shelter, which it then partially consumes: the pig ate an entire side of his "sty" (86.28). The royal pig is then lost, escapes through mismanagement, or is misappropriated by Festy himself. Regardless of the manner in which it occurs, Festy commits a serious transgression through his involvement with the pig.

During the trial, remarkable evidence (86.32) is presented by the witness "W.P." (86.34). According to W.P., during the three-day festival, "Tournay, Yetstoslay and Temorah" (87.8), one H.O.D., on the fair green, attempted to single-handedly "sack, sock, stab and slaughter" (87.16) two of the other old kings (86.16–17); "bad blood" (87.20) existed on the ground of the "boer's trespass" (87.20–21); and this fight on the green might be for the favors of a woman (87.22–23). After W.P.'s testimony, Festy is questioned on his knowledge of secret Druidic languages and Ogham alphabets (89.29–34). Two more witnesses, "Camellus" and "Gemellus," the famous doorkeepers at Tara (McHugh, *Annotations*, 90), describe their version of a fight, and the indictment concludes with an ominous thundering (90.31–33).

Festy is given a chance to speak (90.33), and his loud outburst of "poesy" (91.3) is permeated with pig puns and porcine allusions: sows, orcs, the sow of Eire, porkers, mucs, torcs, and reference to "Anthony" (the smallest pig in a litter). His denial is as obscure as are the charges against him: Festy would swear that if "live thurkells" (91.9 [Old Irish, *torc caille*, "forest swine"]) followed him about, that was "no steal" (91.10); and then Festy emphasizes, during a dramatic point in his deposition, that he absolutely "did not fire a stone" (91.11–12) either before or after that particular time (91.8–13).

Given the absurdity of both the charges and the defense, Susan Swartzlander notes, in "Multiple Meaning and Misunderstanding: The Mistrial of Festy King," "Critics have never fully understood the Festy King section of *Finnegans Wake*" (465). Salient points, though, have been addressed.[9] In her *Second Census*, Adaline Glasheen, citing the reference to "flying cushats," suggests that the primary charge against Festy is "stealing coal" (140). The second charge ("making fesses immodst his forces") is certainly an allusion to the "Buckley and the Russian General" episode. Philip L. Graham interprets "fesse" in its heraldic sense and argues that Festy/HCE is a solar king, charged with claiming the right to bear heraldic insignia to which he is not entitled; Festy's right to the title of solar king is questioned. Both Swartzlander and Graham note that the numerous porcine allusions seem consistently symbolic of Ireland, her "history and religion" (Swartzlander, 468). The central charge, then, is that during a festival and in some fundamental way, Festy King "betrayed the pig" that is symbolic of Ireland. F. X. Matthews emphasizes that readers should see Shakespeare's Feste lurking in the shadow of Joyce's character. Matthews connects Festy King with the European tradition of the Festival of the Fools, when the "King of the Bean" was elected on Twelfth Night to reign over a kingdom of misrule, a Christian medieval event derived from the pagan ritual regicide of the waning solar king. Even with these various points of elucidation, the episode—especially with its emphasis on the pig material—remains essentially obscure, as Swartzlander concludes: "The pig material has little to do with Festy King's alleged offenses. Selling a pig or sneaking into a fair with one is hardly a capital offense. The meaning cannot be resolved—at least not on this narrative level" (469). However, on another narrative level, the meaning of the plotline *can* be resolved; and the "pig material" has everything to do with Festy King's offenses.

The "Pig Material" at the *Teamhur Feis*

The backdrop of Festy's trial, describing a three-day festival, held in March after the calends and associated with agricultural and seasonal cycles, attended by all classes and races of Irish, involving a ritual bonfire on a hill where a "solar king" lights a fire, where rivals for the kingship fight for the "affections of a woman," and a tournament ("Tournay") involving ritual combat ("Yetstoslay") at Temora (that is, Tara) is a fair summary of the main events of the *Temora Feis*. And R.A.S. Macalister, whose own work (that is, specific phrases from his *Secret Languages*) is alluded to in the "Festy King" episode (89.29–34), makes some important observations regarding the *Feis*, the solar king, his fire, and his important "pig material": "The king, as representative of the divinity that kept the fire of the sun alight, was naturally bound to maintain a perpetual fire at Tara, and to cause it to blaze up and to be the source of all common fires at . . . the Vernal Equinox" (*T*, 167). This sacred fire was always described in "pig" terms: "swine of the fire," "fire pig." In *Da Derga's Hostel*, the sacred bonfire is described in the obscure Old Irish term *torc caille* ("forest swine"), very close to the term used by Festy ("thurkells" [91.9]), when he speaks in his own defense.

The "pig" at the *Teamhur Feis* inhabited a pyramidal structure of logs called both *torc tened* ("fire boar") and *torc caille*. When this structure was consumed by fire, the embers were taken, and "stones placed in the . . . fire"—that is, the fire was slowed down so as to be kept alive during the year; and the "fire boar" of the following year was lit from it (*T*, 167).

If the "Trial of Festy King" is interpreted within the context of this ancient tradition, a meaning to this obscure event may be elicited. A faltering and threatened festival king (HCE) is arrested while attempting to light a ritual fire at the vernal equinox, the fire proclaiming ascendancy for the one who lights it. The first charge leveled against Festy is trying to steal coals; the second charge is falsely presenting himself as a solar king. The proceedings then state that Festy King was sneaking into the festival with a "pedigree pig." The "pig" is placed in a wooden house, which it partially consumes, that is, the king attempted to light a bonfire. The "pig"— "symbol of Irish history and religion"—is misappropriated, an act perceived by the festival attendants as an ultimate betrayal of Ireland herself, as "bad blood on the ground of the boar."

Festy's two-part denial is also directly related to the accusation that he attempted to light the ritual fire. Festy states that if the "thurkells" follow him, he is not responsible for it; he then denies using the *torc caille* coals to build the fire, claiming that he "did not fire a stone." Misappropriation of the *torc caille* at the *Teamhur Feis* is a major violation of a royal *geis*. *The Book of Rights* underscores the serious nature of this offense: "Patrick goes afterwards to Fearta Feir Feic [Slane]. A fire is kindled by him at that place on Easter Eve. Laegaire is enraged as he sees the fire, for that was the *geis* of Teamhair among the Gaedhil."[10] Sneaking a "pig" into a fair is indeed a betrayal of Irish religion and history and a capital offense. It is the very act committed by Patrick at the Rites of Tara in chapter 17 of the *Wake*.

"The Prankquean's Tale" and the Rite of *Lommrad*

"The Prankquean's Tale": A Summary

During a night in Ireland when bonfires are blazing on hilltops and a festival is under way, the Prankquean arrives at the closed castle of the king ("van Hoother"), who is inside with the two "jiminies" (21.11 [*gemini*, "twins," and *gamina*, Celtic, "season change"]) and their younger sister, the dyadic emanation of the Prankquean herself. The king is in seclusion within the citadel, "laying cold hands on himself" (21.11 [masturbating, attempting to warm himself, attempting to heal himself, attempting to kill himself]). The Prankquean demands entrance; implicit in her demand are requests for sex with the king, hospitality, recognition of her true identity, and affirmation of her relationship with the jiminies and their sister. The Prankquean poses a riddle to the king: "Mark the Wans, why do I am alook alike a poss of porterpease?" (21.18–19). The king, angered because the Prankquean "made her wit" (21.16 [urinated, expressed her riddle]) against the "dour" (21.16 [door, dour one]), slams the door in her face. Incensed, the Prankquean takes one of the "jiminies" and travels "Tourlemonde" (21.27), the circuit of the world. During this journey (the cycle of which is forty), the jiminy transforms into his opposite.[11]

The Prankquean returns to the castle, and again there is a festival with bonfires on hilltops. The Prankquean presents a variation of the "poss of porterpease" riddle and is again insulted and rebuffed. The Quean removes the other jiminy, takes him on the quarantine circuit of the world, and he too transforms into *his* opposite.

Once more the Quean returns to the castle after her cyclical journey and again poses the porterpease riddle. The king, exasperated by the riddle and the demands, rushes at the Quean and insults her to her face. The princess now turns on the king and slams a shutter against him, which produces a peal of ominous thunder. The king himself is now shut out of the castle, and shut out from the Quean—indicating his fall, defeat, or death. The Quean and her dyadic counterpart now merge. Along with the others, the young/old Quean engages in a feast that involves imbibing the mysterious ale (the porter) alluded to in the riddle. The tale ends with the feast under way, a call for a truce, and plans for a wedding ceremony.

Critical Observations Regarding "The Prankquean's Tale"

In "Seasonal Change and Transformation in 'The Prankquean's Tale,'" Michael Kaufmann argues that the Prankquean episode is enacted within the context of a Celtic seasonal ritual. Kaufmann cites details surrounding the Prankquean's visits to the castle: the hilltop bonfires and the weather conditions suggesting seasonal festivals, the transforming *gamina* who personify the changing seasons. These indicate a "pattern of Celtic seasonal festivals on which Joyce structures the tale" (437). The transformation of the Twins occurs as a result of the seasonal changes taking place. HCE (as the king) and Anna (as the Prankquean) personify natural forces impelling the seasons round the calendar; the parents' identities as natural forces explain the jiminies' changes that, in Celtic tradition, were "ritualized in the festal points of the calendar" (441).

In *The Riddles of Finnegans Wake*, Patrick McCarthy notes that allusions to the Tara Triangle (Finn, Grania, Diarmaid) appear throughout "The Prankquean's Tale," and that this triangle "seems to be the single most important source for the thematic implications of the Tale" (108). McCarthy notes that both "The Prankquean's Tale" and "The Pursuit of Diarmaid and Grania" share the following important components:

- A dyadic queen rejects an older man and selects a younger male.
- The woman acts as both creator and destroyer.
- The woman is the one who chooses and is the one with the real power in the situation.
- The old and young males are closely related, introducing an Oedipus-like theme.
- The elopement of the queen and young male is deliberately connected to the seasonal cycle.
- The issue of sexual virility is implicit in the selection of the man.
- A magical and intoxicating liquid is instrumental in the structure of both stories.

McCarthy further observes that the fairy-tale quality, the traditional Celtic tripartite structure, and the ancient Fenian themes combine to turn the Prankquean episode into "a ritualistic action of cosmic significance" (119).

For many *Wakean* scholars, the most intriguing aspect of "The Prankquean's Tale" is the strange riddle upon which much of the action and meaning of the tale hinges. After examining Joyce's early drafts and comparing these to the final edition, McCarthy believes Joyce constructed the riddle to convey at least three levels of interlocking meaning: "a request for porter, a question about why the Prankquean wants (or likes) porter, and a metaphoric riddle about the Prankquean's similarity to a pot of porter" (112). McCarthy believes that the riddle implies both sexual desire and sexual request on the part of the Quean. The riddle "might in fact be rephrased to indicate a desire to 'pass the *porte* [door], please,' which in turn would imply a desire for sexual union"; the Quean demanding entrance suggests a sexual challenge to the king inside (110). McCarthy, like Kaufmann, perceives an element of Celtic tradition in the riddle: "Prankquean is really a druidic satirist, for the satirists were fond of pulling pranks and were able to perform magical conversions. posing the riddle three times, she is not only challenging . . . but also threatening him" (119).

E. L. Epstein suggests that the riddle is fundamentally a religious question on the nature and identity of a triune divinity: "'Why do I am alook alike a poss of porterpease?' might be glossed 'Why do the three members of the Trinity resemble each other so completely?'" (McCarthy, 113). In Epstein's gloss, there is the indication that the riddle might involve the recognition of a triune divinity represented by the Quean herself.

William York Tindall believes the nature of the relationship between the Quean, the king, and the twins is the core of the riddle: "A.L.P. looks like the twins (who are as like as two peas in a pod) because she is their mother" (McCarthy, 113–14). Accordingly, the riddle should be interpreted: "Why am I like a pot of porter please?" (Mrs. Porter is one of Anna's names throughout the *Wake*) or "Why am I like a pod for Porter's peas?" The answer in either case is because the Quean, as their mother, held the jiminy twins (alike as peas in a pod) in her own womb (pod).

Grace Eckley, in "Petween Peas Like Ourselves: The Folklore of the Prankquean," connects the Prankquean's riddle with the nursery rhyme "Pease porridge hot" and the children's singing game "Oats, peas, beans, and barley grows," citing several passages in the *Wake* where the riddle and the children's games merge. Making this connection between the riddle and rhymes from folklore, Eckley suggests that the riddle and the entire "Prankquean" episode itself may be related to earlier pagan rites: "'Oats, peas, beans' in folklore means a springtime vegetation or fertility ritual" (184). Eckley also suggests that Irish rites of kingship may offer a clue to the resolution of the "Prankquean" episode itself: "The relation between Irish kings and their realm is often portrayed as a marriage, and the inauguration feast of a king is called a wedding-feast. The country is a woman, the spouse of the king, and before her marriage she is a hag or a woman whose mind is deranged" (186). Eckley suggests that the Prankquean, as a Celtic goddess, attacks the "king" in the sense of kidnapping the children. The "king" must resolve this royal struggle before there can be peace in the marriage, the castle, and the land (186).

Margaret Solomon emphasizes the sexual nature of the riddle, and would translate it as: "Mark I, why am I and a poss of porter as much alike as peas in a pod?" Her answer is that, "like the porter (ale), she, too, is firewater, and is the cause of man's fall" (McCarthy, 114). The ale/firewater is also the urine with which the Quean "made her wit" and is suggested in the word *porterpease* (that is, Porter pees), symbolizing the Quean's cyclical nature: on a microcosmic level, the cycle of imbibing, assimilating and eliminating; in a larger cycle, rain, river, sea, and rain. The Quean's request for porter (the red ale, and the king, Mr. Porter) is a metaphor for her desire for sex with the king; but by slamming the door, he rejects her advances. In some mysterious and significant way, the Prankquean is herself the porter or firewater, "because she, like the red ale, is a cause of man's fall, and because she is identified in the tale with fire and water: 'she lit up and fireland was ablaze' and 'into the shandy westerness she rain, rain, rain'" (McCarthy, 114). The identity of the Quean with "firewater" is further strengthened by her identity with other intoxicating liquids throughout the *Wake*: Tea (goddess and drink), piessporter wine, Tara water, and Bass's Red Ale (with its prominent red triangle on the label). All of these are associated throughout the *Wake* with micturition, sexuality, cyclical processes in nature, rivers, wells, springs, fertility, creation, and quintessential feminine divinity and power. The mysterious liquid intoxicant at the core of this fecund riddle—the "sacramental ale" as Patrick McCarthy calls it—is, in some magical or ritualistic sense, at once the drink, the act of sex, the challenge to kingship, the great cycle of nature, and the powerful and perhaps divine Quean herself.

The Wakean *Quean as Irish Sovereign*

The *Wakean* Quean who is both creator and destroyer has attributes that strongly identify her as the Sovereign of Tara. Both Prankquean and Sovereign manifest as single Queen, as the dyadic *puella senilis* of princess and queen or, as Epstein observed, a divine trinity. The Sovereign, like the Prankquean, is the mother of the Twins, the transforming young males, the gemini/*gamina*, who represent Samhain and Beltane, the two seasons of the ancient Celtic solar year. She is the divinity manifest within the Queen of Tara.

As Solomon observed with the Prankquean, the Sovereign is strongly identified with springs and rivers. As Medb, Ana, or Tea, she is all the flowing liquids that sustain life, bestow royalty, and engender fertility. The Sovereign, in all of her emanations, is associated with "dispensation of drink, promotion of fertility, and bestowal of kingship" (Enright, 273).

In Irish tradition, the identity of the Sovereign with life-giving liquids is *so* complete that the *Filidh* typically referred to the goddess with puns (like Joyce's "porterpease") that deliberately merged the identities of the liquid, the goddess, and the magical powers of both. *Medb* ("Mead") literally means "The Intoxicant"; the pun intentionally connects the fiery enthralling beauty of the Tara Queen, the drink of "firewater" (mead), the heady power of kingship she bestows, and the intoxication of sex with the goddess herself. Another of the early names for the Sovereign is *Dergflaith* ("Red Sovereignty"). The name is a well-crafted pun on two early Irish words, *Flaith* ("Sovereignty") and *Laith* ("Ale"): "*derg flaith*, a name which can mean both 'red ale' and 'red sovereignty' . . . is a bride, the server of a powerful drink, and the drink itself" (Rees and Rees, 75–76).

As Ireland's palladium of fecundity, the Sovereign is obligated to mate with the king, presumably the best male candidate possible. The Queen and king *must* have sexual relations as a necessary rite of sympathetic magic to maintain the fertility of Ireland, the well-being and fecundity of the people, the animals and vegetation, and the regular change of Samhain into Beltane and back again. The Sovereign's choice of king and consort is based on the collective criteria of *Fir Flathemhan*. Promulgated through the *Audacht Morainn* and other texts related to the rites of pagan kingship, the qualities of *Fir Flathemhan* as required by the Sovereign are identical to the Prankquean's demands at the castle of van Hoother: the king's participation in the favorable transformation of the seasons, his hospitality and generosity at court, sexual virility and relations with his queen, personal responsibility in promoting fertility, absence of niggardliness and excessive pride, personal health and hygiene, and recognition of the goddess of Sovereignty herself.

Like the Prankquean, the Sovereign traditionally tests the *Fir Flathemhan* of her consort with a mysterious riddle. The mythic paradigm for this test is described in the visionary tale *Baile an Scál,* found in the oldest extant copies of *The Tripartite Life,* one of Joyce's principal sources for Patrician lore. During the seasonal rites at Tara, the high king Conn is conveyed to the royal palace in the Otherworld. Conn meets the Sovereign standing next to a silver cauldron filled with a magical red liquid and holding in her hand a goblet of *Dergflaith.* The Queen, "a diadem of gold upon her head," turns to Conn and poses a mysterious riddle: "Who shall this *Dergflaith* be served to?" The king is taught the correct answer to the Queen's riddle: *Dergflaith* is his Queen, his lover, the sacramental red ale, and the intoxicating sex that underscores his *Fir Flathemhan* and thereby legitimizes his reign as king. Conn understands the riddle and is thus accepted by the Queen. Conn then hears the regnal list of future kings, all described by the Sovereign in terms of the *Dergflaith* riddle:

> Art shall drink it after forty nights, a mighty hero . . . Cormac shall drink it up; an ancient drink . . . Coirpre shall drink it, a fitting contestant, with righteousness of rule [that is, *Fir Flathemhan*]. Fiachri shall demand it . . . till Broadfaced Daire shall distribute it for a plenteous month. . . . Finnachta who shall pour shall drink it.[12]

The Lommrad

Conn of the Hundred Battles, a model king, correctly answers the Queen's riddle and conducts his reign according to the precepts of *Fir Flathemhan.* This, however, is not always the case. A king who fails the regnal riddle and falters in his adherence to the precepts of *Fir Flathemhan* now acts through *Gó Flatha* ("falsehood of a king"). The Sovereign not only abandons such a king, she typically becomes the dark Queen and the agent of his destruction: "the goddess of sovereignty reappears as the goddess of death to unjust kings and withdraws sovereignty" (E. Bhreathnach, 113).

In an event called the *Lommrad* (the act of laying bare, the act of melting away, the act of shearing), the Sovereign becomes the destructive queen and uses her power to take back all of her gifts from the failed king: health, virility and fertility, the seasonal *gamina,* his right to residence in the castle.[13] After the *Lommrad,* the king is no longer legitimate. Like van Hoother, he is stripped of his gifts and powers and shut out by the goddess—the prelude to his destruction.

In order to prevent Ireland from becoming the Wasteland, a new king and consort must be found. The cycle personified by *Dergflaith* begins again at the *Teamhur Feis,* the great Celtic seasonal festival where hilltop fires are blazing, where the goddess calls a truce, where her mysterious drink is served, where she is reunited with her *gamina*, and where she plans her next wedding—exactly as the *Wakean* tale relates.

The Grail Myth in "The Prankquean's Tale"

The salient features of "The Prankquean's Tale" also suggest another and much more familiar Celtic pattern: a Celtic king who is sexually dysfunctional but associated with fertility commits a transgression against a woman. The transgression is the violation of a code of honor and is, in some fundamental way, a sexual sin. The woman insulted is associated with royalty and divinity, and a mystical cycle of regeneration. The woman is also connected in a numinous way with a sacred red liquid that is the essence of divinity and regeneration. A deliberate pun emphasizes this connection. A riddle built around the pun must be correctly answered for the king to heal his relationship with the woman. If he fails, he suffers and dies, and his children and kingdom suffer as well. If he answers correctly, he becomes the new king and the land becomes fertile once again.

While this is the pattern of Joyce's fairy tale, it is also the pattern of the Grail Romance: the aging king who is sexually ill and wounded in his "thigh"; the Grail itself holding the divine red liquid; the pun on the name *San Graal* (Holy Grail) and "*Sang Real*" (Royal Blood); the riddle that must be answered ("Who does the Grail serve?"); the failure leading to the death of the king and the Wasteland; the successful response identifying the new king. Many *Wakean* scholars have sensed that the Grail Legend is deeply embedded in the cycle of the *Wake*; but the Grail Legend, as Jessie Weston and others demonstrate, is itself based upon much earlier Celtic rituals. While "The Prankquean's Tale" resembles the Grail Legend, the closer pattern to Joyce's tale is found in the rite of *Lommrad* enacted at the *Teamhur Feis*. The Grail Legend, though resonant with the story of the Prankquean, is itself derived in large part from the Rites of Tara, making it the more recent surface inscribed on Joyce's ancient palimpsest: "Thou in shanty! Thou in scanty shanty!! Thou in slanty scanty shanty!!!" (305.23–24).

Regicide through Word and Deed

Verbal Weapons of the Irish Filidh

The belief that a Druid or *Fili* could, through the power of words alone, bring favorable or ill fortune is a fact well attested in Irish literature and folklore. This ability, known as *moladh agus aoir* ("praise and satire"), is illustrated in many medieval texts through the claim that a skillful *Fili* had two little compartments in his tongue, one holding honey, the other containing poison (Ó hÓgáin, *Sacred Isle,* 82–83). These little compartments, however, were hardly used with equivalent frequency: the Irish *Filidh* typically placed much greater emphasis on satire and curse than on praise and accolade.

Vivian Mercier connects this poison-tongue preference directly to the Irish pagan tradition: satire (*aer, aoir*) was originally a magical rite inherited from Druidism. A Druidic *aer* "was believed to have power to cause . . . even death, in its victim"; and the Irish *Fili* undoubtedly acquired his much feared verbal powers from this Druidic tradition (*ICT,* 106). The word *aer,* which eventually came to mean "satire" (in the most general sense), originally signified a Druidic "spell" or "enchantment."

A malevolent *aer* delivered by Druid or *Fili* was typically aimed at a very specific individual. As a probable result of its Druidic origin, Irish satire usually takes the form of a personal attack rather than a generalized satire. However, since Ireland has adopted the English law of libel, Mercier notes, "such lampoons now rarely find their way into print, though Joyce had both 'The Holy Office' and 'Gas from a Burner' printed at his own expense" (*ICT,* 106). Much like his Druidic precursors, "Joyce held the archaic, magical view that words are weapons—and lawful weapons" (*ICT,* 107). And some of the most colorful of these "lawful weapons" are voiced once again at the *Wake.*

"Hosty's Rann*" as the bria-mon is meth righe*

One of the verbal weapons used by the *Filidh* was a song, a *rann,* publicly performed against a king already in his decline and guilty of violating the tenets of *Fir Flathemhan.* This vituperative recital was known as *bria-mon is meth righe* ("the word-play that constitutes the decline of reign") (Ó hÓgáin, *Sacred Isle,* 82). The *bria-mon is meth righe* is both satire and blame, and the emphasis in its composition is placed on the culpability of a waning king who has earned the displeasure of the people as a whole and of the *Filidh* in particular. The king's lack of honor, his increasing age, the failure of crops and animals, human illness, bad weather, and general decline of services are the specific topics of this Bardic *rann.* The intention of the *bria-mon is meth righe* was to publicly place the blame for misfortune where it belonged—the failing and hapless king—and in so doing shape public opinion against him, thereby encouraging, if not initiating, a series of subsequent acts that would eventually lead to regicide. "Hosty's Rann," the slanderous little song entitled "The Ballad of Persse O'Reilly" (44.35–47.32), easily translates as a modern rendition of the *bria-mon is meth righe* that was sung at ancient Tara.

In the *Wake*, at the great festival, all the Irish tribes of "Scotia Picta" (43.30) have gathered: a great overflowing meeting of all the Irish, a single-minded supercrowd, fully represented in all sections and cross sections of Ireland (42.20–23). The event they anticipate is Hosty's Rann, his lay for the great but fallen leader: the "rhymers' world" (42.12) will be, with good reason, the richer for Hosty's ballad, his "lay" of the "vilest bogeyer" (42.15) and the most attractive avatar the world has ever explained (42.11–16).

Hosty's composition (Hosty's the man to rhyme the *rann*, the king of all the *ranns* [44.15–17]) addresses all the traditional grievances found in the *bria-mon is meth righe*. The *rann* cites the literal fall of the king, how he fell with a roll and a rumble (45.2). The king, once the fecund vessel of the Spirit of Vegetation, has deteriorated into an old and rotten parsnip (45.8), even though he was at one time the king of the castle (45.7). The fallen king, also failing in virility, is blamed for infertility in the Irish people as well: he is responsible for the "immaculate contraceptives" (45.14) of the populace. In the course of the ballad, the king is cited as the father of all schemes that bother us (45.13), including illness, bad harvests, failing animals, and overall mendacity. Hosty then accuses the king of various crimes and concludes his *rann* by urging that the assembled Gaels use the festival itself as the opportunity to murder their failed leader: "Then we'll have a free trade Gaels' band and mass meeting / For to sod the brave son of Scandiknavery. / And we'll bury him down in Oxmanstown / Along with the devil and Danes" (47.22–26). Hosty's Rann at the *Wake* contains all the characteristics and malicious spirit of the *bria-mon* at the *Teamhur Feis*.

The Glam Dichenn *at "The Banging at the Gate"*

"The Banging at the Gate"

Even more vicious than Hosty's *bria-mon* is the violent curse delivered by the Cad Magrath in the episode Campbell and Robinson refer to as "The Banging at the Gate" (63.20–74.19). Here too, Joyce patterns Magrath's curse on an older Druidic tradition. In this episode, Magrath, a "process server" (63.31–32), after undertaking a clan march (70.14) from the middle west of Ireland (70.14) through the Belfast Mountains (70.15–16), arrives at the threshold of the "houseking's" (70.19) residence near a sacred hill. In this "drema of Sorestost Areas" (69.14–15 [dream, drama, of the Irish Free state]), Magrath, the "unsolicited visitor" (70.13), performs a series of bizarre activities while positioned at the "stonehinged gate" (69.15) of the king's residence. Magrath, like a "starling bierd" (70.16 [starling bird, startling bard]), does a "long dance" (70.16) at HCE's gate. With HCE watching through the keyhole in his door, Magrath then throws a handful of dry cereal (Quaker's oats, possibly) through the keyhole into HCE's face: "blew some quaker's (for you! Oates!) in through the houseking's keyhole to attract attention" (70.18–19). (The term *quaker's* is more than a brand name: *quaker's* suggests that the cereal itself, for some unknown reason, causes HCE to become a "quaker," as he is now quaking and shaking with fear.) Magrath's next action only intensifies HCE's already panicky state.

Screaming in an "eeriesh" (70.4 [eerie, Irish]) mythic tongue of mixed languages (70.4), Magrath delivers a violent threat against HCE: he "bleated" (70.19) through the "gale" (70.20 [Gael]) that he would break his [HCE's] head (70.19–22). Magrath, now identified as a hog-caller or hog-catcher (70.20–21), continues at a "wicked rate" (70.32), railing against the houseking in mixed metaphors and ordering him to come out to be executed, "Amen" (70.31–35). Then Magrath, in an absolute "rage" (73.13), screams: "a brisha a milla a stroka a boola" (73.12–13 [Irish, *ag briseadh,* "breaking"; *ag milleadh,* "destroying"; *ag stracadh,* "tearing"; *ag buaileadh,* "beating"]) and levels a curse intended to render HCE dead and/or insane: "Gog's curse" (73.6–7) on HCE, "burst" (73.7) him until he is completely "dizzy" (73.7), and then build a cairn of rocks over him (73.9). Magrath's curse is apparently extemporaneous and comprises a catalog of abusive names addressing HCE's faults and age, with references to the recurring criminal charges leveled against him. The curse is also ritualistic: Magrath's curse, as William York Tindall notes, is exactly 111 execrations, a number used in the *Wake* to imply cyclical process and completion (78–79). HCE, now scared speechless (72.18), hides until Magrath finally leaves: he suspects his death is near. The strange and ominous episode concludes with a foreshadowing of a resurrection described in the imagery of the Green Man, the Spirit of Vegetation who is slain in order to rise again in the spring of the year: HCE shall wake from "earthsleep, *h*aught *c*rested *e*lmer" [hce] (74.2), "Greenman's Rise O (lost leaders live! The heroes return!)" (74.2–3).

The *Glam Dichenn*

Magrath's activities at the "stonehinged gate" of the "houseking"—his birdlike dancing, throwing dry cereal at HCE and thereby causing tremendous fear, delivering a ritual execration in an "eeriesh" mythic tongue, positioning himself on an ancient threshold—are the precise components of the Druidic curse known as the *glam dichenn*. The most compelling of all ritual curses, the *glam dichenn* would have been directed at a disgraced leader or failed king and delivered only by a powerful Druid, such as the "process server" Mog Ruith—the most powerful Druid of all.

The *glam dichenn* was one of the most feared of the magical abilities attributed to Irish Druids, a powerful rite of malediction recognized by the Irish Celts that ensured the authority of the Druids and the efficacy of their edicts. The *glam dichenn* was a ritualized execration, a curse, intended to put its victim—one subsequently shunned by all levels of society—under shame, sickness, and even death (Ellis, *Dictionary*, 136–37). The *glam dichenn* was frequently delivered in conjunction with a birdlike dance or balanced posturing ("one hand, one foot, one eye") intended to augment the force of the curse, and traditionally known as the "crane-stance" (MacKillop, *Dictionary*, 224). Joyce's "namesake," P. W. Joyce, describes the modus operandi of this ritual curse: "While in this posture [the "crane-stance"] he [an Irish Druid] uttered a kind of incantation or curse, called *glam dichenn*, commonly extempore"; the curse was "intended to inflict injury on the maledicted person. . . . It was chanted in a loud voice, as the word *glam* indicates, meaning . . . 'clamour' or 'outcry.'"[14]

P. W. Joyce also cites an episode in the "Bruden Da Derga" where two adversaries of the high king of Tara—one a "hog-catcher" like the *Wake*'s Magrath—perform the crane-stance and the *glam dichenn* against the doomed King:

> King Conari was on his way to the Bruden, [when] he was overtaken by two rough monstrous big-mouthed misshapen goblins, man and wife, the man—whose name was Fer-Caille ("Man of the Wood")—"with his one hand, and one eye and one foot," carrying a great black squealing hog on his back. And just before the tragedy in which this king was slain, a horrible spectral-looking woman came, and, standing at the door of the house, she croaked out some sort of incantation "on one foot, one hand, and one breath." (*SH*, 1:241)

As with hog-catcher Magrath, the *glam dichenn* directed against the fated king of Tara is purposely delivered on a threshold. In Druidic tradition, threshold and liminal locations are the optimal loci for harnessing and generating magical power. Liminal locations—for example, "the threshold separating the inside of the room or house from the outside world"—can be utilized by a Druid as "the source of extraordinary powers because the liminal transcends normal distinctions between separate categories" (Nagy, "Liminality," 135–36). A Druid would use these liminal places (for example, near a door, on the boundary between civilization and wilderness) to create a magically charged "atmosphere" in order to "help generate the power necessary for ritual" (Nagy, "Liminality," 138). Magrath, cursing HCE from the stonehinged gate, and the wailing banshee at the portal of the Bruden Da Derga, are both capitalizing on the Druidic concept of liminality when they deliver their malefic vituperations.

Though the *glam dichenn* was believed powerful enough to cause shame, sickness, or even death, it was on special occasions augmented with the *dlui fulla*. The most dreaded of all the necromantic powers attributed to the Irish Druids was perhaps the ability to inflict madness (Irish, *dasacht*). And *dasacht* was believed by many Irish to be often brought on by a malignant magical agent—usually the work of a Druid. For this dark purpose, a Druid prepared the *dlui fulla*, the "madman's wisp" (*SH*, 1:224). The *dlui fulla* was a handful of grain chaff or cereal straw into which a Druid "pronounced some horrible incantations, and, watching his opportunity, flung it into the face of his victim, who at once became insane or idiotic" (*SH*, 1:224). In *Finnegans Wake*, Magrath sees the houseking HCE pressing his face to the keyhole; seizing his opportunity, Magrath flings his handful of dry cereal—a *dlui fulla*—into HCE's face, an act that certainly gets his attention, causing him abject terror.

Both the *dlui fulla* and the *glam dicchen* would have been performed in the ritual speech of Druids and Bards, the secret language referred to in "The Colloquy of the Ancients" and elsewhere as the "Dark Tongue." The speech of "eeriesh" myth used so effectively by Magrath, along with his threshold dance and his dry-cereal projectiles, re-creates the same Druidic curse performed by Magrath's ancient counterpart, Mog Ruith, at Tara.

Regicide

In the "Bruden Da Derga" and at the Rites of Tara, the *glam dicchen* is delivered, as it is in *Finnegans Wake*, shortly before the actual murder of the king. In the *Wake*, HCE, sensing his "melancholy death" (97.33) is imminent, began to fear for his days (97.28). In the course of his flight, HCE hears a strange noise, the same sound the cursed king at Tara would have heard and feared, the roaring *Roth Romach* that drives him insane with fear: its wires hummed (98.14); its cracking "cricked" (99.4); the aerials "buzzed" (99.10); and the noise of its roar drove him mad (98.3–4). At the height of his terror, HCE once again encounters his powerful adversary, Magrath (98.9), wielding his mysterious piece of wood (98.26) imbued with divine powers (98.27). And on an ancient tumulus used for the inaugural rites of Irish kings, HCE is murdered the day before the ritual bonfire is lit (100.8–13): the king (99.24) with a mansion in a place of inauguration (99.24), on the hill of "Tullymongan" (99.26–27), suffered real murder (99.27), of the "rayheallach royghal raxacraxian variety" (99.27–28).

Marion Cumpiano suggests that elements of this passage and the more complete report of HCE's death (99.24–100.4) are based upon the account in *The Annals of the Four Masters* describing the assassination of Tighearnan Ua Ruairc at the Hill of Tlaghtgha in 1172:

> Tighearnan Ua Ruairc, for a long time a powerful chieftain, was treacherously slain at Tlaghtgha by Hugh de Lacy. . . . He was beheaded and ignominiously carried to Dublin; his head was placed over the towngate, and his body was gibbeted with his feet upwards, on the north side of the city, a woeful spectacle to the Irish![15]

Cumpiano suggests that Joyce deliberately alters the account given by the Four Masters, changing the location and thereby deliberately imbuing the murder of HCE with a more ritualistic significance. Joyce changes the site of the actual murder from the ancient cemetery Hill of Tlaghtgha . . . to "a place of inauguration on the hill of Tullymongan" (99.26–27). The Hill of Mongan in East Breffney was ruled by the O'Reilly Clan, and this fact is found in the eighth thunder word: "-tullaghmongan-" which is preceded by "-parrassannuaragheallach-" (332.05), which Brendan O Hehir translates as: "Piers the Descendant of Ragthallach (O'Reilly) of the Hill of Mangan (*tullach*, hill)." In the passage cited above, the "real murder, of the rayheallach royghal raxacraxian variety" (99.27) is thus the ritual murder and resurrection of the kingly HCE Perse O'Reilly-O'Rourke, and the place of martyrdom of the sacrificed king becomes the place of his inauguration (85). Like the kings of Tara, HCE is thus murdered at the site of his own impending resurrection and the locus of royal inauguration. But before these events can occur, and much like all the god kings of Ireland's past murdered at the Rites of Tara, the *Wakean* god king must first travel to the Celtic Elysium, *Tir na Nog*.

HCE's Journey to *Tir na Nog*

Joyce's Familiarity with the Lore of Tir na Nog

Of the numerous paradigms from Irish mythology utilized by James Joyce, the traditions of the Celtic Otherworld, *Tir na Nog*, are perhaps the most easily recognized. Joyce's familiarity with the defining features of the Irish Elysium is, as Maria Tymoczko notes, "the aspect of Irish mythos that is most overdetermined in the sources Joyce had to hand" (*IU*, 185). The literature of the Celtic Revival is replete with material about *Tir na Nog*; and Joyce's sources for lore related to the Irish Otherworld certainly include essays by Yeats; Yeats's early narrative poem "The Wanderings of Oisin" (1889), which describes many of the features of the Otherworld; and works by other Celtic Revivalists such as Æ. Other sources would include P. W. Joyce's translation of *Echtra Conlai* (*The Adventure of Connla*); the *Immrama* tales translated by Whitley Stokes; the compilation of Irish wake customs by the folklorist Lady Wilde (cited by Adaline Glasheen in her *Census*); and J. A. MacCulloch's essays on *Tir na Nog* (cited by Campbell and Robinson in *Skeleton Key*). These sources provided Joyce with the lore, themes, and mythic imagery that characterize the Irish pagan conception of the afterlife. And in the *Wake*, this essentially pagan perception of the Otherworld is reenacted as HCE's journey to *Tir na Nog*.

The Nature of the Irish Otherworld, Tir na Nog

In "Nearness of Heaven, Earth, and Purgatory," William Butler Yeats observes: "In Ireland this world and the world we go to after death are not far apart. . . . Indeed there are times when the worlds are so near together that it seems that our earthly chattels were no more than the shadows of things beyond" (*Celtic Twilight*, 98). The Celtic Otherworld, unlike the Heaven of Christianity or even the *Avernus* of Greco-Roman religion, is not a distant world but rather an otherdimensional reality more or less coterminous with the physical realm. In many ways, the Otherworld resembles the earth plane, but in a pristine state, an "idealized mirror image of the human world," a realm of primal power and primary forms (Green, *Dictionary*, 167). The Celtic Otherworld is the most sacred of places and contains more power than any other person, place, or object. Furthermore, it is the source of *all* power and sacrality—including that which is located in the physical world. Thus the Otherworld "plays the mythic role of establishing archetypes or models for powerful actions and events, objects, and people" (Brenneman and Brenneman, 25).

The Otherworld is *the* matrix of spiritual power, and as such, it is also the ultimate source for regeneration and renewal. All mortals returning to the Otherworld retain their youth if young, return to youth if aged. The most frequently applied appellation for the Otherworld certainly conveys this belief: *Tir na Nog* literally translates as the "Land of the Ever-Young." The ever-young, however, are not the most numerous of Otherworldly denizens.

One of the consistent features of the Celtic Otherworld is its avian population. Birds are everywhere: messengers of the gods, harbingers of springtime, emblems of transcendence, singers of song, embodiments of joy. The song of birds—mellifluous, transcendent, eldritch, and dream-inducing—is a constant feature of *Tir na Nog*—just as the song of Rhiannon's birds induced in its listeners a gentle and warm euphoria and a loss of all sense of time for over eighty years. In "The Wanderings of Oisin," the young Fianna is awestruck by his first impression of *Tir na Nog* and its sheer number of birds, joyfully singing as the sun sets:

But now a wandering land breeze came
And a far sound of feathery quires;
It seemed to blow from the dying flame,
They seemed to sing in the smouldering fires.
The horse towards the music raced,
Neighing along the lifeless waste;
Like sooty fingers, many a tree
Rose ever out of the warm sea;
And they were trembling ceaselessly,
As though they all were beating time,
Upon the centre of the sun,
To that low laughing woodland rhyme.
And, now our wandering hours were done,
We cantered to the shore, and knew
The reason of the trembling trees:
Round every branch the song-birds flew,
Or clung thereon like swarming bees;
While round the shore a million stood
Like drops of frozen rainbow light,
And pondered in a soft vain mood
Upon their shadows in the tide,
And told the purple deeps their pride,
And murmured snatches of delight. (lines 165–87)

In the "Voyage of Tadhg mac Sein," Tadhg travels across the Otherworldly ocean accompanied by great flocks of joyfully singing birds. In the Otherworld, they meet the goddess Clidna who gives magic birds to Tadhg for entertainment and guidance.

> And then they came across to the *sidh* and the bird-flock came and perched on the cornices and couches of the *sidh*. And thirty of the birds were into the house of the weapons where Caeilte was, and they made a chorusing inside. Cascorach seized his stringed instrument, and with every piece that he played, the birds joined in. "We have heard much music," said Caeilte, "and we have not heard music as excellent as that."[16]

Many of the Otherworldly birds in Irish lore are not actually avian but rather shape-shifters who for various reasons appear in avian form. Some of these magical birds are divinities assuming their totem aspect: Cerridwen as a hen, Mor-Rigu as a raven. Sometimes these birds are mortals transformed by the gods: the swans of Lir, the birds of Rhiannon and Clidna. On rare occasions, even some powerful mortals could transform themselves into an avian form.

In order to venture successfully to the Otherworld and back, usually on a mission connected with kingship, some Druids had the power to shape-shift into birds to facilitate their other-dimensional journey. To do this, a Druid would "become" a bird: don the *Tugen* (a long bird-skin cloak covered with hundreds of bird feathers), and place on his head the *Encennach* (the bird mask that completely covered his head and face). Mog Ruith, the Druid with personal ties to the *Wake*, provides a good example. To become a birdman in *Tir na Nog,* Mog Ruith dons "his speckled bird-dress with its winged flying [cloak], and his druidic gear besides. And he rose up, in company with the fire into the air and the heavens" (Ross, *Pagan Celtic Britain*, 333).

Of far more consequence than the hosts of birds flocking to *Tir na Nog* is the Sovereign goddess, whose true home *is* the Otherworld. Here she resides, manifest in her most beautiful and alluring aspect. In "The Champion's Ecstasy" for example, Conn, transported to the Otherworld, recognizes the goddess as his own earthly consort but in a far more beautiful, refined, and divine form. The bevies of ethereal Celtic vixens and fey Irish beauties portrayed in the Otherworld tales of the *echtra* and the *immrama* are all emanations of the Sovereign, the reason the pagan Irish also refer to the Otherworld as *Tir na mBan*, "The Land of Beautiful Women."

Given that *Tir na Nog* is the matrix of youth, health, and beauty for both genders, sexuality is inherent to the Otherworld and is certainly one of the alluring reasons for staying there. Otherworldly goddesses seek the love of mortals—heroes and kings—and mortals certainly desire to visit *Tir na mBan* because of their enticements. The sexuality of the Otherworld, however, is always "without sin, without crime"; and this belief—as J. A. MacCulloch observes—indicates "the existence of ritual sex-unions at stated times for magical influence upon the fertility of the earth, these unions not being regarded as immoral, even when trespassed on customary tribal law" (MacCulloch, *Religion*, 385).

The archetype and paradigm for these ritual sex-unions is the mating of the Sovereign and her royal consort, the act through which she bestows kingship upon her chosen lover. This sexual union first occurs in the Otherworld and is then reenacted on the earth plane as one of the central rites of *Banais Righe* so integral to the *Teamhur Feis*. The legitimate succession of Irish kings therefore has its ultimate origin in this sexual union initially occurring in the Otherworld.

The Sovereign, too, plays a role in her consort's return to *Tir na Nog*. When an Irish king dies, or is murdered, he returns to *Tir na Nog*, where he is restored to his youthful and powerful form. The exemplar of Celtic kings, Arthur, mortally wounded during the Battle of Camlann, is conveyed by ship back to the Otherworld by the Sovereign, his true consort, whose earthly manifestation was Guinevere, a "shining phantom." In the matrix of renewal, the Once and Future King, through the powers of both *Tir na Nog* and the Sovereign, is mystically restored. When the time is appropriate, the god-king, now in his youthful and renewed form in *Tir na Nog*, will return to the earth plane and begin the great cycle once again.

Legitimate succession of Irish high kings thus required verification directly from *Tir na Nog* to correctly identify the new king—a main reason for the Otherworld's other title, *Tir Tairngire*, "The Land of Prophecy." One method of verification was a quest to *Tir Tairngire*, the shamanistic and visionary "flight" sometimes performed by Druids. Another method was entering *Tir Tairngire* through the earthly portal of a *sidh* or *forradh*. A third strategy, the *Tarbh Feis*, is a divinatory rite specifically identified with the Rites of Tara. Æ notes that entry to the Otherworld, always a risky venture, can also occur during sleep: "Many go to . . . Tir-na-nog in sleep, and some are said to have remained there, and only a vacant form is left behind without the light in the eyes which marks the presence of the soul."[17] The journey to the Otherworld, however, is most frequently portrayed as the crossing of an animate sea. Irish paganism, as with many traditional religions, is imbued with a deep belief in pan-psychism, and the ocean itself is perceived as a living entity. In many of the voyages, the sentient sea responds to the travelers upon it, and its waves acquire human traits. During his sea voyage to *Tir na Nog,* Oisin tells of such humanlike waves:

> Fled foam underneath us, and round us, a wandering and milky
> smoke,
> High as the saddle-girth, covering away from our glances the tide;
> And those that fled, and that followed, from the foam-pale distance
> broke;
> The immortal desire of Immortals we saw in their faces, and
> sighed. (Yeats, "The Wanderings of Oisin," 3:1–4)

The Otherworldly waves are usually associated with the death voyage of a great leader. As they swell and ebb in the immense ocean, they assume a transitory life of their own. And in this fleeting existence—perhaps for the pagan Celts evocative of the cycle of human life itself—the waves speak. They utter prophecy, as in *Da Derga's Hostel,* where the mysterious "man at the wave" predicts dire events in the ill-fated reign of King Conaire. They offer lamentation for the deceased; they review the life and events of the voyaging dead. At the Battle of Ventry for example, the sea spoke, "telling the losses, and the waves raised a heavy, woeful great moan in wailing them." In other cases in Ireland, by a spell put on the waves, or by the intuitive knowledge of the listener, the ocean waves reveal that they are wailing for a death, or describing some distant event in the life of the deceased. In the beautiful song sung by the wife of Cael, "the wave wails against the shore for his death"; and in Welsh myth the waves bewailed the death of Dylan, "son of the wave," and were eager to avenge it. In Ireland, the voice of the waves, the roaring of the sea, was thought to be prophetic of a king's death (MacCulloch, *Religion,* 179).

To negotiate these Otherworldly waves requires an Otherworldly craft: a glass boat, a crystal ship, an invisible sailing vessel created through Druidic rites. The prototype for this other-dimensional craft is the *Aigean scuabadoir,* "Ocean-sweeper," the gift of Lugh Lamfhada to Manannan mac Lír, the magical craft capable of navigating to these different realms more than oceans apart. In "Connla's Voyage," the two young lovers use just such a craft to traverse the Otherworldly ocean:

> A land of youth, a land of rest,
>   A land from sorrow free;
> It lies far off in the golden West,
>   On the verge of the azure sea.
> A swift canoe of crystal bright,
>   That never met mortal view—
> We shall reach that land ere fall of night,
>   In that strong and swift Canoe;
> We shall reach the strand
>   Of that sunny land,
>   From druids and demons free;
>   The land of rest,
>   In the golden west,
> On the verge of the azure sea.[18]

All of these Irish pagan conceptions regarding the Otherworld—the magical ship, the alluring goddess, inherent youthfulness, archetypes related to king and Sovereign, sexual union, renewal of the aged, birds and bird men, the animate waves—are found in the death voyage of HCE.

The Death Voyage of HCE

Late at night in his tavern (380.6), "His Most Exuberant Majesty" (381.24–25), the monarch of all Ireland (380.34), HCE, passes out—dead, dead drunk, dead to the world. HCE finds himself on his own magical ship to the Otherworld, the stout ship *Nancy Hans* (382.27), sailing from "Liff away" (382.27). HCE, the king who has come, now returns to the Otherworld in his ship (382.28): "Goodbark, goodbye!" (382.28–29). HCE sails away on the *Nancy Hans* and his Otherworldly adventure begins. The "monarch of all Ireland"—as Campbell and Robinson explain this episode—"now sails forth like a sea wanderer returning to the bounding deep, on a ship of dream . . . a dream of the honeymoon voyage of Tristram and Iseult" (*Skeleton Key*, 248). HCE's physical frame, helpless and unconscious on the floor, becomes the aged King Mark of the story; but his spirit, "rejuvenated in the sonlike image of the successful lover, will know again the joys of youthful love." The dream ship of HCE is "surrounded by waves and gulls, and these become the presences of the Four Old Men" who will now bear witness to the dream of their "broken master" (*Skeleton Key*, 248).

Voyaging to the Land of the Ever-Young, HCE, like all other Irish kings returning to *Tir na Nog* in their dream ships, finds himself in his renewed and youthful state. He is no longer the worn-out shell; he becomes his own youthful successor with whom he is mystically identified. One of the rolling ocean waves rises up, and like the animate waves of the Otherworldly ocean, utters this enigmatic prophecy: "Exeunc throw a darras Kram of Llawnroc . . . kirked into yord. Enterest attawonder, Wehpen, luftcat revol, fairescapading in his natsirt. Tuesy tumbles" (388.1–4). William York Tindall explains and "translates" the prophecy of the wave-man: "To signify the end of things and a fresh beginning Joyce used the device of reversal." And the reversal of names abounds in this section: "Kram of Llawnroc," his "Wehpen," and "Tuesy" (388.2–4) take the places in this exchange of Mark of Cornwall, his nephew Tristan, and Iseult (*Reader's Guide*, 211). And to further signify the mystical renewal of the monarch, Joyce, much like his pagan predecessors, uses the imagery of the sea and its perils or successes of voyaging.

Like every other Irish god-king before him, the renewed "Wehpen"/HCE travels to the Otherworld with one of "romance's fadeless wonderwomen" (395.30–31), a stunning modern yet ancient Irish "priscess" (396.7–8): the Sovereign in her most alluring form. The "priscess" (precious, princess, and priestess) chooses the regenerated HCE as successor and lover, and in the "otherworld of the passing of the key of Two-tongue Common" (385.4–5), young HCE and the gorgeous goddess have sex that is literally and figuratively out of this world—exactly as they should according to pagan tradition and the rites of *Banais Righe*: then, a pretty thing happened (395.26); the vivid girl, deaf with love (395.29), and with a queer little cry of "joysis crisis" (395.32), "renulited their disunited" (395.33) while the renewed HCE, as quick as a greased pig (395.35), and with one arrogant thrust, drove the massive missive of his virile victory flash past (395.35–36) and "rightjingbangshot" (396.1) into the goal (396.2). At this very moment—the Otherworldly union of king and Sovereign—renewal begins as well on the earth plane, exactly in accordance with the pagan tradition. A "caschal pandle" (397.26–27 [Paschal candle]), reversed (hence renewed), lights the Irish Easter rising of king and goddess. Lazarus comes forth (398.26) to the tune of "Auld Lang Syne"; and "Miss Yiss," who, like the Prankquean, "ran, when wit won free" (398.17–20), utters Mrs. Bloom's great "yes" (Tindall, 218). As William York Tindall explains, "Miss Yiss or Iseult is renewal's agent, but Tristan, with a part in her, has had a part in it"; "Heroest champion of Erenn," Tristan the *tanaiste*, is the new HCE (218).

One of the remarkable features of HCE's Otherworldly ocean voyage is the number of birds in accompaniment: the winged ones (383.16), sea hawks, seagulls, curlews, plovers, kestrels, all the birds of the sea called out right boldly when they saw the big kiss of "Tristan" and "Isolde" (383.15–18). As in the pagan tradition, the birds fly overhead, singing and talking as if human, watching and commenting upon the voyagers themselves. The singing of birds begins and ends the chapter. Some of these humanlike birds also act as the agents of the death/renewal theme at the center of HCE's voyage. They mock and vilify the fallen and aged king; they witness and comment upon the ritual sex of the goddess and her new consort. Some are reminiscent of the "Birdmen" of *Tir na Nog*—the shape-shifting Druids on their Otherworldly mission. Gulls and other birds verbally attack "King Mark," who, they say in their introductory verses, will be replaced by Tristan, whose bedding of Iseult is what the gulls are looking at and "shrillgleescreaming" (383.15) about. These talking birds are "either the four old men with feathers on . . . or else the gulls are shipmates" (Tindall, 214).

As with the Otherworldly voyages of earlier Irish kings, the rolling waves surrounding HCE's dream ship take on human characteristics. The waves become the big Four (384.6), the Four Master waves of Erin (384.6). The Four listen (384.7), and often they pray together (384.9), rightly enough, in this "bausnabeatha" (384.9 [death of life]). The waves, vociferous and ephemeral, swell and ebb in succession. As they manifest in the deep dark blue of the "Ossian roll" (385.36), each speaks out in turn upon the "seatuition"(385.30) on the azurian deeps (387.32). The Men of the Waves, like their ancient counterparts, reflect and prophesy upon the life of the royal voyager. One swells, speaks, then recedes, and is replaced by another, providing flowing commentary for the entire voyage.

Renewed from his journey to the Otherworld, reunited with the Sovereign, and regenerated in the matrix of sacral power of *Tir na Nog*, HCE, like all the god kings of Ireland, will soon return to earth plane—reborn during the Rites of Tara. First, however, the participants of the *Teamhur Feis* and the *Wake* must honor their fallen king and their mythic dead with elaborate funeral rites—the original Irish wake, the funeral games at the valley temple of Tara.

5

The Funeral Games at Valleytemple

Funeral Rites at the *Wake* and the *Feis*

During "The Inquest," one the Four Elders, speaking to the unconscious subject under interrogation (Shaun), makes an important demand regarding the wake rites in *Finnegans Wake*: "I want you, witness of this epic struggle . . . to reconstruct for us . . . inexactly the same as a mind's eye view, how these funeral games, which have been poring over us . . . took place" (515.21–25). The reconstructed funeral games pouring over us in the course of the *Wake* took place in exactly the same mind's-eye view as they did for the witnesses of the epic struggle at the Rites of Tara. In their broad frameworks, *Finnegans Wake* and the Rites of Tara both have their origin in a primeval Irish wake. The funeral games of both *Finnegans Wake* and the *Teamhur Feis* pay tribute to the epic struggle of a recently departed leader; and they also honor the mythic and ancestral dead, especially Finn MacCool. Both celebrate their wake rites at the great tumulus of a valley temple ("The Games funeral at Valleytemple" [602.21–22]) during a national truce; for both the *Wake* and the *Feis,* this tumulus is at once a burial mound, a cultural matrix, and the locus for a large Irish gathering and legislative Assembly. Like the funerary festivities in the *Wake,* the rites of the ancient *Feis,* though "bound up with a cult of the dead," were nevertheless "also connected with the annual phenomena of seasonal change" celebrated at the vernal equinox (*IPC,* 290–91). The funerary events of both the *Wake* and the *Feis* thus commemorate death *and* rebirth; and in a very broad and significant sense, both celebrate a wake *and* an awakening that is at once personal, cultural, seasonal, and spiritual.

The funerary events of the *Wake* and the *Feis* also share important connections on a more detailed and specific level. The complete array of funerary rituals and events performed at the primordial wake of the

Teamhur Feis was collectively referred to as the *Nosad*; in turn, the *Nosad* encompassed three large categories of activities:

1. *Cluiche Caointe* are the rites directly related to the funeral and burial conducted at the *Feis*. These rites include the initial *Guba* (a funeral song relating the deeds of the deceased): the *Caoine* (the keening); the *Ecnaire* (a panegyric); the *Amra* (a form of stylized elegy); the *Aire* (the watch over the corpse); the presentation of funerary offerings by Druids and Fianna, and the ringing of the *Es* (the death bell).

2. *Druidecht*, Druidic lore and rites, mostly in the nature of auguries, portents, and divinations, were a key component of the *Nosad* at Tara. During the *Feis*, the great Druidic College of Ollam Fodhla also convened at Tara to further the training in *Druidecht* for the students of Irish Druidism.

3. *Cúitech Fúait* are the diverse and colorful assortment of games, events, rituals, and rites comprising the actual wake at the *Feis*. At Tara, the *Cúitech Fúait* were performed *after* the actual funeral. If the honored dead were associated with Tara and were of great distinction, the wake was traditionally repeated on the anniversaries of the funeral or at other talismanic points on the Celtic calendar (such as the *Teamhur Feis*). (At the numerous celebrations of the Rites of Tara, the wake of Finn was celebrated repeatedly in this manner.) The events of the *Cúitech Fúait* include drinking, music, sports events, ribald games, a ritualized feast (*Fled Cro Lige*), the recitation of stories and dramatic enactments from the "sacred canon" of Fenian lore, and fertility rites involving ritual lustration of Brigit's priestesses and a sacred drama replete with elements of sexuality and sympathetic magic. Given the large number of people gathered for the *Cúitech Fúait*, it was also the occasion at Tara for various legislative assemblies to convene.

All of the specific rites of the *Nosad*—as conducted during the *Teamhur Feis*—are reenacted in *Finnegans Wake*. Each of these reenactments is discussed in this chapter.[1]

Cluiche Caointe

Like *Finnegans Wake*, the *Teamhur Feis* was held at the burial site of the mythic dead, where the entire event "seems to have . . . arisen from the burial there of some great or renowned personage" (*MC*, 1:cccxxvi). The *Teamhur Feis* has its origin in funerary rites; and the initial rite in this ancient wake at Tara was the performance of the *Guba* or *Cepog*, a dirge sung by a Bard and a mourning chorus, a retelling in song of the key events in the life and death of the fallen hero, complete with refrains where the "mourners" would join in. In ancient Ireland, the earliest gatherings at Tara were for these funeral rites; the principal function of the Irish crowd was to join in the mourning chorus of the *Guba*, and this primordial assembly was called the *Aenach Guba*, or "Mourning Assembly." And from this primary gathering, the *Feis* of Tara developed into an elaborate festival, a party complete with wake games, feasting, conclaves of various kinds, and a general Assembly. In the old accounts, the *Guba* is so central to the wake at Tara that the name itself is used as a synecdoche for the entire event. In like manner, the *Guba* of *Finnegans Wake* is the Irish-American ballad "Finnegan's Wake": the song itself recounts the key events in the life of the mythic hero; Finnegan's wake necessitates a great Irish assembly at an ancient burial mound; the gathering becomes the occasion for an elaborate array of rites, events, and episodes; and all are collectively identified by the name of the *Guba* itself: *Finnegans Wake*.

The *Mná Caointe* ("Mourning Women") at Tara are called in the *Wake* "Tarra's widdars" (9.21); they gather and begin their keening while others sing in the *Guba* chorus: "Macool, Macool, orra whyi deed ye diie? of a trying thirstay mournin? Sobs they sighdid at Fillagains . . . wake" (6.13–15). At this great Irish assembly, all the hooligans of the nation (6.15), while prostrated in consternation (6.15–16), keened in a "profusive plethora of ululation" (6.16–17); they mourned, with "shoutmost shoviality" (6.18–19) their mythic dead. At this celebration (6.20), most of them "agrog" (6.19), some sang the *Guba* in "kinkin corass" (6.21), while others joined in "kankan keening" (6.21).

The Fianna, the "fenians" (25.1), and Druids (25.2) assembled for the *Cluiche Caointe* offer the fallen leader their funerary gifts, the offerings of the field (25.3–4): "Mieliodories" (25.4 [Irish, "a thousand tears"; Greek, "honey gifts"]), poppy sap as a passport out (25.5), milk (25.8), and honey, the holiest thing that ever there was and the food for glory (25.5–7).

With the keening of "Tarra's widdars" in the background, the short *Ecnaire* indicates a royal funeral for a high king of Ireland; the speaker notes that there was never a warlord in Great Erin or Britain like HCE (25.27–28), neither a king nor an "ardking" (25.29 [high king]) who could hoist high the stone that "Liam failed" (25.31 [*Lia Fail*, the coronation stone at Tara]).

The *Amra* emphasizes the death/rebirth theme of the wake and, as at the Rites of Tara, relates the cycle of the fallen leader to the cycle of the seasons: the house of HCE has fallen in the dust (55.3), verging on blight like the "mundibanks" (55.4 [mountebanks, muddy banks]) of "Fenny-anna" (55.5 [Fianna, fen of Ana]); but these "deeds" (55.5 [deeds, dead]) are bound to go and arise again (55.5); "Life" (55.5), as HCE himself once said, *is* "a wake" (55.7). The bells (*Es*) sound throughout the *Wake* and are concurrently the death knell of the fallen king and the joyous tintinnabulation of the pagan springtime festival Sechselauten—thus resonating in complete concordance with the theme of death and rebirth so fundamental to both the *Feis* and the *Wake*.

Druidecht at the Rites of Tara

Druidic lore and Druidic rites comprised a significant aspect of the *Nosad* held at the *Teamhur Feis*. The seasonal threshold on which the *Feis* was celebrated, the mythic events associated with the *Feis*, and the death/rebirth principle inherent to the *Feis* itself made this occasion both powerfully liminal and highly charged—the kind of fecund matrix so favored by the Irish Druids for the performance of their rites. In addition, Tara was the center of Druidic training for all of pagan Ireland. Consequently, the *Teamhur Feis* was the largest and most important congregation of Druids and their students in ancient Ireland, the occasion for Druidic training, and the optimum event for the performance of their rituals.

Druidic Divination at the Wake *and the* Feis

As with other Celtic transitional and seasonal festivals, many of the Druidic rites performed during the *Teamhur Feis* were divinatory in nature; some rites relied upon the implementation of *Da Shealladh*, the second sight; and each rite involved a curious modus operandi: ogham letters; clouds and weather; birds, especially the wren; water in a basin; viewing tubes; the banks of a sacred river. Druidic rites involving all of these various methods are reenacted at the *Wake*.

Ogham Divination

The Irish ogham alphabet is a gift from the All-Father Ogma, as described in the *Wake*: all the Irish "signics" (223.4) of her "helpabit" (223.4) came from "Father Hogam" (223.4). The ogham characters each represent a tree, and the "trees" could "tellabout" (361.8) things by speaking twisters in the Irish tongue (361.6–7): "Quicken, aspen; ash and yew; willow, broom, with oak for you" (361.7–8). Like the runes, the "Talking Trees" were imbued with a magical potency; carved into wood—usually on long sticks or branches—they were used as a tool in casting spells, conveying secret messages, and divination. On "holyyear's day" (569.13), at a site favored by Druids for divination, "wateredge" (569.17), at a "clear springwell" (571.2), a divinatory rite is conducted with the use of the Talking Trees. Magical spells are first cast upon the "bookstaff branchings" (571.5–6), and the "leaves" (571.6) are cut on the trees (571.6 [that is, ogham characters are inscribed on the sticks]). And some can ken their "tantrist spellings" (571.7 [*tanaiste* spellings, tantric spells]): "Elm, bay, this way, cull dare, take a message, tawny runes ilex sallow, meet me at the pine" (571.7–9).

Neldoracht

Augury through observation of weather phenomena was one of the fundamental divinatory practices of Irish Druids. *Neldoracht* involved a symbolic reading of the weather and cloud conditions, which, in turn, provided a weather forecast that was also prophetic in nature. Perhaps the best example of the rite occurs in the story of the high king Dathi, and involves the Archdruid of Ireland, who performs *Neldoracht* as a prelude to the *Teamhur Feis*.

In the seventeenth and most auspicious year of his reign, Dathi, High King of Tara, requests an augury from Daghra, Archdruid of Ireland, regarding two important events: the convening of the *Teamhur Feis* and the possible conquest of Scotland. The Archdruid retreats to a sacred hill known as the "Ridge of the Druids" and performs *Neldoracht* before returning to King Dathi:

> At the rising of the sun in the morning, the Druid repaired to the king's bedroom, and said: "Art thou asleep, O King of Erinn and Albain [Scotland]?" "I am not asleep," answered the monarch, "but why have you made an addition to my titles? For, although I have taken the sovereignty of Erinn, I have not yet obtained that of Albain." "Thou shalt not be long so," said the Druid, "for I have consulted the clouds of the men of Erinn, and found that thou wilt soon return to Tara, where thou wilt invite all the provincial kings and the chiefs of Erinn, to the great Feast of Tara and there thou shalt decide with them upon making an expedition into Albain."[2]

During the wake party in HCE's tavern, HCE describes an event analogous to the *Neldoracht* performed by the Archdruid Daghra. From the very vantage point used by the Archdruid Daghra, that is, "dhruimadhreamdrue" (320.21 ["The Ridge of the Druids"]), the traveler experiences the extremes of weather—blazing sun, snow, and squalls (320.29–30)—and subsequently understands that these climatic conditions are actually signaling "gael warnings" (321.12). Shortly after the "gael warnings" are forecast, a detailed weather report interrupts the party; like the *Neldoracht,* the weather conditions can be interpreted as divinatory pronouncements regarding central events of the *Wake*. The prediction for HCE, "a sotten retch of low pleasure" (324.31–32 [a sudden ridge of low pressure]), "missed [mist] in some parts" (324.31–33) is: worsening conditions leading to the "allexpected depression" (324.27). HCE will weather the ritual test of *Casal Ríg* when he is "unwalloped in an unusuable suite of clouds" (324.29–30 [enveloped in an unusual suit of clothes]), and will successfully traverse the Portal of Blocc and Bluicne when he filters through the middle half of the "same gorger's kennel" (324.31 [St. George's Channel]) on his "wage wealthwards" (324.31 [way westwards]). (The test of *Casal Ríg* requires ECH to fit into a closely fit garment; the rite is reenacted in the *Wakean* episode known as "Kerse and the Sailor." The Portal of Blocc and Bluicne is a ritual test at Tara that is enacted again in the *Wake* as HCE makes his passage through the middle of various portals. Both of these rites are discussed at length in the next chapter.) The conclusion is forecast as a royal marriage at Temorah and a solar resurrection: "the outlook for tomarry . . . beamed brider" (324.33–34).

Aviomancy

When Stephen Dedalus, in *A Portrait of the Artist*, first consciously apprehends his connection with the ancient *Filidh* tradition, avian imagery provides the link between the past and present. Like the *Tugen*-clad Birdmen of pagan Ireland, the bird is Stephen's totem animal; and like an ancient Irish *Fili,* Stephen carefully notes the mannerisms of his totem: "He watched their flight; bird after bird; a dark flash, a swerve, a flash again, a dart aside, a curve, a flutter of wings. . . . He listened to the cries: like the squeak of mice behind the wainscot: a shrill twofold note" (*P*, 224). And for young Dedalus, aviomancy provides the bond with his Druidic past: "And for ages men had gazed upward as he was gazing at birds in flight. The colonnade above him made him think vaguely of an ancient temple and the ashplant on which he leaned wearily of the curved stick of an augur. A sense of fear of the unknown moved in the heart of his weariness, a fear of symbols and portents" (*P*, 225).

Young Dedalus, like a Druidic *haruspex*, observes the two characteristics of birds traditionally required for aviomantic interpretation: the complex flight patterns birds engage in and the subtle variations in their cries. Birdsong especially seems to have fascinated the early Irish augurs. Eugene O'Curry notes that elaborately detailed descriptions of the nuances of birdsong were kept by the pagan Irish, so meticulous that "some of the distinctions taken respecting the sounds made by birds are very curious, almost suggesting the recognition of some species of language among them" (*MC*, 2:223–24).

One bird in particular was the favored subject for Druidic augury: the wren, the king of all the birds. Mythologists, whose writings span well over a thousand years, have recorded an array of traditions associating the wren with Irish Druids, with rituals of kingship, and with rites of augury. Bishop Cormac identifies the wren as the "*Drui-én*," the "druid-bird," a bird that makes prophecy: "*drui-én magis avium eo quod aliquibus praebet augurium* [the wren is called the bird of druids because to certain individuals it furnishes auguries]" (*Cormac's Glossary*, 60). James Bonwick notes that, for the pagan Irish, the wren "symbolized the sun," and Irish Druids "employed a wren to symbolize the sun's divinity" (225). Sir James Frazer records that this "worshipful animal" was killed with great solemnity once a year; the first to strike down the sacred bird was proclaimed the new "king," who then led his murderous entourage into town in procession, carrying the dying bird with them, "that each of his worshippers may receive a portion of the divine virtues that are supposed to emanate from the dying god" (623). Frazer sees in this folk custom the vestige of earlier ritual regicide. Robert Graves notes that the wren is hunted when "the wheel of the year has gone full circle" (186). Holly and ivy are ritually connected to the wren; ivy is the nest of "the old king, the wren"; holly is "the tree of the tanist—the one who kills the aging king and succeeds him" (Graves, 186, 298). Wood-Martin calls the Druid bird "an object of superstitious veneration among the pagan Irish" (298). In the *Lorica of Columcille* (translated by Richard Best), the great Irish saint warns against paganistic divination traditionally associated with the wren:

> Ní adraim do gothaib én,
> na sreód na sén for bith che,
> ná mac ná mana ná mnai.
> Is é mo drai Críst mac Dé.
>
> I adore not the voices of birds,
> nor sneezing nor lots in this world,
> nor a boy nor omens nor woman.

My Druid is Christ the Son of God. (43)

Campbell and Robinson identify the "Scapegoat wren" as "a folk reduction of the crucified god, and as such is an appropriate figure for HCE" (*Skeleton Key*, 62).

Throughout the *Wake*, avian divination and the *Drui-én* are used in the same manner as in the old Druidic tradition. Through the "auspices" (189.33) of a cloud of ravens (189.33), and by the "auguries" (189.34) of rooks in parliament (189.34), HCE, soon to become the "dying god," has his dire fate foretold: "death with every disaster" (189.34). Aviomancy also predicts a much more positive final outcome for the resurrected "King of all Wrens" (431.13): "Birdflights" (324.36) confirm the approaching nuptials (324.36–325.1). Several participants at the *Wake* carefully listen to the "twattering" (37.17) of "bards" (37.17) in the twilight between "Druidia"(37.18) and the "Deepsleep Sea" (37.18); and like the Irish Druids at Tara, some interpret the sounds as auguries: at dark (383.19), they listen as hard as they can (383.22) to solans (migratory birds), wild geese, gannets, thrushes, and the auspices of all these birds (384.1–3). The *Wakean Drui-én*, from its prophetic nature, its "bard's highview" (504.16), will "burble"(504.17) to us in "strict conclave" (504.17). The burbling provided by the *Drui-én* throughout the *Wake* is, as it is for Stephen Dedalus, a present link with the ancient Druidic past.

Hydromancy

One of the stranger *Wakean* activities ascribed to HCE/Finn is a curious attempt at combining face washing and divination: one yesterday, he sternly stuck his head in a tub (4.21–22), to "watsch the future of his fates" (4.22 [wash the features of his face; watch the future of his fates]). This passage alludes to a form of hydromancy credited to Finn, performed by Irish seers, and described in *The Colloquy*: "Then a basin of bright gold was brought to Finn, and he washed his white hands and his ruddy bright face. He put his thumb under his tooth of knowledge, and the truth was revealed to him then, and falsehood was concealed from him."[3]

Finn's custom of washing his face before divination, as described in *The Colloquy*, is recognizable as a seer's rite: the washing suggests a ritual purification prerequisite to shamanistic divination and reflects "the archaic metaphorical connection between light/brightness and supernatural knowledge" (Nagy, *Wisdom*, 22). In *The Colloquy* passage quoted above, the verb usually translated as "washes" (*niamaid*) literally means "brightens." Significantly, the name *Finn* itself means "bright" and comes from the same Indo-European root from which derive various Irish words meaning "to know," "knowledge," and "knowledgeable"; the name *Finn* thus designates a possessor of "bright" knowledge who himself becomes resplendent with it (Nagy, *Wisdom*, 22).

When HCE/Finn, of the "Stuttering Hand" (4.18), attempts to perform this ancient rite of hydromancy in the opening episode of the *Wake*, he finds that all the water in his basin has "eviparated" (4.24). Unable to either wash the features of his face (as a prelude to divination) or watch the future of his fates through divination, HCE begins to lose the bright knowledge—a dire portent and the prelude to his fall.

The *Frith of Brigit*

The augury which Brigit made for her Foster Son:
She made a pipe of her palms:
"I see the Foster-Son by the side of a well,
Teaching the people without doubt." (*Frith of Brigit*)

The augury made by gentle Mary for her Son:
The Queen of Virgins looked through her palms:
"Did you see the King of Life?"
The Queen of Virgins said what she saw. (*Frith of Mary*)[4]

Though both of the above poems are ostensibly Christian, the *Frith* is an Irish pagan rite of seership, usually performed under the auspices of Brigit, the goddess and patroness of insightful Druids and visionary *Filidh*. To perform the *Frith*, the seer first makes a "*frithing* tube" by curling the fingers over the palms (as Brigit does in her poem) or by using some flexible material (vellum, parchment, and so on) curled into a tube and held in the palms. Frequently, gestures and chant meant to induce *Da Shealladh* accompany the *Frith*. The augur then uses this "seeing tube" as a means to gain insight into the issue at hand, to review what has been lost or forgotten, or to acquire a new perspective.

Frithing tubes and *frithing* rites proliferate at the *Wake*. Shaun, for example, desires to perceive and openly relate the "tireless secrets" (407.20–21). With an announcement of "Tubetube!" (407.21), Shaun performs a *Frith*. With the palms of his hands lifted (407.23), with his "handshell cupped" (407.23), with gestures conveying negation, affirmation, caution, supplication, repulsion and prostration (McHugh, *Annotations*, 407), and with a chant of "Helpsome hand that holemost heals!" (407.25), his vision comes: memories of the past (407.31–32), and "hicnuncs" (407.32 [the here and now]) of the present (407.32) embellishing the music of the future (407.32–33).

Shem, curious to gain some insight into Irish politics and history, attempts his own *frithing* rite at the *Wake*. Shem takes a "tompip [peepingtom] peepestrella" (178.27 [peep and *finistrella*, Italian, "small window"]) through a "threedraw eighteen hawkspower durdicky [Gipsy, *dur-dicki mengre*, "far-seeing thing"] telescope" (178.27–28). Like the old Druidic *frithers*, Shem chants for a clear vision: he prays to the "cloud Incertitude" (178.31–32) to find out for himself whether true political reconciliation was forging ahead or falling behind (178.32–34). Shem then perceives the essential nature of his query and gets the "charm" (179.1) of his "optical life" (179.1–2) when he finds himself blinking down the barrel of an "irregular revolver" (179.3) of the Bulldog [that is, English] pattern (179.4). (*Ulysses* is three books, eighteen chapters. Shem's *frithing* tube, the "eighteen hawkspower" telescope on Irish history and politics, is Joyce's *Ulysses*.)

Elsewhere at the *Wake*, the seeing tubes perform a variety of visual and visionary purposes. A "*helioscope*" (341.24) is employed to view the horse race, *The Irish Race and the World*. "Jaun" uses the "eroscope" (431.14) to view the "apparition" (431.15) of his beautiful sister (431.15), and the "neviewscope" (449.34) is appropriated for sunrises. Other seeing tubes include the "*inconoscope*" (349.19), "fathomglasses" (386.16), the "marmorial tallowscoop" (9.34), the "myrioscope" (127.35), the "faroscope" (150.32), the "tailoscrupp" (10.13), and the "macroscope telluspeep" (275.L2).

One of the more insightful of the *Wakean frithing* tubes appears as the answer to question 9 in "The Quiz Show" (143.4–28). The question embedded in this meandering interrogative passage might be succinctly stated in this manner: If one could envision the entire historical pattern of Ireland, what would it resemble? "Answer: A collideorscape!" (143.28). Look through this *frithing* tube, the "collideorscape," to get the perspective on Irish history. "Collide" with the invaders, the Parthalonians, the Nemedians, the Fir Bolg, Fomorians, Tuatha De Danaan, Celts, Jutes, Vikings, Normans, and English; "collide" with them socially, culturally, genetically, and on the field of battle. "Orscape" to North Armorica (as Celts did circa A.D. 450) or to North America (as they did later). Escape the new colonist in Ireland and become the new colonist yourself. Reverse the roles, like Mutt and Jute, and continue the process in a modified fashion. Like the view in a kaleidoscope, the collide/escape pattern seen in the "collideorscape" repeats itself with infinite variations. And like the kaleidoscope, each cyclical turn of the "collideorscape" changes the immediate details while preserving the overall pattern. The "collideorscape" of question 9 is, of course, *Finnegans Wake*, Joyce's ultimate lens for gaining perspective on the patterns of Irish history. Place *Finnegans Wake* in the palms of your hands. As indicated by its punctuation, connect the last sentence of the last page with the first word on the first page. When the *Wake* is completed in this manner, the ends of the book are joined. The *Wake* thus forms a tube in the palms of your hands, to be used—like the earlier eighteen hawkspower *Ulysses*—to gain perspective on Irish history and culture. The best *frithing* tube in the *Wake* is the "book of Doublends Jined" (20.15–16) itself.

Druidic Scrying at a Sacred River

The Wakean Washers at the Ford. Chapter 8 of the *Wake*—"The Washers at the Ford"—features the *Wake*'s female trinity: Maiden Issy, Mother Anna, and Crone Kate. Joyce describes the roles of the three women and the pattern of the chapter as "a chattering dialogue across the river by two washerwomen who as night falls become a tree and a stone. The river is named Anna Liffey."[5] Campbell and Robinson note that the Crone and Maiden are evoked, "like spirits, from the countryside, the elder from a stone, the younger from a whispering elm"; at dusk, both "will melt back again into their elemental forms" (132–33). Given the weird and elemental manifestations of both elder and younger women, their dyadic roles as washerwomen, and the eldritch atmosphere of the episode itself, they are intended to represent banshees, sometimes referred to in Irish folklore as the "Washers at the Ford"—"shadowy Celtic sisters of the Germanic Norns . . . and the classical Fates" (*Skeleton Key*, 133). In this episode, as Campbell and Robinson suggest, these shadowy Celtic sisters enact many of the mythic patterns related to the banshees of Irish myth.

At the beginning of the episode, Maiden and Crone are washing and rinsing the soiled clothing of the failing HCE; the Crone tells the Maiden to wallop it well with a "battle" (196.17), that is, a "beetle," a short bat used to beat dirt out of clothing. Their activity on the banks of the river elicits an ensuing exchange about HCE, Anna, and their dirty laundry: commentary on their soiled past, gossip about HCE's tattered relationship with Anna, predictions for a washed-up future. The river itself is integral to their conversation; indeed, much of their riparian dialogue is itself composed *of* rivers—literally hundreds are named and punned in the course of their conversation. The river Anna even communicates with the Washers, telling them that she, by her earth and the clouds in her sky (201.5), badly needs a brand new consort, another "bankside" (201.5 [backside]) partner, for the petty affair she has [that is, HCE] is worn out (201.7). Anna explains that her old hoddie-doddie companion (201.8) cannot "*wake himself*" (201.11) out of his "*winter's doze*" (201.11) and "*bore me down*" (201.11) like he used to (201.11–12).

After hearing the message of the river goddess, the conversation of Maiden and Crone turns to Anna. They discuss her polyandry as a young goddess (pages 201–4) and her micturition, her pure and simple "pee" (204.12) that creates the river (204.12–18). The dialogue about Anna is interrupted when the Washers stop to inspect and wash "Mrs. Magrath's" (204.34) undergarments, the "drawars" (205.12) of "Kinsella's Lilith" (205.11), and joke about her apparent sexual activity through a strange allusion to John the Baptist: "Baptiste me, father, for she has sinned!" (204.36).

The river Anna flows forth and then bequeaths her gifts to all her Irish children; the catalogue of her offerings is presented by the Washers themselves (205–12). At dusk, while the two women are finishing their wash, they are startled by a vision of the Great Horseman, the great "Finnleader" (214.11) himself proudly riding a high horse (214.10–12). Frightened by the apparition they see in the gloaming, the women attempt to dismiss their disquieting vision by considering other possible interpretations—perhaps they only see a blackberry bush (214.32–33) or the gray ass owned by the Four Elders (214.30–33). In this highly charged crepuscular setting, the Washers then shed their human identities and melt back again into their elemental forms: tree and stone on either bank of the river. Maiden, Mother, and Crone are, in their most primal manifestation, the features of the land itself.

The Wakean Washers as Banshee Figures. As Joseph Campbell and others have observed, the Washers at the Ford are traditional Irish banshees; and Irish banshees are traditionally of two types: the *Sí*-Woman and the *Badhbh*-Figure.[6] The *Sí*-Woman is hardly a frightening presence; she manifests as a young and beautiful maiden, usually with long blonde or golden hair, and an overall gentle demeanor. She possesses the visionary abilities, *Da Shealladh* and *imbas forosnai*, that give her knowledge of the future and preternatural insight in the present—abilities that she uses in her role as banshee.

In *Cogadh Gaedhel re Gallaibh* ("The War of the Gael with the Gaul"), just such a *Sí*-Woman appears as the beautiful banshee Aoibheall, who, the night before the Battle of Clontarf, gently informs King Brian Boru of his imminent death on the field of battle the next day (Lysaght, 194). The *Badhbh*-Figure is far less appealing. In Irish mythology, she appears as a witch or Crone: a querulous, hideous, withered hag with long disheveled hair, frequently seen squatting on the bank of a river ford, gazing into the water as if scrying, or beetling the garments of those about to die. The ominous *Badhbh*-Figure appears as the Washer at the Ford in mythological texts that range from the medieval to the early modern Irish period. Thereafter, this mythic model seems to have lost her generative force in the literary tradition; she remains, however, in the oral tradition of the banshee: "the Washer at the Ford in her ancient context—beetling in a stream" (Lysaght, 201). Both the *Sí*-Woman and the *Badhbh*-Figure manifestations of the banshee "originally symbolised the sovereignty of the land" (Lysaght, 206). Both, then, are aspects of the Sovereign goddess Ana, who, as in her *Wakean* representations, can present herself in two antinomial emanations (for example, *puella/senilis*, youthful and aged, the beauty and the hag) or through her triune nature (Maiden, Mother, Crone).

The two Washerwomen at the *Wake* reenact quite accurately the ancient mythic patterns associated with the Irish banshee. Maiden and Crone Washerwomen easily correspond to *Sí*-Woman and *Badhbh*-Figure; both in turn are emanations of the Sovereign goddess Ana. Their gossip concerning Anna's polyandry, the failing sexual prowess of HCE, and his potential replacement, suggest the issue of *Fir Flathemhan* so critical to sacral kingship. Their association with rivers—the hundreds of river names, the creation of the river through micturition, the wealth of rivers—furthers their identity as Sovereign figures. The *Wakean* banshees possess the ability of *imbas forosnai*. They can hear the voice of the river—the mysterious message of Anna—and understand it as prophecy: the aging HCE is failing and he must be replaced. (The strange interlude where the banshees wash the drawers of "Kinsella's Lilith" and make reference to John the Baptist also relates to prophecy: Magrath gains tremendous magical power as the slayer of John the Baptist, and this power allows him to win and wed Lily Kinsale.) Like their pagan prototypes, the *Wakean* banshees also possess *Da Shealladh*. At the riverbank in the gloaming, the banshees receive their troubling vision of the Great Horseman—the epithet for the high king—the one soon to die. At the end of the chapter, the banshees return to the features of the land, the primordial form of the Sovereign.

Scrying at the Feis. Many of the allusions to the Washers at the Ford found in the medieval myths—especially the frequent references to their riverside scrying—are the vestigial accounts of an important Druidic rite of divination actually conducted by *Ban-Druí*, female Druids, at the fords of rivers.[7] The ford of a river—the liminal brink between two worlds—is a powerful locus for access to the Otherworld and therefore especially appropriate for exercising the rites associated with *Da Shealladh* and *imbas forosnai*. (Finn MacCool, for example, the greatest of all Irish seers, acquires both *Da Shealladh* and *imbas forosnai* on the banks of the River Boyne.) The *Ban-Druí* were understood to be especially responsive to rites associated with rivers, since rivers are the domain of their goddess, Ana. Priestesses, acting as the Washers at the Ford and trained in the arts of seership and divination, were called upon to give prophecy before impending and important events, such as the seasonal rites at the vernal equinox and the kingship rites of the *Teamhur Feis* (J. Matthews, 111–12). The *Wakean* banshees, as humorous and ridiculous as they are, nonetheless reenact the mythic and ritualistic patterns first performed by their pagan prototypes long ago at the ford of a river sacred to Ana, during the vernal equinox at the Rites of Tara.

"The Study Period" at the Wake *and the* Feis

> It is not for nothing that the *Tripartite Life of Saint Patrick* calls Temair 'cend ídlachta ocus drúidechta na hÊirenn'—"head of idolatry and druidry in Ireland." (*TB*, 283)

> The chief college of the Druids was at Tara. There was held the national convention of the Teamorian Fes. (Bonwick, 260)

As the *Teamhur Feis* was the optimum occasion for a great Druidic convocation, the most important Druidic school in Ireland, the College of Ollam Fodhla, held session during this period and was an intrinsic component of the *Teamhur Feis* itself. At the College of Ollam Fodhla (named after its founder, "The Learned Man," a.k.a. Dagda), students were trained in Druidic lore and the various subjects and esoteric philosophies comprising the Druidic canon of pagan Ireland. In the *Wakean* reenactment of the *Teamhur Feis*, Joyce would certainly include a version of this important Druidic event; and as suggested through the following discussion, the reenactment of the studies at Ollam Fodhla may be found in the most esoteric section of the *Wake*, chapter 10, named "The Study Period" by Campbell and Robinson.

Joyce's Druidic Amalgamation

Joyce, drawing upon the works of Blake, Bruno, and Blavatsky, believed Druidism to be a primal component in the same matrix from which a diverse array of Western esoteric systems emerged: Cabalistic lore, the Egyptian Hermetica, Platonism (especially as presented in the *Timaeus*), and Pythagorean theories of music and mathematics.[8] William Blake (certainly a significant and avowed influence on Joyce), in *Jerusalem: The Emanation of the Giant Albion*, addresses Jews on the Cabala, which, like Joyce, he believes is ultimately derived from Druidic sources:

> Your Ancestors derived their origin from Abraham, Heber, Shem, and Noah, who were Druids: as the Druid Temples (which are the Patriarchal Pillars & Oak Groves) over the whole Earth witness to this day.
>
> You have a tradition, that Man anciently contained in his mighty limbs all things in Heaven & Earth: this you recieved [*sic*] from the Druids. (171)

Joyce himself, in "Ireland, Island of Saints and Sages" (1907), makes a similar connection between Irish Druidism and the Hermetica of ancient Egypt: "The religion and civilization of this ancient people, later known by the name of Druidism, were Egyptian. The Druid priests had their temples in the open, and worshipped the sun and moon in groves of oak trees. . . . Irish priests [that is, Druids] were considered very learned" (156). In J. Lewis McIntyre's *Giordano Bruno* (which was reviewed by Joyce in the *Daily Express* [Dublin], October 30, 1903), Joyce would have certainly read Bruno's statement and subsequent argument that the Cabala "derives from the Egyptians, among whom Moses was brought up" (130).[9] In *Isis Unveiled* (which Joyce recommended to friends), H. P. Blavatsky argues a connection between the Cabala and "the cosmological theory of numerals which Pythagoras learned from the Egyptian hierophants"; Blavatsky adds further that the Platonism expressed in the *Timaeus* was itself based on the same sources as the Cabala (1:7–8).[10] According to Joyce, the teachings of Irish Druids were thus fundamentally Cabalistic, Hermetic, Platonic, and Pythagorean in nature.

"The Study Period" as a Druidic Amalgamation

"The Study Period," more than any other episode in the *Wake*, reflects this "Druidic" blend of Western esoteric traditions. The columned structure of the chapter is analogous to the Cabalistic Tree of Life; and as Campbell and Robinson note, the entire section is laden with "the esoteric doctrines of the Cabala" (*Skeleton Key*, 163). The balance and interplay of antinomials, a fundamental precept of the Hermetica ("The tasks above are as the flasks below, saith the emerald canticle of Hermes" [263.21–22]) are represented by the Shem and Shaun columns on each page. These reverse identity in midchapter, as they should, to reflect the process of *Enantiadromia*—a concept fundamental to these various esoteric and "Druidic" traditions. Pythagorean mathematics, sacred geometry, and music theory are the basic teachings in "The Study Period."

There are, however, some distinctively Irish Druidic lessons taught in the *Wakean* "Study Period" as well. Irish history (270), Fenian lore (277, 291–292, 306), and divinatory techniques (281) are subjects that certainly would have been taught at Ollam Fodhla during the *Teamhur Feis*. Perhaps the most uniquely Irish lesson taught in "The Study Period" is the mnemonic technique used by Finn MacCool, by Irish *Filidh* and Druids, and known as *dichetal do chennaib*. Adjacent to the right-hand commentary "AUSPICIUM AUGURIA" (282.5–6R), Shaun explains the technique of *dichetal do chennaib*. First, Shaun identifies his fingertips, his four cardinal points [fingers] and thumb (282.20–23) and explains that you always recite from the four cardinals, "arecreating" (282.28) from them in "lumerous" (282.29 [numerous, luminous, numinous]) ways (282.24–27).

Shaun demonstrates the process on pages 282–83. He begins by counting on his fingers (282.30–283.3), but soon his fingers recall more than just numbers—the fingers are actually mnemonic devices, and he then utters an extemporaneous recitation (283.3–20) with implications and insights well beyond simple counting. John Bishop, commenting on Shaun's five-finger descant, notes that this finger recital, as childish as it appears, results in the "sudden popping up of a memory" (*Book of the Dark*, 319).

Shaun's curious form of digital memory is nearly identical to the archaic Irish technique of *dichetal do chennaib*, explained in the early accounts as "recital from the ends of the fingers" (*SH* 1:243–44). *Dichetal do chennaib* was essentially the utterance of prophecy and insight, or the voiced expression of memory, or the recollection of poetry, accomplished with the aid of mnemonic contrivance in which the fingers played a principal part, and by which the poet was enabled to pour forth his verse (*SH* 1:243–44). As a rule, *dichetal* recitation begins with the thumb (the "rude rule of fumb" [283.20] as Shaun calls it). Each fingertip and finger joint is assigned a letter, or number, or both. Some texts illustrate the technique by drawing a hand and assigning the correct letter to each part of the finger, very reminiscent of the hand drawn at the end of "The Study Period" chapter, on page 308. This drawing may be alluding to Finn's famous thumb (which *he* used in his own performances of *dichetal do chennaib*), and it may be Shem thumbing his nose at authority—but it is also Joyce giving all *Wakean* students the Druidic finger of *dichetal do chennaib*, the mnemonic contrivance for recollecting the lessons taught at the College of Ollam Fodhla, "The Study Period" of the *Teamhur Feis*.

Cúitech Fúait

The Original Irish Wake

The *Wakean* crowd that initially assembles at the burial tumulus for the *Guba* and other events of the *Cluiche Caointe* gathers again at HCE's tavern in chapter 11, "Tavernry in Feast," for the "glory" (309.6) of a "wake" (309.7). Bernard Benstock identifies most of their activities at the tavern as representative of the funeral games of a traditional Irish wake.[11] And Adaline Glasheen notes: "It is also plain that Joyce had and used in *FW* a great deal of information about wake games" ("Flesh and Blood Games," 100). From his sources (O'Curry, P. W. Joyce, Lady Wilde, Gwynn, Croker, Prim, Wood-Martin, Macalister, and MacCulloch), Joyce would have known the unanimous belief of these scholars—that most, if not all, of the traditional activities performed at Irish wakes had their origin in the earlier pagan *Cúitech Fúait*. This event, in turn, was first conducted at the *Oenach* or *Feis*, making the *Feis* of Tara, in a very real sense, the original Irish wake. And the games and events of the *Cúitech Fúait* of Tara are the very ones performed at the *Wake*.

Even though the staid proceedings of the *Feis*—the trials, regicide, inauguration, and religious rituals—were its essential components, the *Feis* was also the occasion for a very raucous and rowdy wake, with copious drinking, music, horse races, sports events, sideshows and entertainments. Consequently, the *Cúitech Fúait* assumed the chaotic tenor of a pagan carnival, and, like the *Wake*, was replete with its representative drunks, rabble, vendors, vaudevillian showmen, grifters, itinerant Fianna, sportsmen, and entertainers: "all manner of strange vagrants—strolling musicians . . . showmen, gypsy fortune tellers . . . vendors of cheap utilities . . . jugglers, buffoons . . . and the like seem to have been an intolerable nuisance in early Celtic days. . . . Many of their antics seem to have been of a very gross description" (*T*, 165–66).

The carnival atmosphere of the *Cúitech Fúait* at Tara, described above, surfaces again at "Tavernry in Feast," providing an elaborate reenactment of the earlier pagan party. The participants, both rural and cosmopolitan Fianna, fans and fawners of Finn—"Finnfannfawners, ruric or cospolite" (309.9–10)—gather at the tavern. Many of these "Hiberio-Miletians" (309.11) are inebriated and begin a brawl that continues throughout the chapter. Music blares in the background while the two buffoon showmen, Butt and Taff, meander through their scatological yarn with the circumlocution indicative of the highly intoxicated. News reports and gossip interrupt other events. Hurley matches are under way; and news of a great horse race, *The Irish Race and the World*, is reported in the midst of other noisy merriment. Vendors of cheap utilities advertise (in the form of a laxative commercial) their products. Other entertainments include a group songfest (with the recurring refrain: "Like waters parted from the sea"), a skit from the "Tales of Yore" (359.24), *The Coach with the Six Insides*, some fortune-telling (324.24–34), and some vague blatherings about the Prophecies of Merlin, the "perofficies of merelimb" (358.15). An announcement of an impending Druidic ritual is broadcast through the din of the party: "'Tis golden sickle's hour. Holy moon priestess, we'd love our grappes [grasp, grapes] of mistellose [mistletoe]!" (360.24–25). The announcement refers to the Druidic rite of cutting mistletoe as the prelude to a ritual sacrifice and banquet. Pliny, in *Historia Naturalis*, describes the ceremony: "The mistletoe, however, is not found but rarely on the oak and when found, is gathered with due religious ceremony, if possible, on the sixth day of the moon. . . . Having made preparations for sacrifice and a banquet . . . the priest ascends the tree and cuts the mistletoe with a golden sickle" (*Historia Naturalis*, 16:249). All of these tavern activities are in accordance with the chaotic events of an ancient Irish wake.

The drinking at the tavern begins promptly with a toast to the deceased. They would deal to death a drink (311.15), and slake thirst and thoughts "awake" (311.16 [away, a wake]) with it: "We rescue thee, O Baaas [Irish *Bas*, "Death"; Boss; Bass Ale; Dutch, *Baas*, "Master"], from the damp earth and honour thee. . . . Up draught and whet them" (311.17–20). Not surprisingly, drinking and toasting were also important elements of the wake at Tara: "Drinking the feast of Tara" was the recognized expression conveying attendance at the wake games (*T*, 168).

Drinking songs alluding to Finn MacCool, Fianna salutes, and games of definite pagan origin are drunkenly performed in the course of the evening. Other tales and skits presented at the tavern—retold by the Fianna members themselves—recount the exploits of Finn MacCool and the deceased king—tales very appropriate for a *Cúitech Fúait*. The circuitous narratives related by these drunken raconteurs are permeated with obscenities, ridiculous double entendre, blasphemous and scatological humor—so much so that Vivian Mercier felt compelled to comment: "I wonder if Joyce fully realized how much the grotesque obscenity of *Finnegans Wake* . . . was in keeping with the traditions of the Irish wake. . . . In so far as the grotesque is present in the phallic, it fuses with the macabre in a playful, even humorous amalgam at a traditional Irish wake" (*ICT*, 52).

The "grotesque obscenity" associated with *Finnegans Wake* has its origin in the earlier pagan wakes, where the "obscenity" was originally connected with rites to secure fertility and rebirth: "Improper songs and performances on such occasions are not in essence mere exhibitions of wantonness: they are a deliberate application of sympathetic magic" (*T*, 164–65). Thus, an element of ribaldry, sexual license, and obscenity is to be looked for, "even in an Assembly [that is, the *Teamhur Feis*] which, morally, may have been strictly policed" (*T*, 165).

"The Building of the Ship"

One of the more significant of these "improper" performances from Irish paganism—traditionally called "The Building of the Ship"—is reenacted during "Tavernry in Feast." The idea of the magical ship to the Otherworld is the basis for this ancient rite performed at traditional Irish wakes—a death custom in which many of the pagan beliefs regarding the Otherworld were still very much alive. In its origin, the ritual undoubtedly springs from the belief in an Otherworld across the sea—a belief among the Celtic and Germanic tribes that also gave rise to boat burials, the placing of little boats in tombs, the setting of the great adrift in burning ships in Norse myth and ritual, and the story of the mortally wounded King Arthur sailing to Avalon for the healing of his wounds. "This belief in a voyage of death is . . . echoed in the ribald games dramatizing 'The Building of the Ship' which were played at wakes for the dead, in Ireland, until recent times" (Rees and Rees, 318).

Lady Wilde, in "The Wake Orgies," argues that "The Building of the Ship" is a remnant of an ancient fertility ritual, conducted by Druids at pagan wakes, but probably even pre-Druidic in its origin (J. Wilde, *Ancient Legends*, 122). According to the extant descriptions, the rite, as it was performed until banned by the Catholic Church in the nineteenth century, was usually conducted late at night after the Christian services for the deceased had concluded. In the same room as the laid-out corpse, several men, usually in an advanced state of alcoholic intoxication, would "build the ship" to launch their dearly departed into the other realm. The men would become parts of the ship: one as the bow, one the stern, another, the helmsman. In the section of the ritual called "The Laying of the Keel," one young man, "the keel," would lie supine on the floor in the center of them all.

The next event in this wake drama has troubled the Victorian folklorists who recorded the rite, all of whom are reticent in their descriptions and restrained in their analysis. P.G.A. Prim's 1853 account is the most complete. Once the "keel" is in place, one of the young and attractive females attendant at the wake joins in. In the Prim version, the young lady goes to "the keel," and with deliberate gestures "strongly indicative of a Pagan origin . . . from circumstances too indelicate to be particularized," performs the especially arousing event called "The Erection of the Mast."[12] Once the mast is up, the ship is fully rigged, and the voyage to the Otherworld gets under way. The ribald and merely symbolic gestures involved in "The Erection of the Mast" are certainly the toned down remnants of ritual sex performed on the funeral "ship" during the pagan wakes. The two great antinomials of existence—life and death—meet in this ancient ritual celebrating our great transitions. The rite that brings life into this world and the ritual that conveys it out unite on this ship to the Otherworld—built once again at the *Wake*.

Late at night in the tavern, following some heavy drinking at the "gettogether" (380.8), and after the "barbecue beanfeast" (380.10–11 [the wake party]) was over, HCE assumes his royal persona as the last "pre-electric" (380.12–13 [freely elected]) king of all Ireland in the "Taharan [Tara] dynasty" (380.21–22). Dressed in his seven articles of regal clothing (381.10–14), and with the midnight thirst upon him (381.26–27), HCE drinks himself under the table, off the "throne" (382.26), onto the floor—dead drunk. While the royal "corpse" is laid out, the men in the tavern, all fairly inebriated themselves, perform "The Building of the Ship." Each man, much like his "ancestors" (382.14) with their "ouldmouldy gods"

(382.15), becomes a part of the magical vessel that allows the "king" to sail "From Liff away" (382.27). The young lad cowering in the corner (382.16–17) becomes the "fore" (382.20 [bow]) for coves and trawlers, to heave ho and leave alone (382.20–21). Larry is on the "focse" (382.22 [fo'castle]), while Faugh MacHugh is at the wheel (382.22)—"one to do and one to dare" (382.22–23); another is on the "flure" (382.23) with his "feats" (382.24 [feet, feats]), with the feel of the fumes in the "wakes" (382.25) of his ears (that is, the wake of his years, the wax in his ears [382.24–26]). And thus sailed their "stout ship" (382.27) from life away (382.27–29). Then, a "vivid girl" (395.28) with a first-class pair of "bedroom eyes" (396.11) comes aboard the wake ship. She completes the last stage of the rite—"The Erection of the Mast"—when she "renulited their disunited" (395.33). Late at night in the tavern, the royal corpse receives a sendoff directly related to the wake rites of Irish paganism.

Fled Cro-Lige: *The Feast at the* Wake

Feasting, in addition to these other activities, is another important component of the *Cúitech Fúait*. One of the fundamental yet highly stigmatized events of the *Cúitech Fúait* was the wake feast, *Fled Cro-Lige,* which at different times in its history involved ritual cannibalism in its literal or symbolic form. This archaic rite is reenacted in the *Wake* at 7.3–19. When the mourners "wake him" (7.3), the great leader is laid out on a board, a loaf of baked bread by his head (7.9–12), a glass of old ale (7.12) at his "tayle" (7.11). The corpse is then presented as food to be eaten by the *Wake* participants: they will "sink teeth" (7.13) through the pith of that "flowerwhite bodey" (7.14) into flesh almost like "rubicund" (7.16 [reddish or pink, woebegone, and German, *wohlbekannt,* "well-known"]) Salmosalar" (7.16 [*Salmo salar,* "salmon"]); a meal "dead off" (7.18 [spoiled]) for some man (7.18); the feasters "schlook" (7.18 [German, *schlucken,* "to swallow"]), "schlice" (7.18 [slice]), and say "goodridhirring"(7.19 [good riddance, good red herring]).

The few scholars who have commented upon this passage treat the implied cannibalism symbolically. William York Tindall sees this scene of god-king, bread, and alcoholic beverage as representative of the Last Supper or the first Christian Communion (35). Campbell and Robinson interpret the scene as a symbolic and communal rite prevalent in many traditional religions: "The theme of eating is always associated in *Finnegans Wake* with the eating of the god: the consuming of the life substance of the father by his sons and retainers" (*Skeleton Key,* 196). Both of these interpretations certainly apply; Joyce, however, with his penchant for historical accuracy, may have had a more literal event in mind when his *Wake* participants carve up and consume the salmon-colored flesh of their dead leader.

Irish Ritual Cannibalism

Two thousand years ago, the Greek geographer Strabo reported the custom of cannibalism prevalent at Irish wakes:

> Besides . . . Britain, there is also a large island, Ierne, which stretches parallel to Britain on the north. . . . Concerning this island . . . its inhabitants are more savage than the Britons since they are man-eaters as well as herb-eaters, and since further, they count it an honourable thing, when their fathers die, to devour them. (*Geography*, 4.5.4)

Since the time of Strabo, various anti-Irish propagandists have used the charge of Irish and Celtic cannibalism as a reason for defamation as well as a justification for incursions and machinations against Celts in general or the Irish in particular.[13] As a result, many Irish apologists (and later, some Celtic Revivalists) have tried to dismiss the slanderous charge by calling Strabo a liar, or anti-Irish, or the gullible reporter of secondhand and dubious information. Certainly, the overwhelming majority of these apologists feel much like Jonathan Swift, when he voiced his personal objection to the always-controversial subject of Irish cannibalism: "it is not improbable that some scrupulous people might be apt to censure such a practice . . . as a little bordering upon cruelty, which, I confess, hath always been with me the strongest objection against any project, however so well."[14] The evidence, however, indicates that in pre-Celtic Ireland many of the tribes would indeed consume the corpse of their dead king as part of their wake rites. Later, the Irish Celts, as part of their *Cúitech Fúait*, continued the rite in a much-mollified form, placing food on or near the corpse and consuming this food as a symbolic assimilation of their honored dead—exactly as Joyce describes it.

As a wake rite, Irish cannibalism was *always* of the ritualistic (rather than the nutritional) variety, and was a means of honoring and perpetuating the memory and qualities of the deceased. In his discussion of this archaic ritual, R.A.S. Macalister has suggested that we of Irish lineage, rather than deny the charge outright, should admit the fact and place it in its proper perspective—and from this, gain an understanding of the rite as well as an appreciation of the honorable motives of our cannibal ancestors; for if perceived in its proper perspective, Irish ritual cannibalism is "not without its element of pathos and even of beauty" (*IPC*, 312). The ritual *Fled Cro-Lige* had nothing to do with the satisfaction of appetite; its meaning is much more subtle. As at the *Wake*, when a great and magnanimous Irish leader died, his character, his greatness, his beloved qualities, could be assimilated—in the most literal sense of the word—by the participants at the *Fled Cro-Lige;* the character and greatness of the deceased thus transferred to the participants, and the deceased himself lived on through those who loved and respected him. *Fled Cro-Lige*, for the pagan Irish, was "an endeavour to force from the mystery surrounding nature an answer to the question, asked at every grave-side . . . *'If a man die, shall he live again?'*" (*IPC*, 312). Through *Fled Cro-Lige* the honored dead do indeed live again, and live through those who most honored them. When the mourners at the *Wake* consume the bread and ale placed near the corpse—or perhaps the salmon-colored flesh of the corpse itself—they are reenacting one of the most important and honorable rites of their pagan heritage. The *Fled Cro-Lige* at the *Wake* thus assimilates—in both its body and its spirit—the same modus and motive of its ancient Irish counterpart.

The Assembly at the Wake

Throughout the course of the *Wake* meanders a huge crowd of Irish who initially collect for the *Cluiche Caointe* of HCE/Finn and subsequently reappear in various episodes in the roles of both spectators and participants. In its origins, and through its defining characteristics and specific functions, this *Wakean* assemblage appears identical to the Irish gathering at the *Teamhur Feis*. Like the *Wakean* crowd, the Irish at the *Feis* initially gather for a funeral and wake. Tara was the burial site of "many illustrious semi-historical personages"; and the public assembly at Tara, "a marked and important feature of social life in ancient Ireland," had its origin in a wake and "Funeral Games" (*SH* 2:434). At the *Feis*, as in the *Wake*, the burial mound is the locus for this great Irish gathering. On one occasion, Finn MacCool was seated upon the Assembly-mound at Tara. The Fianna in his entourage joined Finn on the tumulus and asked, "Whose burial place is this?" They assumed, as a matter of course, that the Assembly-mound was also a place of burial (*T*, 160).

The national gathering at this Assembly-mound at Tara was possible in large part due to a truce and armistice agreed upon by all tribes and all participants at the wake. The *Dindshenchas* relates that such a truce was indeed enacted to allow all wake participants, spectators, and mourners to safely congregate at Temora.[15] This tradition explains the corresponding truce announced at the beginning of the *Wake*: there will be an "armitides" (11.13) tonight, "militopucos" (11.14 [Esperanto, "war peace"; and "my little pookas"]) and "toomourn" (11.14 [tomorrow, to mourn, Temora]), a gorgeous "truce" (11.15) for the happiest children everywhere [hce] (11.15–16). And because of this truce, the *Wakean* assembly is nationwide, an "overflow meeting" (42.20) of all the clans, sections, and tribes that becomes a "singleminded supercrowd" (42.22) representing "all sections and cross sections" (42.23) of Ireland.

The ancient Assembly (also called the *Oenach*) at the Tara wake was also a nationwide and representative event, a meeting indeed of "all sections and cross sections" of Ireland (*TB*, 366). As it is in the *Wake*, the Assembly at Tara was *not* confined to the tribes in whose territories their rites were situated but was a convention of the whole country (*TB*, 366). And like the *Wakean* assembly, the *Feis* at Tara was a unifying national event—a point worth noting, for there is an ongoing assumption that, in Ireland, there was no sense of unity in the country at large until it was imposed from without (*TB*, 366). The "overflow meeting" at the *Wake*, as well as the tradition of the Tara Assembly, both suggest that one of the strongest unifying forces in Ireland was the ancient wake Assembly.

The Irish "supercrowd" convening for the *Wake* manifests other characteristics as well—all in accordance with the traditions of the pagan *Feis*. During the making of Hosty's Ballad (42.17–44.21), the gathering becomes an angry mob and exults in the denunciation of their failing king. The *rann* circulates among the assembly (44.7), and they join in with Hosty in his satirical song, threatening a "mass meeting" (47.22) to depose and murder the aging leader. The Washers at the Ford describe the incident: the maudlin rabble around him caused a fracas (206.1) with their "timpan" (206.2 [timpani, tin pan]) and their "crowders" (206.2 [crowds, fiddles]). The crowd is present during the arrest and trial of Festy King; the mob pursues him like "hounds" (97.17) on a fox hunt; and they gather to witness his execution.

The crowd functions, in part at least, under the aegis of a legislative body that is apparently convening during the course of the *Wake*. Referred to throughout as the "thingaviking" (609.19), "Thing" (215.24, 313.13), "Assembly men" (97.28), "Thing Mod" (118.21), and "folkmood" (590.16), this Irish Assembly similar to the Scandinavian "Thing" is behind some of the major events at the *Wake*. After HCE's trial comes the disclosure that his "Thing" (58.12) might have undone him (58.12). The Assembly decrees the death and burial of HCE: the "thinghowe" (76.14), through a number of their committees having power (76.14), by fit and proper legal resolution (76.17), and following a court's order (76.17–18), made him, while he was still alive (76.20), their present of a "protem grave" (76.21). In "The Inquest," the spirit of HCE (532.6) desires to exonerate himself by speaking on his own behalf at the Great Assembly, the "Thing of all Things" (536.31), with the intention of securing the right to return. In his self-defense, HCE boasts of his achievements as a member of the Thing, claiming to have received letters, widely signed petitions, and even poetry (543.6–7) proclaiming his "monumentalness"(543.7–8) as a "thingabolls" (543.8). When HCE *does* return, resurrected as "Solsking the Frist," he is officially recognized by this same Irish Assembly, hailed by the "folkmood" (590.16), and acclaimed conclusively by the Irish "Thing" as the new "Nebob of Nephilim!" (590.16–17).

The Irish "folkmood" convening throughout the course of *Finnegans Wake* that functions as a legislative organization and legal body had an identical counterpart at the *Teamhur Feis*. Pagan Ireland consisted of four quarters further divided into three sections each, and these twelve sections sent a given number of representatives to the *Oenach*, "held at the theoretical centre" of Ireland, Tara (Rees and Rees, 150–51). The occasion for this national Irish Assembly was the *Teamhur Feis*; and according to the *Dindshenchas*, one of the chief functions of the Irish Assembly convening during the *Feis* was the public adjudication of important lawsuits:

> Legal cases to review,
> Laws to publish and declare—
> This the business of the Fair.[16]

Legal cases affecting the nation as a whole were tried and decided at the *Feis*, the outcome of each case proclaimed to the entire gathering. In the *Wake*, the Trial of Festy King is conducted at such a gathering as described in the *Dindshenchas*. Other important cases such as *Honuphrius* [HCE] *vs. Magravius* [Magrath] (572.17–573.34) and *Tango vs. Pango* (573.35–576.8) are presented to the Assembly, adjudicated, formally decided, and publicly decreed during the course of the *Wake*—exactly as they were at the *Teamhur Feis*.

The Wake of Finn

Finn of the Wake

The lore of Finn and the Fianna provides the most pervasive presentation of mythological allusions in the entirety of *Finnegans Wake*.[17] Finn MacCool, in Joyce's words, casts "a great shadow" over his protagonist, HCE (*Letters III*, 473). HCE seems an emanation of Finn; and Finn is the mythic parallel and *comimeadh* of HCE. The *Wake* itself celebrates the life, death, and return of Finn as much as it does the modern Everyman HCE, or even the ancient god-king, ECH. The *Wake* is the great occasion for all the Fianna of Ireland to gather in celebration and remembrance of their renowned leader. As Joyce indicates, *Finnegans Wake* "signifies at once the wake and the awakening of Finn" (*Letters III*, 473).

The entire Fenian Cycle, from Finn's conception to the death of the last Fianna, is woven throughout the text of the *Wake*. "The Cause of the Battle of Cnucha" presents the story of Finn's birth and parentage and introduces his lifelong adversary, Goll Mac Morna. Finn's father, Cumal (pronounced "Cool"), "Cooloosus" (625.21), is one of the colonized Fir Bolg but is also *Rígfennid* ("King of the Fianna") of the high king, Conn. As a Fir Bolg and one of the socially marginalized Fianna, Cumal is, regardless of his title of *Rígfennid*, a low-status social outcast who will never attain equality within the Milesian community. Cumal falls in love with "Highbosomheaving Missmistress Morna" (189.25) of the "allsweetheartening bridemuredemaenor" (189.26), Tara aristocrat, daughter of Tadg, and one of the leaders of the Milesian ascendancy. Cumal abducts Morna (or she elopes voluntarily, depending upon who tells the tale). King Conn demands the return of Morna and threatens force: "Steadyon, Cooloosus! Mind your stride or you'll knock" (625.21–22). Cumal refuses, and Conn sends his army to retake the now pregnant Morna. The battle is joined between Fir Bolg Fianna and Milesian army at Cnucha: the "Real Hymernians [Hibernians] stringing strong at knocker knocker" (376.12); "Knock knock. War's where! Which war?" (330.30–31). At the "knock out in the park" (3.21), Cumal is killed by Goll ("One-Eyed") Mac Morna who becomes *Rígfennid* of Tara and archenemy of Finn MacCool. Like HCE, Finn's non-Celtic ancestry virtually guarantees his status as an outsider the duration of his life. Finn, like HCE, is shadowed throughout his life by a mysterious, sinister, and partially blind adversary.

Finn's family tree, as presented in "The Cause of the Battle of Cnucha," shows a recurring pattern among the males: they typically come in pairs that "represent individually the diverse sides of the hero, as do Finn's father Cumal and his grandfather Tadg" (Nagy, *Wisdom,* 20). One figure in each of the pairs is characterized as a social outcast, a Fianna; the other is portrayed as a respectable and even prestigious member of society. The existence in the Fianna lore of these paired and antinomial characters serves to emphasize, through their contrast, the paradoxical nature of Cumal's famous son, the poet and the outsider Finn MacCool. In the *Wake,* the same dualistic pattern is clearly evident in HCE's family: Shem the social outcast, artist, and poet, and Shaun the privileged official with no imagination. HCE, like Finn, reconciles the opposing traits within his own character.

In "The Boyhood Deeds of Finn," the "holy child of Coole" (531.33) (now known as "Demne") is rejected by his mother and raised in secrecy by two Druidesses, "Babdols" (376.27) and the "Grey One" (376.27), who train the youth in tracking, hunting, weaponry, and martial arts. After this physical preparation, young Demne plans to return to Tara to claim the position held by his father. On his way, guided by the River Boyne herself, he meets an old Druid and *Fili* named Finnecces (literally, "Finn the poet"). The "finnecies of poetry" (377.16–17) lives on the banks of the Boyne searching for Fintan ("the ancient Finn"), the Salmon of Wisdom, the "foyneboyne salmon" (41.26–27) in the "Salmon Pool" (174.28). It has been prophesied that whoever eats this salmon will acquire the Three Illuminations: *imbas forosnai* ("incantations on the palms," "knowledge that enlightens"); *teinm laegda* (intuitive perception, "knowledge from the pith," mantic utterance); and *dichetal do chennaib* (the ability to recite and recall by using the fingers). Finnecces catches Fintan and orders Demne to cook it. When almost done, a blister rises on the skin of Fintan, which Demne presses with his thumb. Demne burns his thumb, quickly places it in his mouth, and thereby acquires the Three Illuminations. Realizing the prophecy has been fulfilled, Finnecces gives both his name and identity to the youth; Demne is now "Finn"—the "Bright," the one who possesses "bright knowledge." Finn is now a *Fili* and can attain insight into any situation, compose poetry, and recall past events by reenacting the ritual thumb-chewing of *teinm laegda*: we know Finn to have used as "chawchaw" his own muscle and bone, flesh and blood (36.2–3); Finn will "sing thumb bit" (625.16), then "wise your selmon" (625.16) on it; Finn "bit goodbyte" (73.16) to his thumb (73.16).

In this Irish myth describing the acquisition of poetic abilities are several themes fundamental to the *Wake*. The elder Finn (Finnecces) and the young man who becomes Finn are mystically the same person. Youth supplants age; but in the great cycle, the rivals share the same identity. The cycle completes itself on the bank of a sacred river—for both the pagan Irish and James Joyce the ultimate symbol and locus for cyclical renewal; and for both, the animate river is itself the guide and *anima* for the hero. In the *Wake* as in the above tale, *teinm laegda,* artistic creation, is always an autophagous ritual. Self-cooking (the salmon, too, is named "Finn") and self-consumption are the requisites for creation—an important theme demonstrated in the *Wake,* especially through the character of Shem the Penman, a.k.a. "Pain the Shaman," in his metatextual lesson on artistic creation in "The Haunted Inkbottle."

Immediately after his acquisition of the Three Illuminations, Finn perceives the bonfires of the *Teamhur Feis* celebrated not far away and proceeds to Tara with his newly acquired wisdom. During the *Feis,* Finn uses both his shamanistic and martial skills to slay an Otherworld entity, and for this act of heroism he is rewarded with the position of *Rígfennid*: young Finn, the "unnamed nonirishblooder" (378.10–11) becomes a "Greenislender" (378.11) overnight. "Finsen makes cumhulments" (624.28–29) becomes the great "Finnleader" (214.11) himself. Around Finn at Tara gather the most famous members of the Fianna, the band of warriors and poets who live on the fringe of society, those "nice boys going native" (374.30): Ossian, the "Rageous Ossean" (139.21), the great warrior poet and son of Finn; Ossian's son "Oscar, that son of a Coole" (68.11); Diarmuid O Duibhne, "dermot" (21.14), "dearmud" (68.14), Finn's nephew who becomes the lover of Grania MacCormac in the Fenian version of the Celtic Triangle; and Conan Mael, the aging, cranky, and humorous malcontent, his "old Conan" (322.3). Finn becomes a great builder at Tara though his own *dun* is at the Hill of Allen, "Ahlen's Hill's" (594.18), "Hillary Allan" (617.23).

Finn, the seventeenth, the greatest, and the last *Rígfennid* of Tara strives to increase the status of his Fenian outcasts. Finn makes initiation into the Fianna a rigorous ordeal; he requires all candidates for the Fianna to possess scholarly skills as well as martial prowess. To this end, he uses the *Teamhur Feis* as the occasion for a public examination of each Fianna candidate on the "Twelve Realms of Knowledge." If successful, the candidate takes the pledge of Fiannaship as part of the ceremonies at the *Teamhur Feis*. In the *Wake,* "The Quiz Show" (chapter 6)—with its public examination based on twelve questions concerning such issues as Finn MacCool and the Fianna, provincial capitals of Ireland, various *Wakean* characters and their roles, visionary insight, Celtic Triangles, and the invasions of Ireland—becomes the parodic reenactment of this ancient test. Question Number 1, probably the longest interrogative sentence ever written, honors Finn through thirteen pages (126.1–139.13) of accolades and allusions to his life and death.

The most significant of the Fianna tales reenacted in *Finnegans Wake* is "The Pursuit of Diarmaid and Grania." As reported in the "Tara Tribune" (375.24), an aging Finn, now a lonely widower (375.26), is soon to be married to Grainne, the beautiful modern yet ancient Irish princess (396.7–8). The "Tara Tribune" notes the big wedding of "Fummuccumul with a graneen aveiled" (375.29) along with his anticipation of the subsequent "hornemoonium" (377.15–16) with its promise of nonstop "marrimont" (375.27 [merriment, marriage mount]). But Grainne has the "eitch" (376.19) in her blood, "arrah!" (376.19), for Finn's articulate young nephew with the irresistible "love spot" on his cheek, Diarmaid, the freckled fresh-cheeked "sweetworded lupsqueezer" (376.19–20). During the wedding feast, the young bride flashes a look at Diarmaid, her beautiful "enameled" (203.28 [enamored]) eyes goad Diarmaid on to the verge of "violetian" (203.28–29). Grania passes a wedding goblet laced with soporifics to Finn and other celebrants, which causes the mighty builder of Tara (377.26) to "fullen aslip" (377.26). Diarmaid, the child who gives the sire away (375.21), "spreed's abroad" (58.11 [speeds aboard, spreads abroad, spreads a broad]) with Grania while Finn's "breach is fallen down" (58.10–11). The couple escapes to "Clanruckard" (376.32) pursued by the "kinn" (376.33 [king, kin]) of all the "Fenns" (376.33). During the elopement, Diarmaid builds a seven-door shelter for himself and Grania, and the couple is aided by Diarmaid's relative, the Otherworld deity Angus (371.1), the keeper of the keys of the seven doors of the "dreamadoory" (371.1–3 [dormitory, drama story]).

"The Pursuit" continues for exactly one complete solar cycle. Angus then makes peace between Finn and Diarmaid. As a gesture of reconciliation, Finn and Diarmaid agree to a hunt. On "the last day of the year," Diarmaid joins Finn in hunting the Wild Boar of Ben Bulben; but the boar is magically identified with Diarmaid's foster brother, by whom he is destined to fall. Diarmaid slays the boar but is wounded by one of its poisonous bristles. Only water from the magical hand of Finn can save Diarmaid, as the dying hero tells his old rival:

> Ór do ghlacais an t-éo fis do uí for Bóinn,$_7$ gidh bé dá ttiubharthá deoch dot bhasuibh do bhiadh sé óghshlán ón uile ghalar dá éis.

> [For you handled the salmon of knowledge which was on the Boyne, and to whomsoever you should give a drink from your palms would be perfectly sound from all diseases after that.][18]

Finn goes for water, gathers it in his cupped hands, then remembers the elopement and allows the healing liquid to trickle out through his fingers. Twice he does this; and by his third trip to the well Diarmaid is dead. "The Pursuit," with its ritualistic enactment of the triangle, its seasonal and cyclical nature, resonates strongly with HCE's own cyclical adventure in the *Wake*.

In "The Pursuit," as well as in the other major tales in the Fenian Cycle, Finn "was regarded as a sort of alternative king" (Ó hÓgáin, *Encyclopedia*, 218). Finn's official title, *Rígfennid*, "King of the Fianna," certainly indicates some form of kingship. *The Colloquy* (cited in VI.B.30 of the Buffalo Notebooks) explains that Ireland was divided into two alternate realms, *Tuatha* and *Fianna*, and as a consequence, Finn, "King of the Fianna," indeed became a shadow king in the alternate kingdom. This dualism of "official king" and "Fianna king" that factors into most of the Fianna tales explains the many parallel themes between High King and Fianna King: the Celtic Triangle at the core of both Fianna rites and rites of kingship at Tara; the theme of antinomial Twins who manifest as siblings, ancestors, or progeny; the mysterious one-eyed Adversaries armed with strange weapons; the "Fall" of both kings through their inevitable aging; the identity of both kings related to the passing of the seasons or the solar cycle; the cyclical return that is both requisite and expected. In turn, these are the same themes that Finn MacCool, the "great shadow," shares with the *Wakean* "king," HCE. The great themes of the Fianna thus correlate with the major themes of *Finnegans Wake* and with those of the *Teamhur Feis*.

Finn's Wake at the *Teamhur Feis*

In addition to retelling the Fianna tales, the *Wake* is the occasion for a gathering to celebrate the life, death, and "return" of Finn MacCool. At this great "overflow meeting" (42.22), all the Fianna gather to honor their dead leader, a vile "bogeyer" (42.15) but the most attractive avatar the world has ever explained (42.15–16). The "faunayman" (25.32) at the funeral (25.32–33) toast their leader with joyous drinks at the "fewnrally" (277.4–5 [funeral, Fianna rally]), where every feaster is a foster brother, Fenians all (277.4–6). They commemorate Finn with the "fiounaregal" (332.26 [funeral, fianna, regal] games of the "oathmassed" (332.26) Fenians (332.26–27). The Fianna celebrate the promised return of their dead leader, the day when Finn shall arise, when he shall wake from his "earth-sleep" (74.2), when their lost leader lives, and the hero returns (73.36–74.2). Significantly, they celebrate Finn's wake at a "fair" (246.19), where the lore of Finn and the Fianna—the fights, the victories, the failures, the elopements, the pursuits, the tales of death and resurrection—is retold and reenacted. At this "fair" that is the *Wake*, the Fianna lore provides a kind of mythological canon that underlies much of the *Wake* itself.

In *Finnegans Wake*, and through the entire course of the Fenian Cycle, Finn MacCool, the Fianna, and most of their major adventures are inextricably linked with Tara. Finn's father is *Rígfennid* at Tara, his mother an aristocrat at Tara, and Finn himself is conceived at Tara. As young Demne, Finn acquires the Three Illuminations within sight of Tara. Finn becomes *Rígfennid* in his own right during the *Feis* at Tara. Finn makes the *Teamhur Feis* the occasion to test and initiate new candidates for the Fianna. Finn marries Grainne at Tara, where the ritualistic "Pursuit" begins. King Cairbre instigates the destruction of the Fianna during a feast at Tara, declaring, "I would sooner die fighting the Fianna, if I could bring them down along with me, than live with Ireland under them the way it is now." Years after their destruction, the few Fianna who survived went to Tara. There, on the Hill of Tara, they placed their bodies face down, put their lips to its sacred earth, and died. The Fenian Cycle begins and ends at Tara. The great wake and "fair" at Tara thus became the matrix of Fianna lore as well as the major occasion for honoring Finn and his associates. An account in the *Irish Chronicle* underscores this connection between the Fianna Lore, Tara, and the *Teamhur Feis*:

> There is in Meath an hill, called the Hill of Taragh
> Wherein is a playne twelve score long;
> Which was named the Kemp-his-hall.
> There the countrey had their meetings and falckmoates,
> At a place that was accounted the high Pallace of the Monarch.
> The Irish historians hammer many fables
> In this forge of Finne Mocke Coyle & his Champions,
> As a Frenche historie doth
> Of King Arthur and the Knights of the rounde table.
> But doubtlesse the place soemeth to beare the shoe of
> An ancient and famous monument.[19]

Much earlier than the *Irish Chronicle* is a poem from the *Dindshenchas* that provides a description of events conducted during the *Teamhur Feis*.

As the poem indicates, the retelling and reenactment of Fianna lore is an important and pervasive component of the Rites:

> Lore of Finn and the Fianna, a matter inexhaustible,
> Destructions, forays, wooings,
> Tablets, and books of lore.[20]

The Fianna lore presented at the *Teamhur Feis* was more than entertainment: the great themes of the Fianna provided mythic paradigms and archetypal examples for those attendant to incorporate into their own lives. These "tales of the tingmount" (53.5–6) were understood to be both powerful and sacred, providing for the participants examples of which "the deeds of other men must be regarded as a reflexion" (Rees and Rees, 211). The lore of Finn and the Fianna thus formed "what is not too much to call a sacred canon" (*T*, 165). As the *Wake* explains: "(full well do we wont to recall to mind) thy oldworld tales of homespinning and derringdo . . . these tales which reliterately whisked off our heart" (431.30–33).

In the *Wake*, as at the *Feis*, the life and deeds of Everyman are regarded as the reflection of the life and deeds of the great Finn. The "sacred canon" of the Rites of Tara is identical to the "the tales all tolled" (275.22) throughout the course of the *Wake*. The *Cúitech Fúait* in honor of Finn were performed again and again at the *Teamhur Feis*; and the wake of Finn, once celebrated at the Rites of Tara, is once again rightly celebrated in *Finnegans Wake*.

Fertility Rites at an Irish Wake

For the pagan Irish, death and birth were deliberately and inextricably linked at the *Teamhur Feis*. The regicide and rebirth of ECH, the celebration of renewal on a great tumulus of the dead, death rites conducted at the vernal equinox, the inherent sexuality in "The Building of the Ship," the wake and awakening of Finn—all reflect archaic Celtic beliefs regarding immortality, the rebirth of a human soul, the cyclical nature of life, as well as the ancient Celtic principle that ritual itself can be used to facilitate renewal and rebirth. With this perspective, fertility rites—rites intended to maintain and promote fecundity and renewal through "deliberate application of sympathetic magic"—were integral to the events performed at Tara during the vernal equinox (*T*, 168). These rites are reenacted in the *Wake*; curiously, the central performers in these rituals are the Twenty-Eight Girls from Saint Brigit's School, that is, the priestesses of the goddess Brigit, the Vestal Virgins of ancient Ireland.

The Irish *Februa*

"Shaun's Sermon" (chapter 14, 429–73), his exhortation addressed to Brigit's girls for the perpetuation of their virginity, is the longest diatribe in *Finnegans Wake*. Shaun presents himself as an official representative of Church and State to the twenty-nine "hedge daughters" (430.1) of Saint Brigit's National Night School (430.2) from Kildare (436.31). Many of the "hedge daughters" are named (430.35–37) prior to Shaun's speech; their names suggest virginity as well as the springtime occasion. The feast of Agatha, the Virgin Martyr, is February 5; the Feast of Our Lady of Lourdes, seen by Bernadette, is February 11; the feast of Juliana, Virgin Martyr, is February 16; the feast of Eulalia, Virgin Martyr, is February 12. Agatha's lamb and Juliana's rabbit also suggest Easter (Tindall, 249).

Shaun further emphasizes the virginity of Brigit's "hedge daughters" when, in the course of his speech, he identifies them with the most famous virgins of antiquity, the Vestal Virgins, keepers of the sacred Vestal light of ancient Rome. Shaun exhorts the virgins to keep their fresh chastity "cool" (440.31), which is far better than parting with that "vestalite" (440.32–33 [vestal light]) of the first importance (440.31–33). When Shaun directly addresses "Brigit," their leader, he refers to her as "Luperca" (444.37), the name of the mythic she-wolf who suckled the Roman Twins, Romulus and Remus. The Vestal Virgins were identified with Luperca and were considered her descendants. The nurturing of Luperca, which gave rise to Rome, was continued through the Virgins' perpetual tending of the Vestal fire, the symbol of Rome itself.

Luperca also gave her name to the Roman ceremony known as the "Lupercalia." During the Lupercalia, one of the fundamental events was a ritual lustration of the Vestal Virgins, referred to as the *Februa*. In the *Februa*, a goat, symbolic of male sexuality, was sacrificed and skinned. The goat hide was then carried by a representative of the *SPQR*, the *Senatus Populus Que Romanus*, who delivered a highly stylized speech to the priestesses—an official exhortation for each Virgin, for the good of the State, to remain *virgo intacta*. The lustration rite of *Februa* later became Christianized as the "Feast of the Purification of the Virgin" (Walker, 557).

Like the *Februa*, Shaun's "Sermon" is an official exhortation for the girls to remain, as Shaun describes them, "viragos intactas" (432.11). Acting in his official capacity as the "seanad and pobbel queue's remainder" (454.36 [Senatus Populus Que Romanus]), the self-appointed representative of Church and State delivers a highly stylized speech wherein he warns the "hedge daughters" against dangerous dalliance and risky scenarios and urges them to maintain their virginity. His speech continues for dozens of pages; among his many admonitions he warns the girls to never park their "brief stays" (433.24) in a man's convenience (433.24–25); never clean their "buttoncups" (433.25) with a dirty pair of scissors (433.25–26); never let the promising hand make free use of their "oncemaid sacral" (433.27–28); never slip a silver key through the gate of golden age (433.31–32); and always "look before you leak" (433.34). Shaun's Sermon concludes with Brigit's "daughters" apparently agreeing to continue their virginal status as they watch Shaun, the "just one" (470.10), take his leave: the "hedge daughters" of February voiced approval in their customary manner by dropping to their knees in tears, and crying together joyously as they all clapped their hands (470.4–8).

Like pagan Rome and *Finnegans Wake*, ancient Ireland had her Vestal Virgins. The virgin "Daughters of the Fire" were referred to as *Inghean au dagha;* and as "Fire-keepers" were called *Breochwidh* (Bonwick, 200–201). The Irish Virgins were twenty-eight in number, and their leader always took the name of "Brigit," whose sacred month is February. The *Inghean au dagha,* Christianized as the "Nuns of Saint Brigit," kept a sacred fire perpetually burning at their shrine in Kildare well into the Christian era, until the archbishop of Dublin, fully aware of its pagan origins, ordered the sacred flame extinguished in 1220. Giraldus Cambrensis claims to have visited the Kildare shrine while the flame and the cult center were still intact. His description, entitled "Of the Hedge Round the Fire, Which No Male Can Enter," explains why the women were referred to as "hedge daughters." Giraldus also alludes to a ritual performed at Kildare, meant, like the goat sacrifice at the Roman *Februa,* to neutralize male sexuality in the vicinity of the shrine.

> This fire is surrounded by a hedge, made of stakes and brushwood, and forming a circle, within which no male can enter; and if anyone should presume to enter, which has been sometimes attempted by rash men, he will not escape the divine vengeance. . . . Moreover, by virtue of a curse pronounced by the virgin [Brigit], goats here never have any young. (*Chronicle,* 97)

Like her Roman counterparts, each of Brigit's hedge daughters was required to be *virgo intacta*. Each of the Irish Virgins was considered something of a living palladium for Ireland. The inherent energy of her sexuality, preserved and focused through celibacy, allowed each of these "unbroken vessels" to become both a matrix of Irish fecundity and a symbolic medium for cultural preservation.

The parallels between Roman and Irish Vestal Virgins extend into the realm of ritual as well.[21] Accordingly, an Irish rite analogous to the Roman *Februa* was conducted either at Kildare or at Tara as part of the rituals usually performed in spring. In this Irish *Februa,* the hedge daughters would undergo a ritual lustration conducted by a representative of the State. Like the Roman *Februa,* this male representative of Ireland would deliver a stylized exhortation to the daughters of Brigit, urging them to continue their virginal roles for the good of Ireland. Shaun's exhortation, replete with puerile puns, ridiculous double entendre, and ribald humor, provides an amusing analogue to one of the more staid rites from the realm of Irish paganism.

The Marriage Mime at the *Wake* and the Feis

A Summary of "The Mime." Chapter 9 of the *Wake,* "The Mime," features the Twenty-Eight Girls from Saint Bride's Finishing School (220.3–4), their leader "Julia Bride," and the Twins, "Glugg" (219.22) and "Chuff" (220.11). The Mime is performed before the Assembly, the "Caesar-in-Chief" (219.11), and his entourage comprised of all the "King's Hoarsers" (219.15) and all the "Queen's Mum" (219.16). The drama is presented through the distinguished patronage of "their Elderships the Oldens" (219.10), who have arrived from the four corners (219.10) of "Findrias, Murias, Gorias and Falias" (219.11). The "Oldens" bear curious names or titles: "Clive Sollis, Galorius Kettle, Pobiedo Lancey and Pierre Dusort" (219.11–12). The Mime is billed as a "Pageant of Past History" (221.18–19), one of the jests, jokes, and jigs for the wake (221.26), culminating in a "Magnificent Transformation Scene" (222.17), a wedding (222.18), and the dawn of peace, pure, perfect and perpetual, "Waking the Weary of the World" (222.18–20).

In a letter to Harriet Shaw Weaver, Joyce draws attention to several themes—children's games, riddling, singing, and a circular rainbow dance—as the salient features structuring the Mime. Joyce notes that the "scheme of the piece" is a children's game called "Angels and Devils" or "Colours," and is "full of rhythms taken from English singing games." The "Angels" (the Twenty-Eight Girls) are grouped behind the Angel (Shaun), and the Devil (Shem) has to come over three times and ask for a color. When he (Shem) is baffled a second time, the girl Angels sing a "hymn of liberation" around Shawn and perform a circle dance involving "the double rainbow in which the iritic colours are first normal and then reversed" (*Letters I*, 295).

The Mime begins as a riddling contest between the boys and girls. In order to "marry" the leader of Bride's Girls, the boy has to correctly answer a riddle: he has to find for himself, by "gazework" (224.26 [guess work, gazing], the color of their underwear (224.25–27). (The correct answer is "heliotrope.") The riddle is initially presented by Julia Bride, the leader with the looks of a queen (223.24). First, Julia Bride announces that the riddle is "A darktongues, kunning" (223.28); then she states the riddle itself: "O theoperil! Ethiaop lore, the poor lie" (223.28) Later, she presents the riddle again, but in a different form: "A window, a hedge, a prong, a hand, an eye, a sign, a head and keep your other augur on her paypaypay. And you have it" (249.16–18). "Glugg" tries three times to answer the riddle and fails all three attempts. He is then symbolically killed and buried for his failure: poor Glugg was dazed and then laid in his grave (240.3–4).

"Chuff" wins the contest, becomes the "sun-god." Chuff is allowed to marry Julia Bride, who now goes by the name *Klitty* (239.18), a name J. O'Sullivan notes as highly significant. In Greek mythology, Clytie, the daughter of Oceanus, pined for love of Apollo and was turned into a heliotrope. The name *Clytie* means "beautiful or shining one"; Apollo, of course, is the handsome and youthful sun god (*Colors*, 152). In this Pageant of Past History, and under the patronage of the Four Old Ones, the young Irish Apollo solves the riddle and will soon marry the woman with the looks of a queen.

In celebration, the Girls of Brigit joyously gather to "chant" (234.36) in "chor" (234.36 [chorus, choir]), singing a paean of praise to their young Apollo (234.34–35). Throughout the course of their singing and throughout much of the Mime, the girls, adorned with garlands, silver jewelry, colorful ribbons, and bright clothing, perform an elaborate circle dance. The purpose of the dance is to unite, to marry, their leader with their Irish Apollo: for though she's unmarried, after the dance she will dress up (226.18) and teach her husband how to hop, hip it and trip it, cheer up and swing (226.17–19). The dance the girls perform becomes a magical circular rainbow. The dancers leap so lovely as they "link to light" (226.26–27) and spell "RAYNBOW" in their sunwise dance (the ancient Irish *Deas-iul*), a "cadenzando coloratura" (226.30) that goes "entrancing roundly" (226.26–35). Reversing direction, they perform the widdershin dance (called, in ancient Ireland, *Ear-tuia-iul*) while spelling "RAINBOW" reversed, "WOBNAIR"; and here they came back (227.14–15), all the "gay pack" (227.15), the Twenty-Eight "florals" of Bride (227.13–15).

Roland McHugh, citing the familiar "superabundance of rainbows" in Irish mythology, observes that the Rainbow Dance is also a "Reign Beau" Dance in that it deliberately attempts, through the mythic associations of the rainbow, to unite the heavens with the earth, and the sun god with the earth goddess—the rainbow being "the bridge connecting earth and sky, and especially the bridge to the gods."[22]

This mythic "marriage" enacted through the RAINBOW Dance is the climactic event of the Mime. Afterward, there is a sense of renewal and reconnection with the past: "ancients" (254.8) are linked with the present as the human chain extends (254.8–9). The Mime is over. The Twenty-Eight Girls, "every blessed brigid" (256.5–6), the Twins, and the audience, "Home all go" (256.11).

Critical Assessments of The Mime. The prominent features of the Mime—its connection with children's games, the circle dance, the marriage theme, and the riddle—have been addressed by a number of *Wakean* scholars. Roland McHugh sees the drama as an "invocatory ritual depending upon gesture and imitation to convey its subtleties" (*Sigla*, 57). Children, knowing the general form of marriage games, would naturally dance in circle form to any ballad verses in which marriage or love and courtship occurs. The circle games (such as the *Wakean* Mime) are vestiges of earlier rituals in which a "homogeneous group of persons" perform "a ceremony of a religious character," a marriage ceremony in particular; the remains of this rite "can . . . be traced in old plays."[23] The children's game, with its circle dance and its courtship riddles, thus imitates earlier pre-Christian marriage rites performed in the British Isles.

The Gaelic folklorist Alexander Carmichael describes another version of the Marriage Mime, the Christianized version of a pagan fertility rite. In early spring, the young maidens of the village, dressed in bright spring colors, garlands, colorful ribbons, and silver jewelry, parade through the village carrying the image of their leader, "Bride." After making the rounds, they go to a house to make the "Bride Feast." Young men from the village go to the house to "honour Bride" but are not allowed entry until they answer the questions and riddles presented by "Bride's girls." When a few boys are admitted, the girls then perform a circle dance and sing. Lyn Webster Wilde argues that this "'respectable' Christian rite" is the desexualized vestige of an Irish fertility ritual enacted in springtime. In the ancient version, the priestesses of Brigit perform the circle dance and the riddles, and their leader, "Bride," engages in an Irish rite of *hieros gamos* with the chosen male who has "come to worship the goddess prior to being initiated into her secrets via the act of sacred sexual intercourse."[24]

Vivian Mercier notes that marriage mimes (such as the one described above) were a fundamental component of early Irish "wake games or mimes" (*ICT*, 5). These "kissing games and mock marriages" performed at wakes prove that "something of the old pagan spirit still survived" (*ICT*, 50). Early Irish wakes "included some quite elaborate mimed dramas, reminiscent of fertility ritual" (*ICT*, 50). Lady Wilde describes some of these under the heading "The Wake Orgies"; Henry Morris argues that these fertility mimes and other wake games "came down in unbroken descent through all the centuries from the Cluichthe [*sic*] Caointe . . . mentioned so frequently in our pagan Irish literature."[25] The salient features of the *Wakean* Mime–the riddling contest, marriage rites, the circle dance of Brigit's girls, the song—are identical to the defining components of the fertility mimes performed at earlier pagan wakes.

The "Heliotrope" Riddle. "Heliotrope" (*Helios*, "sun"; *trope*, "a way," "a turn," "a manner")—the emblem of the Mime and the improbable answer to its riddle—is something of a riddle in itself and has elicited its own responses from various commentators. Patrick McCarthy emphasizes the "Heliotropic" aspects of both Chuff and Brigit's Girls. "Heliotrope" indicates "Bride's" preference for "Chuff," the sun god who is worshipped by the "holytroopers" (223.11); Bride focuses her attentions on Chuff who, "as the son and the sun, represents a new generation and the promise of a new day" (138–39). McCarthy further notes that Joyce, in his choice of "heliotrope" as the answer to the riddle, is "looking for an idea rather than a color"—the denotative significance of "heliotrope" is its real significance, for Joyce's symbolism in the *Wake* is more often semantic than visual. All Twenty-Eight Girls are "holytroopers" (223.11), that is, heliotropic worshipers of "Sunny" Chuff, and they are appropriately represented as a rainbow, which, since it must face the sun, is by its very nature "heliotropic" (McCarthy, 144).

Margaret Solomon interprets the primary meaning of "Heliotrope" as symbolic of renewal, rebirth, and fertility: [Heliotrope] "seems at first to be the password for opening the gate for a son-change—in effect, a rebirth—a crossing over into a new cycle of marriage, or fertile sex" (30–32).

J. O'Sullivan notes that in the *Wake*, seven references to "Heliotrope" appear in "The Mime" section, and all seven have to do with the girls' colors and Glugg's guesses; several other references to "heliotrope" in the

Wake are associated with Issy or the two girls in the park, or woman as object of man's desire; O'Sullivan further notes that he "can find no other pattern or significance" with the riddle involving "Heliotrope" (150–51).

The Riddle in Irish Tradition. Another significant pattern relevant to the heliotrope riddle may be found, however, through a consideration of the Irish tradition regarding the use of the riddle itself. As Alwyn and Brinley Rees emphasize, in the oral tradition of the *Filidh*, riddling was no children's game: "We have relegated riddles . . . to the kindergarten, and it is disconcerting to find that for the seers and sages of old they enshrined the deepest wisdom" (350). For the Irish *Filidh* and Druids, the riddle was a form of sympathetic magic. When used skillfully, the riddle "has the power to breach the constraining boundaries of the finite" and elucidate the secret connection between apparent disparities (Rees and Rees, 351). The Irish riddle was an evocation used as a means to discern the correspondences between seemingly unrelated things. Through the ritualistic play of riddles, "the great connections and the major equivalences are discovered; it is a subterfuge designed to admit the ineffable into human discourse" (Rees and Rees, 351).

Because the ancient Irish understood the riddle as a magical means of connecting opposites and disparities, riddles were used as one of the rites to unite women and men in marriage, or even as a means to connect the seasons at the great transitional phases of the year. (Consider for example, the Prankquean's riddle.) In Celtic marriage rites, obstacles and "impossible tasks" were frequently placed in the path of the bridegroom. The impossible tasks, by their very nature, could only be accomplished in a figurative sense—as in the solving of a riddle. And because of their power to connect antinomials, the Celtic riddling contests associated with fertility and matrimony "also figured in certain seasonal rituals," such as the rites associated with the vernal equinox (Rees and Rees, 269).

Finn MacCool, a *Fili* skilled in the technique of riddling, provides a good example of the riddle used in marriage rites. In "The Wooing of Ailbe," Finn, enamored of Ailbe MacCormac (Grainne's younger and more attractive sister), banters with Ailbe in the secret language used by Irish poets. Finn is impressed that Ailbe knows the poetic tongue; he is further impressed with her when she holds her own in their ensuing riddling contest:

> What is sweeter than mead?—Intimate conversation.
> What is blacker than the raven?—Death.
> What is whiter than snow?—Truth.
> What is swifter than wind?—Thought.

What is sharper than the sword?—Understanding.[26]

Each riddle requires verbal "magic" for its solution: the answers require the metaphorical transmutation of the adjective in each question. Each answer unites two seemingly disparate realms. The original contest was in a language known only to a very few, *bélra na filed,* frequently glossed in English as the "Dark Tongue." To the others who happened to overhear the Dark Tongue speech of Finn and Ailbe, their conversation sounded like so much gibberish, but the use of a Dark Tongue technique—riddling—itself united the couple. The union of these two opposites, male and female, deepened through the riddles; this ritualized riddling led, shortly afterward, to their marriage.

In the *Filidh* tradition, the most skillful riddles presented in the mythological tales manifest a kind of holographic quality. The phrasing in which the riddle is framed may indicate the larger issues at play in the story itself. The answer responds not merely to the immediate question but to the entirety of the drama. Both question and answer might encapsulate the major theme of the tale. The "solution" to the question may lie in the riddle itself.

One of Finn's better riddles involves the other MacCormac sister, Grainne. Lonely and forlorn after the death of his wife, Finn is introduced to the young princess. Attracted to her, Finn begins his courtship with flirtatious bantering that soon takes the form of a riddle meant to both confuse and impress her:

"What is hotter than fire, swifter than wind?"
was the question Finn posed to Grainne.
"The thought of a woman between two men,"
was the answer she gave back to him.[27]

Finn is taken aback by Grainne's feisty and unexpected response, which makes her, in his assessment, even more intriguing and desirable. The riddling episode leads shortly to their marriage. At their wedding feast, Grainne's thought turns away from Finn to the young and handsome Diarmaid. Their attraction is immediate and hot; their flight from Finn is swift. The pursuit of Diarmaid and Grainne that begins at the wedding results in death for Diarmaid and eventually for Finn himself. The pursuit exacerbates the internecine strife already within the Fianna and is one of the reasons for its final destruction at the Battle of Gabra. With the destruction of the Fianna, Ireland is considerably weakened and much more susceptible to foreign invasion. The riddle imposed by the great *Rígfennid* upon the much younger Grainne was meant to confuse and impress the youthful woman through its cleverness—suggesting a certain arrogance and perhaps an element of hubris on the part of Finn. Grainne's response reflects the basic traits of her own character: a type of acuity quicker and sharper than most of the men around her, tempestuousness, and a passionate but fickle heart. The question and response collectively imply the Celtic Triangle—the older man of high status in love with the younger woman in love with the younger man of lower status—that is the fundamental theme of the most famous of Fenian myths. The riddle that is the initial marriage rite for Finn and Grainne encapsulates the dynamics that lead not to the fidelity, love, and children hoped for in marriage but to their opposites, the deaths, dishonor, and strife that end the entire Fenian tradition. The riddle, a fundamental technique of the Dark Tongue, can thus act as a microcosmic emblem for an entire event.

The "Heliotrope" Riddle as a Dark Tongue Technique. In the *Wakean* "Mime," the initial and most elaborate presentation of the "Heliotrope" riddle is introduced as "A darktongues, kunning" (223.28), suggesting that both the riddle and its occasion are ritualistic, possibly connected with marriage and seasonal rites, and that it partakes of the attributes of the traditional Irish riddles in the ancient Dark Tongue. The riddle given is "O theoperil! Ethiaop lore, the poor lie" (223.28). One of the Dark Tongue techniques, *Ogam Uird,* can be appropriated for the solution to this riddle. *Ogam Uird* is, essentially, the use of anagrams; but the anagrams themselves should reflect characteristics of the concept they are meant to secretly convey. All three phrases of the riddle are anagrams of "Heliotrope." "O theoperil" suggests the trial or test ("peril" from Latin, *periculum,* "trial") of "theo," a god. "Ethiaop lore" suggests arcane or ancient knowledge. "The poor lie" might be litotes for "truth."

In its second elaborate presentation, the riddle is more obscure: "A window, a hedge, a prong, a hand, an eye, a sign, a head and keep your other augur on her paypaypay. And you have it" (249.16–18). Another Dark Tongue technique, *Ogam romesc Bres* ("The Ogham which bewildered Bres") works well in this instance. In *Ogam romesc Bres,* the *Fili* writes the name *of* the letter *for* the letter; "Joyce," for example might be written (more or less) as "Jay Owe Why See He." The name of this cipher is explained by a story to the effect that a message thus concealed was given to the ancient hero Bres as he was going to battle; Bres then lost the battle because he was trying to decode the riddle instead of focusing on the struggle at hand (*SL,* 46–47). The riddle is solved when the words are first recognized as the names of Hebrew or Phoenician letters and the Dark Tongue technique is then applied:

Word	Hebrew	English
Window	*He*	H
Hedge	*Cheth*	E
Prong	*Lamed*	L
Hand	*Yod*	I
Eye	*Ayin*	O
Sign	*Taw*	T
Head	*Rosh*	R

The remaining three letters "OPE" are found in the rest of the sentence: "augur" as German *Auge*, "eye," provides another "O" and the "P" is more or less pronounced ("paypaypay" [249.18]).[28] The "Heliotrope" riddle appears several more times in "The Mime"; each of its presentations can be solved with the application of a Dark Tongue technique.

"Heliotrope" is "A darktongues, kunning," which suggests that it may be a riddle connected with ancient Irish marriage rites and seasonal festival. As a Dark Tongue riddle, "Heliotrope" should reflect (as it does) the dynamics at play in "The Mime" episode. The Twenty-Eight Virgins are "heliotropers" as they perform the circle sun dance around their Apollo. As sacred votaries of Brigit, they are the "holytroopers." The color of the holytrooper's panties is heliotrope, obviously associating heliotrope with sex and fertility. Klytie/Bride is a "heliotroper" through marriage with her Apollo. Heliotrope is the flower of early spring, and follows the sun in its deosil dance through the heavens. Chuff, their Irish sun god, is himself a sun-turning heliotrope. As "A darktongues, kunning," "Heliotrope" thus implies marriage or fertility ritual, conducted at a seasonal juncture, and encompassing all of the above meanings of the word *Heliotrope* itself: Klytie and her holytroopers, sun god marrying Bride, seasonal festival and circle dance. And in the seasonal Rites at Tara, a sacred drama nearly identical to the "Heliotropic" Mime was performed as part of the wake and seasonal rites of the *Feis*.

The Mime at the Teamhur Feis. Classical writers as diverse as Pomponius Mela, Strabo, and Pausanias describe a cult of virgin priestesses in the northern Celtic realm who perform "a magical ceremony to hasten the coming of the spring" that includes a "remarkable dance in honour of Apollo."[29] These classical references strongly indicate the virgin priestesses referred to are the cult of the Twenty-Eight Virgins of Brigit associated with Kildare and Tara (*TB*, 394–97). Diodorus Siculus, drawing extensively on the account of Hecataeus, states that on an island "no smaller than Sicily," with "a mild climate" but far to the north in the domain of the Celts, a sacred drama is performed in "a huge temple of rotund form." The site of this drama is the home of the island's hereditary kings, who are all offspring of the sky god in horse form. On the vernal equinox, the "Celtic Apollo" is invited down from the heavens to the temple, where he dances with the priestesses. The sun dance performed was circular: "an attempt, by sympathetic magic, to keep the sun revolving in its appointed course" (*TB*, 392).

At Tara, the home of the hereditary "horse kings" (that is, the variant forms of "ECH"), a young man was selected to personify the sun god as part of the sacred drama performed by the Twenty-Eight Virgins and their leader, Bride. The drama was a ritual meant to strengthen the sun in its course through the heavens and to foster the vegetation that would hopefully return in early spring. The drama was a fertility rite, enacting the marriage of the sun god and earth goddess, which would facilitate the fecundity of the animals and crops. The circle dance was intrinsic to the drama, necessary for both the progress of the new sun in its seasonal course, and an essential rite meant to unite heaven and earth. There is evidence that similar fertility rites involving circle dances were performed throughout Ireland, at ancient sites such as *Achadh Greine* (the "Sunfield") near the stone circle called the "Piper's Stones" (County Wicklow), and at *Rannach Cruim Duibh* ("Wheels of Cromm Dubh") near Loch Gur (*TB*, 392). The Rites of Tara, however, were the center for this ritual in Ireland. So central was this sacred drama to the *Teamhur Feis* that the medieval scribes typically glossed the Gaelic word for the Rites of Tara, *Oenach*, as *Theatrum* (Rees and Rees, 183–84).

Joyce, very deliberately, locates the *Wakean* Mime at Tara as well. The Mime is performed under the "distinguished patronage" of the "Elderships the Oldens" from the four corners of "Findias, Murias, Gorias and Falias." The four places named are the four mythical cities of the Tuatha De Danaan, located at the four corners of the world. Each city was home to a powerful talisman, as described in "The Second Battle of Moytura":

> (1). The Tuatha De Danaan were in the northern isles of the world, learning lore and magic and druidism and wizardry and cunning, until they surpassed all the sages of the arts of heathendom. (2).

> There were four cities in which they were learning lore and science and diabolic arts, to wit, Falias and Gorias, Murias and Findias. (3). Out of Falias was brought the stone of Fal, which was in Tara. It used to roar under every king that would take (the realm of) Ireland. (4). Out of Gorias was brought the Spear that Lugh had. No battle was ever won against it or him who held it in his hand. (5). Out of Findias was brought the Sword of Nuadu. When it was drawn from its deadly sheath, no one ever escaped from it, and it was irresistible. (6). Out of Murias was brought the Dagda's cauldron. No company ever went from it unthankful.[30]

After the victory of the Tuatha De Danaan over the Fomorians at the Second Battle of Moytura, the Tuatha De Danaan made Tara their new religious and political capital. To Tara they brought their four ancient talismans. These sacred objects—the Four Hallows—are ceremoniously presented in the *Wake* at the beginning of "The Mime," with the Assembly, the queen, and the high king of Ireland looking on: "Clive Sollis" (Glave of Light), "Galorius Kettle" (Cauldron of Plenty), "Pobiedo [Russian, 'Victory'] Lancey" (Spear), and "Pierre Dusort" (Stone of Destiny). In his "Notebooks," Joyce carefully worked out the correspondences between the Four Hallows, the cities of their origin, their designated cardinal points, their corresponding elements, and their related Celtic deities:

N—solid	Falias	Midyir	Stone of Destiny
S—fire	Gorias	Nuada	Spear of Victry [*sic*]
E—cloud	Findias	Ogma	Sword of Light
Water [*sic*]	Murias	Dagda	Pot of Plenty

(VI.B.11.94)

1) Sword of Light
   Ogma, Findias
   cloudy, E
2) Nuad, spear of
   Victory, Gorias
   flame, S
3) Dagda, Cauldron
   Plenty, Murias
   water, W

(VI.B.35.32)

4) Midyir, Stone of
Destiny, Falias
earth, N
(VI.B.35.33)

The Four Hallows were essential accoutrements to the rites at the *Teamhur Feis*—displayed to bestow divine sanction upon ritual events, and in some instances used as instruments to perform the rituals themselves. The presentation of the Four Hallows at the beginning of the Mime places the event squarely at Tara; the themes of renewal, marriage, and fertility, along with the riddling and deosil dance make "The Mime" an accurate if somewhat playful rendition of one of the archaic fertility rites of Irish paganism.

As a fertility rite, the Mime enacted at the *Teamhur Feis* was replete with elements of sympathetic magic. The deosil dance was meant to both symbolize and facilitate the progression of the great wheel traversed by the sun god. The ritualistic riddling is also a form of sympathetic magic—meant to unite male and female, god and goddess, old cycle with the new. The "marriage" enacted by the performers of this ritual—obviously a fertility rite—magically facilitates the divine marriage of ECH and Ana. At the *Teamhur Feis*, the intended results of this sympathetic magic come to fruition: the sun god, whose death and wake occur at the *Feis*, returns, reborn and renewed. And in the rites of investiture also enacted at the *Feis*, the renewed sun god marries Ana. The great wheel of the sun comes full circle, and the ascendant arc of the great wheel is also celebrated at the Rites of Tara—and at the *Wake* as well.

6

The Return of Solsking the First

The Ascendant Arc of an Irish God-King

While the *Teamhur Feis* is the occasion for the downfall, divestiture and death rites of the *ard rí*, the ascendant arc of this great cycle—the rebirth, return, and investiture of a renewed solar king—comprises an equally important portion of the choreographed rites and events conducted at ancient Tara. At the *Feis*, ECH will arrive, as he does in the *Wake*, "renascent" (596.3). Through the process of ritual tests and arcane rites of investiture, and in great procession, the primal solar king will return: "Solsking the Frist" (607.28) will "processingly" (607.29) show up (607.29).

Accordingly, at the *Teamhur Feis*, a series of rites were performed to facilitate the return of the "Solsking," archaic rites used to identify the new king, verify his identity, and invest him with the powers of royal office. During the *Feis*, the séancelike *Tarbh Feis* was conducted by four elder Druids to make contact with entities in the Otherworld, and from them obtain the identity of the new king. A series of magical tests involving horses (*Carpat Na Flatha*), a tight-fitting royal mantle (*Casal Ríg*), and symbolic portals (Blocc and Bluicne) were conducted to verify the findings of the *Tarbh Feis*. The new ECH was then invested with the power and identity of sacral kingship through the ceremonies comprising *Banais Righe*—"marriage rites of kingship"—which included ritual imbibing of the sacramental ale; coition with the royal consort; baptism in a well, a spring, or river sacred to the Sovereign; and a fourteen-stage procession around the royal hall of Tara. As in the *Wake*, the ceremony is completed through the lighting of the *torc caille*. Table 6.1 outlines these events and their reenactments in the *Wake*. These events at the *Feis* and their *Wakean* analogues are discussed in this chapter.

Table 6.1. The Rites of Investiture at the *Teamhur Feis* and their correspondences in *Finnegans Wake*

Event at the *Teamhur Feis*	Description of Event	Correspondence in *Finnegans Wake*
Tarbh Feis	Four Elder Druids give a man with mediumistic propensities a ritual meal, place him supine on ground in trance state, and interrogate entities that speak through him.	In "The Inquest of Shaun," the Four Elders give Shaun a huge meal, place him supine on ground, place him in trance, and interrogate entities that speak through him.
Carpat Na Flatha	The Royal Candidate is placed in a cauldron with his totem animal, the horse; king must ride and exhibit control over horses.	Shaun is placed in or near the "holy kettle" with a donkey; victorious HCE enters on horseback and displays control over horses.
Casal Ríg, The Cloak of Kingship	"Test of the Mantle": the candidate must perfectly fit into a tight-fitting garment; if it does not fit, he cannot marry the queen.	In "The Sailor and Tailor," the Sailor cannot marry unless and until his Tailor-made suit fits perfectly.
The Voice of Fal	The "Voice of the Thunder God" must be heard throughout the *Feis* as a sign of divine validation.	"Thunderwords" heard throughout the *Wake* are the "Voice of the Thunder God."
Blocc/Bluicne, The Portal Test	The Candidate must traverse the space between stones or through a portal.	HCE carefully traverses "The Hole in the Wall" and "The Stonehinged Gate."
Banais Righe, "Wedding Feast of Kingship"	Royal inauguration and marriage of king through union with goddess in three of her manifestations. *Banais Righe* involves 3 rites: (1) drinking intoxicating liquid, (2) coition with queen, and (3) immersion in her sacred well.	(1) HCE as "King of Ireland" sucks up all drinks in tavern; (2) HCE has sex with his "queen/goddess"; (3) HCE/Kevin is immersed in the sacred waters of Anna.
Deisil of *Tech Midchuarta*	King performs a ritual procession of 14 stages.	Shem's 14-stage procession called the "Via Crucis."
Relighting the *Torc Caille*	Ritual bonfire is relit at the vernal equinox and proclaims ascendancy of one who lights it.	Saint Patrick lights the Paschal fire at Tara at the very moment the pagans expect the relighting of the *torc caille*.

The *Wakean* Inquest and the *Tarbh Feis* of Tara

A Summary of "The Inquest"

In the compendium of strange, dark, and ostensibly nonsensical episodes comprising the *Wake,* "The Inquest" (474–554) is certainly a contender for the most bizarre section of all. The central character in this segment, "Yawn," remains on his back in a trance the entire chapter. Yawn functions as a medium in a psychic investigation conducted by the Four Elders (who are also known as the Four Watchers), the strange scenario described by John Gordon: "the ventriloquial conductor . . . emitting a welter of different voices . . . a supine unconscious subject being observed from on high by watchers who arrive and begin to question him in an inquisition" (*Plot Summary,* 237–38). The theories offered for this episode include: a study of multiple personalities evoked through hypnosis and psychoanalysis; a re-creation of the nonrational dream-state; and a parody of a séance. A consideration of the key features of "The Inquest" certainly suggests elements appropriated from all of these theories.

Late at night, shortly before the Inquest, Shaun gorges himself in preparation for the strange upcoming events, recruiting his strength through meals comprised of "spadefuls" (405.30) of mounded food (405.29–30). The catalogue of Shaun's gorging extends for almost two pages; in his "Gastronomic Postscript," he concludes by thanking the Four Elders, telling them that he enjoyed their fine hot luncheon (456.1–2), the most tender "bully" (456.3) he ever ate—suggesting that Shaun's huge meal of "bully" was provided at the expense of the Four Elders. Shortly after his meal, Shaun requests an unusual gift from the Four, a coat made of animal hide, and notes that if the Four will buy him this "coat" (456.12) with the very best fur (456.12), he will certainly try to put it on (456.12); Shaun notes that the furry coat is in fairly good order (456.12–13), and no doubt it will "serve to turn" (456.13). Shaun gets his requested coat and decides to wear it "skinside out" (507.6).

At the beginning of the Inquest, Shaun, now called "Yawn," is lying supine on a mound at one of the most ancient boundaries in Ireland, the Eiscir Riada (475.22), a broken ridge of low hills extending from Dublin to Galway Bay, forming the traditional borderland between the "Half of Conn" and the "Half of Mug Nuadat" (a.k.a. Owen). Yawn is moaning in a "semiswoon" (474.11) and is met at this liminal location by the Four Elders, identified with the four Irish provinces and the four points of the compass: "three kings" (474.18) and a "crowner" (474.19), from all of their cardinal points (474.19). In the gloaming (474.21), the Four Elders hop it up the mountainous hill (474.22) to wonder at what class of a "crossroads puzzler" (475.3–4) Yawn would likely be, with one-half of him in Conn's half (475.6), but the other nevertheless in "Owenmore's" (475.7).

Leaning over and encircling the unconscious Yawn, the Four Elders chant a "sevenply sweat of night blues" (474.24–475.1): "Feefee! phopho!! foorchtha!!! aggala!!!! jeeshee!!!!! paloola!!!!!! ooridiminy!!!!!!!" (475.1–2), altogether a nightmarish incantation; each word of power permeates the body of Yawn and produces a reaction within him (475.11–18). The chanting has the cumulative effect of putting Yawn into a deeper level of trance. William York Tindall finds this strange singing perplexing, and suggestive of a magical incantation: "Although the first three of the seven words suggest a fearful giant, the sequence is puzzling. Of no common tongue, the words may be . . . like the 'nebrakada femininum' of *Ulysses* (242), the nonsense of a spell or incantation"; this septenary chant is "Hermetic enough to please a magician" (*Reader's Guide*, 2). Ian MacArthur cites the sources for the incantatory words, all evidently selected for their nightmarish connotations. In *Letters I*, (225–26) Joyce describes the seven-part chant as "words expressing nightmares": "feefee" (English, "fear"); "phopho" (Greek, φοβια, "phobia"); "foorchtha" (German, *Furcht*); "aggala" (Gaelic, *eagla*]; "jeeshee" (Japanese: *jishi*, meaning "a child," or "treachery"); "paloola" (from the Italian *paura*); and "ooridiminy" (Assyrian, the star group called the "gruesome hound") (MacArthur, "Textual Study," 92). Given the meanings of the seven words, the incantation is intended to induce fearful dreams and nightmares in the entranced subject.

The Four, much like the "watchers of Prospect" (476.11 [Prospect Cemetery; Latin *prospectus*, "distant view"]), are evidently satisfied with the result of their chanting. They take their places around Yawn and prepare to conduct an inquiry with their unconscious subject: a crack quadrature of stenographers they made (476.13–14), solons and psychometrists (476.14–15), with Yawn lying there (476.18–19), all "asprawl" (476.19).

The interrogation begins on page 477; and for nearly eighty pages the Four Watchers present the unconscious Yawn with dozens of questions about Irish history and mythology, future events, personal issues, and inquiries into his true identity. Yawn responds, but shortly into their inquest the Four arrive at an impasse with their increasingly recalcitrant subject, who begins to evade their line of questioning by speaking in pidgin and promising his assistance at a later time: "Me pigey savvy a singasong anothel time" (485.31–32). The Four refuse to accede to Yawn's tactics.

They put an end to his "sob story" (486.1) and demand to know his real name and other aspects of his identity (486.1–2). To acquire this knowledge, one of the Four produces a wand carved to resemble a snake with the head of a ram, a "serpe with ramshead" (486.21), explained by Campbell and Robinson as "a mystic symbol intended to stir . . . memory of the past" (*Skeleton Key*, 298). The Elder holding the wand touches the end of it to Yawn's temple (486.15), then to his lips (486.22), and then to his breast (486.29). Each touch of the wand evokes a different image: the images surface from increasingly deeper and older levels of consciousness. First, the wand evokes the era of Saint Patrick and Irish Christianity; then, "the pre-Christian period of Celtic warriors and myths, the age of Cuchulinn, Finn MacCool, and the Fairy Queens"; finally, the wand, also suggestive of a phallic monolith from pre-Celtic times, conjures "a simple age of semi-primitive agriculture and fertility dances" (*Skeleton Key*, 298). After the application of the serpentine talisman, Yawn becomes more cooperative; he continues, and discusses among other things the "triptych vision" (486.32) and the coming of Patrick.

The voice of a woman comes through (491.26), possibly Anna, and relates HCE's indiscretions. A ghostly voice, identified by the Four as an "earthpresence" (499.28), is asked about ancestors in a tumulus. After responding, the "earthpresence" tells the Four about the fall of the great king. Another entity, chanting Patrick's *Lorica*, breaks through (500.12). Shortly after "Patrick," Yawn returns (501.10). The Four, sifting through the maze of voices, understand they are on a search and seem to have their own strange agenda. "The inquisition of the inquisitive four" (as William York Tindall describes it) takes the forms of "a fishing, a hunting, a séance, a trial in court, an analysis in depth, and the sounding of an ocean" (253).

The interrogation continues. More voices, more entities, speak through Yawn, are dismissed and replaced by yet others. The controlled questioning deteriorates into argument between Yawn and the interrogators (520.27). At 522.26, Yawn informs the Four: "I have something inside of me talking to myself." The Four demand to hear this mysterious interlocutor (523.1). At this command, six of Yawn's invisible friends speak through him in succession (523). Next, a young woman (possibly Issy) speaks; then an older woman (possibly Kate) talks through the entranced subject (530.36). At this point in their inquest, Matt Gregory—the toughest interrogator of the Four—has had enough of the vociferous ramblings of this farrago of spirits. He abruptly ends the blathering of "Kate" and the other elemental spirits with the command: "All halt!" (531.27). Tired of this "finicking" (531.28) about Finn and fiddling with "faddles" (531.28–29), Gregory now demands a final "ballot" (531.29) to remove all doubt: by all the sylphs and salamanders, trolls and tritons (531.29–30), he means to tip the tap of this test at last (531.29–31). And the next voice from Yawn is that of a most powerful and regenerated HCE: "*E*ternest *c*ittas, *h*eil [ECH]!" (532.6). ECH announces that he is here once again (532.6–7), brought up through dynasties long out of print (532.7–8), and known throughout the world (532.9–10), by both saints and sinners alike (532.13–14), as a "cleanliving man" (532.16). The Four Elders allow this new voice, the new HCE, to continue speaking. The entity identifying himself as HCE or ECH explains to the Four the great civilization that he has previously founded (536–40). HCE states that he is the husband of the land (542–46). He recounts his conquest of, and mating with, the Sovereign (546–52). This is evidently both the response and the person that the Four are seeking. The Inquest comes to an abrupt halt. The Four, impressed with both the powerful entity and the dramatic story they have just heard, end the interrogation with a triumphant salutation to the new HCE: "Hoke!" (552.31–34 [German, "Heil!" "Hail!"]).

The Inquest at the Rites of Tara: The Tarbh Feis

The Inquest in the *Wake* has a strikingly close correlate in one of the most important Druidic rituals conducted during the Rites of Tara: the *Tarbh Feis*. Since both the new king and his legitimate succession originate in the Otherworld, identification and verification of the royal successor begin in the Otherworld as well. The Irish Druids formulated the *Tarbh Feis* to accomplish this goal.

The *Tarbh Feis* requires five people to perform: four senior Druids, called the "Four Watchers," and a younger man chosen for his mediumistic propensity. The young man is given a huge meal, usually beef (hence the name *Tarbh Feis*, "bull feast"), though some accounts suggest other meat as well. After gorging himself on this ritual meal, the man wraps himself in the hide of the slaughtered animal as a kind of protective psychic envelope. (Shaun puts his own animal coat on "skinside out against rapparitions" [507.6–7].) The man is brought to a boundary or threshold location, one of the liminal power spots typically selected by Druids for their rituals. Here, the Four Watchers, representing the four cardinal points of the compass and the four ancient provinces of Ireland, place the young man supine on the ground and arrange themselves around him "with the intention of forming a magic circle" (Ettlinger, 31). Next, the "four druids chanted over his body an *ór firindi*, or spell of truth" (*TB*, 238). Now in an entranced state, the sleeper would "commune with the Otherworld" (O'Rahilly, 325). A host of "invisible friends," a "swarm of dimunitive spirits," would then begin to speak through the mouth of the supine subject (Spence, 96–97). The *Tarbh Feis* is indeed a psychic investigation. The Four Watchers engage the "invisible friends" in an interrogation. Presenting questions and analyzing the Otherworldly responses, the Four seek verification for the identity of the legitimate successor to the throne of Ireland. R A.S. Macalister summarizes the entire ritual as it was conducted at the *Feis* of Tara: "Someone . . . glutted himself . . . then went to sleep. As he slept, four druids stood over his body, chanting a 'spell of truth.' The appointed king would appear to the sleeper amid the nightmares naturally induced by his overfed condition" (*T*, 130). Quite possibly, the "spell of truth" chanted by the Four Watchers carried with it "some hypnotic suggestion" (*T*, 130).

The *Tarbh Feis* is such an important and intrinsic component of the rites performed at the *Teamhur Feis* that quite a few renditions of the ritual have survived in the mythological texts. Eugene O'Curry cites, as a representative account, an excerpt from "The Story of Lughaidh Reo-derg":

> A meeting of the four great provinces of Erinn was held at this time (at Teamair) to see if they could find a person whom they could select. To whom they would give the sovereignty of Erinn; for they thought it ill that the Hill of Sovereignty of Erinn, that is Teamair, should be without the rule of a king in it; and they thought it ill that the people should be without the government of a king, to administer justice to them in all their territories. For the men of Erinn had been without the government of a monarch . . . until this great meeting of the four great provinces of Erinn, at Teamair of the kings. . . . There was a Bull-feast made by them there, in order that they might learn through it who the person was to whom they would give the sovereignty. This is the way in which that bull-feast was made, namely, a bull was killed, and one man ate enough of its flesh and its broth; and he slept under that meal; and a true oration was pronounced by four Druids upon him: and he saw in his dream the appearance of the man who would be made king of them, his countenance and description, and how he was occupied. The man screamed out of his sleep, and told what he had seen.[1]

P. W. Joyce cites an example of the *Tarbh Feis* in *The Book of the Dun Cow*: "A white bull was killed, and one man ate enough of its flesh, and drank of the broth: and he slept under that meal; and a spell of truth was chanted

Figure 2. Cernunnos with Rams-Headed Serpent. Graphic design by Mary Davis, Abita Springs, Louisiana.

over him . . . by four druids: and he saw in a dream the shape and description of the man who should be made king" (*SH* 1:245). In "The Destruction of Da Derga's Hostel," the *Tarbh Feis* is again used to determine the succession at Tara: "Then King Eterscel died. A bull-feast was prepared by the men of Erin in order to determine their future king; that is, a bull was killed by them and thereof one man ate his fill and drank its broth, and a spell of truth was chanted over him" (Cross and Slover, 97).

In conducting the *Tarbh Feis,* the Four Watchers would employ magical means to "delude the spirits" or even to elicit information from recalcitrant entities, living or dead (Spence, 96–97). In the *Wake,* when pidgin-tongued "Yawn" becomes evasive and refractory, one of the Four produces the wand carved like a "serpe with ramshead" (486.21). By touching the unconscious body with his wand, the Elder is able to educe information from the reluctant subject. This wand is decidedly Celtic. The serpent with ramshead motif is a symbol of power identified with the god Cernunnos ("The Horned One"). (A Pan-like deity associated with the cycle of regeneration, replete with horns and cloven feet, Cernunnos is usually portrayed holding a *torc* in one hand and the ramsheaded serpent in the other.) In Celtic tradition, such a wand was believed a powerful instrument helpful in facilitating the psychometric ability known as *teinm laegda.*

Cormac's Glossary describes the use of such a wand and the rite of *teinm laegda* as performed by the blind *Fili,* Lugaid, in the story of "Breccan's Cauldron" (a great whirlpool between Ireland and Scotland). Breccan had fifty currachs trading between Ireland and Scotland, until they fell into the whirlpool there; all were lost and their fate unknown. Lugaid, the Blind Poet, came to Bangor, was presented with a small skull found on the strand of Inver Bece, and was asked questions regarding its identity. Lugaid said, "Put the end of the poet's wand upon it." This was done, and the *Fili* then spoke: "The tempestuous water, the waters of the whirlpool, destroyed Breccan. This is the head of Breccan's dog; and it is little of great, for Breccan was drowned with his people in that whirlpool" (*Cormac's Glossary,* 41–42).

The "Commentary on the Introduction to the *Senchus Mór*" (the *Senchus Mór* is cited in the *Wake* at 397.31 and 398.23) defines the ritual use of the wand, describes its modus operandi, and offers the reason for the ritual's discontinuance:

> Before St. Patrick's time it [*teinm laegda*] was performed differently. At that time the *Fili* placed his staff on the person's body or head (*fors in colainn no fors in cend*) . . . and found his name . . . and discovered every unknown thing which was put to him (*co de nomaide do dala no tri*); and this is *teinm laegda* . . . for the same thing used to be revealed through them. . . . But Patrick abolished those things from among the poets, because they were heathen rites.[2]

In "The Inquest," Joyce's description of the "serpe with ramshead" wand, its application, and the results produced collectively provide a very accurate rendition of the ancient Druidic ritual of *teinm laegda.*

The overall purpose of the *Tarbh Feis* is to correctly identify the next king—the new manifestation of ECH—through his connections in the Otherworld. Once the identification is made, the Four finalize the ritual, as they do in the *Wake.* When the Four are satisfied that the new HCE has made contact with them, they close the event with a ritual salutation (sometimes referred to as the *Gairm Ríg*). At this point in the Rites of Tara, the ritual of *Tarbh Feis* is completed and the new king identified in the Otherworld—exactly as it is enacted in *Finnegans Wake.*

The *Wakean* Inquest contains all of the precise features required for the *Tarbh Feis* ritual conducted at the Rites of Tara: the huge meal, the mediumistic subject wrapped in animal skin, the Four Watchers associated with the cardinal points, the liminal location of the ritual, the nightmarish chant, the interrogation of spiritual entities by the Four Watchers, the magical wand with ram-headed serpent design, the goal of identifying the new king and the new ECH. Joyce's rendition of this ancient Druidic rite—a rite specifically and strongly identified with the *Teamhur Feis*—is, perhaps, the most complete performance of the *Tarbh Feis* in the entire corpus of Irish mythological lore. Joyce certainly understood the *Tarbh Feis* and its importance at the Rites of Tara; accordingly, he developed "The Inquest" into the longest single episode in *Finnegans Wake*.

Equine Rites at the *Wake* and the *Feis*

"Shaun's Dialogue"

The *Wake*'s important equine theme first appears in chapter 1 (with "Willingdone" falling off his horse) and culminates in chapter 17 (with HCE as Solsking the First riding triumphantly in royal procession). The most elaborate presentation of the theme, however, occurs in "Shaun's Dialogue" (403–28), where Shaun and the ass associated with the Four Elders present themselves in a surrealistic public performance.

At the beginning of the episode, the young man appears before the assembled Irish, dressed like an earl in all of the "correct wear" (404.16–17); his "correct wear" is the seven articles of different-colored clothing, the defining attire of the kings of ancient Ireland and the ever-present apparel of HCE. By assuming this traditional dress, Shaun is attempting to claim the role of his father, or, as William York Tindall states, "Shaun is becoming the new H.C.E." (223). In front of the crowd, Shaun gathers his strength

Figure 3. The White Horse at Uffington. Graphic design by Mary Davis, Abita Springs, Louisiana.

(405.29–30) through a meal whose main courses are a "stockpot dinner" (406.1), an "Irish stew" (406.11), and a "saddlebag steak" (406.10), with copious amounts of "broth" (406.13) included in the mix (406.13–14). After publicly gorging himself on meat and broth, the candidate engages in dialogue with the crowd. Shaun attempts to convince them of the legitimacy of his claim as successor to HCE. He asserts that he has the "permit" (409.10) as well as the "order" (409.10) to succeed HCE as the new royal messenger. Early in the proceedings, Shaun claims to act through divine authority, stating "there does be a power coming over me . . . from on high" (409.36–410.1). The Irish multitude is not convinced; and the episode takes the form of a test, with Shaun employing various strategies to convince the crowd of his claim as successor. Shaun explains that he is thinking from the "prophecies" (412.2), that he knows the sacred teachings of Ireland (409.27–28), and that he is the true royal successor, the next "tarabred" (411.22).

Much of this episode is related not by Shaun but by his curious and close associate in this chapter, the ass or donkey that belongs to the Four Elders. After viewing Shaun in his royal clothing, the animal comments on the archaic nature of the scene ("What a picture primitive!" [405.3]) and introduces himself as the "poor ass" (405.6), the "dunkey" (405.6–7) associated with the four tinkers (405.6–7). The ass then notes that Shaun in proper person stood before him (405.9–11); and the donkey then becomes integral to the entire interrogation of Shaun. The ass, now a plaintive "we," joins with the voice of the assembled Irish (404.7) to ask Shaun, "Who gave you the permit, the authority, to decree yourself 'king of the hill' and 'prophetic message bearer'?" (Gordon, *Plot Summary*, 222). The ass now assumes the roles of both speaker and interpreter for the remainder of Shaun's interrogation before the Irish throng.

Joyce's odd choice of a donkey as narrator has generated critical speculation on its role and purpose. The donkey, always in extremely close proximity to the young royal candidate, is an aspect of Shaun; Shaun's ass, as many have noted, is obviously a part of Shaun himself. In "The Complex Ass," Ian MacArthur notes that, although acting as both narrator and interpreter, the ass actually presents itself more as a spirit, a totemic presence, or a "familiar" (94). Blake Leland sees the thematic imagery of a new king, a mystical donkey, the Four Elders, and the assembled crowd in a primarily Christian interpretation. The new king, Jesus, enters Jerusalem upon an ass; the story appears in all four Gospels (the works of the Mamalujo quartet); and in Revelations, Jesus reappears upon the ass, now apotheosized into a white horse ("Complex Ass," 65). William York Tindall suggests an underlying association of the donkey with a pagan deity: the "Ass" associated with the Four is the Danish *as*, or "god" (330). Joyce himself comments on the donkey twice in the Buffalo Notebooks, where he calls it the "totem/ass" (VI.B.14.142), and, the "ass=caricature of a horse" (VI.B.41.123).

Collectively, the critical commentary suggests several important structural elements in this episode: cooking and eating, a claimant to a throne, a mystical or totemic ass or horse connected with both the king and the Four, and a crowd witnessing this event. The most notable structural detail in this episode, however, may be that the entire event occurs with Shaun, along with his ass, standing near—or even in—a vat or cauldron half-filled with liquid. Shaun calls this vessel a barrel (414.13) and later identifies his barrel as the "holy kettle" (426.29) and himself in it as the "waterlogged king of Eire" (414.20). Shaun's appearance before the Irish multitude, his feast of meat and broth, the entire argument for his claim as successor, and the narration of the ass all occur while the two are in or near the "holy kettle." And as surrealistic and bizarre as this episode is, it has a very close correlate in the rituals performed at pagan Tara.

The Totem Horse and the Holy Kettle at Tara

In the series of investiture and inaugural rites conducted at the *Teamhur Feis*, one of the most colorful of these events dramatized the magical connection between the royal candidate and the horse, the totem animal of Irish kings, through a ritual "cooking" of the man and beast. Cooking renders that which is raw, unusable, wild, and even dangerous into that which is accessible, usable, nourishing and safe. Cooking is thus a transformative act, capable not only of changing the nature of that which is cooked, but also of merging or blending that which was separate and immiscible when "raw." "Cooking"—in the sense of a magical process of metamorphosis—plays a key role in the making of an Irish king.

The candidate, a "raw" mortal, must be rendered into a suitable vessel for the "Great Horseman," who will invest the human with the authority of divine kingship. The young candidate must also blend with the totem animal of ECH, the horse. If the "raw" candidate fails to unite with the horse deity, he cannot be king. Accordingly, a "cooking" test is used to determine the legitimacy of the candidate's claim to royal succession.

In front of the crowd assembled for the *Feis*, a large cauldron is positioned. A horse is led in, slaughtered, and the parts placed in the cauldron and cooked. Then the young male claimant to the throne comes before the Four Elders and the assembly, and he too is placed into the holy kettle. While standing in the warm liquid, he then gorges himself on this "stockpot dinner"—the meat and broth of his totem animal—and merges with the spirit of the horse. As Shaun describes it, "there does be a power coming over me . . . from on high"; and it is this power—the totemic horse spirit—that speaks through him now. If the candidate fails the test, he is rejected as the prophetic messenger from the Otherworld. If successful, he may become the next waterlogged king of Eire.

This exact ritual is described by Giraldus Cambrensis (named in the *Wake* as old "Marsellas Cambriannus" [151.31–32]), the Welsh chronicler and anti-Irish propagandist, who compiled his *Chronicle of Ireland* in the late twelfth century. Touring Ireland circa 1185, Giraldus claims to have witnessed the Irish perform "a most barbarous and abominable rite in creating their king." In his short descriptive essay entitled "Of a New and Monstrous Way of Inaugurating Their Kings," Giraldus first apologizes for the "filthy story" he is about to relate and then explains, "what is shameful in itself may be related by pure lips and decent words." He then goes on to describe the very same "filthy story" presented by James Joyce in the *Wake*: the assembly of paganistic Irish, the holy kettle placed before them, the presentation of the young candidate for kingship, the totemistic horse associated with Four Elders, the "cooking" of both man and horse in the cauldron, the feast of meat and broth, the "unrighteous rites" necessary to determine the legitimate succession.[3]

Within the course of the last century, however, most Irish scholars reviewing Giraldus have reached a consensus that this report was not the eyewitness account that Giraldus claims, nor did this rite even occur during his tour of Ireland, and should therefore be considered spurious at best. Nonetheless, R.A.S. Macalister argues that there is a foundation of truth in the old account, and the basis for the tale can be found in the inaugural rites at Tara. Giraldus, according to Macalister, reports strictly "from hearsay evidence, and has erred in assuming that the rites were still maintained in his own time" (*T*, 131). Even so, the inauguration rite as Giraldus reports it is "too complete, too much in accordance with similar practices elsewhere, necessarily unknown to Giraldus, to have been the fruit of his not over-nice imagination" (*T*, 132). The conclusion Macalister presents is that Giraldus actually reports a ritual conducted not in his lifetime, but an investiture rite practiced much earlier—at pagan Tara.

Figure 4. Inauguration of an Irish King. From the *Topographia Hiberniae* and *Expugnatio Hibernica* by Giraldus Cambrensis. Courtesy of the National Library of Ireland.

The Chariot of Kingship

During the *Teamhur Feis,* the royal candidate had further encounters with horses. One rite, called *Carpat Na Flatha,* is also a test for kingship and focuses on the equestrian abilities of the king or his successor. The human representative of the Great Horseman certainly must live up to his appellation. The king must prove himself an able horseman and master of his totem animals—either by riding them or maintaining control over them while driving the royal chariots—hence *Carpat Na Flatha,* "Chariot of Kingship."

In the *Wake,* three short episodes reenact the important aspects of *Carpat Na Flatha.* At the *Teamhur Feis,* the king is required to ride horses as a symbol of his authority and test of his power: "Failure to control them would in all probability mean death: perhaps the victim in such a case would himself serve as a fertility sacrifice" (*T,* 133). In the "Museyroom" episode, the central event described by Kate is the fall of the "king," "Willingdone," off his big "wide harse" (8.21 [white horse, wide arse]). The leader's great fall off the horse is presented as his Waterloo. In accordance with the Rites of Tara, his failure to control the horses does indeed lead to his death as a fertility sacrifice.

When "The Inquest of Shaun" reaches its conclusion and the Four Watchers hail the new king (552.31–34), the regenerated HCE boasts that from his "vongn" (554.2 [Danish, *vogn,* "carriage"]), his "tilburies" (554.2), "noddies" (554.2), "shays" (554.1), and gigs (554.2)—all two-wheeled horse-drawn carriages (that is, chariots)—he controls all the horses of the realm. With his whip and through his power, he makes all the horses obey. Through his commands, they parade and dance for the pleasure and amusement of his sovereign lady: Clydesdales with Arabian steeds (553.35), madly ridden mustangs (553.36–554.1), aggressive bucking broncos (554.1), mule, hinny and jennet (554.5), mustard hued nag and piebald Shetlands (554.5–6), all stepped lively for her pleasure (553.35–554.9).

Finally, in one of the climactic scenes in the *Wake*, the exultant HCE as Solsking the First (607.28) impresses and astounds the Irish crowd when he enters the festival triumphantly astride a horse: HCE may be "humpy" (606.34), he may be "dumpy" (606.34), but there is something "racey" (606.35) about this sailor on the horse (606.34–35); as soon as the crowd sees him they get a "sprise!" (606.34–36). In the *Wake*, as at the Rites of Tara, the Great Horseman has once again arrived.

The Mantle Test and "The Story of the Sailor and Tailor"

Salient Features of "The Story of the Sailor and Tailor"

"The Story of the Sailor and Tailor" (311.5–332.9), also known as "The Norwegian Captain's Tale" and "Kerse and the Sailor," is one of the most obscure episodes in the *Wake*. The story, described by Joyce as a "wordspiderweb" (*Letters III*, 422, note 1), occurs in the middle of the *Wake*, probably narrated by a very inebriated HCE late at night in his tavern crowded with drunken customers (the Twelve Morphios and the Four Elders). HCE weaves his tale through his own intoxicated meanderings, with frequent asides from the customers, and with overlaying broadcasts from the radio playing in the background.

In HCE's tale, a young sailor (that is, the youthful HCE, renewed from sailing to *Tir na Nog*) inquires of a shipping agent as to where he can acquire a rightfully deserved and well-fitting suit. The context and nature of his question imply that the "suit" (311.22) he seeks is at once a suit of clothes, a marriage suit, and a legal suit, a legitimate pursuance to an undisclosed claim. The sailor is directed to the old tailor, Kerse, a version of the older and failing HCE, who is presented as the representative of the ancient firm of Ashe and Whitehead or "white hat" (322.1).

Campbell and Robinson identify the Whitehead and ("white hat") with Finn MacCool in his initial encounter with the high king at Tara; the allusion to Finn suggests the young hero about to overthrow the old. As a boy of fifteen, Finn proved himself superior to many older athletes in a hurley match at Tara. The king, present at the match, notes the superiority of the boy and cries, "Who is that *fin cumhal* ["white cap"]?" (*Skeleton Key*, 206). The "Ashe" too, has significance to Tara and kingship. The *bile*—the sacred Yggdrasil of the Irish—was an ash tree, and one such *bile* at Tara was used in the inaugural rites of the new king. The young sailor meets with Kerse for his "suit," and the tailor makes a model (he drew out the "moddle" [311.7]) of a close-fitting "jerkin" (311.7). At this initial meeting an agreement, a suit, is made between the two (311.21–23). The sailor leaves, like the Prankquean, on a distant and cyclical journey of forty days.

For the second "tryon" (320.18) of the jerkin, the sailor journeys back from his "dhruimadhreamdhrue" (320.21 [Irish, *druim a` dhreama dhruadha*, "The Ridge of the Druids"; "dream come true"]). The sailor meets with the tailor and they argue over the fitting of the jerkin. The sailor tries on the suit and it is so close-fitting and strange-looking that it completely changes his identity—his own "fitther" (322.12 [fitter, father]) would not even know him (322.12–13). After much quarreling (and through various overlays), the old tailor, tired of fighting the young sailor over the suit, proposes peace through the union of the contenders. The "nowedding" (325.27) captain gets his close-fitting suit and is then permitted to marry the young and beautiful daughter of the old tailor. The daughter is the Sovereign goddess "Banba" (325.24); Banba's breasts are her "soilers" (325.24 [farmers, sailors, soil]) and her "toilers" (325.24 [workers, tailors]). "Banba" is another name for Ana; her "breasts" are also the "Paps of Ana" (two hills near Killarney).

As part of the wedding service, the sailor, wearing his new and tight-fitting suit, undergoes a ritual baptism that is also part of his inauguration ceremony. The baptizer "pured" (326.5) the "ouishguss" (326.5 [water]) over HCE to "popetithes" (326.6) him unconditionally, as the "*h*ero *c*hief *e*xplunderer" (326.9 [HCE]) of all the "clansakiltic" (326.9); and from this "douche" (326.11) the royal pledge was given (326.5–14).

All the "pukaleens" (325.11–12 [Irish, *buachaillin*, "young men"; and "little pukers"]) at the wake (326.12) are also part of the great wedding feast of Eire, the "Eriweddyng" (327.32–33) celebrated near the Stone of Destiny, the *Lia Fail* ("liamstone" [331.4]), the sacred tree (331.5), and the great Assembly-mound (331.18). The pukaleens comment on the significance of the upcoming marriage: the entire "Thingavalley" (328.27 [Thing at the valley, that is, Assembly at Tara]) knows that their "raptist bride" (328.28) is their "aptist breed" (328.29), who is nothing less than their own "fiery quean" (328.31), upon the night of the "making" (328.32).

On the night of the making of the king, the "Eriweddyng," not just the pukaleens, but the famous residents of Tara, the ancient stars of Macpherson's *Temora*, are included among the celebrants at the royal wedding feast. Cannmathon and Cathlin sing together (329.14–15); and surly Tuhal smiles upon dear Dar-Thula (329.16–17), while Roscranna's man beguiles the daughter of Cormac (329.17–18). The wedding is an awfully posh (329.28–29) jubilee (329.30), with enough noise, license, and mirth (329.19) to bring down the "rain of Tarar" (329.14–35 [rain and thunder, reign of terror, reign of Tara])—the "grandest bethehailey" (329.35–36) ever seen or heard on earth (329.35–36).

The story of Sailor and Tailor concludes with the royal couple finally united in matrimony (until "deaf do his part" [321.5]). Both partners gain through marriage that which they each desired when single: he got a "berth" (330.28)—a home, a lover, a birth into a new life; she got a "ménage" (330.28)—a bed, a man, and a ménage. The narrator observes in conclusion: "Such was the act of goth" (332.10) amidst the "fiounaregal games of those oathmassed fenians" (332.26–27).

Critical Assessments of the Story

Campbell and Robinson, among others, have remarked upon the purposeful theme of birth/rebirth that runs through the tale, and note references to Thomas Carlyle's *Sartor Resartus*, with its clothing imagery and rebirth theme, woven into "The Sailor and Tailor" text. Campbell and Robinson also recognize in this *Wakean* tale the ancient idea that clothes "represent the material sheaths," which the immortal soul assumes as part of the process of incarnation (*Skeleton Key*, 199). The *Wakean* sailor, floating in a salty sea for forty days (the symbolic gestation period) until he gets his close-fitting and highly personalized suit, can then be baptized—all part of the "berth" (330.28) he so strongly desires and attains.

According to Richard Ellmann, the core and origin of the "Kerse and the Sailor" story is an anecdote that John Joyce told about a Norwegian captain "who ordered a suit from a Dublin tailor, J. H. Kerse of 34 Upper Sackville Street. The finished suit did not fit him, and the captain berated the tailor for being unable to sew, whereupon the irate tailor denounced him for being impossible to fit" (*JJII*, 23). Not surprisingly, James Joyce reported a completely different source to another researcher. In December 1936, Joyce reported on the Norwegian Captain episode and said it was "chiefly or in great part about—Gideon, (Book of Judges, chap. 6, verse 36 et seq.)" (*Letters III*, 393). The dash [—] before "Gideon" was meant to emphasize the name that was almost identical with that of his correspondent, Carola

Giedion-Welcker. Joyce did in fact use almost all of the incident taken from the Book of Judges; these additions "served to make the tangled tale of sailors and tailors and ship's husbands and brides and customers more confusing and intractable than it had been up to that time" (Senn, 25).

In the Book of Judges, Gideon uses his cloak as a test of divine sanction; the cloak will verify his divine right to assume the leadership of the Israelites:

> 37: Behold, I [Gideon] will put a fleece of wool in the floor, and if the dew be on the fleece only, and it be dry upon all the earth beside, then shall I know that thou wilt save Israel by mine hand, as thou hast said.
>
> 38: And it was so: for he rose up early in the morrow, and thrust the fleece together, and wringed the dew out of the fleece, a bowl full of water.

Fritz Senn, in "Seeking a Sign," has identified nearly all of the phrases in the above biblical passage in Joyce's story, mostly in the form of very short passages excerpted from Gideon and then woven into the "Sailor and Tailor" yarn. Senn demonstrates that the primary connection between both tales is the garment itself, its association with a wedding, and its explicit usage as a test and signifier of divine sanction. A fleece can be a primitive kind of garment, and as such it fits well in the story about a tailor. The fleece in the story also conveys a sexual meaning, especially when it is "assatiated with their wetting" (314.33 [associated with their wedding, satiated with their wedding, saturated with their wetting]). For Gideon, however, "the fleece is a convenient means to arrive at certainty, to make sure that the sanction is divine" (Senn, 28–29). In the Douay Bible, Gideon says, "I try once more, seeking a sign in the fleece" (6:39); and the Vulgate has it as "signum quarens in vellere" ("seeking a sign in the fleece"). As Senn notes, "a fleece, in this context, is what might justly and functionally be called a 'signifier,' if ever there was one" (28–29).

The Cloak of Kingship at the Teamhur Feis

Joyce's strange signifier of divine sanction, the close-fitting suit that leads its wearer to baptism and marriage, to kingship of the Clans-a-Keltic and a new birth, has a very strong correlate in the Irish rite known as *Casal Ríg*, "The Cloak of Kingship." Before the candidate for kingship could undergo the *Baisteadh Geinntlidhe* (a ritual of baptism) and the *Banais Righe* (marriage to the queen), "a mantle was put upon him which was required to be close-fitting" (*TB*, 334). The *Casal Ríg* was a test of divine sanction: if the cloak did not fit, if it were either too loose or too tight, the candidate was rejected as king and consort of the queen. If the garment fit snugly, his suit for marriage and kingship was honored, and he could then be baptized and married, and was considered reborn into the life of king and consort.

Rebirth is the central theme of the *Casal Ríg* drama. Immediately before the ceremony at the stones of Blocc and Bluicne [Tara megaliths named after the Twins], the candidate "had to put on a mantle which, if it were too large, would disqualify him from office" (*T*, 134). The mantle "had to be close-fitting: and we see in this an obvious representation of the pre-natal life" (*T*, 134). The mantle cannot be regarded as merely a ceremonial robe, "for it is put on before the rebirth rite: and in any case a ceremonial robe would be more likely to be full and flowing" (*T*, 134).

The ritual drama of *Casal Ríg* at the Rites of Tara was, as in the *Wake*, conducted publicly before all the oath-massed Fianna, "pukaleens," and nobility assembled on the ridge of the Druids, all gathered for the big wedding party later. Appropriately, Joyce places the *Wakean Casal Ríg* near the *Lia Fail*, the "liamstone," that also plays a key role in the rites of royal inauguration.

HCE's Portal to a New World

Throughout the *Wake* are recurring images of ancient portals: a rift of biblical proportions between rending rocks, a secretive hole in an old wall, the small cleft between megalithic standing stones, a door or gate guarded by Twin porters. The portals are all associated with HCE, and in the context of their presentation imply challenge and danger in their traversal. HCE's passage through these perilous thresholds is an act associated with themes of rebirth, Easter, initiation, and the transition from the old world to the new.

One manifestation of these perilous portals are the rending rocks; and allusions to "Rendningrocks" (258.1) appear throughout the *Wake*: "ragnor rocks" (19.04); the "renting of his rock" (88.26); "Rocknarrag" (221.23); "Rock rent" (221.32); "rages rocked" (227.21); "Rendningrocks roguesreckning reigns" (258.01); "ragnowrock rignewreck" (416.36); "rackinarockar" (424.22); "rocked of agues, cliffed for aye!" (505.17). "Ragnarok" is the twilight of the pagan gods, heralding the end of their world. The "rocks rent" is a direct allusion to Matthew 27:51: "the earth did quake and the rocks rent." The cleft in the rocks enacts the split between the Old and New Dispensations, which at that very moment was occurring on the Cross at Golgotha. The coalescence of the pagan and Christian terms—Ragnarok and "rocks rent"—suggests the clash of pagan and Christian realms, the death of one and birth of the other, the rift between these realms occurring at, or connected with, Easter.

The portal appears again as an ancient megalithic gate at HCE's tavern. In the "drema" (69.14) of Saorstát Éireann (69.14–15), a "stonehinged gate" (69.15), which was also an "iron gape" (69.24) was, by ancient custom, left open (69.14–24). The gate was locked on HCE on purpose (69.25–27) by his two faithful "poorters" (69.26) in order keep HCE inside (69.26) in case he [HCE] felt like sticking his chest out too far, and tempting "providence" (69.28) by a stroll on the people's "eggday" (69.27–29). In this dream-drama of the Free State of Ireland, there is an ancient gate, "gape," or gap between standing stones (like Stonehenge); and the "gape" between these ancient stones is guarded by "poorters," the Twins acting as threshold guardians. On Easter, HCE is challenged by the porters from traversing the gape—going through this portal is, for HCE, tantamount to tempting providence or testing divine authority.

In this same section of the *Wake*, the portal appears as the "Hole in the Wall," the pub located on the boundary of Phoenix Park. The house is located near a turnstile ("turn wheel") at a "wallhole"; the turnstile, the original "stonehinged" gate, connects HCE's garden with Phoenix Park. To this side of the house are the remains of a stone wall with gate and railings. The turnstile is set in a hole in that part of the park wall, which is within the confines of the garden to the house. The pub has long been known as the Hole in the Wall (Rose, 15). Easter weekend, late at night after the wake, HCE, dead or dead drunk, passes through the Hole in the Wall and enters his youthful rebirth into the Otherworld. Here too, the portal suggests the transition to another realm and also conveys the rebirth theme intrinsic to Easter.

During the Trial of Festy King, detailed evidence is given concerning the portal located in ancient Ireland and guarded by two porters called Camellus and Gemellus. The occasion is "wildfires night" (90.9–10) on all the hills and tumuli (90.9–10). The portal is called "Guinney's Gap" (90.13–14), located in the middle of the "garth" (90.15 [enclosed yard]) of the mountain fortress of the god king, Saturn (90.15–17). "Camellus" (90.18) tells "Gemellus" (90.18) that HCE "mustn't touch it" (90.15), alluding to the "whole in the wall" (90.21–22) and "eluding from the whole of the woman" (90.22–23). "Wildfires night" on the hills and tumuli suggests a Celtic seasonal festival. "Guinney's Gap" refers to the Ginnungagap of Nordic paganism, the rift between different worlds and ages; to negotiate the Ginnungagap is equivalent to rebirth into a new world. "Camellus" and "Gemellus" are famous porters at Tara; Camellus and Gemellus stood on either side of the main portal of "Saturn's mountain fort," the Assembly Hall of the god-king at Tara, allowing only the designated participants into the royal wrath where many of the Rites were conducted. The "whole of the woman" indicates the birth symbolism suggested in passage through the portal. The warning that whoever goes through the opening "mustn't touch it" suggests danger, risk, or taboo involved in the act itself.

The Portals at the Teamhur Feis

The *Wakean* portals—ancient and "stonehinged," guarded by Twins, dangerous to traverse, implying a test of divine sanction, symbolically representing birth into a new age—collectively provide an accurate rendition of the "Test of Blocc and Bluicne" conducted during the Rites of Tara. "Blocc" and "Bluicne" were originally a version of the Tara Twins and guardians of portals at Tara. Later, these Twin porters gave their names to two standing stones placed close together near the king's hall. As a divine sanction of his legitimacy, the king had to undergo the Test of Blocc and Bluicne: he must pass through the cleft between the stones or crawl through a "hole in the ground," an "opening in a rock," or a "space between two objects set close together" (*T*, 133–34). The king must not touch the sides of the rending rocks; for him to do so suggests divine rejection. If he succeeds, he is reborn into a new dispensation. This ritual test at the Rites of Tara was performed as "a test for legitimacy" and as "a test of worthiness" for the kingship; if successful, "the candidate is regarded as being reborn into a new world" (*T*, 133–34). The physical description of the Test of Blocc and Bluicne at Tara, its Twin porter guardians, its performance on the occasion of a Celtic seasonal festival, the sense of taboo and risk involved in traversing the cleft, and the themes of rebirth and divine sanction associated with successful passage of the cleft, are all in total accord with the portal theme in the *Wake*.

Immediately before the Ricorso, Luke Tarpey (one of the Four Elders) reports that at the "folkmood" (590.16 [the pagan Assembly at Tara]), HCE, once again dressed in his royal septenary colors (590.7–8), has triumphantly passed this final test of kingship: HCE's last "tryon" (590.9) was to march through the "grand tryomphal arch" (590.9–10). In his next scene in the *Wake*, HCE awakes and begins his life anew, reborn into a new dispensation.

Banais Righe: The Wedding at the *Wake*

Marriage Rites of the Triple Goddess

As with other significant names and concepts in Irish mythology, the pagan *Filidh* have provided more than one etymology for the word *feis*: *festum* (Latin, "feast," "festival") and *foaid* (Irish, "to spend the night with"). Together, they indicate one of the central purposes of the *Feis*: the inaugural rites that culminate in the marriage of the king and Sovereign. At the *Feis* of Tara, the defining rite in this inaugural cycle is the *Banais Righe*, the "wedding feast of kingship"—the union of king and Sovereign.

The specific events comprising the "wedding feast of kingship" are strongly associated with fundamental characteristics of the Sovereign goddess herself. True to her triune nature, three dimensions of the goddess play key roles in the *Banais Righe*. The Sovereign manifests through the consort of the king; she is also a mystical and intoxicating liquid—Mead, Red Ale, *Dergflaith*—that is the essence of sacrality and regal power at Tara; and she is the source of this mystical liquid itself, the well, spring, or sacred vessel identified with the Sovereign. A royal candidate cannot become king until he is united with the Sovereign in all of these manifestations; and only through their complete union is legitimate kingship conferred.

Accordingly, the specific rites of the *Banais Righe* enact the union of the king with the Sovereign in these three aspects: the drink, the well, and the female identified with both. The king performs the initial rite of *Banais Righe* by imbibing the sacred and intoxicating liquid, *Dergflaith*, shortly before assuming his throne in the royal hall, *Tech Midchuarta*, "The House of the Circulation of Mead." The second event, also performed in the *Tech Midchuarta*, is the actual sexual union of king and Sovereign. The act of coition was legally required for the inauguration to be valid; therefore, a few important witnesses were usually present to verify the consummation of the marriage—much like the tradition of employing official witnesses at royal marriages in other parts of Western Europe. The third component of the *Banais Righe* was the *Baisteadh Geinntlidhe*, a ritual immersion or baptism of the newly made king in the well, river, or spring identified with the goddess. These rites were "regenerative as they took place at the critical times of seasonal transition" and were "central to the rite of inauguration of kings that ritualized the periodic renewal of the earth as divine mother and queen of the king" (Brenneman and Brenneman, 22).

The mythic paradigms for the rites of *Banais Righe* can be found in the inaugural myths associated with the kings of Tara. In *Baile in Scál,* Conn of the Hundred Battles unites with *Dergflaith,* the drink, the great cauldron that is its source, and the beautiful goddess who proffers the sacred liquid to the future king. Niall, before he is the famous "Niall of the Nine Hostages" (or as Joyce calls him, "Mrs. Niall of the Nine Corsages" [96.4–5]), travels deep into a forest during a hunting trip to fetch water. He finds a sacred well, but a loathly crone owns it and guards it carefully. She offers a cup of her water to Niall on the condition that they engage in sex. Niall complies with her demand, and during this act she transforms into a beautiful goddess. The goddess offers her cup of liquid to Niall. She identifies herself as the Sovereign and proclaims Niall the next high king of Ireland. Sovereignty, sexuality, and the drink *Dergflaith* converge at the sacred well of the goddess who bestows kingship.

In a third inaugural myth, as told in "The Second Battle of Moytura," the emphasis is placed on the acts of sexual union and ritual immersion. In this version of *Banais Righe,* the Dagda finds the Morrigan straddling her river. Significantly, her hair is braided into nine distinctive tresses. The Dagda approaches the river goddess, and while immersed in the river the two engage in sex. The Dagda thus becomes the prototype of high kings, and this key moment of union between the All-Father and Mother Ana is "the model for the inauguration ritual of chieftains that occurred at the center of the world (Tara) with the guardian of the spring, the lady" (Brenneman and Brenneman, 31–32). The straddling of the river by the goddess symbolizes the waters of life flowing from her womb, thus presenting her as the source, or the spring, as well as the mother goddess. The nine tresses identify her as the supreme form of the Celtic Triple Goddess and correspond to the nine hazel trees of Segais, the well at the center of the Otherworld. The thrice-three tresses also indicate that she is possessor of the complete wisdom and power of the Triple Goddess, Maiden, Mother, and Crone (Brenneman and Brenneman, 31–32).

This ninefold power of the goddess, known as the *Toradh* of Ana, is especially potent at wells and springs. The specific components of the *Toradh* are described in "Nine Gifts of the Cauldron":

The Cauldron of Life-Work
gives and is replenished,

promotes and is enlarged,
nourishes and is given life,
ennobles and is exalted,
requests and is filled with answers,
sings and is filled with song,
preserves and is made strong,
arranges and receives arrangements,
maintains and is maintained.
Good is the well of measure.[4]

The immersion in a water source sacred to Ana unites the king with the Sovereign, allowing him to receive the nine gifts of Ana, the ultimate power of sovereignty, the *Toradh*.

Wakean *Analogues to the Rites of* Banais Righe

The three rites comprising the *Banais Righe* of the *Teamhur Feis*—ritual drinking, royal coition, ninefold immersion—are all reenacted in the *Wake*. Late at night, HCE, the "mannork" (378.6) of Ireland, circulates through the mead hall and imbibes all the sacred firewater before he sits upon his throne. As the eminent king of all Ireland himself (380.19–20), HCE goes "heeltapping" (381.9) around his own royal table (381.8–9) with the midnight thirst upon him (381.24–27), "reemyround" (381.30) the room to imbibe whatever surplus dregs and rotgut were left (381.28–32). After his circulation through the mead hall and his copious drinking, HCE, like his ancestors (382.14) in the "Taharan dynasty" (380.17–22), slumps onto his "throne" (382.26).

When HCE awakens the next morning in bed with Anna, they find themselves in the "House of the cedarbalm of mead" (558.26–35 [House of the Circulation of Mead])—exactly as they should for the sexual rite of *Banais Righe*. In this "Chamber scene" (559.1–584.25), HCE and Anna unite sexually; and as in the old ritual at Tara, the entire event is witnessed and noted by several official observers. The description of this act (provided by the official observers) indicates that the sexual rite is successful. Once again, the king and the land are one: HCE's huge buttocks merge with the land itself, specifically, part of Phoenix Park. The Four Elders, with a profusely fine bird's-eye view from "beauhind" (564.6–7), note that "Finn his park" (564.8) is the admiration of all (564.8–9) with its straight road down the center that "bisexes" (564.11) the entire park itself (564.10). The largest of its kind in the world (564.11–12), the park is tufted in many places (564.15–16) and is enlivened throughout by "gentlemen's seats"

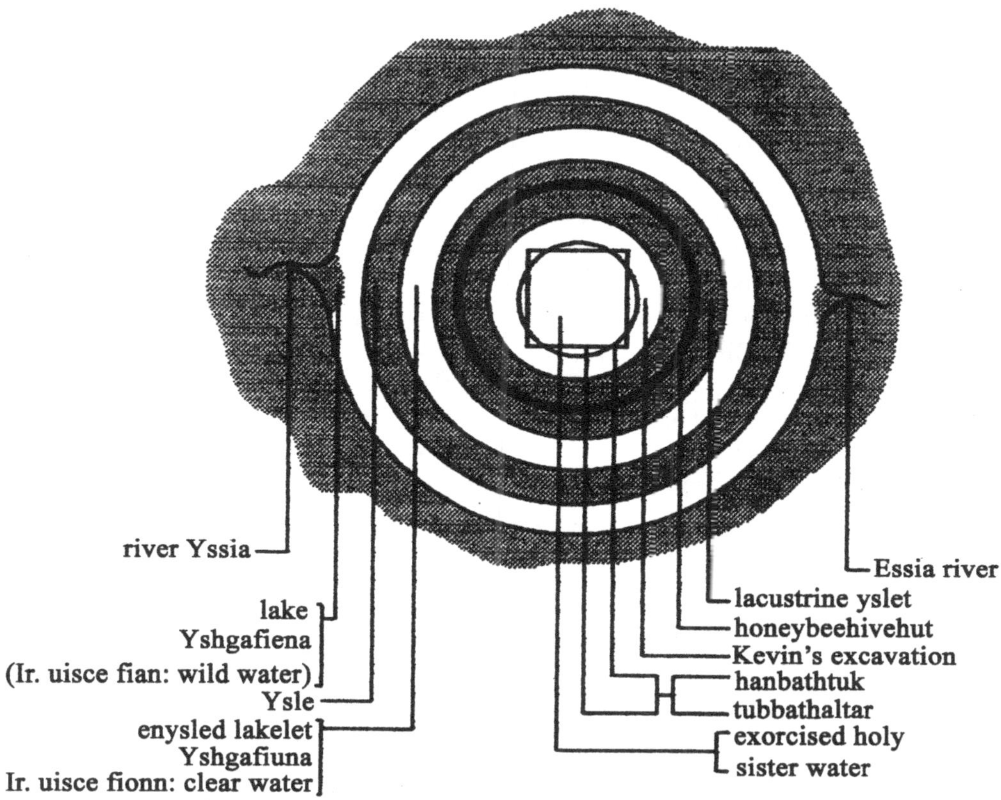

Figure 5. The Nine Waters of Anna. Illustration by Simon Evans for his essay "The Ultimate Ysland of Yreland." Courtesy of Gilliland Press.

(564.6–17). When their consummation rite is (more or less) concluded, HCE and Anna are presented as the new royal couple with their official entourage. In their royal sleeping chamber, the court goes into their morning session (566.7) with the Four Seneschals, Beefeater Sackerson, the Twelve Chief Barons, the Twenty-Eight Bride's Maids (who are all festooned in bright colors), the First Mother (acting as Dame Dowager), along with the Two Princes, and Isabella, who is requested to "do obeisance" (566.23) to the First Father (566.6–25).

The concluding rite of *Banais Righe*, immersion in the ninefold *Toradh* of Ana, occurs in the Ricorso, where, as William York Tindall notes, Saint Kevin plays the role of "the regenerated HCE" (315). HCE, in a sacred cauldron filled with "translated" (606.3–4 [sanctified]) water, immerses himself in the nine waters of the goddess.

The goddess, in her "well understanding" (606.1), fills the cauldron, the "tubbathaltar" (606.2), to its mid height (606.1–2); and therein, the blessed HCE is "ninthly enthroned" (606.3) in the center of the translated water (606.1–4). In this "sate of wisdom" (606.6–7), and through the primal sacrament of ritual baptism (606.10–11), the renewed king continuously meditates on the regeneration of all mankind through ritual "affusion" (606.11) in sanctified water (606.6–12).

Simon Evans, in "The Ultimate Ysland of Yreland," demonstrates that Kevin/HCE, while immersed in his "tubbathaltar," is actually in the center of a series of concentric circles of water—all feminine, all manifestations of the goddess—and the pattern of concentric water circles is ninefold, hence the "ninthly enthroned" (605.03) baptism of the regenerated HCE (b). If Kevin's water is "translated" into pagan terms, his baptism is a very accurate account of immersion and union with the *Toradh* of Ana.

The *Deisil* of *Tech Midchuarta* and the *Wakean* "Via Crucis"

The Deisil: *The Ritual Procession at Tara*

The *Deisil*, one of the oldest ceremonies performed at the Tara *Feis*, is a ritual procession, a form of sympathetic magic, performed at the Rites by the king. As an act of union between the sun god and the land, the king completes a solar-oriented and clockwise (that is, deosil) circumambulation around the realm he is to "husband" and govern. Since the king of Tara was considered the ruler of all Ireland, the *Deisil* procession at Tara was symbolic. The *Deisil* was not performed around the entire circumference of Ireland; rather, the king performed the rite by circumambulating Tara Hill or, more likely, the royal hall upon it, the House of the Circulation of Mead, which was, in itself, deliberately designed as the microcosm of the entire island. The name of the hall even suggests the ceremony of the *Deisil*: "Mead" is the name for both the Sovereign and her drink, indicating the concept of *Dergflaith* intrinsic to kingship. "Circulation" suggests sharing Mead within the hall as well as the ritual circumambulation around it. These deliberate polysemes connected with the royal hall at Tara thus suggest the king bonding with the realm of the goddess at the symbolic center of the land. The idea of this ritual is that through the power of proximity and relationship, the one who circumambulates takes in the power of that which is circumambulated, and vice versa. Thus the *Deisil* establishes a magical bond between the king and the center—"exactly what transpires in the Irish king's inauguration" (Brenneman and Brenneman, 34).

The power acquired by the king through the *Deisil* procession was understood to be comprised of fourteen separate attributes. The *Senchus Mór* (397.31) delineates these fourteen qualities necessary for a great leader:

> Honesty and dignity,
> daily work, genealogy,
> *imbas forosnai* and *dichetal,*
> *anamain* ["inspired verse"] and judgement,
> *teinm laegda* and ocean of song,
> purity of hand and of marriage,
> purity of lips and of study.[5]

These regal qualities were integral to the design of the *Tech Midchuarta* itself, symbolically represented as the fourteen portals of entry to the royal hall:

> In chathir gríanach glan-sin
>   fledach fianach co fondsib,
> inde fri soichli solus
>   dá secht ndorus de dorsib.
>
> [This sunny shining citadel,
> festive, martial, with cask-staves,
> therein, amid radiant hospitality,
> were doors twice seven in number.][6]

R.A.S. Macalister suggests that the ritual circuit, when actually performed at Tara, was not simply a mere circular walk; rather, the *Deisil* was more in the nature and pattern of a Celtic spiral or labyrinth. Macalister cites a petroglyph of an ancient Irish labyrinth found near Tara that he believes outlines the pattern of the royal circuit and is the symbol of the *Deisil* itself. The evidence—textual and archaeological—indicates that the *Deisil* was a ritual bonding of king and land, a rite in which the king "marries" the Sovereign of Ireland, acquiring the fourteen elements of kingship through circumambulating a labyrinthine pattern woven around the *Tech Midchuarta.*

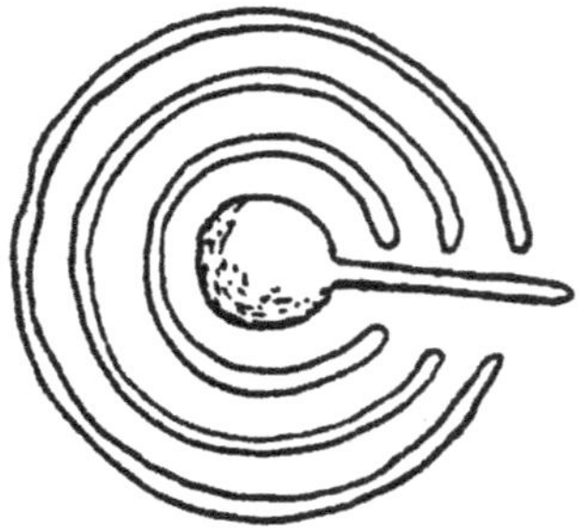

Figure 6. The *Deisil* Labyrinth at Tara. From "Temair Breg," by R.A.S. Macalister.

The Wake's *"Via Crucis" Compared with the* Deisil *of Tara*

Embedded within chapters 13 and 14 of the *Wake* (409–70) is a "procession" by Jaun that is remarkable in its similarities to the ancient *Deisil* of Tara. Joyce, in a letter to Harriet Shaw Weaver (dated 24 May 1924), states that Jaun is in a procession or circuit, and the structure of this section is "written in the form of a via crucis." The fourteen stations of the "Via Crucis" are represented in the fourteen questions appearing in this section.

Ian MacArthur, in his analysis of the "Via Crucis" section of the *Wake*, identifies all fourteen Stations of the Cross in these fourteen questions—but he also emphasizes some important anomalies uncovered in his analysis. Even though the Via Crucis is identifiable in the fourteen questions, the overall theme permeating the section is less Christian than it is pagan and sexual: "The underlying theme is that introduced on the first page of *FW*, the male invader baptizing/raping the female Ireland" ("Structure and Motif," 72). The entire "procession" of Jaun is more descriptive of the marriage and sexual bonding of a male candidate and female Ireland than it is reminiscent of a religious tradition of Christian Easter ("Structure and Motif," 73).

MacArthur also points out that while all of the fourteen "stations" can be identified in the fourteen questions in the *Wake*, Joyce has deliberately altered the numerical sequence of the "Stations." Joyce rearranges the Stations of the Cross in this order: (3, 2, 1), (5, 10, 7, 8, 9, 6, 11, 4), (12, 13, 14). This rearranged sequence, MacArthur notes, yields three groups: an initial triad reading from right to left, a concluding triad reading from left to right, and a complex central group of alternating odd and even numbers reading in sequence from right to left. Why Joyce deliberately rearranged

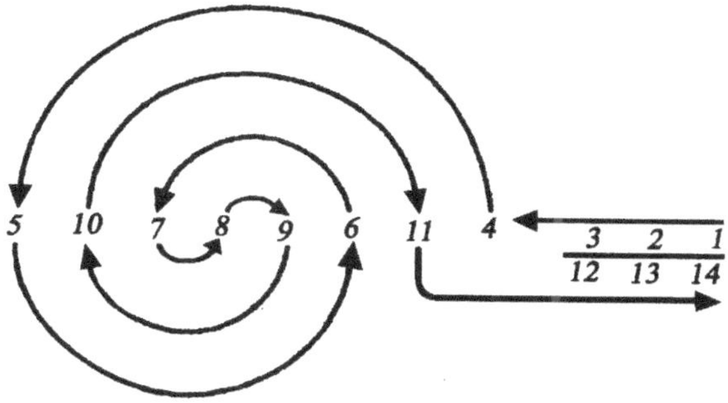

Figure 7. The Labyrinth of the "Via Crucis." Illustration by R. Beck. Courtesy of Gilliland Press.

the numerical sequence is, in MacArthur's assessment, unknown ("Structure and Motif," 67–73).

R. Beck, working from MacArthur's data, demonstrates that Joyce intentionally designed an ancient Celtic pattern through the numerological sequence cited above. Beck notes that if we employ MacArthur's terminology and describe the right to left sequence as descending and the reverse as ascending, we see that in addition to the cross-pattern in the center, we also begin with a descent and end with an ascent. Then, taking the numerical sequence in itself, the central group describes a double spiral, beginning and ending on the right. This, in turn, suggests that the initial triad be placed at the other end, where it would unfold properly, and be connected to the entrance of the spiral. By deliberately rearranging the numerical sequence of the fourteen divisions of the *Wakean* procession, "Joyce creates a spiral labyrinth . . . presumed to represent the descent to and return from the underworld. Similar patterns appear at barrow tombs in Celtic areas" (Beck, 1). The *Wakean* spiral labyrinth is reproduced above:

A comparison of the *Deisil* pattern found near Tara and the Via Crucis pattern in the *Wake* indicates some remarkable similarities. Both present a circular or spiral labyrinthine design meant to indicate a processional pattern. Both are constructed of triple whorls, and both have an "entrance" above the "exit." Furthermore, the *Deisil* associated with the Rites of Tara is, like the *Wakean* Via Crucis, deliberately designed as a procession containing fourteen divisions. Both the *Deisil* and the Via Crucis convey the theme of marriage and sexual union of the male "invader" and female Ireland. Both processions suggest the themes of death and rebirth, as well as the union of antinomial opposites. These striking similarities in design and theme strongly suggest that the Via Crucis in the *Wake* is the deliberate reenactment of the *Deisil* of Tara, one of the most archaic rites at the *Teamhur Feis*.

Two Important Themes in the Deisil *Procession*

A further consideration of the *Deisil* procession around the Mead Hall at Tara suggests two of the fundamental themes intrinsic to most of the rites performed at the *Teamhur Feis*: its microcosmic quality, and its intention be all-inclusive. For example, the Mead Hall of Tara, with its fourteen portals, is deliberately designed as the microcosm of Tara; and Tara was deliberately designed to be the microcosm of Ireland. The fourteen portals of the Mead Hall are meant to be inclusive of *all* attributes necessary for a powerful and righteous king. The *Deisil* procession itself is deosil, sunwise, and is a microcosm of the sun king's cyclical traversal and possession of the *entire* island of Ireland. The *Deisil* indicates kingship over the entirety of Ireland—*all* of its land and rivers, *all* of its people, *all* of their qualities and attributes.

The Mead Hall and the procession around it thus reflect these two central themes of the *Teamhur Feis*: its microcosmic quality, that is, the deliberate attempt on the part of the organizers of the *Feis* to make the *Feis* a reflection of the entire worldview of the Irish; and the inclusive quality of the *Feis*, that is, the deliberate attempt to make the *Teamhur Feis* resonant with, and significant for, all participants. These qualities are so intrinsic to the Rites of Tara that two important etiological myths regarding the *Teamhur Feis* are used to explain them. These two myths (discussed in the next chapter) have a remarkable resonance with *Finnegans Wake*, and may help to explain the microcosmic quality and the deliberate inclusiveness so fundamental to *Finnegans Wake* itself.

7

The Etiological Myths

The Etiological Myths of the *Teamhur Feis* and Their Analogues in the *Wake*

In the *Filidh* tradition of ancient Ireland, just as multiple etymologies are frequently given for the name of a significant person or place (such as "Ana" or "Teamhur"), more than one etiological myth is sometimes offered to explain the origins of an important event, such as the *Teamhur Feis*. The *Dindshenchas, Lebor Gabála Érenn*, "The Settling of the Manor of Tara," and "The Tale of the Ordeals" collectively relate two dramatically variant etiological myths regarding the Rites of Tara: the Dream of Old Finn, and the Cauldron of Restitution. These two stories certainly endeavor to explain the origins and the raison d'être of the *Teamhur Feis*; more important, however, they introduce significant mythic paradigms to explain some of the extraordinary characteristics and qualities inherent in the *Feis* itself: its re-creation and reenactment of the entire span of Irish history, the structuring of the *Feis* as a microcosm of the world, and its deliberate inclusion of the entirety of knowledge, science, art, and lore.

These two key myths pertaining to Tara both have their analogues in the etiological lore associated with *Finnegans Wake*. More important, perhaps, the ancient paradigms found in these myths—the paradigms used to explain some of the extraordinary and unique features of the *Teamhur Feis*—can also explain the presence of these identical features in *Finnegans Wake* itself.

Old Finn's Dream of Recovery

The etiological tale James Joyce conveyed to many friends and critics regarding *Finnegans Wake* is that his book originates in the dream of the enigmatic character "Old Finn," whose dreaming recovers the entire cycle of Irish history in the course of the *Wake*. Ellmann notes that Joyce conceived of the *Wake* as "the dream of old Finn lying in death beside the river Liffey and watching the history of Ireland and the world—past and future—flow through his mind like flotsam on the river of life" (*JJII*, 544). Weaver observes that Joyce "regarded the dream form with its shiftings and changes and chances as a convenient device, allowing the freest scope to introduce any material he wished—and suited to a night-piece" (Atherton, 17). Wilson relates that the *Wake* is "apparently to occupy itself with the single night's sleep of a single character" (91). Stuart describes the *Wake* as "a miniature *universal* history as recalled by a sleeping Dubliner in a series of dreams."[1] Ogden calls the *Wake* "the timeless condensation of the dream" (x-xi).

The Morphean quality of the dream-state allows Old Finn to shift and change his identity as needed to experience and relate any historical occasion. The horological and chronological fluidity of the *Wakean* dream permits Old Finn to condense the entirety of Irish history into the occurrence of a single night. Through the dream of Old Finn, Joyce conjures the entire chronological and mythological past of the Irish nation into the present moment of the *Wake*.

This primordial character, Old Finn, dreams the invasions of Fomorians, Tuatha De Danaan, and Milesians. He remembers the great feasts, destructions, courtships, victories, and defeats that constitute Irish history. Old Finn transforms himself through space and time to relive history through the identities of other people—while in some manner still retaining his own identity. All the characters of both past and present in the *Wakean* dream/drama are therefore connected with Old Finn. And Old Finn is connected to all of the key moments from Ireland's past and present—even though the *Wake* is but a single night's sleep.

During the long night of the *Wake*, only once is the dreamer really awakened from his dream-state—awakened by the shaking of a branch from an "overlisting [over-listing, everlasting] eshtree" (503.30), the ash tree adjacent to his window. The shaking branch of this overlisting ash sounds the recurring onomatopoeia, "Zinzin" (500.5, 500.9, 500.20, 500.26, 500.34, 501.1). And in the sleeper's dream state, the arboreal "Zinzin" has provided an aural component to his dreaming: the sound is interpreted in his dream as "the noise of jubilee at the wake."[2] The ash tree, too, is in his dream; but in the dream-state this tree is perceived not as the familiar ash outside the pub but as "our sovereign beingstalk" (504.18–

19), the sacred Yggdrasil, the "eggdrazzles" (504.35). We are nourished by the Yggdrasil's forest (503.36), we are clad in its wood (503.36), we are "burqued" (503.36 [birthed, berthed]) in its bark (503.36–504.1), and our lectures are its leaves (504.1); this sacred tree is the king of all the "crans" (504.1 [Irish, *crann,* "tree"]), high and holy (504.1–2). The jingling "Zinzin" of the overlisting/everlasting ash transports the sleeper (as well as readers of the *Wake*) from dream-state to waking and back again.

In the Ricorso, the sleeper finally awakens—with complete memory of all that he has dreamed in the course of the long *Wakean* night. All of Irish history is present at the *Wake,* recovered through the shape-shifting and time-traveling dream of Old Finn. The celebration in the Ricorso is, in large part, commemorating the dream of Old Finn, his awakening, and his recovery and reenactment of the entirety of Irish history.

Old Finn's Dream at the *Teamhur Feis*

In the archaic tradition of Ireland, Old Finn (in Old Irish, "Fintan") is the primordial manifestation of Finn MacCool. Fintan is the archetypal *Fili,* shaman and *shanachie,* and has acquired the ability to shape-shift in his dream-state through a rite the ancient Irish termed the *Tuirgin.* The *Tuirgin* allows Old Finn to change shape and identity during sleep, to travel through time and experience history firsthand through various identities. Bishop Cormac attempts to define the *Tuirgin* as "birth that passes from every nature into another . . . a transitory birth which has traversed all nature from Adam and goes through every wonderful time down to the world's doom."[3] (Stokes's edition of *Cormac's Glossary* lists numerous translations and interpretations of the concept of *Tuirgin* as offered by various scholars. Collectively, these translations suggest that the Celtic concept of the *Tuirgin* may be akin to accessing the Collective Unconscious of the Jungians, the *Anima Mundi* of Yeats, the Golden Dawn, and other Celtic Revivalists, or perhaps even the *Akashic Memory* of the Theosophists. All of these concepts were certainly familiar to Joyce.)

Fintan uses this extraordinary ability—the *Tuirgin*—to recover all of Irish history. Indeed, Fintan is credited with recovering the major "historical" texts *of* early Ireland. In the *Dindshenchas,* Old Finn introduces himself as the historian/narrator, alludes to his shape-shifting ability, and notes that he is celebrated at Tara for the recovery of this history.

Is misc Fintan fili
nirsam écne óen-lindi;

is and romtócbad co mblaid
ar in fót-brug os Temair.

[I am Fintan the Fili
I am a salmon not of one stream;
it is there I was exalted with fame,
on the sod-built stead, even Tara.][4]

In the *Lebor Gabála Érenn* ("The Book of the Taking of Ireland"), the most famous of the Irish "histories," Old Finn is again the historian and narrator. Referring to himself in the third person, Fintan explains that his shape-shifting through time allowed the recovery of history as recorded in the *Lebor Gabála Érenn*. One of Old Finn's emanations for this particular project is another historian, Tuan, who also gathers historical information through "changing his shape during sleep" (Matthews and Matthews, 93).

> God fashioned him [Fintan/Tuan] in many forms in many times and that man survived alone from the time of Partholon to the time of Findian of Mag Bile and to Colum Cille so that he related to them the "Taking of Ireland" from the time of Cessair, the first who took Ireland to that time of the saints and of Diarmait MacCerbaill, King of Ireland. For it is Fintan who arranged the settlement of the household of Temair for Diarmait and it is clear that Fintan was Tuan.[5]

Old Finn's most celebrated role, however, is explained in the important Middle Irish text "The Settling of the Manor of Tara" (from *The Yellow Book of Lecan*), where he acquires fame at the Rites of Tara for his recovery of Irish history. During the *Teamhur Feis*, the participants gathered for the feast soon reach a state of discord, arguing over political divisions of the land. The legal decisions necessary to resolve the crisis require knowledge of Irish history and historical precedents for their just resolution. The participants, however, have forgotten their history and soon realize that their collective amnesia portends much future strife. Because of this ominous realization, all in attendance refuse to partake of the collective feast. To resolve this dangerous situation, Old Finn is summoned to the *Feis*:

> A great welcome was given to Fintan in the banqueting house, and all were glad at his coming to hear his words and his stories. And they all rose up before him. . . . And he said to them "there is no need to make rejoicing for me, for I am sure of your welcome as every son is sure of his fostermother, and this then is my fostermother," said Fintan, "the

> island in which ye are, even Ireland, and the familiar knee of this island is the hill on which ye are, namely, Tara. . . . And I am skilled in its feasts and its cattle raids, its destructions and courtships, in all that have taken place from the Deluge until now."[6]

Old Finn then recalls the entire cycle of Irish history for the participants at the *Feis*: the invasions, defeats, victories, elopements, lore, and traditions—all that is "indispensable to help us in the matter of our discussion" ("The Settling of the Manor of Tara," 105).

Fintan explains to the assembly that once before this same ominous situation—the loss of Irish history—occurred. Centuries earlier, during a *Feis* held on the first Easter, another great *Fili* walked into the assembly carrying a branch cut from the Yggdrasil, the ash tree in the Otherworld; and in one evening this great *Fili* recalled all of history for those present. This Irish shaman gave Fintan seeds from the Otherworldly branch he carried; Fintan planted these seeds, and the trees that grew from this act became the sacred *bile* of Ireland. In honor of this event, every *Fili* and *shanachie* in ancient Ireland carried the *craeb sida*, the "silver branch"—symbol of their vocation—all cut from one of the sacred ash trees initially sown by Old Finn himself. The *craeb sida*, for the Irish Celts, acts as "an agent of transference from one reality to another"; the silver branch became the "symbol of office" for the *Filidh* and symbolically indicated the fact that they retold the ancient history and lore through the endeavor of Old Finn and under the aegis of "the great tree of the otherworld"—the sacred ash of which their branch was a scion.[7]

Because of Old Finn's recovery of history at Tara, the *Feis* became *the* great occasion to reenact and recount the history, lore, and heritage of the Irish: "in the presence of the kings, the nobles, and the people, the whole mythological and chronological past of the nation was conjured into the present by the shanachies" (Rees and Rees, 169). This re-creation of Irish history—condensed into a single magical event in present time—was a powerful and sacred rite intended to renew both individuals and society. Mundane time with its debts and quarrels was suspended during "the sacred phases" of the *Feis* when "the whole heritage of the people was accurately and vividly remembered" (Rees and Rees, 172). And this unifying experience promoted a state of mind that was conducive to the settlement of differences, the recognition of a primeval legacy, and the reconnection of each person with the ancient heritage and history: "Fortified by its tradition and purified of its contentions, society could begin life anew" (Rees and Rees, 172).

During "the sacred phases," of the *Feis,* when the dream tales of Old Finn were retold, the *Fili* would typically hold aloft his silver bough (which was frequently adorned with tiny silver bells) and shake it. This silvery tintinnabulation—the "Zinzin" sound from his quaking ash—identified the narrator as a poet in the ancient tradition, signified the Otherworldly and dream-state source of his historical narratives, and honored the dreamer himself, Old Finn, whose recovery of Irish history is one of the central events reenacted and celebrated at the Rites of Tara.

In the *Wake,* once again is heard the sound of the silver bough, the "Zinzin" of the quaking ash of the Otherworld; its silvery tintinnabulation identifies the narrator as a *Fili* in the ancient Irish tradition, signifies the Otherworldly and dream-state source of the historical episodes, and honors the dreamer, Old Finn himself, whose recovery of Irish history is one of the central events reenacted and celebrated at the *Wake.* As in the Rites of Tara, "Zinzin" is indeed the sound of jubilee at the *Wake.*

The Cauldron of Restitution

The *Wake* as Microcosm

As decades of readers have observed, the *Wake* is deliberately designed as a microcosm, intended to contain the world and invoke the presence of the universe and all of its component parts. Campbell and Robinson refer to the *Wake* as the "macro-microcosm" (*Skeleton Key,* 4). Glasheen describes the *Wake* as "a simulacrum of the world" (*First Census,* ix) and a "model of our universe" (*First Census,* xviii). Atherton identifies the *Wake* as the "microcosm . . . to God's macrocosm" (16) and further suggests that every section and even every word of the *Wake* tend to reflect in their own structure the larger structure of the *Wake* itself (34, 53). Very purposefully, and for reasons never divulged, Joyce included in the *Wake* catalogues, collections, and compilations of everything; literally, every subject, and "all kinds of more or less complete sets of different kinds of objects" can be found within the *Wake* (Atherton, 45). But as Atherton, among many others, has also noted: "nobody has ever been able to suggest what purpose is served by this inclusion" (45). Decades after these early observations, the microcosmic construction of the *Wake* has become a truism in *Wakean* lore, while the reason for this intentional design remains elusive.

One important result of the microcosmic design of the *Wake* is its extraordinary ability to provide meaning—if not sustenance and support—for all readers regardless of their personal or professional interests, psychospiritual development, or social identities. The universality of the *Wake* virtually guarantees that all participants will find in it a resonance with their own beliefs; John Bishop observes that "any reader can go into *Finnegans Wake* and discover everywhere within it whatever he or she wants or already knows" (Introduction, xii). And, as Bishop emphasizes, this deliberate and "infinitely accommodating" quality is "part of the glory of *Finnegans Wake*," because "it invites the participation of all" (Introduction, xii).

As the *Wake* is quintessentially an Irish and Celtic document, students of Irish culture and politics have even seen in this "infinitely accommodating" feature of the *Wake* "a model of the kind of understanding perhaps necessary to cooperative living in the postnational late twentieth century" (Bishop, Introduction, xii). Rather than adhering to a crumbling politics of identity and maintaining that single terms (like "Irishman" or "Celt") must refer essentially to only one thing, the *Wakean* microcosm, with this infinitely accommodating quality, offers a new paradigm: regardless of diversities, every Celt, every Irish woman and man, every person, can find in the *Wake* support for their own worldviews, connection with their own values, affirmation for their own unique sense of identity. And as with the *Wake*'s other great features and themes, this paradigm has its ancient parallel in Irish myth.

The Microcosm at Tara

Joyce's carefully designed fourfold microcosm—with its concomitant ability to accommodate all participants—has an important precedent in Irish culture, and the model can be found at Tara. Tara was deliberately conceived by its founders as "the microcosmic symbol" of Ireland; further, at Tara "the world was symbolized by a series of microcosms, each set within the other" (Rees and Rees, 154, 159). Accordingly, Tara was designed with the "four provincial halls" (representing the four provinces, cardinal directions, elements, and all other quadratures in Irish mythology) arranged around the Central Hall (representing Meath, the center), and "the plan of the whole state was further reproduced within the Central Hall itself" (Rees and Rees, 147). Within this *temple quadrata* that "symbolized the cosmos," the divisions of the land and seasons, the solar and lunar cycles, the polarities of chaos and cosmos, *tuatha* and *fianna*, male and female, space and time, were symbolically reproduced through spatial divisions within the hall (Rees and Rees, 163). This complex arrangement was a deliberate attempt to re-create the entire universe and embody the principle that "every unit, however small, tends to have a structure which mirrors that of the whole" (Rees and Rees, 145). This fourfold microcosm that deliberately attempts to re-create the entire universe wherein the parts tend to mirror the whole is, of course, a perfectly fitting analogue of *Finnegans Wake*.

Tara was the form of the microcosm, and the *Teamhur Feis* imbued the form with life. The activities and events of the *Feis*—like Tara itself—were designed to symbolically represent the entire Irish universe. Describing the *Feis* at Tara, the *Fili* narrating the *Dindshenchas* conveys this universality as he delineates its amazing catalogue of components. In their commentary on this passage, Rees and Rees note that the *Fili*, in his ebullient and expansive declamation, "seems to invoke the presence of the universe and its component parts" (169).

> "Heaven, earth, sun, moon, and sea,
> fruits of earth and sea-stuff,
> mouths, ears, eyes, possessions,
> feet, hands, warriors' tongues.
>
> "Horses, swords, chariots fair,
> spears, shields, and faces of men,
> dew, mast, sheen on leaf,
> day and night, ebb and flow—
>
> "The hosts of Banba, free from enduring sorrow,
> gave all these completely
> that it [the *Feis*] should not lie under gloom of disputes
> to interrupt it, every third year.
>
> "Lore of Finn and the Fiana, a matter inexhaustible,
> Destructions, Cattle-raids, Wooings,
> Tablets and wooden books,
> Satires, keen riddles:
>
> "Proverbs, maxims of might,
> and truthful teachings of Fithal [Finn's "respectable" brother],
> dark lays of the Dindshenchas for thee,
> teachings of Cairpre and Cormac [kings at Tara];
>
> "The great feast of Tara and other feasts,
> the assembly of Emain and other assemblies;

annals there, this is true;
every division into which Ireland has been divided;

"The story of the household of Tara, that is not scanty,
the knowledge of every cantred in Ireland,
the chronicle of women, tales of armies, conflicts,
Hostels, Prohibitions, Invasions:

"the tenfold Testament of hundreded Cathair
to his right pleasant offspring kingly of stature;
the estate of each man as is due
so that all may listen to it."[8]

This ritual declamation possesses "the force of a creation rite," intended "to reestablish the foundations of the tradition at the inception of a new period of time" (Rees and Rees, 170). The subject matter of the *Feis* is selected by its creators to intentionally encompass and embrace the entire cosmos. The rites are performed, as they are in the *Wake*, with the objective of reaffirming the status of its participants and renewing the world itself.

The extremely diverse array of subjects addressed at the *Feis* was intended, as indicated by the *Fili*, to give each "as is due." The historical reenactments, musical contests, inaugural pageantry, athletic competitions, poetry readings, philosophical debates, magical rituals, wake rites, theater, games, food and drink, skits, legislative and judicial assemblies, special studies for Druids and Fianna were meant to accommodate all diversity. As in the *Wake*, these events were conducted and performed by women and men who themselves represented divisions of the land and seasons, forces of the cosmos, and abstract principles.

The universal and microcosmic quality of the *Teamhur Feis* is perhaps best illustrated through the important etiological myth found in "The Tale of the Ordeals."[9] During the *Feis*, when Irish from all provinces were gathered in the Central Hall, a divisive problem arose because of a legal decision made in Northern Ireland. The politics underlying Irish identity, status, and rights deteriorated to the point that "each man again encroached" on the other. Seeking a means to cooperative living, acceptance of diversity, and mutual respect among those assembled, the high king initiated the tradition of the *Coire Aisic*, the Cauldron of Restitution, which became the symbol of the *Teamhur Feis* itself. The cauldron was positioned in the middle of the Central Hall. In it was placed every form of sustenance used by the Irish. Further, "lords and poets and wizards"—representatives of all the sciences and arts—each performed an incantation over the cauldron, instilling it with all the knowledge of their particular subject. The Cauldron of Restitution, the microcosm at the center of the world, contained the entire worldview of the Irish. Each component of the universe was magically rendered into the microcosmic mix—blended in the cauldron through the skill of the *Filidh*.

During the *Feis*, every participant was invited to partake of the cauldron. Because of its special nature, it was infinitely accommodating: "it was called *coire aisic*, 'cauldron of restitution,' because it used to return and deliver to every company their suitable sustenance." Every participant could derive meaning for himself, support for his beliefs, and affirmation of his identity. The Cauldron of Restitution consistently provided the appropriate sustenance for each, always according to the personal and professional interests, psychospiritual development, and social identity of the participant: "Now each in turn was brought to that cauldron, and every one was given a fork thrust out of it. So then his proper portion came out to each.... Wherefore in that assembly his proper due fell to each" ("The Tale of the Ordeals," 269).

The Cauldron of Restitution—symbol of the universality and the infinitely accommodating properties of the *Teamhur Feis*—is a most appropriate emblem for *Finnegans Wake*. Once again, each participant is invited to partake of the magical sustenance at the *Wake*—infused with the universe through the magic of the *Fili*, James Joyce. As during the Rites of Tara, once again we are all invited to the magical feast—each of us guaranteed to find therein our proper portion and our proper due.

8

The Recovery of the Dark Tongue

For that first language, spoken by the theological poets . . . was a fantastic speech.

—Giambattista Vico, *The New Science*

The *Wake*'s Bilingual Colloquy

In the book whose most striking characteristic is its language, a verbal confrontation in two different tongues is a fitting rite for its climactic conclusion. Pagan Druid and Christian Saint clash at the Rites of Tara over the issues of vision and perception (611.3–613.14), and their conflicting philosophies are presented in two languages as different as the worldviews they each convey: the native Druidic "pidgin" and the "English" of the Invader Patrick.

The Archdruid is arrayed in all the colors of the spectrum, with his *heptachrômatikos* (Greek, "seven-colored"), *septicoloratus* (Latin, "seven-colored") mantle (611.6–7). In "pidgin," he relates his richly hued perception of reality, the "photoreflection" (611.16) of the several "iridals gradationes" (611.17) of solar light (611.16–17), and explains how a seer in the seventh degree of wisdom (611.18 [that is, a Druid, or *Fili*]) is able to accurately perceive the true "inwardness of reality" (611.18–19). For the Druid, all objects show themselves in their truest of colors, always resplendent with their "sextuple gloria" of light (611.22–23). The Archdruid is capable of seeing the "Ding hvad in idself id est" (611.21): the *Ding an sich*, the King as he is in himself, and the thing that is itself. The language spoken by the Druid is as esoteric and colorful as his philosophy: multilingual, replete with puns and polysemes, and extremely circumlocutional in its presentation. Its sense is deliberately obscured, suggesting either esoteric elitism or ostensible gibberish. The language of the Druid is, as William York Tindall and others have noted, also the language of *Finnegans Wake*:

"That Berkeley [the Archdruid], the artist, speaks pidgin English . . . seems odd until we reflect that, to the public, the *Wake* sounds like pidgin English. Berkeley, the Irish 'archdruid' . . . confronts a foreign invader . . . Patrick the archbishop" (319).

Patrick, starkly dressed in black and white, sees his orthodox reality strictly in terms of black and white. Patrick neither follows nor comprehends his opponent's argument but rather hums to himself during the Druid's colorful presentation. When he does speak, his language is as blank as his clothing and perception. Linear, shallow, and simplistic, the language he uses is intended not for an elite few but for the assembled masses. The message is exactly what they can comprehend and what they want to hear—appropriately delivered in the language of colonizer and invader—and deliberately calculated for mass market acceptance: "Shamwork" (613.10) was in his "scheining" (613.10 [shining; German, *Erscheinung*, "appearance" or "phenomenon"]).

Joyce, in a letter to Harriet Shaw Weaver, indicates that the diverse tongues of Druid and Christian spoken at the Colloquy at Tara are very much connected to the central purpose of *Finnegans Wake*: "Much more is intended in the colloquy between Berkeley the archdruid and his pidgin speech and Patrick the (?) and his Nippon English. It is also the defense and indictment of the book itself" (*Letters I*, 406). A closer examination of the languages involved in the Colloquy at Tara does indeed suggest a significant yet unrecognized intent on the part of Joyce regarding the language of the *Wake*.

The White Language versus the Dark Tongue

As Joyce indicates in his above statement, the Archdruid of Ireland actually *did* speak a form of "pidgin" as obscure, polysemous, and circumlocutional as the soliloquy of Archdruid "Berkeley" or even the language of the *Wake* itself. In Old Irish, this artificially constructed tongue was known as *bélra na filed*, "language of the *filidh*," and was striking in its outrageous presentation, colorful characteristics, and nearly impenetrable obscurity. *Bélra na filed* (also called the "Dark Tongue") is a language nearly incomprehensible in its polyglot logorrhea; language sometimes blathering, at other times ranting, ribald, profound, or scatological, and everywhere laden with absurd catalogues of everything; language rife with riddles, and riddled with puns, neologisms, and a plethora of polysemes and portmanteaus; language literally loaded with thousands of words misspelled and malformed, bent, folded, twisted, mutilated or torn into pieces—all of this according to a bizarre set of "rules" and techniques that consistently apply, known to the *Filidh* but unfathomable to the uninitiated.

The linguistic techniques used in *bélra na filed* compositions are ritualistic and magical in both their origin and nature; these techniques, in turn, formed an important part of the spiritual training of Druid and *Fili*. *Bélra na filed* was the language of ritual; but it was also the language of history, religion, poetry, and law within the pagan Irish tradition. This deliberately obscure form of speech, the "pidgin" of the Archdruid at Tara, was also the privileged language of the *Filidh* and Druids, and was therefore the fundamental semantic medium of power, tradition, and knowledge in pre-Christian Ireland. And the Colloquy at Tara was, in many ways, the *ricorso* of that fantastic speech, that first language spoken by the *Filidh*, the theological poets of ancient Ireland.

Immediately after his ritualistic victory at the *Teamhur Feis*, Patrick, now in collusion with King Leary, furthers his semiotic conquest of Ireland by gaining control over the very medium of Irish pagan tradition. At Tara, the newly victorious Patrick convenes a synod; a committee is formed to purge Irish history, poetry, and knowledge, and place it under the control of the new dispensation. Leary, in the wake of his subjects' conversion to Christianity and at the insistence of the colonizer Patrick, orders that the entire native tradition transmitted via *bélra na filed*—oral performance, ritual, myth, history, lore, poetry and law—be reviewed and judged. At Tara, the "Christian invaders" and their committee edit the indigenous *senchas*—sorting the "acceptable" from the "unacceptable"—into a form and language controlled by the Christian clerics, not the native *Filidh* (Nagy, *Angels*, 204). The Christian attack is specifically directed at the secret language itself. Any of its principles or techniques of composition deemed too pagan, magical, or powerful are made illegal. The control of language—and therefore the control of the indigenous tradition—is placed in the hands of Christian scribes, as explained in the *Prologue* of the *Senchas Mór*.

> Co tainic patraic tra ni tabarta urlabra acht do triur I nerinn: fer comgne fri asndeis $_7$ scelugud, fer certa fri molad $_7$ air, Breithem fri breithemnus a roscadaib $_7$ fasagaib. O tainic immurgu patraic, is fo mam ata cach urlabra dona fiib so do fir in bérla báin .i. ina canoine.

> [Before Patrick came, the right to speak was not given to anyone except three people: the chronicler, for recounting and storytelling; the man of art, for composing praise and satire; and the man of law, for issuing judgments by way of pronouncements and maxims. But since Patrick came, each of these kinds of speech is under the yoke of the man of the white language—that is, of the Bible.][1]

In this ultimate act of colonization, the language that was the heart of the indigenous Irish tradition, the language that held its history, its religious and spiritual precepts, its poetry and mythology, is banned by the non-Irish Invader now celebrated as the patron saint of Ireland. The stark black-and-white orthodoxy of the *fir in bérla báin*, "the man of white language," outlaws the colorful philosophy of the *heptachrômatikos* Archdruid. The White Language replaces the Dark Tongue.

Bélra na filed: The Extant Sources

Though *bélra na filed* was dismantled at Tara, knowledge of this Druidic language survives to the present. An inherent tendency among the Irish Celts towards syncretism, coupled with a traditional Irish respect for Druidic learning that even Patrick could not erase, certainly mollified the Christian ban on the Druidic tongue. And Irish Christian scribes curious about—if not actually sympathetic to—the indigenous pagan tradition, along with classical writers fascinated with Celtic culture, recorded much of the tradition and lore of this banned language.

Consequently, a host of writers, scholars, and poets, over the span of two millennia, have provided written accounts and commentary regarding the outlawed Dark Tongue. Many of these sources are also recognized as sources Joyce used in researching the *Wake*; these include the following:

• Fianna Lore. Finn MacCool is the greatest of all the Irish *Filidh*, and as such, allusions to the language of the *Filidh* are found throughout the Fenian material. Finn's prophetic speech, his mnemonic skills, his abilities to discern the hidden nature of people and things, are all manifestations of the Three Illuminations (*imbas forosnai, dichetal do chennaib, teinm laegda*), which, in turn, are shamanistic techniques strongly identified with *bélra na filed*. On several occasions in the Fenian stories (for example, *The Wooing of Ailbe*), Finn shifts his speech from the vernacular to *bélra na filed* in order to specifically address those familiar with the secret language while concealing his intentions from all others. Finn's ability to speak *bélra na filed* is one of his defining characteristics, and Fenian lore provides numerous examples of the Dark Tongue and its techniques.

• Classical Commentators. Diodorus Siculus (in *Historiae* 4.3) discusses the secret tongue spoken by Celtic Druids, which he describes as a "divine language" used to translate the mystical experiences of the Otherworld into concepts accessible to human understanding. Diogenes Laertius (in *Vitae*), also familiar with the Druidic tongue, observes that the Druids "make their pronouncements by means of riddles and dark-sayings."

• Samuel Butler (identified by both Ellmann and Atherton as a source for the *Wake*). In *Hudibras* (part 1, Canto 1), Butler provides a poetic description of the ancient Druidic tongue when a Gaelic Druid confounds his listeners with *bélra na filed*:

> But, when he pleas'd to shew't, his speech
> In loftiness of sound was rich;
> A Babylonish dialect,
> Which learned pedants much affect;
> It was a party coloured dress
> Of patch'd and py-ball'd languages:
> T'was [Irish] cut on Greek and Latin
> Like fustian heretofore on satin.
> It had an odd promiscuous tone,
> As if h'had talk'd three parts in one;
> Which made some think, when he did gabble,
> Th' had heard three labourers of Babel;
> Or Cerberus himself pronounce
> A leash of languages at once.[2]

Butler obviously knew enough about *bélra na filed* to present this accurate and poetic description of the Dark Tongue and its "Babylonish dialect"; his description could easily apply to the language of the *Wake*.

• Scholarship during the Celtic Revival. Kuno Meyer, in *Revue Celtique* (xiii, 1892), edited a well-known tale replete with passages in *bélra na filed*: *The Story of Baile the Sweet-Spoken*. Meyer comments on the riddles, punning, "obscure modes of diction," and the polyglot of archaic, vernacular, Latin, and Hebrew that characterizes Dark Tongue composition; his following passage is representative:

> We have here, in fact, an instructive example of that delight in obscure modes of diction, which Irish poetry so often shows in its use of kennings, extinct forms of language, antiquated native, and lastly even foreign words. We know that a regular training in the use of such expressions formed part of the curriculum of the aspiring *fili*, and I think that it was these various modes of expression that were comprehended under the name *bérla na filed* [*sic*], "the language or dialect of the poets," which the young *fili*, then called *anroth*, was required to master. (220)

Meyer provides further information regarding the characteristics of *bélra na filed* in several of his other works, especially his commentary on *Sanas Cormaic* and *The Scholar's Primer*. In his annotations to *Sanas Cormaic*, Meyer presents a lengthy presentation on the qualities and characteristics of *bélra na filed*. Eugene O'Curry, in *Manners and Customs*, discusses the archaic speech of the *Filidh* and describes it as "language so obscure as to be almost unintelligible" (2:20). Whitley Stokes, in *Thesaurus Palaeohibernicus* (1903), cites ancient spells and curses used by the *Filidh* involving the puns, polysemes, and verbal permutations that constitute the techniques of *bélra na filed* construction.[3] Stokes also edited and annotated *Cormac's Glossary*, which contains many entries from the realm of *bélra na filed* and *Filidecht*. P. W. Joyce, in *A Social History*, details the training regime of the *Fili* and discusses many of the techniques utilized in *bélra na filed*.[4] R.A.S. Macalister, among others, presents a translation of a well-known story replete with allusions to and examples of Dark Tongue: *The Colloquy of the Two Sages*. In *The Colloquy*, two *Filidh*, Nede and Ferchertne, vie for the position of Ollave in the court of Conchobor mac Nessa. They conduct their entire dialogue in "dark tongue" that is clear to them but so multilingual, enigmatic, and obscure that, as King Conchobar notes, no one but the *Filidh* themselves can follow their argument: "These people keep their judgments and their knowledge to themselves. We know not the meaning of what they say" (*SL*, 12). *Revue Celtique* and *Zeitschrift für celtische Philologie* both provide numerous articles on *bélra na filed* and its principles, characteristics, and construction techniques.

• *The Secret Languages of Ireland*. One of the more detailed and comprehensive examinations of *bélra na filed* is found in *The Secret Languages of*

Ireland by R.A.S. Macalister, who was considered by some (such as Robert Graves) to be *the* authority on the subject. In the February 1963 edition of *A Wake Newslitter*, the feature article is "*Finnegans Wake* and *The Secret Languages of Ireland*," by Adaline Glasheen. Glasheen pores over the text of the *Wake*, collects dozens of terms and allusions specific to *The Secret Languages*, and then emphatically announces: "The book is mad fun and Joyce used it" (1). In *The Secret Languages*, Macalister examines *Hisperica Famina*, an extant manuscript written in *bélra na filed*. Based on his analysis of *Hisperica Famina* and other important *Filidecht* texts (including *Auraicept na n-Éces*), Macalister provides a lengthy analysis and examination of the rules and techniques for constructing (or reconstructing) the Dark Tongue. In *The Secret Languages*, in his chapter on *Hisperica Famina* and its Dark Tongue techniques, Macalister enters into a lengthy discussion, comparing *bélra na filed* to the language of *Finnegans Wake* (portions of which he had read prior to the *Wake*'s publication). *The Secret Languages*, however, was published in 1937, a relatively late date in relation to Joyce's own research for the *Wake*—indicating that while Joyce used *The Secret Languages* and its concomitant information on *bélra na filed* in *Finnegans Wake*, *The Secret Languages*, important for the reasons already listed, cannot be Joyce's initial or primary source of material on the Dark Tongue.

• *Auraicept na n-Éces*. The most comprehensive extant work on the lore and techniques of *bélra na filed* is *Auraicept na n-Éces*, a.k.a. *The Scholar's Primer*. *Auraicept na n-Éces* presents the etiological myths and other lore associated with the Dark Tongue and describes in detail and at length the array of bizarre linguistic techniques used by Irish *Filidh* to construct *bélra na filed*. *The Scholar's Primer* was translated by George Calder and published in 1917; even before Calder's translation was published, however, many Celtic philologists known to Joyce (for example, Heinrich Zimmer Sr., Kuno Meyer, Whitley Stokes, and R.A.S. Macalister) were themselves thoroughly familiar with *Auraicept na n-Éces* and used *Auraicept na n-Éces* as a primary source for their own research and commentary regarding *bélra na filed*.

Collectively, these sources present a comprehensive body of knowledge regarding the defining characteristics of *bélra na filed*: its essential obscurity, its association with darkness and night, its predication upon magical and arcane principles, and the bizarre array of linguistic techniques utilized in its construction. These characteristics are identical to the defining characteristics of the dark language of *Finnegans Wake*.

The Dark Tongue and the Language of the *Wake*

If there is a single, fundamental, characteristic of *bélra na filed* it is its overwhelming and nearly impenetrable obscurity. *Auraicept na n-Éces* emphasizes this trait to such a degree that in the first twenty-three lines of the text, this characteristic is addressed, alluded to, and commented upon repeatedly. Fenius Farsaidh, cited in *Auraicept na n-Éces* as a prototypical *Fili* and the ostensible creator of *bélra na filed,* first collects "every obscure sound that existed in every speech and in every language" and then "on account of obscurity" incorporates the most murky of these sounds into the secret language. The *Fili* Gaedel, along with other early *Filidh,* add to the language "by way of obscuration" (*Primer,* 3). Appropriately, Fenius creates this *Bérla Fortchide,* "Obscure Language," at the Tower of Babel. At Babel, Fenius goes to great trouble in the creation of the Obscure Language: first, he collects a wide and representative compendium of babble; and from this collection, he purposely and intentionally selects the most obfuscating linguistic material he can find (*Primer,* 103).

Bélra na filed is thus deliberately obscure; but the obscurity is not an end in itself. Rather, this obscurity is, in large part, intended to conceal the lore, rites, and rituals contained within. Julius Caesar in *De Bello Gallico* noted this, and believed that the Druids concealed their lore because they were unwilling to allow their system of knowledge and lore to be "bruited abroad among the common people" (6.13–14). And this trait, this fundamental tendency to obscure and thus conceal, is quintessentially Celtic. The very word *Celt* (etymologically associated with *ceilt,* "an act of concealment") is derived from an ancient expression meaning "the hidden people" because of this Celtic proclivity to conceal their lore and their rituals by means of oral tradition and obscure language (Ellis, *Dictionary,* 58). The obscurity of *Finnegans Wake,* like its equivalent in the Dark Tongue, is an ancient Celtic means of concealing the lore, rites, and rituals contained within: the obscurity of the *Wake* cloaks the lore, rites, and rituals of the *Teamhur Feis.* The *Wake*'s obscurity, perhaps its most striking quality, is also one of its most profoundly Celtic characteristics—not an end in itself, but a time-honored means of encapsulating and preserving pagan Irish tradition.

In Irish tradition, *bélra na filed* is emphatically identified with darkness, and was ritualistically created and used by the *Filidh* as a nocturnal tongue—a language of the night in both a literal and figurative sense. The *Filidh* understood *bélra na filed* to be imbued with several qualities of darkness:

• *duibhe*, "blackness," in the sense of obscurity, because *bélra na filed* was intentionally designed to sound like gibberish to the uninitiated;

• *dorchatu*, "darkness," in the sense of the mysterious, the arcane, or the enigmatic, because of the magical and shamanistic aspects of the language; and

• *dlúithe*, "compactness" or "density," a reference to the language's ability to identify and express new connections and concepts through the techniques of semiotic and linguistic compression—arcane techniques traditionally applied during nighttime.[5]

The inherent "darkness" of *bélra na filed* is especially crucial in the creation of literary works using this obscure tongue. One early Irish text notes that *bélra na filed* is always "found" (that is, created) *i ndorchaidhéta* "in darkness" (Ó hÓgáin, *Sacred Isle*, 89). In Ireland, a specific rite was employed by the *Fili* for the creation of literature in *bélra na filed*. Applying the magical techniques of *bélra na filed*, the *Fili* ritualistically composed while in complete darkness, usually late at night—the idea being that connections and meanings invisible and unfathomable to daytime linear rational consciousness could be revealed through the language of the night. Because of its inherent "darkness," its ability to reveal hidden connections, and its nocturnal origin, *bélra na filed* was typically glossed by medieval scribes simply as the "Dark Tongue." Joyce's own comments regarding the language of the *Wake* clearly suggest the Dark Tongue qualities of *duibhe*, *dorchatu*, and *dlúithe*: "In writing of the night, I really could not, I felt I could not, use words in their ordinary connections. Used that way they do not express how things are in the night, in the different stages—conscious, then semi-conscious, then unconscious. I found that it could not be done with words in their ordinary relations and connections."[6] The dark nature of the *Wakean* language, and the reasons for its nocturnal origins, are no different than those of the ancient Irish Dark Tongue.

Bélra na filed, like the language of the *Wake*, is based upon a belief system archaic and magical in nature. In the lore of the *Fili* (that is, *Filidecht*), words of the Dark Tongue are believed to be living entities that exist apart from speech and apart from the *Fili*. Dark Tongue words are intrinsically talismanic in nature and are mystically united with the thing, object, concept, or action that they identify and express. Correspondences (or near correspondences) and other relationships between words can thus indicate correspondences and relationships between these different things, objects, concepts, or actions. For the *Fili*, the Dark Tongue and its concomitant array of linguistic techniques were therefore used as tools for prophecy, for acquiring insight, inspiration, and knowledge of the hidden connections, obscured patterns, and invisible relationships between things.

Like an ancient Irish *Fili*, Joyce believed that the *Wakean* words were "Words of silent power" (345.19), and the *Wake* itself a "work of magic" (Atherton, 15). In creating the *Wake*, Joyce "believed that somehow the spirit of language was working through him of its own volition" (Atherton, 15). According to Joyce, some *Wakean* passages seem to foretell the future—thus proving the *Wakean* tongue to be "unconsciously prophetical" (Atherton, 15). Like the Irish *Filidh*, Joyce believed that his nocturnal words were living entities possessing an inherent power, existing apart from their speaker, talismanic in nature, and intrinsically connected with the thing they name:

> Did Joyce, perhaps, adopt a principle described by Lévy-Bruhl as being almost universal among primitive people? They believe that there is a real connection between a man and his name; and many peoples are confused between a name and a thing. . . . It is not impossible that Joyce himself had some such idea in mind, indeed he frequently claimed that to be mentioned in his book had an effect on the people named. . . . He seems to have had some odd idea that his work [*Finnegans Wake*] could subsume the things it named, and it seems to have been something very close to the primitive belief which he must have thought to contain some element of truth. (Atherton, 45)

Joyce's version of "associative mania," his belief in the talismanic potency of words "trivial" and "quadrivial," and his personal beliefs regarding the verbal magic of the *Wake* are in complete concurrence with the ancient *Filidecht* regarding the Dark Tongue—so much so that F. L. Radford suggests that Joyce's self-image as a writer "is closer to that of the ancient Irish *filid* [*sic*] than to any other cultural analogue" (268).

The linguistic techniques used to construct the Dark Tongue are numerous and bizarre, and they resonate with suppositions archaic and shamanistic in nature. *All of these colorful techniques find their exact counterparts in Joyce's construction of the language of the Wake:*

• "Babylonish hotchpotch" (*SL*, 225). As *The Scholar's Primer* and other texts emphasize, the Dark Tongue is a polyglot patchwork of languages. The mother tongue of the speaker provides the basic language and the syntactical framework upon which a variety of languages are grafted. The number and variety of languages composing the "hotchpotch" varies, depending upon what linguistic material is available to the speakers. In Druidic Ireland, vernacular Irish provided the framework and syntax; the patchwork languages included doggerel Latin, Argot, Greek, Hebrew, various dialects found in Ireland, archaic words, neologisms, and a dosage of undeterminable gibberish. In the *Wake*, the "mother tongue" of the speaker is English, not Irish, and the syntactical framework is that of English. The number of accessible languages has considerably increased, but the hotchpotch construction pattern remains the same.

• Vocabulary "little short of diabolical" (*SL*, 82). The vocabulary includes the mother tongue in both its present and archaic forms, vernacular, foreign, classical, colloquial, slang, dead, Argot, dialects, esoteric terminology, and neologisms. Foreign words are appropriated with complete disregard to their native syntax. (Hebrew words, for example, might be written from left to right rather than the Hebraic right to left.) Proper nouns and names are frequently unprivileged, that is, written without capital letters. And though the framework of the Dark Tongue is the mother tongue, no privilege is given to any one language or word over another. Argot is as valid a building block in the framework as standard or canonical vocabulary. Further, all words can be distorted morphologically for magical or occult purposes.

• Magical and arcane rules, "for torturing one poor word ten thousand ways" (*ICT*, 97). One of the fundamental precepts of Dark Tongue linguistics is that *words are things that exist independently of their speaker*. In *Auraicept na n-Éces*, one of its ostensible authors, Amairgen White-Knee, the first Gaelic Druid of Ireland, illustrates this arcane belief by formulating an analogy between a spear and a Dark Tongue word: both have an existence apart from their senders; both have a point, a haft, and a shaft;

both require technique and skill to deliver effectively; both can be sent with varying intent. And like a spear, a word must be appropriately modified by "science" to suit the intent of its sender (*Scholar's Primer*, 125–34). Accordingly, *Auraicept na n-Éces* provides a fascinating plethora of rules for transforming a normal, rational, waking-consciousness word into a verbal spear, a native weapon honed for usage in Dark Tongue composition:[7]

Cendfochras allows the alteration of the first or final consonant of a word "for arcane or etymological purposes."[8]

Gleselgi ("the track of the hunt") permits the merging of two words by hinging them on a shared syllable or by interlacing the syllables of both words. The *Wakean* "portmanteau" words are a fine example of *gleselgi* application.

Fertot a telgud noe is the formulation of neologisms, especially those of a technical, arcane, or scientific nature. Neologisms—as a form of reverse pun—are also encouraged to illustrate connections for which no apparent word exists.

Delidin sillabacda breaks a word into its syllables and then strews the syllables among the words in a sentence to allow for new meanings and connections to be made manifest.

Deletin litterda applies metathesis or complete reversal of the letters in one word to reveal its inner meanings. In the *Wake*, "ECH" and "HCE," and "Nephew" and "Wehpen" exemplify this technique.

Condall adds a new syllable to a word.

Cotut deletes a syllable from a word.

Lorga Fuach adds various syllables to complete or enhance a word's meaning.

Filltigthi combines numerous words into one long word to increase its intensity.

Fer tot is an onomatopoetic word that, when analyzed, contains the meanings of the very word it aurally imitates. In Dark Tongue terminology, the "thunderwords" of the *Wake* are an ingenious application by Joyce of both *Filltigthi* and *Fer tot*.

Rofota and *Lumbrosa* involve spelling the sound of a word; the spelling can then indicate a further or deeper connection or relationship.

Airchell calaid allows for the "theft" (that is, "dropping") of a final letter.

On any given page of *Finnegans Wake*, many—if not most—of the above rules are applied.

• Synchronistic slips of the tongue and the pen. In Dark Tongue composition, there is no such thing as "accident" or "coincidence"; rather, these slips are perceived as integral components in the arcane rite of Dark Tongue composition itself. "Unrecognizable forms" that may be either "factitious inventions" or "corruptions due to the scribes who have transmitted the text" thus become valid components of the esoteric and magical message (*SL*, 82). An anecdote related by Richard Ellmann indicates the identical practice in the *Wake*:

> Beckett was taking dictation from Joyce for *Finnegans Wake*; there was a knock on the door and Joyce said, "Come in." Beckett, who hadn't heard the knock, by mistake wrote down "Come in" as part of the dictated text. Afterwards he read it back to Joyce who said, "What's that 'Come in'?" "That's what you dictated." Beckett replied. Joyce thought for a moment, realizing that Beckett hadn't heard the knock; then he said, "Let it stand." The very fact that the misunderstanding had occurred in actuality gave it prestige for Joyce.[9]

• "The enthusiasm of the author for periphrastic expressions" (*SL*, 82). The invention of new, lengthy, and complex adjectival forms is an accepted and encouraged practice. In *Filidecht*, circumlocution requires and develops the mental acuity necessary to follow the extensive train of thought; logorrhea in the extreme intensifies the inherent obscurity. An example of this procedure can be found on nearly every page of *Finnegans Wake*.

• Oral-formulaic catalogues and long lists of epithets and appellations. The recitation of lists and catalogues is an archaic practice that reflects the awesome mnemonic skills possessed by the Irish *Filidh* and also the shamanistic belief that to name a person or a thing is to evoke its essence. Like the *Filidh*, Joyce possessed the same mnemonic abilities and magical sensibility regarding his *Wakean* catalogues. Examples of these in the *Wake* include his mellifluous catalogue of riparian allusions in "The Washers at the Ford," the thirteen pages of appellations for Finn MacCool, and the 111 monikers ascribed to Anna Livia Plurabelle.

• Puns, Near-Puns, Polysemes, and Multiple Etymologies. Harriet Shaw Weaver, after her initial reading of the *Wake*, was rather disappointed in Joyce for wasting his time and genius concocting innumerable puns. The "Wholesale Safety Pun Factory"—her description of *Finnegans Wake*—

suggested to Weaver (and others) a lapse by Joyce into puerility rather than an endeavor worthy of his talent. Punning, however, is an archaic magical tradition, a verbal rite essential to *bélra na filed* that attempts to discover the hidden connections between things—the single word that, as Joyce states it, connects "two thinks at a time"(583.7). A word that has the ability to manifest the invisible connections through puns, polysemes, and multiple etymologies is a powerful tool in *Filidecht*. Rees and Rees note that punning is an ancient and important technique in Irish *Filidecht* and was "not indulged in merely for fun" (348–49). In Irish *Filidecht* there is, in the concepts of polysemes, multiple names, and puns, "an ambiguity, or a multiplication or concentration of meaning which makes them fitting symbols for the unmanifest, which is itself the world of chaos and at the same time the ground of all being" (Rees and Rees, 248–49). (Or, as William York Tindall puts it: "The pun is mightier than the word" [7].) Vivian Mercier emphasizes that Joyce's use of the pun, "so brilliantly demonstrated in *Finnegans Wake*," clearly indicates Joyce's affinities with the ancient Gaelic tradition: "*Finnegans Wake* is the apotheosis of the pun"; and in Irish *Filidecht*, "we can be almost certain" that the pun is one of the oldest of the magical techniques used by the *Fili*: "Once again, Irish archaism helps to explain the Irish comic genius" (*ICT*, 78–80). Joyce's wholesale use of the pun is in complete accordance with the ancient Irish tradition of punning in *bélra na filed*.

• Subordinate Orthography. In both the Dark Tongue and the *Wakean* language, orthography is *always* subordinate to the ability to make puns and thereby discover hidden connections. Alternate spellings and near-spellings that allow polysemous readings of a word are practices both valid and encouraged.

• *Ail*, "the insult of a nickname which clings." Many of the members of the *Sigla Group* are given secondary names that carry some pejorative connotation. Anna is our "wee wee mother." Shem the Penman is called "Sham the Punman." The Twenty-Eight Virgins of Brigit are referred to as the "Lunar Sisters' Celibacy Club" (92.24–25). Sly Saint Patrick is the "Pea Trick" and "Mr. Trickpat" (487.23) and Pea Trick's famous symbol of Irish Christianity, the shamrock, is seen as the "Shamwork."

• *Aer*, satires, parodies, and insults, "litanies of spite which were essentially pagan in spirit" (*ICT*, 127). One fine example (among many) in the *Wake*:

"In the name of the former and of the latter and of their holocaust. Allmen" (419.9–10).

• Deconstruction through *belre n-etarscartha,* "the language of separation." *Belre n-etarscartha* is an ancient shamanistic technique of linguistic deconstruction discussed at length in *Auraicept na n-Éces* and used by Irish *Filidh* to reveal and disclose the hidden or inner meaning of a word or concept. The technique involves breaking a word into smaller components (the *Wakean "abnihilisation of the etym"* [353.22]) and then interpreting these "original" elements to discover their esoteric essence.

> The so-called *belre n-etarscartha* or "language of separation" had been elevated to a science. . . . To resolve a word into its "original" elements, each of them a separate word . . . a superficial similarity in sound or meaning was sometimes enough. This method of interpretation seems to have had its roots in the pre-Christian tradition. . . . What we are dealing with here is basically a primitive sort of learning which survived outside the Roman imperium and was dominated by magical beliefs. Within this intellectual horizon, correspondences between words pointed to correspondences between the objects they named, and so language itself was seen as a source of knowledge. For the initiated, this juggling with synonyms and homonyms (or near-synonyms and near-homonyms), punning, even a slip of the tongue, represented indispensable instruments of inspiration.[10]

Throughout the *Wake,* Joyce splits words apart, revealing smaller "original" components with their own separate etymologies—an invitation by Joyce to apply *belre n-etarscartha.* An appropriate demonstration of this ancient technique might be made with Question 9 of "The Quiz Show" (143.3). Question 9 concerns the hidden processes underlying the course of Irish history. In the question, the very word itself—*History*—is broken into two components ("his" and "tory" [143.12]) whose separate etymologies can then be examined to thus reveal the inner meanings of Irish "history." "His"—the masculine possessive—indicates the patriarchal bias of chronological historical narrative, the reduction of history to "his" story. The second component of history, "tory," is not without its own etymological and Irish significance. "Tory" is derived from the ancient Irish *toraige,* originally meaning "wanderer." A *toraige* was a native Irishman, dispossessed by the English invaders, forced through hardship and homelessness into banditry; *toraige* then became a term for any criminal or marauder. Later, *tory* became a term of abuse for Irish Catholic Royalists and supporters of James II. After 1689, a "tory" was any Englishman opposed to the Glorious Revolution. Finally, "tory" came to mean a conservative or reactionary—one who would oppose, among other things, Irish independence and support English colonial policy. Originally used to designate a victim of English colonialism, "tory" came to signify colonialism's strongest supporters. The outrageously ironic concept of "tory" thus illustrates, in a particularly Irish fashion, one of the fundamental principles of both Irish *Filidecht* and *Wakean* his tory: the process of *enantiadromia*, the idea that reality manifests in polar opposites that tend to mutate into each other. "History" is broken into its original components, and *belre n-etarscartha* reveals its inner principles: its underlying patriarchal bias, its outrageous irony, and the cyclical process of *enantiadromia*.

All of the Dark Tongue techniques listed above—from "Babylonish hotchpotch" to *belre n-etarscartha*—have their application in *Finnegans Wake*; conversely, *all* of the peculiar "rules" Joyce applies to construct the language of the *Wake* have their exact parallels in *bélra na filed*. This striking similarity was noted even before the *Wake* reached publication in 1939.

Macalister's Comparison of the Dark Tongue with the Language of the *Wake*

Vivian Mercier, who had connections with R.A.S. Macalister, wrote a letter to the editor of *A Wake Newslitter* that appeared in the June 1963 issue. Mercier states that Macalister read the sections of *Finnegans Wake* that were circulated before its publication (under the heading of *Work in Progress*) and was struck by the close similarities between the Dark Tongue techniques of *Hisperica Famina* and the linguistic devices used by Joyce in *Work in Progress*—so much so, that *Finnegans Wake* is discussed at length in *The Secret Languages*. *The Secret Languages* contains, Mercier notes, "a long passage in which Macalister compared what he had seen of *Work in Progress* with the *Hisperica Famina*" (7). Mercier then adds that "Macalister never mentions Joyce or *Work in Progress* by name, hence they don't get into the book's index, hence few Joyceans have realized the relevance of the book" (7). In Macalister's somewhat supercilious commentary in *The Secret Languages*, he refers to Joyce in the plural, he identifies Joyce's techniques in the *Wake* as the exact ones used in *Hisperica Famina*, he calls the *Wakean* language the "modern antitype" of the old

Druidic tongue, and he likens it to the Dark Tongue speech found in *The Colloquy of the Two Sages*:

> If I may generalize from these fragmentary data, their [that is, Joyce's] language is fundamentally English: but the sense, if any, is placed beyond the reach of ordinary persons by anarchic neologisms of idiom, accidence, and vocabulary; by artificial deformation of words, and violent wrestings of their orthodox meanings; by an occasional admixture of French . . . and by interspersed combinations of letters, not always pronounceable, and to me, at least, unintelligible. I am quite ready to admit the possibility that these writers [Joyce] may have grounds for self-congratulation, hidden from my undiscerning eyes. . . . But originality is not to be reckoned among these assets. Every one of the vagaries above enumerated was anticipated twelve or thirteen hundred years ago by the authors of *Hisperica Famina*: the only novelty which has been introduced into the modern antitype [that is, *Finnegans Wake*] is an occasional affectation of moral irresponsibility. The language of *Hisperica Famina* is fundamentally Latin: but the sense is often rendered at least elusive by anarchic neologisms of idiom, accidence, and violent wrestings of their orthodox meanings; and by an occasional admixture of doubtful Greek, along with a faint suggestion of Hebrew, and a little unrecognizable gibberish. If those who contrived this jargon [that is, James Joyce] were able to speak it with any fluency, they would have puzzled any ordinary Latinist, at least as completely as the disputing judges puzzled king Conchobor. And this is precisely the effect at which they were aiming. (*SL*, 78–79)

Though Macalister acknowledges the exact similarities between the language of the *Wake* and the Dark Tongue, he chooses to see the *Wakean* language as either Joyce's surreptitious appropriation of ancient linguistic techniques or, more likely, as a mere (and somewhat unfortunate) coincidence between the language of Joyce's novel and his own work in *The Secret Languages*. For several important reasons, however, both of these assessments are lacking. Joyce knew of the Dark Tongue and had access to much of the same material regarding this language as Macalister did—Joyce even used Macalister's own work as a source. The *Wake*, as argued in the previous chapters, is the re-creation of the Rites of Tara; and the Dark Tongue is *the* language of the Rites. Joyce's own beliefs regarding verbal magic are in complete concurrence with those of the ancient speakers of

Dark Tongue. The defining and highly unique characteristics of the Dark Tongue and the *Wakean* language are identical. And perhaps most important, for James Joyce—especially in regard to the creation of *Finnegans Wake—there is no such thing as "coincidence."*

"A darktongues, kunning" (223.28)

If the language of the *Wake* is indeed the reincarnation of the ancient Dark Tongue, then, as Joyce stated, "much more is intended in the Colloquy at Tara with the Archdruid and his pidgin speech." The secret language used to perform the Rites of Tara, the verbal "spear" of the ancient Irish *Filidh*, the language that Patrick banned, is the very language Joyce uses to re-enact the Rites of Tara once again as *Finnegans Wake*. James Joyce (as Seamus Heaney observes) transformed English from an "imperial humiliation" into a "native weapon."[11] The "native weapon" wielded by Joyce in *Finnegans Wake* and the one honed by Amairgen White-Knee in ancient Ireland are one and the same.

In the book whose ultimate purpose *is* renewal and recovery, there is no more appropriate means for Joyce to express this purpose than through his deliberate re-creation of the very language that was banned by the Invader at Tara so long ago—making the Dark Tongue truly the language of the Ricorso, and its recovery in *Finnegans Wake* the defense and indictment of the book itself.

Coda

The Meta-Celtic Canon

The evidence presented in the preceding chapters indicates that the *Teamhur Feis* provides the interpretive model that elucidates much of the obscurity of *Finnegans Wake*. The date of the *Teamhur Feis* and its extraordinary convergence of Christian, pagan, and seasonal events, resolves the decades-long controversy over the day and event underlying the *Wake*. The performers and enactors of the Rites of Tara have their identical counterparts in the dramatis personae of the *Wake*, the *Sigla Group*; both are nearly indistinguishable in their names, numbers, and functions. The entire choreographed sequence of rituals and events conducted during the Rites at Tara is fully re-created as the various episodes of the *Wake*. The inherent characteristics of the *Teamhur Feis*—its origin in the dreaming of Old Finn, its microcosmic construction, its deliberate universality and infinitely accommodating qualities, and its very language—are the same intrinsic and unique characteristics of *Finnegans Wake*. The principles enacted through the *Teamhur Feis*—the Celtic Triangle, the superannuation of the All-Father, death leading to rebirth, a great Irish wake for the mythic dead, the personification and interplay of antinomials as a cosmic pattern, the Irish rite of *hieros gamos* that equally honors both masculine and feminine energies, the celebration and restitution of Everyman and Everywoman, the process of cyclical return manifest in both the seasons and the human soul—are the very principles enacted in *Finnegans Wake*. Collectively, these patterns indicate an underlying, comprehensive, and intentional structure to *Finnegans Wake*—a structure based upon Joyce's vision of the *Teamhur Feis*, the most important event in the religion of pre-Christian Ireland. In its most fundamental sense, *Finnegans Wake* is thus a radical (Latin, *radix*, "root") religious text—as Joyce himself stated.

And as James Atherton and many other *Wakean* scholars have already noted, Joyce's own attitude regarding *Finnegans Wake was* religious. Joyce sincerely believed he was an Irish prophet assigned the enormous task of introducing a new religion to the West. According to Joyce, *Finnegans Wake*, in its most radical sense, is the sacred canon of this religion: the depiction of its pantheon, the presentation of its mythic paradigms, the formulae of its rituals, the statement of philosophical and spiritual principles upon which this religion is based. As argued in the preceding chapters, the sacred canon of Joyce's new faith is structured on the earlier religion celebrated through the *Teamhur Feis*. The *Wakean* canon is thus fundamentally Celtic; but through the genius of James Joyce, it is now transmutated and universalized, and might appropriately be called "Meta-Celtic."

This Meta-Celtic canon—its fundamental precept, cyclical renewal—is the reincarnation of the old religion of Ireland as it was celebrated through its most important event, the *Teamhur Feis*. Appropriately, its resurrection in the *Wake* occurs through "sacred coincidence"—the enactment of the same rites and rituals that were conducted at its earlier demise. Through the dark and talismanic events of seventeen chapters and through the labor of seventeen years—seventeen, the sacred number of regeneration for the pagan Irish—the *Fili* James Joyce celebrates the *Wake* Rites once again.

Notes

Chapter 1. Introduction

1. The terms quoted here, *talismanic* and *sacred coincidence,* are taken from Ellmann's *James Joyce,* First Revision (523, 325); Ellmann uses both terms in reference to Joyce's birthday.

2. See Edel Bhreathnach, *Tara* (34–35), for a complete discussion regarding the etymology of "Tara" and "Teamhur."

3. Kaufmann, in "Seasonal Change and Transformation" (452), reiterates the views regarding the *Teamhur Feis* that are held by most modern historians; Joyce's alternate sources of information on the *Teamhur Feis* are discussed later in this chapter.

4. I am greatly indebted to Maria Tymoczko for much of the bibliographical material and evidence used in this section.

5. Stanislaus Joyce, in *My Brother's Keeper* (171, 123), provides further evidence of his brother's interest in Celtic lore and Irish mythology.

6. See Radford, "Daedalus and the Bird Girl" (254, 273 n. 4).

7. John Kelleher notes this assessment throughout his essay "Identifying the Irish Printed Sources for *Finnegans Wake*"; Sultan notes this in *Eliot, Joyce, and Company* (42–48).

8. William Irwin Thompson's quote is cited by Tymoczko in *Irish Ulysses* (223) and is taken from William Irwin Thompson, *The Imagination of an Insurrection: Dublin, Easter 1916: A Study of an Ideological Movement* (13).

9. Kelleher, in "Identifying the Irish Printed Sources for *Finnegans Wake*" (161–62), and Tymoczko, in *Irish Ulysses* (7–12), discuss these reasons at length.

10. See Frank Budgen, *James Joyce and the Making of "Ulysses"* (36, 325).

11. See Craig Carver's essay "James Joyce and the Theory of Magic" for a comprehensive discussion of Joyce's occult interests, especially Joyce's interest in the Western esoteric traditions.

12. See Scholes and Kain, eds., *The Workshop of Dedalus* (63). See also Carver, "James Joyce and the Theory of Magic" (213 n. 1).

13. O'Connor's apocryphal tale is retold in Tymoczko's *Irish Ulysses* (161–62) and is taken from O'Connor's essay "Joyce and Dissociated Metaphor" (301).

Chapter 2. The Day of the *Wake*

1. Throughout Irish mythology, the number seventeen is consistently used as a numerological symbol for transformation, renewal, and the beginning of a new cycle; for example:

- In *Dunaire Finn*, there are two rival factions for control of the Fianna (Clan Mhorna and Clan Bhaoisgne), each represented at Tara by sixteen men. Finn MacCool, accepted by both factions as their seventeenth man and their leader, resolves the strife, becomes the new leader, and thus begins a new cycle in the history of the Fianna.
- Prior to Finn, there were sixteen leaders of the Fianna; Finn, the seventeenth and greatest, transforms the Fianna into one of the most renowned organizations of Ireland's Golden Age.
- King Mongan, who was identified by Caoilte mac Ronan as the reincarnation of Finn, spends the first sixteen years of his life in the Otherworld, the Land of Promise; in his seventeenth year, he returns to earth plane, marries, and then becomes king.
- The pre-Celtic settlers of Ireland, the Partholonians and Nemedians, collectively cleared sixteen plains; these sixteen, plus the Old Plain of Elta, fashioned by God, defined the settlement areas of Ireland and allowed for a new chapter in the history of Ireland.
- The Battle of Tailtiu, which transformed Ireland into a Celtic realm, began on the seventeenth day of the moon.
- Saint Patrick, the initiator of the new dispensation in Ireland, is celebrated on the seventeenth.

In the creation of *Finnegans Wake*, Joyce uses the numerical significance of seventeen in the same manner as his ancient counterparts:

- The *Wake* is composed of sixteen chapters plus the Ricorso, the seventeenth chapter of transformation and renewal.
- The *Wake* itself gestates for sixteen years and is "born" on Imbolc of its seventeenth year.

Given Joyce's knowledge of both numerology and Irish lore, the incorporation of this important aspect of Irish numerology is hardly accidental. Joyce deliberately fashions the *Wake*—in both its spatial organization and its chronological development—within frameworks based on divisions of seventeen, the ancient Irish number of renewal and regeneration.

2. See McHugh, *The Sigla of "Finnegans Wake"* (108). In *The Sigla*, McHugh revisits and reviews much of the argument initially presented by Clive Hart for an Easter Ricorso.

3. Muirchú's Latin account from *The Book of Armagh* (1.19.1–2) and Bieler's translation (1979, 92.3–7) are both cited in Nagy's *Conversing with Angels* (88).

4. The date of Joyce's letter is February 19, 1935. The original is in Italian; I have used the translation included as footnote number 1 on page 346 of *Letters III*.

5. In antiquity, due to a different reckoning of the calendar, the equinoxes (and solstices) were observed several calendar days later than they are at present; this different reckoning accounts for the late date of the vernal equinox cited by Nathan Halper in his essay.

6. See Bieler's translation of Muirchú's Latin account in *The Patrician Texts* (84–85).

Chapter 3. The *Sigla Group* at the *Teamhur Feis*

1. See Glasheen, introduction to *Third Census*. In her introduction, Glasheen identifies and discusses the primary and secondary characters of the *Wake*, from which much of the above summary is taken.

2. Some *Wakean* scholars believe there is another *Siglum*, the mysterious "F" *Siglum* that may represent the spirit of Finn MacCool at the *Wake*. The inclusion of the "F" *Siglum* would certainly lend support to the claims made in this chapter, but it is excluded because of its inconclusive nature.

3. See Macalister, *Secret Languages* (22). Macalister reproduces the characters of the Formello-Cervetri alphabet from which a close comparison with the *Sigla* can be made.

4. See *The Annals of the Four Masters, anno mundi* 3267 and following for further information regarding the Fir Bolg Eochu. See also MacKillop, *Dictionary of Celtic Mythology* (162–66), for a listing of the many variants of "Eochu" in Irish mythology.

5. The equine rituals conducted at the Rites of Tara and referred to in this passage are examined in detail in chapter 6.

6. See Ross and Robbins, *Life and Death a of Druid Prince* (54–59), for references to Irish kingship from the classical writers Athenaeus and Posidonius and for a discussion of the vulpine imagery associated with Celtic kings.

7. For the complete story of Lindow Man, see Ross and Robbins, *Life and Death of a Druid Prince*.

8. Bowen's essay "Great Bladdered Medb" appears in *Éire-Ireland* 10, no. 4 (1975):14–34, and is cited by Tymoczko in *Irish Ulysses* (111–17).

9. See Tindall, *Reader's Guide* (56). Tindall's description of the older male being replaced by the younger is identical to the pattern in Celtic and Irish mythology of the king being challenged and (usually) replaced by the younger *tanaiste*. In Celtic myth, this Celtic Triangle typically involves an elder male (the king) in love with a much younger female who, in turn, loves a young man of lower status than the king. Famous examples of this Celtic Triangle include: Finn/Grania/Dermot; Mark/Isolde/Tristan; Conchobar mac Nessa/Deirdre/Naoise; and Arthur/Guinevere/Lancelot (or sometimes Mordred). Among Celtic scholars, the consensus is that these romantic triangles from Celtic lore all have their origins in the pagan rites associated with royal succession, especially the rites of royal succession as practiced

at the *Teamhur Feis*. In some presentations of the triangle, the Sovereign is presented in her manifestation as the Mother; in other cases, the Sovereign is presented as the Maiden. Both of these versions are found in the *Wake*.

10. Hugh Kenner, in "The Look of a Queen," argues that many of Joyce's female characters share strong resemblance to the Sovereign goddess of Irish myth and ritual. Maria Tymoczko, throughout chapter 4 of *Irish Ulysses*, reaffirms Kenner's claims and provides further evidence for the Sovereign pattern underlying many of Joyce's female characters.

11. See Rees and Rees, *Celtic Heritage* (219–21) for a synopsis of the Ess/Mess story at Tara.

12. See Green, *Celtic Goddesses* (117, 135), and Rees and Rees, *Celtic Heritage* (291–96).

13. See Straffon, *Earth Goddess* (35–52), for a detailed discussion of the relationship and identity of the Sovereign and the *Cailleach*.

14. The quote from Diodorus Siculus is from 4.56. Diodorus is quoted by Macalister in *Tara* (112), in reference to Macalister's discussion of the Twins at ancient Tara.

15. This excerpt from *The Colloquy* is translated by Joseph Falaky Nagy and is found in his *Wisdom of the Outlaw* (30).

16. MacCulloch, in *The Religion of the Ancient Celts* (353), provides examples of the "Transformation Combat" as found in Irish lore and literature. Macalister, in *Tara* (109–14; 116–17), discusses the mutual hostility and combat of the Twins as found in Irish lore. MacCulloch in *Celtic Mythology* (57–59) discusses "Transformation Combat" as a folktale formula.

17. Macalister, in *Tara* (110), quotes Rendell Harris's *Boanerges* (30) regarding the Twins, thunder, and religion. The thundering sound heard at the *Teamhur Feis* that played a key role in the Rites is discussed at length later in this chapter in relation to the important character named "Magrath."

18. See Rees and Rees, *Celtic Heritage* (150–54), for an examination of the Twelve and their relationship to various Irish kings. The texts cited by Rees and Rees in the passages quoted, "Da Derga's Hostel" and "The Wooing of Emer," are both found in Cross and Slover's *Ancient Irish Tales*, a text well known to James Joyce.

19. McHugh, in *Annotations* (398), diagrams the numerous quadratures as described in Joyce's letter.

20. See Mary Condren, *The Serpent and the Goddess* (67–78), and Miranda Green, *The World of the Druids* (103–4), for a discussion of the Celtic priestesses at Tara.

21. See O'Curry, *Manners and Customs*, 1: clxxi n. 285, for further details on the Nine Barrigenae. O'Curry also refers to the classical writer Pomponius Mela (*The Description of the World*, book 3) regarding the Celtic priestesses.

22. Muirchú's Latin account and Bieler's translation (1.10; 74.13) are taken from Nagy, *Conversing with Angels* (46–47).

23. As indicated, this assessment of the Magrath character is taken from Glash-

een's *First Census* (81–82). It may be interesting to note that in her discussion of Magrath in her much later *Third Census,* Adaline Glasheen adamantly disavows the possibility of any connection between the Druid Mog Ruith and the *Wakean* Magrath—a complete reversal of her assessment in *First Census.*

24. Macalister, "Temair" (344–59), recounts this lore from Keating, from *The Book of Ui Maine* and from "The Siege of Druim Damhgaire." Further discussion of the Mog Ruith lore can be found in K. M. Lisowski's "Texte zur Mog Roith Sage," *Zeitschrift für celtische Philologie* 14 (1922–23).

25. See Macalister, "Temair" (344–51), for a detailed description of the Druid Mog Ruith.

26. Macalister is the translator of this section of *Lebor Gabáia Érenn* (4.57).

27. In his discussion of the *Roth Romach* as bull-roarer and its connection with Mog Ruith and the *Teamhur Feis,* R.A.S. Macalister clearly admitted that he made this connection against the better judgment of his peers, who pointed out that there was no archaeological evidence whatsoever of the device known as the "bull-roarer" ever existing north of the Alps. However, *The Ulster Journal of Archaeology* (38 [1976]: 16–18) reports that a bull-roarer of ancient origin was found (in 1976) at Glenviggan, in County Tyrone.

Chapter 4. The Fall of the All-Father

1. This short poem is found in Bonwick, *Irish Druids* (94).

2. The name *Porter,* like *HCE,* has a special significance in the pagan tradition of Ireland. In certain initiatory rites involving access to the Otherworld, one person was selected as a threshold figure, a guardian of the secret rites, and called the "Porter," or more frequently, "Porter in Hell." To be assigned "Porter in Hell" was, curiously, a position of both penance and honor. "Porter" was one who had committed a crime or sin that had to be expiated; but "Porter" was also one selected as a future candidate for special initiation. Until the atonement of this "sin" is accomplished, the "Porter in Hell" remains the Outsider, aware of the Otherworld but unable to attain it, while simultaneously alienated from the mundane world by his connection with the other. The pagan Porter reappears in Christian lore as Saint Peter, guilty of thrice denying Christ, now assigned the role of gate guardian at the threshold of heaven. The "Porter in Hell" also appears as a character in several of the older paganistic ballads. In "The Cruel Mother," her punishment is "seven years a Porter in Hell." In "The Well below the Valley," an old Irish ballad deliberately excluded from the repertoire of many singers because of its sinister themes and pagan underlay, evidence of a dark sex crime is uncovered at the well of life; the crime can only be redressed through becoming the "Porter in Hell." All of these themes related to Porter in Hell—the Outsider, the mysterious "sin," the expiation that both stigmatizes and honors, the initiation into the Otherworld—apply equally as well to Porter in Dublin. James Joyce, professional ballad singer, certainly knew the ballad tradition of his native land. (See "Foundations of the Hidden Tradition in Song and Balladry," in R. J. Stewart, *The Underworld Initiation,* for a discussion of the "Porter in Hell";

also, an excellent version of the ballad "The Well below the Valley" is performed by "Planxty" on the audio CD of the same title.)

3. Amairgen's poem is found in *Lebor Gabála Érenn*, 5.114–17.

4. This rare account of the Welling rite is reprinted in Matthews and Matthews, *Encyclopedia* (292), and is taken from *Sacred Waters*, by Janet and Colin Bord.

5. For a complete listing of the Fenian allusions and references in the Buckley tale, see McHugh, *Annotations* (337–55).

6. Richard Ellmann is quoted by Nathan Halper in "Another Anecdote" (90).

7. Caoilte's tale can be found in its Gaelic original and English translation in Nagy, *The Wisdom of the Outlaw* (143–44).

8. Maelodran's tale can be found in its Gaelic original and English translation in Nagy, *The Wisdom of the Outlaw* (145–46).

9. Susan Swartzlander, in "Multiple Meaning and Misunderstanding: The Mistrial of Festy King," summarizes various commentaries (from Glasheen, Matthews, Graham, and others) regarding Festy King, which I have used in this section.

10. This excerpt from *The Book of Rights* is quoted by Bonwick in *Irish Druids* (203).

11. In Celtic tradition, the number forty has a very special significance in relation to the important seasonal festivals: Imbolc, Beltane, Lugnasad, and Samhain. All four of these feast days were traditionally held forty days after the solstices and equinoxes. (Imbolc, for example, was calculated to occur forty days after the winter solstice.) The idea behind the forty-day calculation seems to be related to a similar pattern found throughout the constellation of Indo-European mythologies—that a duration of time based on increments of forty was a natural period of gestation required to bring a new force from its inception to its complete manifestation. The forty-part circuit of "Tourlemonde" traveled by the *gamina* and Prankquean agrees with this ancient tradition and lends support to Michael Kaufmann's assessment that Celtic seasonal festivals structure "The Prankquean's Tale."

12. This excerpt from *Baile an Scál* is from O'Curry, *Lectures* (618–21).

13. For a synopsis of the concept of *Lommrad*, see E. Bhreathnach, *Tara* (3). For a more extensive discussion of *Lommrad*, see Ó Cathasaigh, "The Theme of *Lommrad* in *Cath Maige Mucrama*" (211–24).

14. This quote is from P. W. Joyce, *A Social History of Ancient Ireland*, 1:240. In a letter to the Irish composer G. Molyneux Palmer, dated April 26, 1909, James Joyce refers to P. W. Joyce as "my namesake" (*Letters I*, 66).

15. Marion Cumpiano, in his essay "Dermot MacMurrough" (105), presents this quote from *The Annals of the Four Masters*, for the year 1172.

16. "The Voyage of Tadhg" is quoted by Anne Ross in *Pagan Celtic Britain* (340).

17. Æ is quoted by Evans-Wentz in *Fairy Faith* (332).

18. This excerpt from "Connla's Voyage" is taken from P. W. Joyce, *Old Celtic Romances* (110).

Chapter 5. The Funeral Games at Valleytemple

1. See O'Curry, *Manners and Customs* 1, for the components of the *Nosad*. Also, see P. W. Joyce, *Social History*, vol. 2, chap. 22 ("Death and Burial") for details of the wake and funeral rites of the pagan Irish. For a discussion of the relationship between the *Teamhur Feis* and funeral rites, see P. W. Joyce, *Social History*, vol. 2, chap. 29 ("Public Assemblies"). For a discussion of the wake at the Rites of Tara and its seasonal and fertility connections, see Macalister, *Tara*, chap. 5 ("The Assemblies of Tara").

2. The story of King Dathi and the prophecy through *Neldoracht* is taken from O'Curry, *Lectures* (284–85).

3. *The Colloquy* is quoted by Nagy, *Wisdom of the Outlaw* (22).

4. The *Frith of Brigit* and the *Frith of Mary* are both in Carmichael's *Carmina Gadelica* and are quoted by Matthews and Matthews, *Encyclopedia* (246).

5. Joyce's description is excerpted from a letter to Harriet Shaw Weaver, dated March 7, 1924 (*Letters I*, 212–13).

6. The terminology used here is borrowed from Lysaght's *Banshee*, perhaps the most comprehensive study of the banshee figure in print. Lysaght also refers to *The War of the Gaedhil with the Gaill*, on page 194, taken from J. H. Todd, *Cogadh Gaedhel re Gallaibh*.

7. For a detailed discussion of this rite, see J. Matthews, "Auguries" (111–12).

8. Much of the following argument connecting Irish Druidism with the Cabala and Egyptian and Platonic philosophy is initially presented by Sheldon Brivic in "The Mind Factory: Kabbalah in *Finnegans Wake*." Campbell and Robinson, in *Skeleton Key* (163) note that much of this section of the *Wake* (Book II, chapter 2, which they name "The Study Period") is laden with "the esoteric doctrines of the Cabala"; Campbell and Robinson discuss these doctrines at length in *Skeleton Key* (193–96).

9. Joyce's review of *Giordano Bruno*, "The Bruno Philosophy," appears in *The Critical Writings of James Joyce* (132–34). The quotation by Giordano Bruno appears in McIntyre (130).

10. Joyce's high recommendation of Helena Petrovna Blavatsky is noted by Sheldon Brivic in "The Mind Factory" (7).

11. See Benstock, *Joyce-Again's Wake* (190–94) for a discussion of some of the wake games in "Tavernry in Feast."

12. Prim's Victorian account of "The Building of the Ship" is taken from his essay "Olden Popular Pastimes in Kilkenny" (334) and is recounted by Vivian Mercier in *Irish Comic Tradition* (50). In the earlier pagan tradition, a child conceived through the enactment of the actual sexual rite involved in "Building the Ship" was typically given the same name as the deceased.

13. One example is Julius Caesar, who used the charges of human sacrifice and cannibalism as partial justification to invade the realm of the Continental Celts.

14. Jonathan Swift's *A Modest Proposal* is found in *British Literature*, 1:956.

15. *Dindshenchas,* "Carmun," verse 30. "Carmun" is quoted by Macalister in *Tara* (158).

16. Ibid.

17. See Rose and O'Hanlon, "Finn MacCool and the Final Weeks of Works in Progress," for a list of Joyce's sources for the Finn material as well as an index of Fenian allusions in the Buffalo Notebooks and in the *Wake*. In addition, Beechold, "Early Irish History and Mythology," provides a compendium of Fenian Lore in the *Wake*.

18. Nagy's translation and the Gaelic original are found in his *Wisdom of the Outlaw* (34).

19. This excerpt is from Holinshed, *Irish Chronicle*, 1577 (69).

20. Gwynn's translation of the *Dindshenchas* is quoted by Rees and Rees, *Celtic Heritage* (170).

21. See Condren, *The Serpent and the Goddess* (67–78), for a discussion of the relationship between Roman and Irish Vestal Virgins and the rite of *Februa*.

22. See McHugh, *The Sigla of FW* (132–33), for a detailed discussion of the rainbows in Irish mythology.

23. Alice Gomme's *Traditional Games* is used by McHugh in *The Sigla of FW* (57) and throughout his discussion of the dance in "The Mime" (57–61).

24. See Lyn Wilde, *Celtic Women* (84). Wilde also discusses the fertility rite described in *Carmina Gadelica* by Alexander Carmichael.

25. Vivian Mercier quotes Henry Morris in *Irish Comic Tradition* (50). Morris's quote originally appears in "Irish Wake Games" (40).

26. This riddle from "The Wooing of Ailbe" is quoted by Rees and Rees in *Celtic Heritage* (350).

27. Finn's riddle is excerpted from "Dan Dheirg" ("Song of the Red"); this particular version of the riddle is translated by Robin Williamson in Stewart and Williamson, *Celtic Bards, Celtic Druids* (97).

28. Credit for solving this version of the "Heliotrope" riddle goes to Adaline Glasheen (*Newslitter* 1, no. 3 [June 1964]: 5). Glasheen was familiar with the Dark Tongue techniques as used in the Mime riddles and as delineated by R.A.S. Macalister, whose book on the Dark Tongue (*Secret Languages of Ireland*) she discusses in *Newslitter*, no. 10 (February 1963): 1–3.

29. See Macalister, "Temair" (393), and Ó hÓgáin, *Sacred Isle* (17–20), for a discussion of the classical references to the Irish circle dance and fertility rite. In *Sacred Isle*, Ó hÓgáin cites Diodorus's *Bibliotheca Historica* 2.47, as well as Carolus Müllerus in *Diodori Siculi* 1, (Paris, 1878), and Ioannes Zwicker, *Fontes Historiae Religionis Celticae*. For Hecataeus and his references to the circle dance, see Lionel Pearson's *Early Ionian Historians* (25–108).

30. This excerpt from "The Second Battle of Moytura" is translated by Whitley Stokes (57–59).

Chapter 6. The Return of Solsking the First

1. This account of the *Tarbh Feis* ritual is found in O'Curry, *Manners and Customs*, 2:199.

2. This excerpt from the "Commentary" is quoted in John Matthews, *Celtic Seers' Source Book*' (67).

3. For a more complete description of this ritual, see Giraldus Cambrensis, *Chronicle*, distinction 3, chap. 25, p. 138.

4. "Nine Gifts" is quoted by Matthews and Matthews in *Encyclopedia* (229).

5. The *Senchus Mór* is quoted in John Matthews, *Celtic Seers' Source Book* (12–13).

6. Edward Gwynn, ed. and trans., "Temair" IV, in *Metrical Dindshenchas*, lines 61–64, pp. 32–33.

Chapter 7. The Etiological Myths

1. Stuart is quoted by Attridge in "*Finnegans Wake*: The Dream of Interpretation" (22). Stuart's quote is originally from "Mr. Joyce's Word Creatures," *Colophon*, part 7.

2. See Campbell and Robinson, *Skeleton Key* (310 n. 28). Campbell's and Robinson's note identifies the "Zinzin" sound on page 500 of the *Wake* as the shaking tree branch outside the window of the pub.

3. See *Cormac's Glossary*, "*Tuirgin*" (158–59). For a discussion of the *Tuirgin* and the dreams of Tuan/Fintan, see Matthews and Matthews, *Encyclopedia* (93, 155, 300–301).

4. This excerpt is from Edward Gwynn, trans., *The Metrical Dindshenchas*, "Temair" I, stanzas 41–44, p. 5.

5. See *Lebor Gabála Érenn*, pt. 2.

6. "The Settling of the Manor of Tara," originally published in *Eriu* 4 (1910), is reprinted in Matthews and Matthews, *Encyclopedia of Celtic Wisdom* (98–114). The excerpt quoted is on page 101.

7. See Matthews and Matthews, *Encyclopedia of Celtic Wisdom* (356); also see O'Curry, *Manners and Customs* (2:316), for a discussion of the traditional silver bough.

8. Gwynn's translation of *The Metrical Dindshenchas* is quoted in Rees and Rees, *Celtic Heritage* (169–70).

9. "The Tale of the Ordeals," ed. Whitley Stokes, was originally published in *Irische Texte* in 1891 and is reprinted in Matthews and Matthews, *Encyclopedia of Celtic Wisdom* (266–80).

Chapter 8. The Recovery of the Dark Tongue

1. Nagy, in *Conversing with Angels and Ancients* (203), translates and comments upon this passage.

2. This excerpt from Samuel Butler's *Hudibras* is quoted by R.A.S. Macalister in

the preface to his *Secret Languages of Ireland*. It should be mentioned that there are actually two literary Samuel Butlers: one the author of *Hudibras*, and the other the author of *The Way of All Flesh* and *The Authoress of "The Odyssey."* James Atherton lists both Samuel Butlers as present in the *Wake*.

3. Stokes's comments are presented and discussed by Vivian Mercier in *Irish Comic Tradition* (6).

4. P. W. Joyce, in *A Social History*, discusses the training of a *Fili* and the techniques of the Dark Tongue in chapter 9, "Paganism," and chapter 11, "Learning and Education."

5. See Ó hÓgáin, *Sacred Isle* (89) for further discussion regarding these dark terms. Kuno Meyer discusses these Dark Tongue terms and techniques in *Sanas Cormaic, Anecdota from Irish Manuscripts*.

6. Joyce's comments to Max Eastman are found in Ellmann's *James Joyce* (546).

7. In his introduction to *The Scholar's Primer*, Calder lists and discusses many of the Dark Tongue techniques cited throughout the *Primer* itself (xiii–lv). Specific references and descriptions to the various techniques are found on the following pages of the *Primer*: *Deletin litterda*, page xliii and line 5308; *Condall*, page xliii and line 5317; *Cotut*, page xliii, line 5287; *Filltigthi* and *Fer tot*, page xlvii, lines 1515, 1529; *Rofota*, page xliii, line 5960; *Lumbrosa*, page xliii, line 5943; *Airchell calaid*, page xlix, lines 1850–51, 1984–85.

8. P. L. Henry discusses the archaic technique of *cendfrochas* in "The Caldron of Poesy" (124).

9. This famous but apocryphal tale is cited by James Atherton in *The Books at the Wake* (15) and is taken from Richard Ellmann, "The Backgrounds of *Ulysses*" (359). Though there are several places in *Finnegans Wake* where the phrase "Come in" can be found, no one has yet been able to conclusively identify the exact place in the *Wake* where (if at all) this particular version of the phrase was incorporated. I have, nonetheless, opted to include this colorful tale as an example of a Dark Tongue principle—primarily because the spirit of the story outweighs, perhaps, the letter of its historical accuracy.

10. See Doris Edel, "The Colloquy in *Cullwych ac Olwen* and Insular Celtic Learning" (256–57). The "language of separation" is also discussed in various sections of *The Scholar's Primer*.

11. The quote by Seamus Heaney appears in Tymoczko's *Irish Ulysses* (338) and is taken from Heaney, "The Interesting Case of John Alphonsus Mulrennan" (40).

Bibliography

Anderson, William. *Green Man: The Archetype of Our Oneness with the Earth.* London and San Francisco: HarperCollins, 1990.

The Annals of the Four Masters. Translated by J. O'Donovan. *Annala Rioghachta Éireann. Annals of the Kingdom of Ireland by the Four Masters from the earliest period to the year 1616.* 7 vols. Dublin: Hodges and Smith, 1848–51.

Atherton, James. *The Books at the Wake: A Study of Literary Allusions in James Joyce's "Finnegans Wake."* New York: Viking, 1960.

Atkinson, Robert, ed. *The Yellow Book of Lecan.* Dublin, 1896.

Attridge, Derek. "*Finnegans Wake*: The Dream of Interpretation." *James Joyce Quarterly* 27, no. 1 (1989): 11–30.

———. *Peculiar Language: Literature as Difference from the Renaissance to James Joyce.* Ithaca: Cornell University Press, 1988.

Aubert, Jacques. *The Aesthetics of James Joyce.* Baltimore: Johns Hopkins University Press, 1973.

Beck, R. "Via Crucis." *A Wake Newslitter.* Occasional Paper. No. 3 (1983): 1.

Beckman, Richard. "Perils of Marriage in *Finnegans Wake.*" *James Joyce Quarterly* 33, no. 1 (1996): 83–100.

Beechold, Henry. "Early Irish History and Mythology in *Finnegans Wake.*" Ph.D. dissertation, Pennsylvania State University, 1956.

Begnal, Michael. *Dreamscheme: Narrative and Voice in "Finnegans Wake."* Syracuse: Syracuse University Press, 1988.

Begnal, Michael, and Fritz Senn, eds. *A Conceptual Guide to "Finnegans Wake."* University Park: Pennsylvania State University Press, 1974.

Benstock, Bernard. *Joyce-Again's Wake: An Analysis of "Finnegans Wake."* Seattle: University of Washington Press, 1965.

Best, R. I. "Prognostication from the Raven and Wren." In *Celtic Seers' Source Book,* edited by John Matthews. London: Blandford, 1999.

———, trans. "The Settling of the Manor of Tara." *Ériu* 4 (1910): 121–72.

Bhreathnach, Edel. *Tara: A Select Bibliography.* Discovery Programme, Monograph 1. Dublin: Royal Irish Academy, 1995.

Bhreathnach, M. "The Sovereignty Goddess as Goddess of Death?" *Zeitschrift für celtische Philologie* 39 (1982): 243–60.

Bieler, L., trans. *The Patrician Texts in The Book of Armagh*. Scriptores Latini Hiberniae 10. Dublin, 1979.

Binchy, D. A. "The Fair of Tailtiu and the Feast of Tara." *Ériu* 18 (1958b): 113–38.

Bishop, John. Introduction to *Finnegans Wake*. New York: Penguin, 1996.

———. *Joyce's Book of the Dark*. Madison: University of Wisconsin Press, 1986.

Blake, William. *The Complete Poetry and Prose of William Blake*. Edited by David Erdman. New York: Doubleday, 1988.

Blavatsky, Helena P. *Isis Unveiled*. Vols. 1 and 2. Wheaton, Ill.: Theosophical Publishing House, 1972.

Bonwick, James. 1894. *Irish Druids and Old Irish Religions*. New York: Dorset Press, 1986.

Bord, Janet, and Colin Bord. *Sacred Waters*. London: Granada, 1985.

Bowen, Charles. "Great-Bladdered Medb: Mythology and Invention in the *Táin Bó Cúailnge*." *Éire-Ireland* 10, no. 4 (1975): 14–34.

Bowen, E. G. "The Cult of St. Brigit." *Studia Celtica*, edited by J. Williams, 8–9 (1973–74): 33–47.

Brenneman, Walter, and Mary Brenneman. *Crossing the Circle at the Holy Wells of Ireland*. Charlottesville: University Press of Virginia, 1991.

Brivic, Sheldon. *Joyce the Creator*. Madison: University of Wisconsin Press, 1985.

———. "The Mind Factory: Kabbalah in *Finnegans Wake*." *James Joyce Quarterly* 21, no. 1 (1983): 7–30.

Budgen, Frank. *James Joyce and the Making of "Ulysses."* Bloomington: Indiana University Press, 1960.

Burgess, Anthony. *Here Comes Everybody*. London: Faber and Faber, 1965.

Burrell, Harry. *Narrative Design in "Finnegans Wake."* Gainesville: University of Florida Press, 1996.

Bury, John B. *The Life of St. Patrick*. London, 1905. Mineola, N.Y.: Dover, 1998.

Caesar, Julius. *The Gallic War*. Translated by Carolyn Hammond. Oxford: Oxford University Press, 1999.

Calder, George, ed. and trans. *Auraicept na n-Éces. The Scholar's Primer*. Edinburgh: John Grant, 1917.

Campbell, Joseph. *The Masks of God: Primitive Mythology*. New York: Viking, 1959.

———. *Mythic Worlds, Modern Words: On the Art of James Joyce*. Edited by Edmund Epstein. New York: HarperCollins, 1993.

Campbell, Joseph, and Henry Morton Robinson. *A Skeleton Key to "Finnegans Wake."* New York: Viking, 1968.

Carmichael, Alexander. *Carmina Gadelica*. Vols. 1–5. Edinburgh: Scottish Academic Press, 1928–72. English text, Edinburgh: Floris Books, 1992.

Carney, James. *Studies in Irish Literature and History*. Dublin: Dublin Institute for Advanced Studies, 1993.

Carver, Craig. "James Joyce and the Theory of Magic." *James Joyce Quarterly* 15, no. 3 (1978): 201–14.

Colum, Padraic. *A Treasury of Irish Folklore*. New York: Crown, 1967.

Condren, Mary. *The Serpent and the Goddess: Women, Religion, and Power in Celtic Ireland*. San Francisco: Harper and Row, 1989.

Connolly, Thomas, ed. *Scribbledhobble: The Ur-Workbook for "Finnegans Wake."* Evanston: Northwestern University Press, 1961.

Cope, Jackson. *Joyce's Cities: Archaeologies of the Soul*. Baltimore: Johns Hopkins University Press, 1981.

Cormac's Glossary. Edited by Whitley Stokes. Translated by J. O'Donovan. Calcutta: O. T. Cutter, 1868.

Cross, Tom, and Clark Harris Slover, eds. *Ancient Irish Tales*. New York: Barnes and Noble, 1996.

Cummins, W. A. *King Arthur's Place in Prehistory*. Godalming, Surrey: Bramley, 1992.

Cumpiano, Marion. "Dermot MacMurrough, Hugh De Lacy, and Tiernan O'Rourke: An Unrecognised Trio in *FW*." *A Wake Newslitter*, n.s., 13, no. 6 (1976): 103–6.

———. "The Flowerpot on the Pole: A Motif Approach to *Finnegans Wake*." *James Joyce Quarterly* 21, no. 1 (1983): 61–68.

Darrah, John. *Paganism in Arthurian Romance*. Cambridge: D. S. Brewer, 1997.

Davies, Edward. *Celtic Researches*. New York: Garland, 1979.

Devlin, Kimberly. *Wandering and Return in "Finnegans Wake": An Integrative Approach to Joyce's Fiction*. Princeton: Princeton University Press, 1991.

Di Bernard, Barbara. "Alchemical Number Symbolism in *Finnegans Wake*." *James Joyce Quarterly* 16, no. 4 (1979): 433–46.

Dillon, Myles. *The Cycles of the Kings*. London: Oxford University Press, 1946.

Diodorus Siculus. *Bibliotheca Historica. Library of History*. Vol. 2. Books 2.35–4.58. Translated by C. H. Oldfather. Cambridge: Harvard University Press, 1935.

Diogenes Laertius. *Vitae. The Lives of Eminent Phiolsophers*. Translated by R. Hicks. Cambridge: Harvard University Press, 1959.

Dixon-Kennedy, Mike. *Celtic Myth and Legend*. London: Blandford, 1996.

———. *Heroes of the Round Table*. London: Blandford, 1997.

Eckley, Grace. *The Steadfast "Finnegans Wake": A Textbook*. Lanham, N.Y., and London: University Press of America, 1994.

———. "'Petween Peas Like Ourselves': The Folklore of the Prankquean." *James Joyce Quarterly* 9, no. 2 (1971): 177–88.

Edel, Doris. "The Colloquy in *Cullwych ac Olwen* and Insular Celtic Learning." *Bulletin of the Board of Celtic Studies* 30 (1983): 253–67.

Eliade, Mircea. *Shamanism: Archaic Techniques of Ecstasy*. Translated by Willard B. Trask. Kingsport: Kingsport Press, 1964.

Ellis, Peter Berresford. *Celtic Women: Women in Celtic Society and Literature*. Grand Rapids: William B. Eerdman, 1995.

———. *A Dictionary of Irish Mythology*. Oxford: Oxford University Press, 1987.

Ellmann, Richard. *A long the riverrun: Selected Essays*. New York: Knopf, 1989.

———. "The Backgrounds of *Ulysses*." *Kenyon Review* 16, no. 3 (summer 1954): 338–86.

———. *James Joyce*. New York: Oxford University Press, 1959.

———. *James Joyce*. First Revision. New York: Oxford University Press, 1983.

———. *Two Decades of Joyce Criticism*. Edited by Seon Givens. New York: Vanguard Press, 1948.

Enright, Michael. *Lady with a Mead Cup: Ritual Prophecy and Lordship in the European Warband from La Tene to the Viking Age*. Portland, Ore.: Four Courts Press, 1996.

Ettlinger, E. "Precognitive Dreams in Celtic Legend." In *The Celtic Seers' Source Book*, edited by John Matthews. London: Blandford, 1999.

Evans, E. E. "The Bull-roarer." *Ulster Journal of Archaeology* 39 (1976): 71.

Evans, Simon. "The Ultimate Ysland of Yreland." *A Wake Newslitter*. Occasional Paper. No. 2. (1983): 5.

Evans-Wentz, W. Y. *The Fairy Faith in Celtic Countries*. New York: Carol, 1966.

Fargnoli, A. Nicholas. "A-taufing in the *Wake*: Joyce's Baptismal Motif." *James Joyce Quarterly* 20, no. 3 (1983): 293–305.

Fargnoli, A. Nicholas, and Michael Gillespie. *James Joyce A-Z*. New York: Oxford University Press, 1995.

Frazer, Sir James George. *The Golden Bough*. New York: Macmillan, 1922.

Fredkin, Grace. "S in *Finnegans Wake*." *James Joyce Quarterly* 23, no. 2 (1986): 189–99.

Garbáty, Thomas, ed. *Medieval English Literature*. Lexington: D. C. Heath, 1984.

Garvin, John. "Some Irish and Anglo-Irish Allusions in *Finnegans Wake*." *James Joyce Quarterly* 11, no. 4 (1974): 266–78.

Giraldus Cambrensis. *The Historical Works*. Edited by Thomas Wright. Translated by Thomas Forester. New York: AMS, 1968.

Givens, Seon, ed. *James Joyce: Two Decades of Criticism*. New York: Vanguard Press, 1948.

Glasheen, Adaline. *A Census of "Finnegans Wake": An Index of the Characters and Their Roles*. London: Faber and Faber, 1956. Cited in this volume as *First Census*.

———. *A Second Census of Finnegans Wake*. Chicago: Northwestern University Press, 1963.

———. *Third Census of Finnegans Wake*. Berkeley and Los Angeles: University of California Press, 1977.

———. "*Finnegans Wake* and *The Secret Languages of Ireland*." *A Wake Newslitter*. No. 10 (February 1963): 1–3.

———. "Flesh and Blood Games." *A Wake Newslitter*. No. 5 (October 1967): 99–100.

Gomme, Alice Bertha. *The Traditional Games of England, Scotland, and Ireland*. New York: Dover, 1964.

Goodrich, Norma. *The Holy Grail*. New York: HarperCollins, 1992.

Gordon, John. *"Finnegans Wake": A Plot Summary*. Syracuse: Syracuse University Press, 1986.

———. *James Joyce's Metamorphoses*. Dublin: Gill and Macmillan, 1981.

Graves, Robert. *The White Goddess*. New York: Farrar, Strauss and Giroux, 1970.

Green, Miranda. *Celtic Goddesses: Warriors, Virgins and Mothers*. New York: George Braziller, 1995.

———. *Dictionary of Celtic Myth and Legend*. London: Thames and Hudson, 1992.

———. *The Gods of the Celts*. Gloucester: Sutton, 1986.

———. *The World of the Druids*. London: Thames and Hudson, 1997.

Gwynn, Edward, trans. "De Shíl Chonairi Móir." "Of the Race of Conaire Mór." *Ériu* 6 (1912): 130–43.

———. *The Metrical Dindshenchas*. Todd Lecture Series, vol. 3. Dublin: Hodges, Figgis, and Company, 1903.

———. *The Metrical Dindshenchas*. Todd Lecture Series, vol. 10. Dublin: Hodges, Figgis, and Company, 1913.

Halper, Nathan. "Another Anecdote in Ellmann." *A Wake Newslitter* 5, no. 6 (December 1968): 90–93.

———. "The Date of Earwicker's Dream." In *Twelve and a Tilly: Essays on the Occasion of the Twenty-fifth Anniversary of "Finnegans Wake,"* edited by Jack Dalton and Clive Hart. Evanston: Northwestern University Press, 1965.

———. "Joyce and Anna Livia." *James Joyce Quarterly* 4 (1966–67): 223–28.

Hanson, R.P.C. *St. Patrick: His Origins and Career*. Oxford: Clarendon, 1968.

Harris, J. Rendell. *Boanerges*. Cambridge: Cambridge University Press, 1913.

Hart, Clive. *Structure and Motif in "Finnegans Wake."* London: Faber and Faber, 1962.

Hayman, David. *The "Wake" in Transit*. Ithaca: Cornell University Press, 1990.

Heaney, Seamus. "The Interesting Case of John Alphonsus Mulrennan." *Planet: The Welsh Internationalist* 41 (January 1978): 34–40.

Henry, P. L. "The Caldron of Poesy." *Studia Celtica* 14/15 (1979–80): 114–27.

Herity, Michael, and George Eogan. *Ireland in Prehistory*. London and New York: Routledge, 1996.

Hofheinz, Thomas. *Joyce and the Invention of Irish History: "Finnegans Wake" in Context*. Cambridge: Cambridge University Press, 1995.

Holinshed, Raphael. *Irish Chronicle*, 1577. London: Dolmen, 1979.

Holy Bible. King James Version. Iowa Falls: World Bible Publishers.

Hull, V., trans. "The Four Jewels of the Tuatha Dé Danaan." *Zeitschrift für celtische Philologie* 18 (1930): 73–89.

Jones, Leslie Ellen. *Druid, Shaman, Priest: Metaphors of Celtic Paganism*. Middlesex: Hisarlik, 1998.

Joyce, James. *The Critical Writings of James Joyce*. Edited by Mason Ellsworth and Richard Ellmann. New York: Viking, 1959.

———. *Finnegans Wake*. New York: Penguin, 1967.

———. *The Finnegans Wake Notebooks at Buffalo*. Edited by V. Deane, D. Ferrer, and G. Lernout. Turnhout, Belgium: Brepols, 2000.

———. "Ireland, Island of Saints and Sages." In *The Critical Writings of James Joyce*, edited by Mason Ellsworth and Richard Ellmann. New York: Viking, 1959.

———. *Letters of James Joyce*. Vol. 1 edited by Stuart Gilbert. Vols. 2 and 3 edited by Richard Ellmann. New York: Viking, 1966.

———. *A Portrait of the Artist as a Young Man*. New York: Penguin, 1985.

———. *Ulysses*. New York: Random House, 1946.

Joyce, P. W. *Old Celtic Romances*. London: C. Kegan Paul and Company, 1879.

———. *A Social History of Ancient Ireland*. Vols. 1 and 2. New York: Benjamin Blom, 1968.

Joyce, Stanislaus. *My Brother's Keeper: James Joyce's Early Years*. Edited by Richard Ellmann. London: Faber, 1982.

Kaufmann, Michael. "Seasonal Change and Transformation in 'The Prankquean's Tale': Implications for Reading the Tale and the Novel." *James Joyce Quarterly* 24, no. 4 (1987): 437–56.

Keane, Patrick. *Terrible Beauty: Yeats, Joyce, Ireland, and the Myth of the Devouring Female*. Columbia: University of Missouri Press, 1988.

Kelleher, John. "Identifying the Irish Printed Sources for *Finnegans Wake*." *Irish University Review* 1 (1971): 161–77.

Kelly, F., ed. and trans. *Audacht Morainn*. Dublin: Dublin Institute for Advanced Studies, 1976.

Kenner, Hugh. "The Look of a Queen." In *Woman in Irish Legend, Life and Literature*, edited by S. F. Gallagher. Totowa, N.J.: Barnes and Noble, 1983.

Kopper, Edward. "Saint Patrick in *Finnegans Wake*." *A Wake Newslitter* 4, no. 5 (October 1967): 85–94.

Lang, Andrew. *Custom and Myth*. New York: AMS Press, 1968.

Layard, John. *A Celtic Quest: Sexuality and Soul in Individuation*. Edited by Anne Bosch. Dallas: Spring Publishers, 1975.

Levin, Harry. *James Joyce: An Introduction*. New York: New Directions, 1960.

Lysaght, Patricia. *The Banshee: The Irish Death Messenger*. Boulder: Roberts Rinehart, 1986.

Macalister, R.A.S. *The Archaeology of Ireland*. Studio, 1906. London: Methuen, 1928.

———, ed. and trans. *The Book of Ui Maine*. Dublin: Stationery Office, 1942.

———, trans. *The Book of Rights. The Book of Ui Maine*. Dublin: Stationery Office, 1942.

———. *Ireland in Pre-Celtic Times*. New York: Benjamin Blom, 1921.

———, ed. and trans. *Lebor Gabála Érenn. The Book of the Taking of Ireland*. Irish Texts Society 34, 35, 39, 41, 44. Dublin: Educational Company of Ireland, 1938–56.

———. *The Secret Languages of Ireland*. Cambridge: Cambridge University Press, 1937.

———. *Tara: A Pagan Sanctuary of Ancient Ireland.* New York and London: Charles Scribner's Sons, 1931.

———. "Temair Breg: A Study of the Remains and Traditions of Tara." *Proceedings of the Royal Irish Academy* 34, sec. 100: 231–399. Dublin: Hodges, Figgs, and Company, 1919.

MacArthur, Ian. "The Complex Ass." *A Wake Newslitter*, n.s., 13, no. 5 (1976): 92–94.

———. "Structure and Motif in Jaun." *A Wake Newslitter*, n.s., 15, no. 5 (1978): 67–73.

———. "A Textual Study of III.4." *A Wake Newslitter*, n.s., 13, no. 1 (1976): 3–8.

———. "A Textual Study of III.3." *A Wake Newslitter*, n.s., 13, no. 1 (1976): 43–48.

Macbain, Alexander. 1917. *Celtic Mythology and Religion.* Hertfordshire: Oracle, 1996.

MacCulloch, J. 1918. *Celtic Mythology.* 1918. Chicago: Academy, 1996.

———. 1918. *The Religion of the Ancient Celts.* London: Constable, 1991.

MacKillop, James. *Dictionary of Celtic Mythology.* Oxford: Oxford University Press, 1998.

———. *Fionn mac Cumhaill: Celtic Myth in English Literature.* Syracuse: Syracuse University Press, 1986.

MacPherson, James. "Temora." In *The Poems of Ossian.* Edinburgh: John Grant, 1926.

Malory, Sir Thomas. "The Quest of the Holy Grail." In *Works of Sir Thomas Malory*, edited by Eugene Vinaver. New York: Oxford University Press, 1971.

Matthews, Caitlin. *Arthur and the Sovereignty of Britain.* London: Penguin, 1989.

Matthews, Caitlin, and John Matthews, eds. *The Encyclopedia of Celtic Wisdom.* Shaftesbury: Element Books, 1994.

Matthews, John. "Auguries, Dreams, and Incubatory Sleep among the Celts of Britain and Ireland." In *Psychology and the Spiritual Traditions*, edited by R. J. Stewart. Longmead: Element Books, 1990.

———, ed. *The Bardic Source Book: Inspirational Legacy and Teachings of the Ancient Celts.* London: Blandford, 1998.

———, ed. *A Celtic Reader: Selections from Celtic Legend, Scholarship, and Story.* San Francisco: Thorsons, 1992.

———, ed. *The Celtic Seers' Source Book.* London: Blandford, 1999.

McAnally, D. R. *Irish Wonders.* New York: Weathervane, 1888.

McCarthy, Patrick. *The Riddles of Finnegans Wake.* Madison, N.J.: Fairleigh Dickinson University Press, 1970.

McGrath, Sheena. *The Sun Goddess: Myth, Legend, History.* London: Blandford, 1997.

McHugh, Roland. *Annotations to "Finnegans Wake."* Baltimore and London: Johns Hopkins University Press, 1991.

———. *The "Finnegans Wake" Experience.* Berkeley and Los Angeles: University of California Press, 1981.

———. *The Sigla of "Finnegans Wake."* Austin: University of Texas, 1976.

McIntyre, J. Lewis. *Giordano Bruno*. London: Macmillan, 1903.

McLean, Adam. *The Triple Goddess: An Exploration of the Archetypal Feminine.* Grand Rapids: Phanes Press, 1989.

Megaw, Ruth, and Vincent Megaw. "Do the Ancient Celts Still Live? An Essay on Identity and Contextuality." *Studia Celtica* 31 (1997): 107–23.

Mercier, Vivian. *The Irish Comic Tradition*. Oxford: Clarendon, 1962.

———. "Letter to the Editor." *A Wake Newslitter*. No. 14 (June 1963): 10.

Meyer, Kuno, trans. "Baile in Scáil." *Zeitschrift für celtische Philologie* 3 (1901): 457–66.

———, trans. "The Expulsion of the Déssi." *Ériu* 3 (1907): 135–42.

———. Introduction to *The Story of Baile the Sweet Spoken. Revue Celtique* Xiii (1892): 220.

———, trans. *Fianaigecht*. Dublin: Hodges and Figgis, 1910.

———, ed. *Sanas Cormaic, Anecdota from Irish Manuscripts.* Vol. 4. Halle (Saxony), 1912.

Mink, Louis. *A "Finnegans Wake" Gazetteer*. Bloomington: Indiana University Press, 1978.

Morris, Henry. "Irish Wake Games." *Béaloideas* 8 (1938): 126–41.

Muirchú maccu Machthene. *The Patrician Texts in the Book of Armagh*. Translated by L. Bieler. *Scriptores Latini Hiberniae* 10. Dublin, 1979.

Murphy, Gerard, ed. and trans. *Early Irish Lyrics*. Oxford: Clarendon Press, 1956.

Nagy, Joseph Falaky. *Conversing with Angels and Ancients: Literary Myths of Medieval Ireland*. Ithaca and London: Cornell University Press, 1997.

———. "Liminality and Knowledge in Irish Tradition." *Studia Celtica* 16/17 (1981–82): 135–43.

———. "Otter, Salmon, and Eel in Traditional Gaelic Narrative." *Studia Celtica* 20/21 (1985–86): 122–43.

———. *The Wisdom of the Outlaw: The Boyhood Deeds of Finn in Gaelic Narrative Tradition*. Berkeley and Los Angeles: University of California Press, 1985.

Norris, Margot. *The Decentered Universe of "Finnegans Wake": A Structural Analysis*. Baltimore and London: Johns Hopkins University Press, 1976.

Ó Cathasaigh, T. "The Theme of *Lommrad* in *Cath Maige Mucrama*." *Éigse* 18 (1980–81): 211–24.

———. "The Semantics of *Sid*." *Éigse* 17 (1977–79): 137–55.

O'Connor, Frank. "Joyce and Dissociated Metaphor." In *The Mirror in the Roadway: A Study of the Modern Novel*. New York: Knopf: 1956.

O'Curry, Eugene. *Lectures on the Manuscript Materials of Ancient Irish History*. Dublin: W. B. Kelly, 1873.

———. *On the Manners and Customs of the Ancient Irish*. Vols. 1–3. Edited by W. K. Sullivan. New York: Scribner, Welford, and Company, 1873.

Ogden, C. K. Preface to *Tales Told of Shem and Shaun: Three Fragments from Work in Progress*. Paris: Black Sun Press, 1929.

O Hehir, Brendan. *A Gaelic Lexicon for Finnegans Wake*. Berkeley and Los Angeles: University of California Press, 1967.

Ó hÓgáin, Dáithí. *Fionn mac Cumhaill: Images of the Gaelic Hero*. Dublin: Gill and Macmillan, 1988.

———. *The Hero in Irish Folk History*. New York: St. Martin's Press, 1983.

———. *Myth, Legend and Romance: An Encyclopedia of the Irish Folk Tradition*. New York: Ryan, 1991.

———. *The Sacred Isle: Belief and Religion in Pre-Christian Ireland*. Woodbridge: Boydell Press, 1999. Cork: Collins Press, 1999.

O'Rahilly, Thomas. *Early Irish History and Mythology*. Dublin: Dublin Institute for Advanced Studies, 1957.

O Suilleabhain, Sean. *Irish Wake Amusements*. Dublin: Mercier Press, 1997.

O'Sullivan, J. Colm. *Joyce's Use of Colors: "Finnegans Wake" and the Earlier Works*. Ann Arbor: U.M.I. Research Press, 1987.

Owens, Cóilín. "Clay (1): Irish Folklore." *James Joyce Quarterly* 27, no. 2 (1990): 337–52.

Pearson, Lionel. *Early Ionian Historians*. Oxford: Oxford University Press, 1939.

Petrie, George. *On the History and Antiquities of Tara Hill. Transactions of the Royal Irish Academy* 18 (1839): 25–232.

Pliny the Elder. *Natural History*. Translated by H. Rackham. 10 vols. London: Harvard University Press, 1992.

Pomponius Mela. *The Description of the World*. Translated by Frank Romer. Ann Arbor: University of Michigan Press, 1998.

Power, Patrick. *Sex and Marriage in Ancient Ireland*. Chester Springs, Penn.: Dufour, 1997.

Poynder, Michael. *Pi in the Sky: A Revelation of the Ancient Celtic Wisdom Tradition*. Cork: Collins Press, 1992.

Prim, John. "Olden Popular Pastimes in Kilkenny." *Journal of the Royal Society of Antiquaries in Ireland* 2 (1853): 319–35.

Radford, F. L. "Daedalus and the Bird Girl: Classical Text and Celtic Subtext in *A Portrait*." *James Joyce Quarterly* 24, no. 3 (1987): 253–74.

Ransom, Timothy. "The p.p.p.power of the Words, Words, Words: *Finnegans Wake* as Words Wake." *James Joyce Quarterly* 9, no. 2 (1971): 259–65.

Rees, Alwyn, and Brinley Rees. *Celtic Heritage: Ancient Tradition in Ireland and Wales*. London: Thames and Hudson, 1976.

Richard, John. *Joyce's Book of Memory: The Mnemotechnic of Ulysses*. Durham and London: Duke University Press, 1999.

Robinson, Marian. "Women Will Water the Wild World Over." *A Wake Newslitter* 15, no. 2 (1978): 19–23.

Rose, Danis. "At the Hole in the Wall." *A Wake Newslitter*, n.s., 13, no 1. (1976): 15.

Rose, Danis, and John O'Hanlon. "Finn MacCool and the Final Weeks of Works in Progress." *A Wake Newslitter* 17, no. 5 (1980): 69–87.

Ross, Anne. *Pagan Celtic Britain*. Chicago: Academy, 1996.

Ross, Anne, and Don Robbins. *The Life and Death of a Druid Prince*. New York: Summit, 1989.

Rutherford, Ward. *Celtic Mythology: The Nature and Influence of Celtic Myth*. New York: Sterling, 1987.

Sandulescu, C. George. *The Language of the Devil: Texture and Archetype in "Finnegans Wake."* Chester Springs, Penn.: Dufour Editions, 1987.

Scholes, Robert, and Richard M. Kain, eds. *The Workshop of Dedalus: James Joyce and the Materials for "A Portrait of the Artist as a Young Man."* Evanston: Northwestern University Press, 1965.

Senchus Mor. Vol. 1. Translated by Alexander Thom. Dublin, 1865.

Senn, Fritz. "Seeking a Sign." *A Wake Newslitter*, n.s., 16, no. 2 (1979): 25–29.

Sharkey, John. *Celtic Mysteries*. Singapore: Thames and Hudson, 1979.

Sharp, E. A., and J. Matthay, eds. *Lyra Celtica: An Anthology of Representative Celtic Poetry*. New York: Haskell, 1970.

Silva Gadelica. Vols. 1–31. Edited and translated by Standish O'Grady. London: Williams and Norgate, 1892.

Solomon, Margaret. *Eternal Geomater: The Sexual Universe of "Finnegans Wake."* Carbondale: Southern Illinois University Press, 1969.

Spence, Lewis. *The Magic Arts in Celtic Britain*. New York: Dorset Press, 1992.

Squire, Charles. *Celtic Myth and Legend, Poetry and Romance*. New York: Bell, 1979.

Stewart, R. J. *The Underworld Initiation: A Journey towards Psychic Transformation*. Guildford: Biddles, 1985.

Stewart, R. J., and Robin Williamson. *Celtic Bards, Celtic Druids*. London: Blandford, 1996.

Stokes, Whitley, trans. *Acallamh na Senórach. The Colloquy of the Two Sages. Irische Texte* 4. Leipzig, 1900; Paris, 1905.

———, ed. *Cormac's Glossary*. Translated by J. O'Donovan. Calcutta: O. T. Cutter, 1868.

———, trans. "The Second Battle of Moytura." *Revue Celtique* 12 (1891): 52–130, 306–8.

———, ed. "The Tale of the Ordeals." *Irische Texte*, 3rd ser. Leipzig: Verlag von Hirzel, 1891.

———. *Thesaurus Palaeohibernicus*. Vol. 2. Cambridge: Cambridge University Press, 1903.

———, trans. "Togail Bruidne Da Derga." "The Destruction of Da Derga's Hostel." *Revue Celtique* 22 (1901): 9–61, 165–215, 282–329, 390–437.

———, trans. *Vita Tripartita. The Tripartite Life of Patrick with other documents related to the saint*. 2 vols. London: Cyebra and Spottiswoode, 1887.

Strabo. *Geography*. Vol. 2. Translated by Horace Leonard Jones. Cambridge: Harvard University Press, 1988.

Straffon, Cheryl. *The Earth Goddess: Celtic and Pagan Legacy of the Landscape*. London: Blandford, 1997.

Streit, Jacob. *Sun and Cross: From Megalithic Culture to Early Christianity in Ireland*. Edinburgh: Floris, 1984.

Stuart, Michael. "Mr. Joyce's Word Creatures." *Colophon*, pt. 7 (1931).

Sultan, Stanley. *Eliot, Joyce, and Company*. New York: Oxford University Press, 1987.

Swartzlander, Susan. "Multiple Meaning and Misunderstanding: The Mistrial of Festy King." *James Joyce Quarterly* 23, no. 4 (1986): 465–76.

Swift, Jonathan. "A Modest Proposal." In *British Literature*, vol. 1, edited by Hazelton Spencer. Lexington: D.C. Heath, 1974.

Thompson, William Irwin. *The Imagination of an Insurrection: Dublin, Easter 1916: A Study of an Ideological Movement*. New York: Harper, 1972.

Thurneysen, R., trans. "Baile in Scáil." "The Poetic Ecstasy of the Phantom." *Zeitschrift für celtische Philologie* 20 (1935): 213–27.

Tindall, William York. *A Reader's Guide to "Finnegans Wake."* Syracuse: Syracuse University Press, 1996.

Todd, J. H., ed. *Cogadh Gaedhel re Gallaibh. The War of the Gaedhil with the Gaill*. London, 1867.

Toulson, Shirley. *The Celtic Alternative: A Reminder of the Christianity We Lost*. London: Century Hutchinson, 1987.

Tymoczko, Maria. "'The Broken Lights of Irish Myth': Joyce's Knowledge of Early Irish Literature." *James Joyce Quarterly* 29 (1992): 763–74.

———. *The Irish Ulysses*. Berkeley and Los Angeles: University of California Press, 1994.

Van Hamel, A. G. *Aspects of Celtic Mythology*. Edmonds, Wash.: Holmes, 2000.

Vico, Giambattista. *The New Science*. New York: Penguin, 1999.

A Wake Newslitter CD-ROM. Old Series Issues 1–18. New Series Issues 1–102. 1962–84. Edinburgh: Split Pea Press, 2000.

Walker, Barbara. *The Woman's Encyclopedia of Myths and Secrets*. San Francisco: Harper and Row, 1983.

Weston, Jessie. *From Ritual to Romance*. Gloucester: Peter Smith, 1983.

Wilde, Jane Francesca Lady. *Ancient Legends, Mystic Charms, and Superstitions of Ireland*. New York: Lemma, 1973.

Wilde, Lyn Webster. *Celtic Women in Legend, Myth, and History*. London: Cassell PLC, 1997.

Wilson, Edmund. "The Dream of H. C. Earwicker." In *The Wound and the Bow*. Boston: Houghton Mifflin, 1941.

Wood-Martin, W. G. *Traces of the Elder Faiths of Ireland*. Vols. 1 and 2. New York: Longmans, Green, and Company, 1902.

Yeats, William Butler. *The Collected Works*. Vol. 1, *The Poems*, edited by Richard J. Finneran. New York: Macmillan, 1989.

———. *Mythologies*. New York: Macmillan, 1977.

Zwicker, Ioannes. *Fontes Historiae Religionis Celticae*. 1–2 Berlin and Bonn: 1934–35.

Index

References to illustrations and tables are indicated by italics.

George Cinclair Gibson has taught English at Louisiana State University in Baton Rouge, Louisiana. He is currently working on a book about Celtic lore and ritual in the ballad tradition of the British Isles.

The Florida James Joyce Series

Edited by Sam Slote

The Autobiographical Novel of Co-Consciousness: Goncharov, Woolf, and Joyce, by Galya Diment (1994)

Bloom's Old Sweet Song: Essays on Joyce and Music, by Zack Bowen (1995)

Joyce's Iritis and the Irritated Text: The Dis-lexic "Ulysses," by Roy Gottfried (1995)

Joyce, Milton, and the Theory of Influence, by Patrick Colm Hogan (1995)

Reauthorizing Joyce, by Vicki Mahaffey (paperback edition, 1995)

Shaw and Joyce: "The Last Word in Stolentelling," by Martha Fodaski Black (1995)

Bely, Joyce, and Döblin: Peripatetics in the City Novel, by Peter I. Barta (1996)

Jocoserious Joyce: The Fate of Folly in "Ulysses," by Robert H. Bell (paperback edition, 1996)

Joyce and Popular Culture, edited by R. B. Kershner (1996)

Joyce and the Jews: Culture and Texts, by Ira B. Nadel (paperback edition, 1996)

Narrative Design in "Finnegans Wake": The Wake Lock Picked, by Harry Burrell (1996)

Gender in Joyce, edited by Jolanta W. Wawrzycka and Marlena G. Corcoran (1997)

Latin and Roman Culture in Joyce, by R. J. Schork (1997)

Reading Joyce Politically, by Trevor L. Williams (1997)

Advertising and Commodity Culture in Joyce, by Garry Leonard (1998)

Greek and Hellenic Culture in Joyce, by R. J. Schork (1998)

Joyce, Joyceans, and the Rhetoric of Citation, by Eloise Knowlton (1998)

Joyce's Music and Noise: Theme and Variation in His Writings, by Jack W. Weaver (1998)

Reading Derrida Reading Joyce, by Alan Roughley (1999)

Joyce through the Ages: A Nonlinear View, edited by Michael Patrick Gillespie (1999)

Chaos Theory and James Joyce's Everyman, by Peter Francis Mackey (1999)

Joyce's Comic Portrait, by Roy Gottfried (2000)

Joyce and Hagiography: Saints Above!, by R. J. Schork (2000)

Voices and Values in Joyce's "Ulysses," by Weldon Thornton (2000)

The Dublin Helix: The Life of Language in Joyce's "Ulysses," by Sebastian D. G. Knowles (2001)

Joyce Beyond Marx: History and Desire in "Ulysses" and "Finnegans Wake," by Patrick McGee (2001)

Joyce's Metamorphosis, by Stanley Sultan (2001)

Joycean Temporalities: Debts, Promises, and Countersignatures, by Tony Thwaites (2001)

Joyce and the Victorians, by Tracey Teets Schwarze (2002)

Joyce's "Ulysses" as National Epic: Epic Mimesis and the Political History of the Nation State, by Andras Ungar (2002)

James Joyce's "Fraudstuff," by Kimberly J. Devlin (2002)
Rite of Passage in the Narratives of Dante and Joyce, by Jennifer Margaret Fraser (2002)
Joyce and the Scene of Modernity, by David Spurr (2002)
Joyce and the Early Freudians: A Synchronic Dialogue of Texts, by Jean Kimball (2003)
Twenty-First Joyce, edited by Ellen Carol Jones and Morris Beja (2004)
Joyce on the Threshold, edited by Anne Fogarty and Timothy Martin (2005)
Wake Rites: The Ancient Irish Rituals of "Finnegans Wake," by George Cinclair Gibson (2005; first paperback edition, 2026)
"Ulysses" in Critical Perspective, edited by Michael Patrick Gillespie and A. Nicholas Fargnoli (2006; first paperback edition, 2026)
Joyce and the Narrative Structure of Incest, by Jen Shelton (2006)
Joyce, Ireland, Britain, edited by Andrew Gibson and Len Platt (2006)
Joyce in Trieste: An Album of Risky Readings, edited by Sebastian D. G. Knowles, Geert Lernout, and John McCourt (2007; first paperback edition, 2026)
Joyce's Rare View: The Nature of Things in "Finnegans Wake," by Richard Beckman (2007)
Joyce's Misbelief, by Roy Gottfried (2008)
James Joyce's Painful Case, by Cóilín Owens (2008; first paperback edition, 2017)
Cannibal Joyce, by Thomas Jackson Rice (2008)
Manuscript Genetics, Joyce's Know-How, Beckett's Nohow, by Dirk Van Hulle (2008)
Catholic Nostalgia in Joyce and Company, by Mary Lowe-Evans (2008)
A Guide through "Finnegans Wake," by Edmund Lloyd Epstein (2009)
Bloomsday 100: Essays on "Ulysses," edited by Morris Beja and Anne Fogarty (2009)
Joyce, Medicine, and Modernity, by Vike Martina Plock (2010; first paperback edition, 2012)
Who's Afraid of James Joyce?, by Karen R. Lawrence (2010; first paperback edition, 2012)
"Ulysses" in Focus: Genetic, Textual, and Personal Views, by Michael Groden (2010; first paperback edition, 2012)
Foundational Essays in James Joyce Studies, edited by Michael Patrick Gillespie (2011; first paperback edition, 2017)
Empire and Pilgrimage in Conrad and Joyce, by Agata Szczeszak-Brewer (2011; first paperback edition, 2017)
The Poetry of James Joyce Reconsidered, edited by Marc C. Conner (2012; first paperback edition, 2015)
The German Joyce, by Robert K. Weninger (2012; first paperback edition, 2016)
Joyce and Militarism, by Greg Winston (2012; first paperback edition, 2015)
Renascent Joyce, edited by Daniel Ferrer, Sam Slote, and André Topia (2013; first paperback edition, 2014)
Before Daybreak: "After the Race" and the Origins of Joyce's Art, by Cóilín Owens (2013; first paperback edition, 2015)

Modernists at Odds: Reconsidering Joyce and Lawrence, edited by Matthew J. Kochis and Heather L. Lusty (2015; first paperback edition, 2020)
James Joyce and the Exilic Imagination, by Michael Patrick Gillespie (2015)
The Ecology of "Finnegans Wake," by Alison Lacivita (2015; first paperback edition, 2021)
Joyce's Allmaziful Plurabilities: Polyvocal Explorations of "Finnegans Wake," edited by Kimberly J. Devlin and Christine Smedley (2015; first paperback edition, 2018)
Exiles: A Critical Edition, by James Joyce, edited by A. Nicholas Fargnoli and Michael Patrick Gillespie (2016; first paperback edition, 2019)
Up to Maughty London: Joyce's Cultural Capital in the Imperial Metropolis, by Eleni Loukopoulou (2017)
Joyce and the Law, edited by Jonathan Goldman (2017; first paperback edition, 2020)
At Fault: Joyce and the Crisis of the Modern University, by Sebastian D. G. Knowles (2018; first paperback edition, 2021)
"Ulysses" Unbound: A Reader's Companion to James Joyce's "Ulysses," Third Edition, by Terence Killeen (2018)
Joyce and Geometry, by Ciaran McMorran (2020)
Panepiphanal World: James Joyce's Epiphanies, by Sangam MacDuff (2020; first paperback edition, 2020)
Language as Prayer in "Finnegans Wake," by Colleen Jaurretche (2020)
Rewriting Joyce's Europe: The Politics of Language and Visual Design, by Tekla Mecsnóber (2021)
Joyce Writing Disability, edited by Jeremy Colangelo (2022)
Joyce, Aristotle, and Aquinas, by Fran O'Rourke (2022)
Time and Identity in "Ulysses" and the "Odyssey," by Stephanie Nelson (2022)
Joyce without Borders: Circulations, Sciences, Media, and Mortal Flesh, edited by James Ramey and Norman Cheadle (2022)
An Irish-Jewish Politician, Joyce's Dublin, and "Ulysses": The Life and Times of Albert L. Altman, by Neil R. Davison (2022)
Beating the Bounds: Excess and Restraint in Joyce's Later Works, by Roy Benjamin (2023)
Genetic Joyce: Manuscripts and the Dynamics of Creation, by Daniel Ferrer (2023; first paperback 2026)
Collected Epiphanies of James Joyce: A Critical Edition, edited by Sangam MacDuff, Angus McFadzean, and Morris Beja (2024)
Guilt and "Finnegans Wake": From Original Sin to the Irredeemable Body, by Talia Abu (2025)
Sensational Joyce: The Psychology of "Ulysses," by John Gordon (2025)
Teaching James Joyce in the Twenty-First Century, edited by Barry Devine and Ellen M. Scheible (2026)
Joyce's Theatrical Poetics: The Novel Language of Drama, by Valérie Bénéjam (2026)

www.ingramcontent.com/pod-product-compliance
Lightning Source LLC
LaVergne TN
LVHW100817200826
845923LV00028B/230